CULTURE ON TWO WHEELS

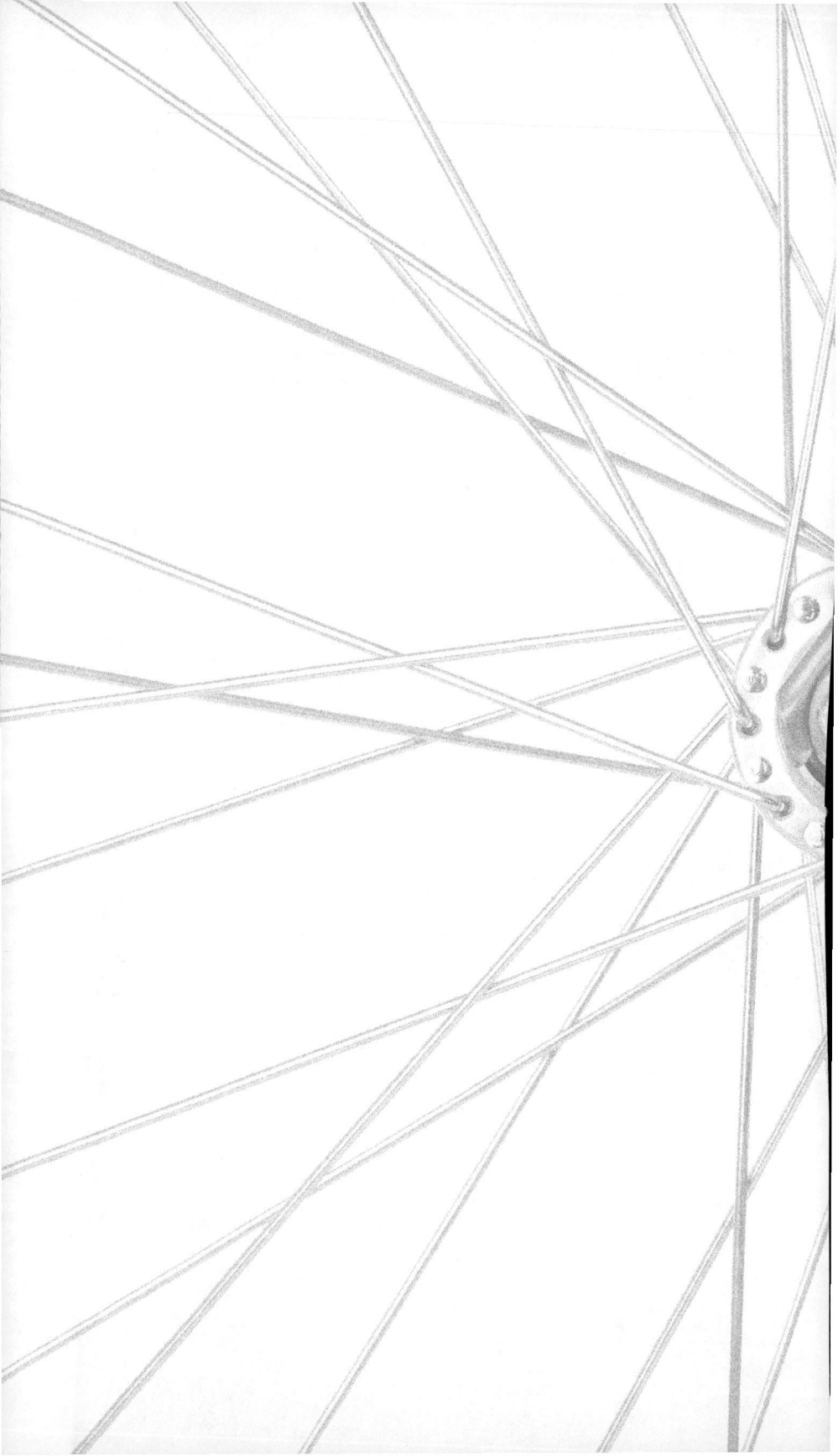

CULTURE ON TWO WHEELS

THE BICYCLE IN LITERATURE AND FILM

EDITED AND WITH AN INTRODUCTION BY
JEREMY WITHERS AND DANIEL P. SHEA

Foreword by Zack Furness

UNIVERSITY OF NEBRASKA PRESS · LINCOLN AND LONDON

Library of Congress Cataloging-in-Publication Data
Names: Withers, Jeremy, editor. | Shea, Daniel P., editor.
Title: Culture on two wheels: the bicycle in literature
and film / edited and with an introduction by Jeremy
Withers and Daniel P. Shea; foreword by Zack Furness.
Description: Lincoln: University of Nebraska Press,
[2016] | Includes bibliographical references and index.
Identifiers: LCCN 2015046481 (print) | LCCN 2016015069
(ebook) | ISBN 9780803269729 (hardback: alk. paper)
| ISBN 9780803290433 (epub) | ISBN 9780803290440
(mobi) | ISBN 9780803290457 (pdf)
Subjects: LCSH: Bicycles in literature. | Bicycles
in motion pictures. | Bicycles—Social aspects. |
BISAC: LITERARY CRITICISM / General. | PERFORMING
ARTS / Film & Video / History & Criticism.
Classification: LCC PN56.B54 C85 2016 (print) | LCC
PN56.B54 (ebook) | DDC 809/.933558—dc23
LC record available at http://lccn.loc.gov/2015046481

Set in Sabon Next Std by M. Scheer.

CONTENTS

List of Illustrations   viii

Foreword   ix
ZACK FURNESS

Acknowledgments   xiii

Introduction: The Bicycle as Rolling Signifier   I
JEREMY WITHERS AND DANIEL P. SHEA

PART 1. BIKES IN LITERATURE

1. Pilgrims on Wheels: The Pennells, F. W. Bockett,
   and Literary Cycle Travels   19
   DAVE BUCHANAN

2. From Charles Pratt to Mark Twain to Frank
   Norris: Horse versus Bicycle, Man versus Machine   41
   PETER KRATZKE

3. "The Face of the Bicyclist": Women's Cycling and
   the Altered Body in *The Type-Writer Girl*   57
   ALYSSA STRAIGHT

4. Bicycles and Warfare: The Effects of Excessive
   Mobility in H. G. Wells's *The War in the Air*   78
   JEREMY WITHERS

5. Like a Furnace: Alfred Jarry's *The Supermale*,
   Doping, and the Limits of Positivism   94
   CORRY CROPPER

6. Albertine the Cyclist: A Queer Feminist Bicycle
   Ride through Proust's *In Search of Lost Time*   116
   UNA BROGAN

7. The Existential Cyclist: Bicycles and Personal
   Responsibility in Simone de Beauvoir's
   The Blood of Others   136
   NANCI J. ADLER

8. Communing with Machines: The Bicycle as a
   Figure of Symbolic Transgression in the
   Posthumanist Novels of Samuel Beckett and
   Flann O'Brien   152
   AMANDA DUNCAN

9. "Hi-Yo, Silver": The Bicycle in the
   Fiction of Stephen King   171
   DON TRESCA

PART 2. BIKES IN FILM

10. "I'll Get You, My Pretty!": Bicycle Horror
    and the Abject Cyclicity of History   191
    MATTHEW PANGBORN

11. Bicycles in Truffaut's *Jules and Jim*:
    Images of Emancipation and Repression   208
    CHARLES L. P. SILET

12. We Hope, and We Lose Hope: The Postman's
    Bicycle in Andrei Tarkovsky's *The Sacrifice*   226
    BENJAMIN VAN LOON

13. Bicycle Borrowers after Neorealism:
    Global Nou-velo Cinema   244
    ANNE CIECKO

14. *Breaking Away* and Vital Materialism:
Embodying Dreams of Social Mobility via
the Bicycle Assemblage   263
RYAN HEDIGER

15. *Beijing Bicycle*: Desire, Identity, and the Wheels   281
JINHUA LI

16. "Swerve! I'm on My Bike": Mediated Images of
Bicycling in Youth-Produced Hip-Hop   300
MELODY LYNN HOFFMANN

Afterword: Form and History in the
Bicycle Sculptures of Ai Weiwei   318
DANIEL P. SHEA

Contributors   329

Index   335

ILLUSTRATIONS

1.1. The Pennells setting out for Canterbury   23

1.2. Pilgrims new and old   26

5.1. Alfred Jarry leaving his house, 1898   101

5.2. Cyclists on a quintuplet   103

5.3. Maurice Garin at the conclusion of
the first Tour de France   109

11.1. Poster for Cycles Gladiator   210

11.2. Poster for De Dion Bouton   212

11.3. A trip up from the beach by Jim, Catherine,
and Jules   216

11.4. A last bicycle ride by Jules, Jim, Sabine,
Catherine, and Albert   219

11.5. Jim at the café   220

FOREWORD

ZACK FURNESS

Having previously spent years of my life riding on, thinking about, talking about, and writing about bicycles, it is safe to say that I have seen images of bicycles and bicycling in just about every format possible, from mass-produced T-shirts and films, to DIY sculptures and fanzines, to tattoos both beautiful and cringe worthy. Consequently, I should not have been surprised last week when I was walking through a Target department store and noticed that, amid the sprawling display of clocks, mirrors, and abstract wall decor, one of the items available for purchase was a multipanel, canvas art print of a single-speed bicycle. However, it was still pretty strange, in the truest sense of the word—as in, I was trying to make out a familiar object rendered momentarily foreign to me. Maybe it was the fact that the encounter took place in my home of Pittsburgh, Pennsylvania, where, just fifteen years ago, bike commuters were something of an alien species on the roads and where the vast majority of adults who actually rode single-speed bikes (like the one in the print) were part of an intersecting counterculture of bike messengers, punk rockers, wingnut artists, and mountain bike diehards with mud-splattered shoes and bags. Or maybe it was because I had taken an extended hiatus from a decade of constantly analyzing bicycling and found myself surprisingly intrigued again by the everyday ways in which bicycles are made meaningful not just through mobility (i.e., riding) but through the culturally entrenched processes of representation.

As I stared at the print, I thought about the conversation that must have taken place between some midlevel executive at Target and the graphic designer commissioned to create a desirable image that speaks to some of the various ideas and tastes that people ostensibly connect to bicycling: the single-speed road bike functioning as a signifier of "urbanness" that gestures toward the fixed-gear cycling trend evident in U.S. cities throughout much of the last ten years, whereas the off-center, silk-screenesque, disjointed pop art aesthetic is likely meant to evoke some kind of connotation with youthfulness, creativity, and leisure apparently befitting those who ride bikes for fun or transportation. I also thought about a much more critical reading that one could give to the print as a symbol of bicycling's thorough commodification—a visual representation thoroughly divorced from the nonconformist, environmentalist, and, at times, anticonsumerist politics that informed a great deal of formal and informal U.S. bike advocacy since the early 1970s. Moreover, there was undoubtedly something that could be said about the availability of this print at a store that sits at ground zero of a massive (and ongoing) gentrification project that has displaced many of the neighborhood's African American residents and businesses and that sits less than a block away from a hip new coffee shop that makes local deliveries by bicycle. Then again, maybe the little kid who walked by me had it right when he stopped, pointed in the direction of my gaze, smiled from ear to ear, and shouted, "Bicycle, Mommy! Bicycle!"

I tell this story not because I think my insights and conflicted interpretations are somehow unique but for quite the opposite reason, which is to say that people have been constructing meaning around and through the image of the bicycle for nearly as long as people have been riding them. Long before the visual rhetoric of advertising became the stock and trade for the auto industry, early bicycle manufacturers had already cultivated richly symbolic images of mobility that located bicycling squarely within the domains of pleasure, fantasy, desire, beauty, independence, and the sensibilities of a technologically modern(ist) world. Champions of the bicycle similarly embraced the narrative form to extol the wonders of cycling for readers of popular magazines and fiction alike. Despite the radical changes in bicycling technologies and practices—not to mention media—throughout the twentieth and early twenty-first centuries, we are still immersed in an ongoing process of defining and debating the meaning of bicycling through the stories we write, the images we capture, the films we watch, and the various digital media we use to interact. Then, as now, people recognized that representations of bicycles and bicycling matter, because they shape our sensibilities in ways that affect, not just our perceptions of specific technologies and practices, but also the real and imagined relationships we have to (among other things) production, consumption, material culture, geography, and each other.

Whereas much has been written about the cultural roles of the automobile and driving in literature and popular culture, there has been surprisingly little analogous work devoted to the bicycle and bicycling, particularly in academia, where cycling is predominantly analyzed through the positivistic lenses of urban planning and injury prevention. At the risk of minimizing the importance of research that provides transportation planners, policy makers, and cycling advocates with a better understanding of where, when, and how people ride bicycles, many of these studies tell us very little about how and why it is actually meaningful to those who do so. Recent ethnographic research on bicycling has dramatically enhanced our knowledge of not only cycling practices, cycling communities, and the everyday lives of bike riders but also the complex cultural, socioeconomic, and political relationships articulated to and through cycling mobilities. Yet even within this diverse and burgeoning realm of scholarship, one still finds relatively few serious engagements with representations of bicycling, despite the fact that, somewhat ironically, cyclists everywhere devote an extraordinary amount of time to the politics of representation: scrutinizing depictions of gender in bicycling ads, critiquing the ways that cyclists are framed in news stories and magazine articles, and even debating whether the very words we use to communicate—for example, "cyclist" vs. "bicyclist" vs. "bike rider"—influence how people identify themselves (to give just a few examples).

This collection helps to fill the gap in critical academic research on bicycling by encouraging us to consider how bicycles fit into the real and fictive stories we tell ourselves about our values, ethics, feelings, politics, bodies, communities, and public spaces. More broadly, the authors ask us to consider what role images of bicycling might play in terms of narrating our hopes and frustrations about the problematics and possibilities of everyday life. Speculating about such issues is necessary work for researchers and absolutely vital if we are to better understand the complex roles that bicycles can and should play in our culture.

ACKNOWLEDGMENTS

The editors wish to thank, first and foremost, the University of Nebraska Press for publishing this collection of essays and for supporting the idea that bicycles deserve to be talked about in a serious, scholarly way. In particular, Robert Taylor, senior editor at University of Nebraska Press, has been an unwavering supporter of this project from the beginning and encouraged us even when this project was just a simple call for papers floating around on the Internet. Additionally, Courtney Ochsner, associate acquisitions editor at Nebraska, has been most helpful in answering our many questions as we worked to put the manuscript together. We thank both Robert and Courtney for their help and support. We would also like to thank Jeremy Hall for the excellent copyediting and Christy Stamey for her assistance with some of the finishing touches in the publication process.

Of course, we would also like to thank our wonderful roster of contributors, most all of whom we have never met in person and have only gotten to know through these essays and through our electronic correspondence. We learned a lot from these scholars, and we are endlessly grateful for their hard work in helping us put together the best book we could. All of our authors have become an important group of colleagues that we look forward to working with in the future.

We would like to thank the many cycling advocates and activists out there who work tirelessly to make the streets a safer and better place for bikes to be. Although our work diverges in many ways from that of more overt bicycling advocacy and politics, we certainly see our book as being in alignment with their goals and values and as contributing in its way to the chorus of voices that strive to raise awareness of what an amazing and often underappreciated technological and cultural artifact the bicycle is.

Jeremy wishes to thank his exceptional coeditor, Daniel Shea. Without Dan's perceptive insights and suggestions, this collection would not be half as good as it is, and without Dan's sense of humor and positive outlook, it would not have been half as pleasurable to work on. Most of all, Jeremy thanks his wife, Abby, for her constant support. Whenever Jeremy was feeling exhausted by the time and effort that goes into putting together an edited collection, Abby's endless enthusiasm for this project always gave him a much-needed burst of energy.

Dan's cycling scholarship and his work on this book was supported by a faculty research grant from Austin Peay State University, and he is grateful for the support of the Department of Languages and Literature and of department chair David Guest. Dan thanks coeditor Jeremy Withers for his initiative, his intellectual insight, and his boundless energy and enthusiasm, all of which have shaped and sustained this project from the beginning. Dan would also like to thank Scottie, Finn, and Nora for sharing his enthusiasm for all sorts of idylls and adventures.

CULTURE ON TWO WHEELS

Introduction

The Bicycle as Rolling Signifier

JEREMY WITHERS AND DANIEL P. SHEA

By most any measure, we are living during a bicycling revolution. Not since the fervor that took hold for all things cycling related in the last few decades of the nineteenth century, when the prototype for the modern bicycle was invented, have we seen the intense interest in cycling that we do now. Many cities across the globe continue to construct mile after mile of on-street bike lanes, while towns and rural areas build off-street bike trails at an astonishing rate.[1] In many of these same cities, bike-share programs sprout up like dandelions.[2] The health conscious embrace the bicycle for the exercise it provides, a form of exercise devoid of the boredom of running in place on a treadmill and of the folly of driving to the gym in order to exercise.[3] Environmentalists celebrate the bike for its low carbon footprint, while young professionals adopt cycling as one solution to the vexing logistics of living and working in culturally exciting yet hypercongested and costly urban centers.[4] After the global financial meltdown of 2008, surely the most people since the energy crisis of the early 1970s perceive the good economic sense of relying on a bicycle as a principal means of transportation. And the surge in popularity of festive, noncompetitive events like moonlight bike rides and the annual RAGBRAI in Iowa show us perhaps one of the biggest reasons for cycling's recent uptick in devotees: cycling is fun.[5]

But of course, people have been recently embracing bicycles in such prodigious numbers for more than these machines' benefits to material practices such as exercising, commuting, and saving money.

Surely, it is also the bicycle's symbolic and connotative significance, in addition to its material advantages and practicality, that are attracting such a range of devotees. For example, bike messengers, hip-hop artists, and punk rockers are jumping onto the saddles of bikes due to the machine's associations with DIY values and anticorporate politics.[6] Bicycles now serve as an origin for sartorial considerations and even as a central, sensual component of some literary and cinematic erotica.[7] In both the art and craft worlds, bicycles are becoming trendy, as evidenced by some recent bicycle-themed art exhibitions and by a search of "bicycles" on Etsy, the popular online craft site, yielding (for the moment) 37,248 results.[8] And although environmentalists cherish the bicycle for its disentanglement from pollution and global warming, surely many of those same environmentalists also use the bike and connect their sense of self to bikes for what that machine symbolizes about a person's commitment to a (supposedly) simpler, purer lifestyle.

In short, although much work remains to be done to make cycling as entrenched in our society as it could be and although it would be premature to proclaim the current cycling revolution as having achieved all that it can, the above examples provide abundant reason to celebrate the state of cycling at the moment. Furthermore, and more importantly, the discussion above sets up two key themes of this book: the idea that a bicycle is a "floating signifier," perpetually taking on new and varied significations, and the idea that bikes are valorized as much (if not more so) for their symbolic as for their material value.

Cycling and Liberation

Though cycling enthusiasts fall into categories and subgroups with divergent, even opposing, interests and identities, the majority of cyclists likely share the common association of cycling with liberation. Kids on BMX bikes exploring the frontiers of their suburbs, Lycra-clad Sunday-morning riders forming brisk minipelotons to tour country roads, and packs of Critical Mass riders meandering down urban byways to reclaim them (even if only temporarily) from automobile traffic—all of these groups are enjoying the bicycle's ability to liberate us from confining schedules and spaces, from sedentary jobs, and from our troubling reliance on petroleum-fueled economic and social structures.

The bicycle has been recognized as a vehicle of liberation as far back as its earliest manifestations in the nineteenth century; and its association with freedom, mobility, and the liberating promise of modernity was secured during its rise to mass popularity following the appearance of the safety bicycle (that is, the pedal-driven machine with two wheels built of a sensibly similar size) in the late 1880s. Bicycles were, for the late Victorians, clearly "geographically liberating," to use Glen Norcliffe's expression—the first cyclists in the late nineteenth century enjoyed the novel opportunity to travel down any road or path they liked, stopping where and when they chose.[9] Though horses, coaches, and even that very symbol of rapid industrial-age travel, the railroad, made extensive travel possible before the bicycle, none of these provided the opportunity for swift exploration and the feeling of complete autonomy that came with the bicycle. Unencumbered by the fixed routes, strict timetables, and relegation to the status of passive parcel that the coaches and railroads demanded and without the exorbitant expense and practical limitations of travel by horse, the cyclist was free to roam. As the author of a series of articles on English cycling excursions in 1886–87 writes, "The road is more pleasant than the rail," and the cyclist must beg pardon for "speaking in praise of the iron steed which enables him to visit with ease and safety, the various places of interest" encountered along the way.[10]

"Ease" and "safety" are relative terms, of course, and the late-Victorian cyclists found that cycling was not always easy and would surely give the novice rider occasion to consider skeptically the safety of cycle travel, particularly in the age of the high-wheeler (which was popular from the 1870s until the appearance of the safety bicycle). Yet despite the hardships, which were amplified by bad roads, mechanical difficulties, and unforgiving machines (one early model of the bicycle was aptly named the "boneshaker"), Victorians nonetheless found that the freedom granted by the bicycle was too compelling to ignore. Indeed, when bicycles became widely available, it quickly became apparent that the residents of big cities in particular longed for the sort of geographical liberation that cycles provided. In the 1880s and 1890s, cyclists began venturing from London into the countryside by the thousands, "flee[ing]," as bicycle historian David Herlihy writes, "the commotion of the city and tak[ing] refuge in the country."[11] Weekend cycling tours of the country became so popular that Andrew Ritchie attributes to them "the beginning of the modern 'weekend.'"[12] Thus, even in the first years of its existence, the bicycle is more than a form of transportation. Instead, it is the means to an escape from the frantic pace of modernity as well as a means of restoring health, rediscovering nature, and reclaiming time from demanding work schedules. Perhaps paradoxically, the late-Victorian bicycles that are produced on an industrial scale in the late-Victorian era become the means of escaping the frantic pace of the industrial age itself; the bicycles simultaneously provide speed and the opportunity to slow down and relax.

English author H. G. Wells, himself an enthusiastic cyclist, depicts the bicycle's growing association with liberation and freedom—Wells calls this association "the psychology of cycling"—in his 1896 novel, *The Wheels of Chance: A Bicycling Idyll*.[13] The novel's protagonist, Mr. Hoopdriver, a young assistant in a draper's shop, begins to expand beyond the bounds of his normal workaday self as soon as he pedals his secondhand bicycle beyond London on his cycling tour of the southern coast. On his holiday, Hoopdriver finds that "all the dreary, uninteresting routine drops like . . . chains fall[ing] about your feet."[14] Hoopdriver's escape is reflected in his bicycle riding, which, in its easy pace, contrasts with the regimented schedule of London and work: "He did not ride fast, he did not ride straight, an exacting critic might say he did not ride well—but he rode generously, opulently, using the whole road and even nibbling at the footpath."[15] In contrast with the regimented directness and straight-line efficiency of the railroads, Hoopdriver absentmindedly carves lazy S curves along the road, delighting in the scenery and the sensation of cycle travel. Not only does Hoopdriver meander along the road, but he begins to dare to consider leaving it altogether, "nibbling at" the idea of eschewing the established pathways and boundaries of modern life and setting his own course entirely.

On his bicycle Hoopdriver becomes someone new; or rather, he has awakened unexercised and unknown parts of himself. He fantasizes about leaving his class identity behind when he hears a bystander mistake him for "a bloomin' Dook" and when another cyclist, clearly a gentleman, addresses him as an equal.[16] In his mind, "the draper Hoopdriver, the Hand, had vanished from existence"; he was free, coasting downhill and emitting a "whoop for Freedom and Adventure!" punctuated by a resounding ring of his bicycle bell.[17] After a few days on the road, "Mr. Hoopdriver was possessed by unreasonable contentment; he lit himself a cigarette and lounged" on the roadside.[18] His thoughts take a romantic turn, and he imagines himself in heroic guise as he aids a young woman who, in an allusion to the significance of bicycling to the late-Victorian women's liberation movement, is escaping an undesirable suitor (and her mother) on her bicycle. In a chapter called "Mr. Hoopdriver, Knight-Errant," he even rises to the occasion and defends her honor in a fistfight, and soon he is inventing elaborate stories about himself, such as one he tells about shooting a lion and riding on the back of a giraffe in South Africa.

Cycling the countryside brings on, Wells notes, "joie de vivre! Albeit with a certain cramping sensation about the knees."[19] As Wells shows us through Hoopdriver, cycling engenders the sort of release that leads from the deadening humdrum of modern work to the invigorating creativity of the imagination. It is unsurprising, then, that bicycles are so often celebrated in literature, film, and art, such as in those texts that the essays in this book analyze and discuss. As the American author Christopher Morley writes, "The bicycle, the bicycle surely, should always be the vehicle of novelists and poets."[20] It is these same associations of cycling with literature and with freedom that lead a more well-known American author, Henry Miller (of *Tropic of Cancer* fame), to refer to his bicycle as "my best friend" and to reflect on how opportune the imaginative space opened up by bicycling is for "think[ing] about nothing but the characters" after "having finished a good book."[21] In particular, Miller tells us he enjoyed reflecting on Dostoevsky's characters; for while riding his bike, the people who populate Dostoevsky's works "were no longer characters from a book, but living creatures, people who haunted my reveries and dream life."[22] However, bicycles are not only liberating devices that free one's mind to think about literature and its ideas; they are also endlessly useful resources for *creating* literature and other kinds of artistic texts.

The Bicycle as Rolling Signifier

Even though we saw in the previous section how the bicycle, from its earliest incarnations, was embraced as a technological marvel associated with newfound mental and physical freedoms, we see the bicycle and its potential meanings increasingly expand, shift, and destabilize in the two decades that span the end of the Victorian era and the beginning of the twentieth century. For example, in the early twentieth century, following the introduction of the automobile, the bicycle goes from being a marker of modernity to one of antiquity and from signifying wealth to signifying working-class status. In fact, throughout its relatively short history, the bicycle has been a symbol in flux and has been associated with both sides of a diverse range of dichotomies: with childhood and adulthood,[23] masculinity and femininity,[24] heteronormativity and queerness,[25] the city and nature,[26] hipness and nerdiness,[27] purity and impurity,[28] the expansion of space and the constriction of space,[29] the public sphere and the private sphere,[30] and so on. Consequently, literature and culture return time and time again to the bicycle because it never remains stagnant for long, either as a vehicle for the transport of bodies or as a vehicle for conveying ideas. Like its real-world counterpart, the textual bicycle is often in motion. An overarching thesis of this collection of essays, therefore, is that a diverse range of texts has found the bicycle to be such a convenient and powerful image because throughout its history the bicycle has served as a blank slate onto which a panoply of values and ideologies can be projected. The various texts analyzed in this collection are interested in the bicycle and find it to be a useful image to appropriate, because the bicycle has always had this motion and this connotative flexibility at its core.

A noteworthy example of the bicycle's ability to serve as a protean, multifaceted symbol is Frances E. Willard's *A Wheel within a Wheel*. Willard, a well-known suffragist and founder of the Women's Christian Temperance Union, composed her book as a history of her experiences with first learning to ride a bicycle while, impressively, in her fifties. She also repeatedly circles back to the image of the bicycle and to her experience of learning to ride it as a useful symbol for various political and religious messages. For example, at one point, Willard draws a connection between the wheel and the human will by stating, "I felt that indeed the will is the wheel of the mind"; therefore, "when the wheel of the mind went well then the rubber wheel hummed merrily."[31] On the next page, however, Willard swiftly transitions to allegorizing the relationship between cyclist and cycle as representing the relationship between a human being and the larger world, a world "upon whose spinning-wheel we must all learn to ride, or fall into the sluiceways of oblivion and despair."[32] As a final example from Willard's text, we might note how convenient the suffragist Willard finds the bicycle when she wants to make a cogent point about the fickle nature of political reforms in general. One time, after both she and her bicycle end up in the gutter after a fall caused by a lack of "forward impetus," Willard tells us that she subsequently said to herself, "It is the same with all reforms: sometimes they seem to lag, then they barely balance, then they begin to oscillate as if they would lose track and tumble to one side; but all they need is a new impetus at the right moment on the right angle, and away they go again as merrily as if they had never threatened to stop at all."[33]

In sum, while learning to ride, Willard "found a whole philosophy of life in the wooing and winning" of her bicycle.[34] What we can glimpse from Willard's *A Wheel within a Wheel* is a succinct example of how endlessly useful the creative mind finds the image of the bicycle. Just as cycling is a deceptively diverse and complex phenomenon that belies the apparent straightforwardness of that term (for cycling, at present, can refer to anything from workday commuting to weekend road racing and from BMX trick riding to monster-bike strutting), so too do literary and cinematic bicycles invite heterogeneity and a wide range of signification and figuration.

Culture on Two Wheels

This book is part of what the sociologist John Urry has called the recent "mobility turn," a phrase that in the context of the social sciences refers to "a turn that emphasizes how all social entities, from a single household to large scale corporations, presuppose many different forms of actual and potential movement."[35] However, rather than looking at formerly neglected mobilities in the entities studied by the social sciences, this collection of essays examines formerly neglected mobilities in the subjects that the humanities study. Specifically, of course, we focus on the particular mobility created by bicycles found in a range of literary and screen texts. Although this book takes as one of its underlying assumptions that bicycles have, for the most part, been overlooked in the creative texts in which they appear, some recent studies have focused on other forms of mobility and transport represented on-screen and in literature. For example, Jonathan H. Grossman analyzes the significance of stagecoach and railway travel in the novels of Charles Dickens and connects Dickens's depiction of various modes of transport to "certain narratological complexities ... especially omniscient narration, simultaneity, serialization, and multi-plottedness."[36] Similarly, Christopher Schaberg examines "the *textuality* of airports" within "the culture of flight." Schaberg defines the latter phrase as "a dispersed set of sensibilities, individual feelings, and collective moods circulating around the subject of air travel," which can be found in creative texts ranging from the F. Scott Fitzgerald short story "Three Hours between Planes" to the Don DeLillo novel *Falling Man* to the Ani DiFranco song "The Arrivals Gate."[37] Of course, scholars have studied for decades now more mundane and commonplace modes of transport, such as travel by automobile and by walking, for their significance in texts of various kinds.[38] Put simply, we see our book's focus on bicycles as part of the larger turn toward issues of mobility in fields like the social sciences as well as part of the move toward a greater focus on representations of transportation in literary and screen studies.

All scholars in all fields of study, of course, owe some debt to those who came before them. *Culture on Two Wheels: The Bicycle in Literature and Film*, admittedly, does not break wholly new ground. A search of the MLA International Bibliography reveals that a few scholars have been (at least sporadically) noticing the importance of bicycles in literary texts since around the late 1960s. For example, examination of an enigmatic reference to "Henry's bicycle" in Hemingway's *The Sun Also Rises* has led to a few early essays written by literary critics who probed the significance of bicycle references in literature.[39] In a much more sustained early analysis of bicycling references, Janet Menzies notes of Beckett's abundant use of cycling imagery, "The bicycle is integral to Beckett's work; the appearance, possession and disappearance coincide with and reflect changes in the physical status of characters and even in the tone of the narrative."[40] James E. Starrs and Alon Raab have edited and written important texts calling attention to the myriad references to bicycles in a wide array of literary works.[41] However, Starrs's book is primarily an anthology of scenes of bicycles in literature, and Raab's essay is an overview description of such scenes. Neither work contains a robust analytical component. The bicycle, in sum, has been noted in literary texts and studied by literary critics for nearly fifty years now, but it has not yet been the subject of any kind of in-depth or consistent critical analysis.[42]

This collection of essays is, therefore, the first sustained examination to date of the significance of bicycles in literary and screen texts, and it will draw on the most recent work done by cycling scholars from various disciplines while also drawing on the most recent work and theories of literary, screen, and cultural studies scholars. This collection of essays aims to fill a lacuna that exists in the scholarship of bicycling, and this gap relates to studies of representations of bicycles in literature and film. Most cycling-related scholarship up until this point has focused either on the technical evolution or on the sociological significance of the bicycle. Represented by important, book-length studies done by historians such as Andrew Ritchie and David Herlihy, the technical approach examines primarily the mechanical evolution of bicycles and often tries to understand which technological innovations moved the bicycle from its earliest incarnations in the two-wheeled but pedalless hobbyhorse of the early nineteenth century through the velocipede, the ordinary, and, finally, the safety bicycle of the latter half of the nineteenth century.[43]

The sociological approach is well represented by Robert A. Smith's *A Social History of the Bicycle*, a work examining how bicycles interacted with and related to discourses of (among others things) religion, fashion, health, and gender in Victorian-era America, and more recently by the essay collection *Cycling and Society*.[44] The analyses of cycling executed in this latter book often center on statistical and quantitative data on cycling, which is often a hallmark of the socio-logical study of bicycling. Additionally, the work done on cycling by scholars associated with research networks such as the Cycling and Society Research Group (based largely in the United Kingdom) and by Bicicultures (based largely in the United States) also trends heav-ily toward sociological, geographical, and anthropological approaches to the study of bicycles and bicycle culture.

Overview of This Collection

This collection of essays complements the above-mentioned scholarly work by analyzing the significance of bicycles in various literary, cin-ematic, and musical texts and is divided into two parts. Part 1, "Bikes in Literature," examines bicycles that appear in a variety of literary texts. This first part covers texts written in time periods ranging from the 1880s, the era of high-wheelers and tricycles, to the late twentieth century, looking at bikes in genres such as novels, short stories, and travelogues. Part 2, "Bikes in Film," focuses on depictions of bicycles in various films of the twentieth and twenty-first centuries and in the music videos of some recent songs. Our contributors draw attention to the ways in which bicycles function not only as literal vehicles in many texts but also as figurative vehicles for those texts' themes; ideas; and social, political, and aesthetic critiques. In order to demonstrate the widespread dispersal of bicycles throughout many different kinds of creative works, the authors in this collection analyze the appear-ance of bicycles both in canonical works such as Samuel Beckett's modernist novel *Molloy*, the Oscar-winning film *Breaking Away*, and the popular fiction of Stephen King and in lesser-known but equally significant texts such as *The Sacrifice*, a film by celebrated Russian director Andrei Tarkovsky, and *A Canterbury Pilgrimage*, a nineteenth-century travelogue by Elizabeth Robins Pennell and Joseph Pennell that retraces the route of Chaucer's pilgrims via bicycle. For our con-tributors, images of cycling in both canonical and noncanonical texts are, to paraphrase the title of Lance Armstrong's best-selling memoir, not always about the (literal) bike—they are also about the image of the bike and the vital role that image plays in communicating a text's larger political, cultural, social, and artistic ideas.[45]

In addition to shifting the analysis of bicycles to a consideration of more literary and cinematic contexts and away from sociological and technical ones, we also shift some emphasis to bicycles appearing in global texts. That is, one criticism that has often accompanied previous studies of cycling, particularly studies looking at the technical evolution of bicycles, is that they focus too much on cycling in white contexts in the United States and Great Britain. Our edited collection aims to avoid such limitations by including essays that go beyond the typical white, Anglo-American contexts in order to consider, for example, cycling in African American culture and in non-Western literature and film. Admittedly, our collection includes analyses of mainstream, canonical texts such as *The Wizard of Oz* and Proust's celebrated French novel *In Search of Lost Time*. However, this collection also includes a chapter on bicycles in American hip-hop music and culture as well as essays on the role of bicycles in global cinema, such as the Chinese film *Beijing Bicycle* and the Saudi film *Wadjda*. Although there is clearly much more work that needs to be done in bringing attention to the significance of bicycles in non-Western texts, we see our collection as contributing in an important, albeit modest, way what we hope will be an ongoing expansion in scholarly focus.[46]

Notes

1. For a useful overview of many of the cycling-related transformations happening in American cities, particularly with regards to policy and infrastructure changes, see Jeff Mapes, *Pedaling Revolution: How Cyclists Are Changing American Cities* (Corvallis: Oregon State University Press, 2009).
2. New York City is, at the time of this writing, the latest high-profile example of a major city that has rolled out a large-scale bike-share program. On the New York City bike-share program, see Eben Weiss, "Bike Share's Rough Ride," *New York Times*, May 23, 2014, http://nyti.ms/1hiFqkY.
3. See chapter 8, "Health and the Bicycle," in Mapes, *Pedaling Revolution*.
4. For an excellent discussion of environmentalism's relationship to the bicycle, see Dave Horton, "Environmentalism and the Bicycle," *Environmental Politics* 15, no. 1 (2006): 41–58.
5. For more on Iowa's annual noncompetitive, border-to-border ride, see Greg Borzo, RAGBRAI: *America's Favorite Bicycle Ride* (Charleston SC: History Press, 2013).
6. For a discussion of cycling's connections to the DIY movement and to subcultures like that of punk music, see chapter 6 in Zack Furness, *One Less Car:*

Bicycling and the Politics of Automobility (Philadelphia PA: Temple University Press, 2010), 140–69.

7. For fashion, see Horst A. Friedrichs, *Cycle Style* (New York: Prestel Publishing, 2012); for erotica, see the zine *BikeSexuality: True Tales of Bicycling and Desire* (2012) and Portland's frequent bike porn festivals.

8. Recent bicycle-themed art exhibits include the Chinese artist Ai Weiwei's massive sculpture *Forever Bikes*, which consists of more than three thousand bikes and is the centerpiece of the 2013 Nuit Blanche art festival in Toronto, Canada, and the sculpture exhibit *Native Kids Ride Bikes*, an art exhibition showing the relationship between bicycles and Native American culture, on display in 2013 at the University of Iowa Museum of Art.

9. See Glen Norcliffe, *The Ride to Modernity: The Bicycle in Canada, 1869–1900* (Toronto: University of Toronto Press, 2001), 23.

10. Unsigned article, quoted in Stephen Channing and Shirley Channing, *A Victorian Cyclist: Rambling through Kent in 1886* (Birchington, UK: Ōzaru Books, 2011), 118, 98.

11. David Herlihy, *Bicycle: The History* (New Haven CT: Yale University Press, 2004), 289.

12. Andrew Ritchie, *King of the Road: An Illustrated History of Cycling* (Berkeley CA: Ten Speed Press, 1975), 89.

13. H. G. Wells, *The Wheels of Chance: A Bicycling Idyll*, vol. 7 of *The Works of H. G. Wells* (New York: Charles Scribner's Sons, 1925). All quotations are from this edition.

14. Wells, *Wheels of Chance*, 14.

15. Wells, *Wheels of Chance*, 16.

16. Wells, *Wheels of Chance*, 18.

17. Wells, *Wheels of Chance*, 20, 21.

18. Wells, *Wheels of Chance*, 97.

19. Wells, *Wheels of Chance*, 22.

20. Christopher Morley, *The Romany Stain* (New York: Doubleday, Page, 1926), 35.

21. Henry Miller, *My Bike and Other Friends*, vol. 2 of *Book of Friends* (Santa Barbara: Capra Press, 1978), 106.

22. Miller, *My Bike*, 107.

23. Throughout the nineteenth century, bicycle manufacturers made only adult models of their bikes. However, during the golden era of suburbanization and of car ownership (the 1950s and '60s), bike sales for children vastly outnumbered adult bike sales, and the bike became more closely associated with a child's toy that one should eventually outgrow. But with the energy crisis of the 1970s, adult bikes once again began to make up a considerable portion of annual bike sales.

24. For a discussion of how the gender associations of bicycles was contested in, for example, the late-Victorian era, see Phillip Gordon Mackintosh and Glen

Norcliffe, "Men, Women and the Bicycle: Gender and Social Geography of Cycling in the Late-Nineteenth Century" in *Cycling and Society*, ed. Dave Horton, Paul Rosen, and Peter Cox (Aldershot, UK: Ashgate, 2007), 153–77.

25. In the early days of the ordinary bicycle (also known as the high-wheeler), cycling was an emphatically masculinist activity associated with rugged athleticism and exposure to danger. However, as Zack Furness argues, in recent times bicycling has been depicted in mass media as an activity of males whose sexual orientation is rendered suspect due to the riding of bicycles. See chapter 5, "Two-Wheeled Terrors and Forty-Year-Old Virgins: Mass Media and the Representations of Bicycling," in Furness, *One Less Car*.

26. See, for example, the above discussion of Wells's *Wheels of Chance*, where the bicycle represents a newfound ability of the working class to escape the city and to access the nature of the countryside. However, with contemporary cycling by fixie enthusiasts, punk rockers, chic young professionals, and so forth, the bicycle is arguably more of an urban phenomenon as of late.

27. See Furness, *One Less Car*, for his discussions of how hipster subcultures are increasingly embracing the bicycle, while at the same time more mainstream culture is viewing bike riding as an activity associated with such negative characteristics as being unhip, unemployed, and sexually unsuccessful.

28. We are referring here, of course, to the doping scandals among Tour de France cyclists, such as those of Tommy Simpson (who died from amphetamine-related heart failure during the 1967 tour) and Lance Armstrong, and how such scandals have problematized the notion of cycling as being a clean and categorically healthy sport.

29. Dave Horton, "Social Movements and the Bicycle," *Thinking about Cycling* (blog), November 25, 2009, https://thinkingaboutcycling.files.wordpress.com/2009/11/social-movements-and-the-bicycle.pdf. Horton writes, "Within contemporary oppositional politics . . . riding a bicycle becomes less a continuation of the search for modern [spatial] freedoms, and more a critique of the negative social and environmental effects of too much 'freedom' in mobility" (11).

30. In its early days, the bicycle was seized on by feminists looking for a technology that enhanced women's privacy by allowing them to escape the watchful eyes of male chaperones. But in recent times, environmentalists and other political groups see the bicycle as a device that enhances public interaction and increases exposure to one's local surroundings. Horton discusses both of these views of the bicycle in his "Social Movements and the Bicycle."

31. Frances E. Willard, *A Wheel within a Wheel* (New York: F. H. Revell, 1895; Bedford MA: Applewood Books, 1997), 26. Citations refer to the Applewood edition.

32. Willard, *Wheel within a Wheel*, 27.

33. Willard, *Wheel within a Wheel*, 28–29.

34. Willard, *Wheel within a Wheel*, 25.

35. John Urry, *Mobilities* (Cambridge, UK: Polity Press, 2007), 6. See also Margaret Grieco and John Urry, eds., *Mobilities: New Perspectives on Transport and Society* (Aldershot, UK: Ashgate, 2012).

36. Jonathan H. Grossman, *Charles Dickens's Networks: Public Transport and the Novel* (Oxford: Oxford University Press, 2012), 7. On the railroads, see also Wolfgang Schivelbusch, *The Railway Journey: The Industrialization of Time and Space in the Nineteenth Century* (Berkeley: University of California Press, 1986).

37. Christopher Schaberg, *The Textual Life of Airports: Reading the Culture of Flight* (New York: Bloomsbury, 2013), 1, 4, original emphasis.

38. On cars, see, for example, Roger N. Casey, *Textual Vehicles: The Automobile in American Literature* (New York: Garland, 1997); Deborah Clarke, *Driving Women: Fiction and Automobile Culture in Twentieth-Century America* (Baltimore: Johns Hopkins University Press, 2007); Jerry W. Passon, *The Corvette in Literature and Culture: Symbolic Dimensions of America's Sports Car* (Jefferson NC: McFarland, 2011). On walking, see, for example, Jeffrey C. Robinson, *The Walk: Notes on a Romantic Image* (Norman: University of Oklahoma Press, 1989); Roger Gilbert, *Walks in the World: Representation and Experience in Modern American Poetry* (Princeton NJ: Princeton University Press, 1991); Anne D. Wallace, *Walking, Literature, and English Culture: The Origins and Uses of Peripatetic in the Nineteenth Century* (Oxford: Oxford University Press, 1995); Donna Landry, *The Invention of the Countryside: Hunting, Walking, and Ecology in English Literature, 1671–1831* (New York: Palgrave, 2001).

39. See Robert O. Stephens and James Ellis, "Hemingway, Fitzgerald, and the Riddle of 'Henry's Bicycle,'" *English Language Notes* 5, no. 1 (1967): 46–49; Fred D. Crawford and Bruce Morton, "Hemingway and Brooks: The Mystery of 'Henry's Bicycle,'" *Studies in American Fiction* 6, no. 1 (1978): 106–9.

40. Janet Menzies, "Beckett's Bicycles," *Journal of Beckett Studies*, no. 6 (1980): 98.

41. James E. Starrs, ed., *The Literary Cyclist: Great Bicycling Scenes in Literature* (New York: Breakaway Books, 1997; originally published in 1982 as *The Noiseless Tenor: The Bicycle in Literature*); Alon Raab, "Wheels of Fire: Writers on Bicycles," *World Literature Today* 86, no. 5 (2012): 22–31.

42. Besides Hemingway and Beckett, another author whose fondness for references to bicycles has been examined for some time now by scholars is Sir Arthur Conan Doyle. See, for example, M. Haddon-MacRoberts, "The Mystery of the Missing Bicycles," *Baker Street Journal* 31, no. 3 (1981): 135–44; Richard Warner, "The Scorcher and the Lady," *Baker Street Journal* 31, no. 3 (1981): 145–46.

43. See Herlihy, *Bicycle*; Ritchie, *King of the Road*.

44. See Robert A. Smith, *A Social History of the Bicycle* (New York: American Heritage Press, 1972); Horton, Rosen, and Cox, *Cycling and Society*.

45. Lance Armstrong, *It's Not about the Bike: My Journey back to Life*, with Sally Jenkins (New York: G. P. Putnam's Sons, 2000).

46. One scholar who has been working especially hard to try to bring more awareness of cycling's deep connections to the non-Western world is Alon Raab. Raab critiques David Herlihy's recent history of the bicycle for the short shrift it gives non-Western cycling. Raab writes, "David Herlihy's much-praised *Bicycle: The History* devoted only 2 of its 480 pages to China and India, nations that comprise a third of the human race and where bicycles are abundant. These omissions ignore the particular flavor and the wealth of experience of every locale." Raab, "Wheels of Fire," 25.

PART 1   **BIKES IN LITERATURE**

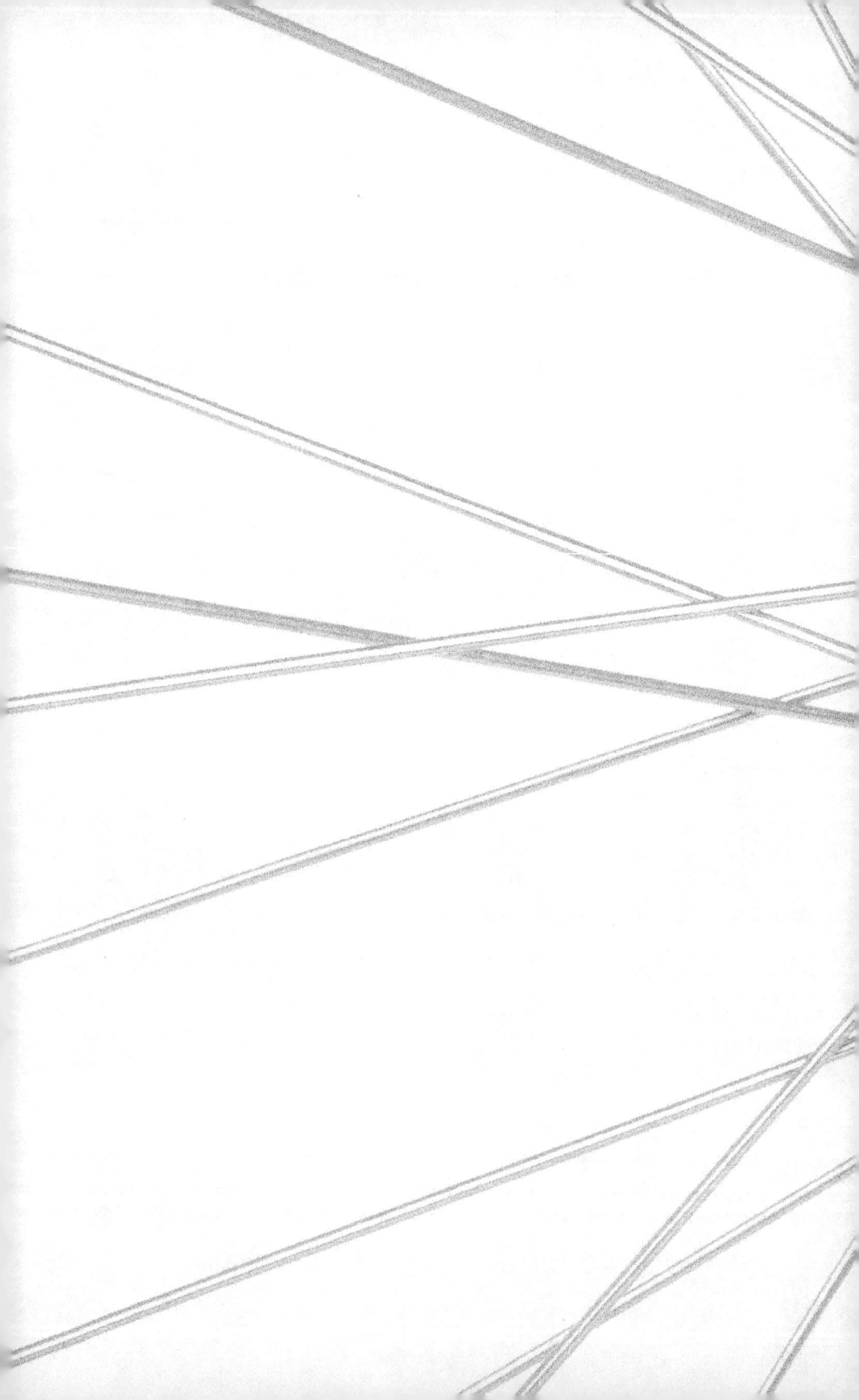

1   Pilgrims on Wheels

The Pennells, F. W. Bockett, and Literary Cycle Travels

DAVE BUCHANAN

Laurence Sterne, eighteenth-century author of *Tristram Shandy* and *A Sentimental Journey through France and Italy*, never rode a tricycle. He couldn't have. The earliest prototype of bicycles and tricycles, the Draisine or hobbyhorse, wasn't invented until after 1810, fifty years after Sterne died. But according to early cycle-travel writers Elizabeth Robins Pennell and Joseph Pennell writing in 1887, Sterne would surely have appreciated leisure cycle travel, at least in the Pennells' tandem-tricycle style; for it was, they claim, perfectly suited to Sterne's meandering, sentimental disposition. In the dedicatory letter to the long-dead Sterne in *Our Sentimental Journey through France and Italy*, the Pennells claim that Sterne would have preferred cycle travel even to a railway carriage and that on a tandem tricycle with its two seats, Sterne "would still have a place for 'the lady,'" a sly nod to the flirtatious tendencies of Sterne's narrator in *A Sentimental Journey*, Mr. Yorick.[1]

Thomas Carlyle, a nineteenth-century essayist and philosopher, never cycled either, at least as far as we know. But that doesn't prevent F. W. Bockett, author of *Some Literary Landmarks for Pilgrims on Wheels* (1901), from imagining Carlyle awheel. Bockett wonders what the notoriously cranky Carlyle might have gained by riding a bicycle. He observes that the "Gentle Art" of cycling "gives inspiration to the poet, health and strength to the plain man, vigour to the man of science, and breadth to the philosopher" and half-jokingly speculates on the potential benefits of cycling for the crotchety Sage of Chelsea: "Imagination fails one in the attempt to conceive what Carlyle might have been had he practised vaulting into the saddle over a pair of sound pneumatics. . . . The adjuncts of cycling would have taken some of the objectionable philosophic starch out of Thomas."[2] Cycling, suggests Bockett, has a way of providing what we might today call *perspective*—something that, in Bockett's view, Carlyle badly needed.

That both the Pennells and Bockett engage in brief imaginative exercises—what-if vignettes—connecting cycling in the late-Victorian present to literature of the past is a striking, if bizarre, coincidence that reveals something about late-Victorian associations between cycling and literature. These hypothetical time-traveling scenarios (Sterne flirting on a tandem, Carlyle letting loose on two wheels) illustrate how cycling in the late-Victorian period possessed imaginative overtones connecting writers of the past with riders, writers, and readers of the present.

Although cycling was a relatively new phenomenon and a technological wonder in the late nineteenth century, in its leisure forms (as opposed to racing, or "scorching" as it was known) cycling was as much an *aesthetic* as an *athletic* activity, one associated with a set of values that looked *backward* more than forward.[3] As a result, cycling offered a particularly apt vehicle for journeys into the literary past, especially pilgrimages to places of literary interest. The newfangled modern machine of the bicycle proved, in fact, the ideal vehicle for nostalgic, bookish travel.[4] In the late nineteenth century, cycling became implicated in the broader trend of what Nicola J. Watson calls "readerly tourism."[5] The cycle-travel writing of the Pennells in the 1880s and of F. W. Bockett around the turn of the century exemplifies the late Victorians' fascination with the old *and* with the new at the same time.[6] These literary pilgrims on wheels connect a yearning for the literary past to a new mode of transportation aligned with the future.

Literary tourism, or the practice of visiting places associated with particular authors or books "in order to savor text, place and their interrelations," is, according to Watson, a relatively recent phenomenon, emerging in the eighteenth century and flourishing in the nineteenth, in Great Britain and North America.[7] The idea may, in fact, go back even further. Ian Ousby suggests that literary tourism developed in England following the Reformation, when a kind of secular version of the religious pilgrimage evolved. According to Ousby, when the Reformation "purged saints from the calendar, stripped idols from churches, and denuded the landscape of shrines, the public need for these things had to find secular equivalents."[8] And the author "provided the ideal hero for a secular culture," becoming a kind of secular saint.

This readerly tourism generally entailed pilgrimages to authors' birthplaces, homes, haunts, and graves and sometimes to the fictional terrain of the authors' books. Shakespeare's Stratford-upon-Avon, Burns's Alloway, Sir Walter Scott's Abbotsford, the Brontë sisters' Haworth, Dickens's London, and Hardy's Wessex were among the favorite destinations of nineteenth-century literary pilgrims; and in the second half of the nineteenth century especially, book-length accounts of these pilgrimage journeys proliferated.[9] Readers went on a pilgrimage to "re-experience the text"—to somehow re-create the sense of authenticity associated with a reader's original encounter with a favorite text or author.[10]

Watson suggests that the decades between the 1880s and the 1920s were the heyday of the notion of literary countries in Great Britain (e.g., "Dickens-Land" and "Hardy Country")—that this was the period when literary tourists, "clasping text in one hand," could most readily be found traipsing around the country "in search of spots infused with sentiment."[11] This golden age of literary tourism happens to coincide with the first era of leisure cycle travel, and the two trends—journeying to places of literary interest and riding cycles for pleasure—overlapped in sometimes surprising ways. This essay argues that cycling, for the Pennells and for Bockett, both enhances and complicates the experience of literary pilgrimage. The new technology of tricycles and bicycles lends a unique kind of authenticity to literary pilgrimage but also undermines it, in different ways for the Pennells and Bockett.

Joseph Pennell and Elizabeth Robins Pennell may well have been the first to establish a link between leisure cycle travel and literary pilgrimage.[12] The Pennells were a husband-and-wife duo (he was primarily an illustrator, she a writer) from Philadelphia but based in London. In the 1880s and '90s, they were pioneers of early cycle travel and prolific producers of cycling literature and illustrations. They published five illustrated books and dozens of illustrated magazine articles about their cycle travels and, in the process, helped invent the idea of leisure cycle touring. In 1887 one anonymous critic credited the Pennells with offering "by far the most important and charming literary treatment of the cycle."[13] By the 1890s they had become "bicycling's most famous couple."[14]

Although all of the Pennells' cycle-travel books feature literary elements to some degree, two of them deal specifically with literary pilgrimages. In *A Canterbury Pilgrimage* (1885), their first book together, the Pennells use their tandem tricycle to trace, as closely as possible, the route of Chaucer's pilgrims from London to Canterbury, exploring the literary geography of Kent along the way. *Our Sentimental Journey through France and Italy* (1887), their third book, tells of the Pennells' journey in France, again by tandem tricycle, a trip inspired by Sterne's classic of a similar name.[15]

Prior to the Pennells, cycle-travel narratives had been rare; and those that did exist, like A. D. Chandler and J. C. Sharp's *A Bicycle Tour in England and Wales* (1881) and the two "Nauticus" books, tended to be largely descriptive, more itinerary than literary.[16] The Pennells, however, struck on a unique and winning formula for the time: taking the literate, slightly satirical, picturesque style of travel writing popularized by Robert Louis Stevenson in *Travels with a Donkey in the Cévennes* (1879) and giving it their unique cycling twist—a kind of *Travels with a Tricycle*.[17]

The Pennells' cycle-travel writing, like Stevenson's book, tapped into an interest in, perhaps even a nostalgia for, preindustrial forms of travel in an age so dominated by the railroad.[18] In the mid-1880s, the public was intrigued by cycling as a new form of travel associated with "modern invention." Although bicycle *racing* had been popular since the advent of the machines in the 1860s, it was really only after the rise of the tricycle in the early 1880s that regular folks began to think of cycles as a means for journeying to places.[19] The Pennells shrewdly capitalized on the public's curiosity about this new leisure-cycling possibility by combining it with the popular trend of literary tourism. The "average cycler," who isn't interested in "hanging around race-tracks," the Pennells suggest, may see the merit of using his or

1.1. Joseph Pennell and Elizabeth Robins Pennell setting out for Canterbury. *A Canterbury Pilgrimage* (1885).

her machine for "making Pilgrims' Progresses and Sentimental Journeys" instead.[20] Essentially, the Pennells ingeniously combined *two* backward-looking trends in Victorian culture—a reactionary travel movement and literary tourism—with a forward-looking, modern one: cycling.

The Pennells' merging of old texts and a new way to travel, however, works better with some texts than with others. My argument is that although both of their literary cycling pilgrimages are, to some degree, sentimental undertakings suffused with a bookish nostalgia, the Pennells' cycle travel turns out to be a better fit with Chaucerian satire than with Sternean sentiment.[21] As a result, while their Canterbury book shows how cycle travel can enhance a literary pilgrimage, their Sterne book reveals how cycle travel can, at least partially, undermine one.

With *A Canterbury Pilgrimage*, the Pennells achieve an elegant fit between text and tricycle, between the style of the author they are tracking and their own approach to travel. *The Canterbury Tales'* brand of medieval-estates satire—which pokes fun at character types from the three estates of clergy, nobility, and peasantry—aligns surprisingly well with both Elizabeth's wry satirical penchant and the way cycle travel allows for close observation of a broad range of social classes en route. Elizabeth points out how "as in Chaucer's day, both rich and poor go upon pilgrimage through Kent."[22] And, indeed, the Pennells do encounter a variety of travelers from across the social spectrum—from tramps, itinerant laborers, and gypsies to clergy and middle-class tourists. In the spirit of The Canterbury Tales, Elizabeth offers several detailed, humorous, Chaucerian sketches of such characters. One, involving a busybody priest they meet at the end of their journey, recalls some of the satirical portraits of the clergy found in The Canterbury Tales.[23] Another sketch depicts an annoying fellow cycle traveler whom the Pennells encounter in Sittingbourne. This latter episode is a particularly good example of Elizabeth adding a late-Victorian twist to Chaucer's estates satire. Interestingly, cyclists, a kind of modern estate, are also a frequent target of satire in the Pennells' cycle-travel writing.

Although the Pennells were great advocates for cycling, they poked fun at certain kinds of (mostly pretentious) cyclists who were becoming commonplace on late nineteenth-century roads.[24] For example, the London watchmaker, traveling by cycle with his wife, accosts the tandem-riding Pennells with the somewhat insulting refrain, "I don't like tandems, do you?" The Pennells politely ignore the watchmaker's repeated complaints. But before long he reveals the extent of his silliness. In response to the watchmaker's interrogation, the Pennells explain that they are American:

"From Canada?" his wife asked.
"Oh, no!" I answered; "from Philadelphia."
"Dear me!" the watchmaker said; "then you're *real* Americans! But you speak English very well!"[25]

This amusing portrait of a rambling, tandem-loathing cyclist recalls, for instance, Chaucer's depiction of the garrulous Monk in The Canterbury Tales, who, like the Pennells' watchmaker, also doesn't know when to stop talking.

The Pennells' close reading and riding of the landscape of Kent uncovers traces of multiple authors and texts, not just Chaucer and his tales. In some ways, the Charles Dickens component of the Pennells' literary pilgrimage is almost as prominent as the Chaucer one. Several of Dickens's novels are set or partly set in this territory, and Elizabeth drops names of classic Dickens characters such as David Copperfield ("a modern pilgrim"), Pip, Mr. Grewgious, "opium-eating Mr. Jasper" from *The Mystery of Edwin Drood*, and "Mr. Pickwick and his friends," whose adventures in the area often ended at the Bull Inn.[26] Passing through sleepy Rochester, Elizabeth points out that Dickens gave it the name "Dulborough" (deservedly, she insists). She also notes, with a hint of sentiment, how Dickens spent the final years of his life nearby at Gad's Hill.[27]

The Dickensian connections were shrewd additions to the Chaucerian thread of the narrative. Dickens's works were still fresh in the minds of readers and much revered by what Elizabeth calls "the scholarly public," who made up a good portion of the Pennells' readers.[28] Dickens and his work had been, and would be, responsible for generating a fair number of literary-pilgrimage books in the years following his death.[29] Readers may well have known the fictional terrain of Dickens Land even better than that of *The Canterbury Tales*.

In addition to being a neat fit with Chaucer, the Pennells' tricycle travel is well suited for a kind of Dickensian blending of sentiment and satire. As the Pennells wheel through rural Kent, they are brought face-to-face with country tramps and migrant hops pickers who line the roadways. (These are sights that rail travelers, in particular, rarely saw up close on their journeys.) The Pennells' descriptions of their interactions with these lower classes are, by turns, sentimental ("whimpering and weary" children lagging behind their overladen mothers) and satirical (compared to one tramp's vacant facial features, "an idiot's face would have been intelligent," Elizabeth jabs), in a manner that recalls Dickens's own mixture of these modes in his fiction.[30]

This unlikely blending of Chaucerian social satire, Dickensian sentiment and satire, and modern cycle travel in *A Canterbury Pilgrimage* was a hit with readers, who in the mid-1880s were both intrigued by nostalgic literary pilgrimages (especially involving beloved authors

1.2. Joseph Pennell and Elizabeth Robins Pennell, pilgrims new and old. *A Canterbury Pilgrimage* (1885).

such as Chaucer and Dickens) and fascinated by the newness of cycle travel. One of Joseph's illustrations shows medieval pilgrims on horseback facing off against modern ones on their "steel steeds," and this image nicely captures the Pennells' unique articulation of the connected pleasures of reading the old and riding the new. With their second literary cycling pilgrimage, however, that double vantage point, looking backward and forward at the same time, proved more difficult to achieve.

In the Pennells' view, cycling is the ideal way to re-create Laurence Sterne's original travel experience in *A Sentimental Journey*. They contend that riding a modern tricycle closely approximates the way Sterne himself must have traveled in the days before rail travel. In *Our Sentimental Journey*'s dedicatory letter to Sterne, the Pennells explain that "the oft-regretted delights of travelling in days of coach and post-chaise, destroyed on the coming of the railroad, were once more to be had by means of tricycle or bicycle."[31] They lament that "nowadays the manner of travelling through France and Italy is by rail, mostly on Cook's tickets, and chaises have become a luxury which we at least cannot afford. The only vehicle by which we could follow your [Sterne's] wheel-tracks along the old post roads was our tricycle, an ingenious machine of modern invention."[32] Paradoxically, it is the *modern* tricycle that offers the best way to re-create an eighteenth-century travel experience—following the same roads, more or less, at a similar pace but with the added bonus of independence (that is, cycle travelers were not beholden to the nuisance of the needs of horses).

While their tricycle helps the Pennells trace key Sternean landmarks, it doesn't always aid their attempts to re-create the sentimental mood of Sterne's text. Consider, for instance, the Pennells' description of the "classic ground" between Montreuil and Nampont, where the infamous "Dead Ass" incident occurs in *A Sentimental Journey*.[33] In Sterne's account, Yorick and his sidekick, LaFleur, are travelling by post chaise between the two towns, when they encounter a dead ass in the middle of the road. Shortly after, in Nampont, they meet the weeping owner of that same dead ass. Yorick is struck by the "simplicity" of the man's grief for his dead animal, and he recounts the man's story of how the ass had been the "patient partner of his journey" over the Pyrenees during a pilgrimage to Spain and had "eat[en] the same bread with him all that way, and was unto him as a friend."[34] Yorick, touched by this tale, concludes, "Shame on this world! . . . Did we love each other as this poor soul loved his ass—t'would be something."[35] It's a classic moment of sentiment—Yorick overcome with emotion at the sight of another's suffering.

However, Elizabeth and Joseph are, in the end, unsatisfied with their visit to this much-anticipated landmark. Although they find what they think might be the "post-house" in front of which "the donkey's master told his pathetic tale," an old man passing by "knew nothing of it," and Elizabeth's prose exudes a touch of the literary pilgrim's disappointment that no one else seems to know or care about the significance of this hallowed landmark.[36] It's a typical literary-pilgrimage moment according to Watson—the visit to hallowed ground ends up feeling anticlimactic. The landmark that has such sentimental value for devoted readers is unnoticed by the rest of the world.[37]

The Pennells' tricycle plays a curious role in this episode of disappointment. The machine allows them to follow Sterne's authentic trail into Nampont. But once there, the Pennells decide to walk their tricycle through the village rather than ride it, as if they don't quite trust the machine to allow them to pick up subtler clues to Sterne's ghostly legacy. The tricycle's modern associations can't quite be reconciled with old-fashioned sentiment; and when Elizabeth mentions the village's new café as "the one sign of modern enterprise in Nampont," she's forgetting about that other "modern enterprise," their machine, which feels somehow out of place there. This divide between old and new is further emphasized when she comments on how Sterne, on the way out of Nampont, overcome by emotion, "went to sleep" in his carriage—"a sweet lenitive for evils," Elizabeth observes, "which Nature does not hold out to the cycler."[38]

As the cycling gets more difficult the farther the Pennells get into France, so grows the tension between sentiment and cycling. Elizabeth tries her best to adopt a Yorick-like approach to travel—meandering and sentimental—but finds such a method antithetical to both her desire to keep moving along and her natural tendency toward sarcasm. She writes more than once of feeling a "duty to be sentimental" and thus seeing sentimentality as now more an obligation than an instinct.[39] In Montreuil, for instance, after meeting some beggars in the street—Sterne's Yorick gets quite sentimental about the "sons and daughters of poverty" he sees there, gradually emptying his pockets for them—Elizabeth admits that "our hearts were hardened against them" after a day of cycling into a howling headwind.[40] Again Elizabeth observes that Yorick had the luxury of sleeping off "the ill-humour of his journey" in a carriage, but she and Joseph do not.[41] She concludes, "I think it was at Montreuil that it first occurred to us that sentiment does not depend on man's will alone."[42] Later in the book, after another day of hard riding, Elizabeth says, "For the hundredth time I admitted to myself that sentiment might do for a post-chaise, but was impossible on a tricycle."[43] It's as if the very technology that has enabled the Pennells to re-create an authentic Sternean pilgrimage experience is now interfering with their ability to feel what Sterne felt, is now working against their attempt to connect with a favorite dead author.

In the Pennells' Canterbury book, then, cycling helps bring the Pennells closer to the authors at the center of their pilgrimage, while in the case of *Our Sentimental Journey*, the tricycle sometimes pushes them apart. Perhaps, then, it is not surprising that the public response to the Sterne book was disappointing. Sales were much lower than expected.[44] One possible explanation is that with the rise of the safety bicycle in the mid-1880s, the short-lived tricycle honeymoon was over, and readers were more interested in travel by bicycle, which was, by then, the way of the future. However, another explanation for the book's relatively poor reception could be that readers and reviewers picked up on this disconnect between the sentiment of Sterne and the satire of the Pennells.[45]

In *Some Literary Landmarks for Pilgrims on Wheels* (1901), F. W. Bockett proclaims that "no ride can compete with one to some place of historic or other interest which you are to see for the first time."[46] In particular, Bockett endorses short (one- or two-day) cycle trips to "historic shrine[s]" of literary significance.[47] His book recounts numerous such cycle pilgrimages in southern England, to birthplaces, homes, and grave sites associated with some of Bockett's favorite famous authors, such as Jane Austen, Percy Shelley, Alfred Tennyson, and Charles Lamb. (He also visits places linked to more obscure—at least to us—literary names: Thomas Day, Abraham Cowley, William Cobbett, Gilbert White.) Nothing compares, Bockett insists, to the "keen excitement" a cyclist experiences riding to a literary landmark. As "you pedal on you draw mental pictures of the spot as you conceive it to be" and ponder how "along this very road the great So-and-so must often have walked, by the girth of that oak tree he might often have lingered under the shade of its wide-spreading boughs."[48]

Bockett is, like the Pennells, a literary cyclist who loves books *and* bicycles equally. He assumes his "gentle reader" is someone like him, "whose dearest treasures" are "well-thumbed books" but who isn't content to sit inside reading all day.[49] Bockett suggests that cycling is, in fact, the best way to carry out literary pilgrimages, and he offers his book as a humble guide to fellow modern pilgrims "who have discarded staff and sandals for the more comfortable and expeditious rubber-tyred wheels."[50] Pilgrimage on foot is a pale comparison. He argues, "To be held down to a snail's progress of four miles an hour by steady toe-and-heel tramping, and then suddenly to be gifted with the power of flying through the air at the rate of fourteen miles an hour with no more exertion . . . this was intoxication."[51] The bicycle, in Bockett's view, offers a new and vastly superior way for pilgrims to reach their destinations.

For the most part, cycling improves the literary-pilgrimage experience for Bockett, as it does mostly with the Pennells, though in a different way. Bockett emphasizes the contemplative and philosophical aspects of cycling and how cycle travel fosters a kind of pilgrim's frame of mind. The tone and temper of Bockett's book owes an obvious debt to Izaak Walton's classic *The Compleat Angler* (1655), which he mentions on the first page. In the seventeenth century, Walton made a charming case for angling as the essential gentlemanly recreational activity, one that is a pastime, "an art somewhat like poetry," and a philosophical activity that lends itself particularly well to reflection.[52] As Walton puts it, "The very sitting by the river's side is not only the quietest and fittest place for contemplation, but will invite an angler to it."[53] Bockett takes Walton's book as a jumping off point for his own book, arguing that now, on the cusp of a new century, cycling, not angling, is "the only truly Gentle Art."[54] Bockett emphasizes the ruminative, reflective element of cycling, advising that one should "never arrange a [cycling] journey without allowing sufficient time for meditation and contemplation."[55] For Bockett, riding a bicycle is equal parts physical and metaphysical activity.

In this sense, Bockett is something of a neoromantic cyclist, inspired by the likes of Hazlitt, Lamb, and Wordsworth. Bockett spends much more time than the Pennells celebrating how cycling brings one closer to the power of the natural world. He sees cycling as "the Gentle Art that has brought nature and man together in a way that not even the arts of poetry and painting have hitherto succeeded in doing."[56] For Bockett, the key natural metaphor of literary pilgrimage is the tree. Several times at pilgrimage sites, he leans his bike against a stately tree and proceeds to praise mighty oaks and majestic elms, which seem to symbolize his favorite authors' legacies. The juxtaposition is striking: the modern, steel, human-made object of the bicycle side by side with the centuries-old, organic object that, like the books he so loves, connects past and present and provides comfort and pleasure to the passing pilgrim. The bicycle-tree combination is a perfect image of the old-new enterprise of Bockett's neoromantic pilgrimage on wheels.

But literary cycle travel is, for Bockett, as with the Pennells, sometimes a sentimental experience. In fact, Bockett's pilgrimage narratives convey much more of a sense of emotional connection with at least some of the authors associated with his pilgrimages. Flashes of this kind of personal connection occur in the Pennells' Sterne book, but Bockett's work is founded on an even more intense, sentimental connection to authors and their texts. Nicola Watson calls the literary pilgrim both "haunter and haunted," at once tracking the trail of the author and also exhibiting signs of being obsessed by, and in thrall to, the author's text.[57] In this sense, Bockett is a more zealous pilgrim than the Pennells; he's got the eye and fervor of the true believer, text in hand, keen to engage in "dialogue with the dead author."[58]

The most vivid illustration of the intensity of the rider-writer connection for Bockett is the chapter "Gentle Folk," about his trip to visit two homes of Charles Lamb, an author he considers "the best loved and best loving of English writers."[59] Whereas the Pennells find that cycling undermines their sentimental connection to Sterne, Bockett's cycle trip, in this case, is more successful in maintaining a cycling-sentiment connection with Lamb. When trying to explain his fondness for Lamb to others, Bockett resorts to hokey praise that sounds like something out of Sterne: "You cannot reason about a man like Charles Lamb. You can only love him."[60] For Bockett, Lamb's life consists of part mirth and part "tenderness and pathos," especially when it comes to Lamb's love life. Bockett claims of the latter, there is "nothing more truly noble and pathetic in the records of human love."[61] At Lamb's Cottage (formerly Bay Cottage) in Edmonton, on the edge of London, Bockett recalls as well the sadness of Lamb's final years when he was caring for his mentally ill sister. Later, at Mackery End, Lamb's onetime farmhouse in Wheathampstead, Bockett lingers for a while, "reading bits of *Elia*," before hopping back on his bicycle and heading off for Hatfield.[62] The presence of his bicycle, in short, only enhances Bockett's devotion to his favorite author.

Bockett's fondness for combining reading and riding like this, however, brings us not just to the particular pleasures but also the tension cycling occasionally causes in his literary pilgrimages. As we saw in the Pennells' books, cycle travel can both bring the pilgrim closer to the dead author and, at times, put the pilgrim at odds with him or her; and that's also true for Bockett, though in a different way than for the Pennells. For Bockett, cycling intensifies and complicates the intensely textual nature of the pilgrimage experience. His favorite books possess such a sacred status for him that he carries them on his cycle journeys; each text is part talisman and part scripture, to be pulled out and read from as appropriate en route. Bockett claims that "all gentle cyclists ride with a book in their pockets," and he packs what he preaches.[63] Bockett repeatedly mentions the texts he brings along on his pilgrimages: a copy of John Denham's poetry for wheeling through Cooper's Hill; a "little sixpenny edition" of *The Complete Angler* for his run to Walton country; a volume of Abraham Cowley's essays, which he peruses during a reading break at the roadside near Jane Austen's Chawton.[64] "How delightfully it read in that pleasant spot!" he proclaims of the Cowley text, revelling in the intersection of his favorite activities: reading, cycling, and contemplating nature.[65] His daily scripture reading completed, Bockett slides the volume "with proper reverence in an inner pocket" of his riding coat and pedals off.[66]

For the most part, cycling is complementary to Bockett's textual impulse and riding intensifies his reading experience. But there is one instance where cycling causes textual trouble for Bockett, and that involves a particular kind of text one is bound to encounter on literary pilgrimage: the memorial tablet, or dedicatory plaque often found at places of literary significance. Most of Bockett's short pilgrimages end with him coming face-to-face with one of these pseudoliterary tablets about, but not by, a favorite author. In fact, Bockett seeks out such tablets; they possess a relic-like status for him, as tangible, textual links to the author's legacy. But Bockett is often disappointed by these tablets, and I would argue that cycling is partly to blame for this.

Take, for instance, Bockett's twenty-eight-mile ride to Wargrave Church, near Twyford, to visit the grave of Thomas Day, the largely forgotten—even in Bockett's time—author of *The History of Sandford and Merton* (c. 1783–89), a once-popular Rousseauian children's book that Bockett fondly remembers from his youth. Once Bockett manages to find where "our old friend" Day is buried (inside the church, under a pew, as it turns out), he locates the text he's been searching for: a tablet bearing an inscription and, in Bockett's view, an unremarkable epitaph—"a plain, commonplace affair," as he describes it.[67] "So good a man deserved at least a better epitaph," Bockett suggests.[68] Like the Pennells in Nampont, Bockett experiences the classic pilgrim's disappointment—the destination fails to live up to his expectations. But here Bockett's disappointment seems especially *textual*. It's not that the place or the people let him down; rather the inscription on the tablet fails to do justice to all that Day represents for the pilgrim.

The problem with these tablets, what makes them so disappointing for Bockett, is that in some fundamental way they contradict the spirit of his preferred mode of pilgrimage on wheels. So much of the joy of his journeys comes from the combination of reading books and pedaling bikes, of *going somewhere* with a text in his pocket, of experiencing texts and landscapes in motion. When Bockett says that "all along the road the imagination is keenly at work," he is referring to cycling as a kind of dynamic reading practice.[69] He loves cycle travel because of the way it prompts contemplation, reflection, and appreciation of nature and of favorite works of literature. These tablet texts, however, are inert, stuck in a particular place, incapable of going anywhere. They can be quoted and reproduced, as Bockett does; but the originals are static, carved in stones that cannot be easily moved. Several times, his encounters with these tablets seem to make Bockett restless and inspire him to hop on his bicycle and get moving again. For instance, in his account of reading the inscription on a granite cross atop the rim of the Devil's Punchbowl near Hindhead, Surrey, Bockett recalls another literary—in fact, fictional—traveller, Dickens's Nicholas Nickleby, reading the very same tablet.[70] But Bockett doesn't linger here. Instead, he hurtles downhill, his next sentence capturing precisely the kind of dynamic energy that the bicycle affords but that the tablet can't: "Down, down, down, the cycle runs with no effort on the part of the rider, and during nearly the whole of the descent there is an ever-changing and ever-beautiful panorama passing before one's eyes."[71] Memorial tablets can't possibly keep up such a pace. Tablets defy the essential impulse of literary cycle travel: while Bockett admires beeches and oaks rooted in place, he prefers his texts on two wheels.

Although cycling complicates the pilgrimage experience for Bockett at times like this, as it does for the Pennells, overall, cycling enhances their journeys and improves their connections to favorite authors and texts. Their modern machines bring the pilgrims closer to what they perceive to be the authentic, old-fashioned travel experience and to the authors themselves. For the most part, the new technology of cycling heightens these late Victorians' experience of reading and savoring old texts.

In general, the literary-pilgrimage phenomenon began to fade around the time of the First World War. But the vogue for literary cycling pilgrimages was briefly revived in the 1920s and '30s by two writers, the American Charles S. Brooks and the Englishman Bernard Newman, both of whom wrote extensively about literary pilgrimages on wheels. Brooks's *Thread of English Road* (1924) and *Roads to the North* (1929) continue the transatlantic pilgrimage tradition; he travels to many of the same English pilgrimage sites that Bockett visited, plus many others. Published a few years later, Newman's *In the Trail of the Three Musketeers* (1934) recounts a cycling trip in the footsteps of Dumas's protagonist D'Artagnan and his classic trio.[72]

By this time, however, cycling was no longer associated with modernity in the same way it had been in the Pennells' or even Bockett's time. The era of the motorcar had arrived; and while the impulse to visit literary places remained for some, modern pilgrims could hop in their cars and head to Stratford and Wessex with much of the independence and freedom formerly only available by cycle. If anything, cycling itself had become a nostalgic exercise by this time. Brooks, especially, exploits the nostalgic aspect of cycle travel, adopting a quirky, sentimental style, a throwback to Bockett's of twenty-five years earlier. Some readers still enjoyed this kind of cycle-travel literature, but for different reasons. By this time, literary cycling pilgrimages had become almost wholly backward-looking endeavors, with little sense of melding old and new anymore. Perhaps as a result, in these works, there are none of the wild imaginative possibilities associated with earlier cycling pilgrimages—no speculating about D'Artagnan on a safety bicycle or imagining Gilbert White and his beloved tortoise Timothy on a tandem tricycle.[73] That late-Victorian moment, when such vignettes reflected the public imagination's link between cycling and literature, was mostly past.

For only those few decades from the 1880s until around 1910 was cycle travel both novel and modern enough to give these kinds of literary cycling-pilgrimage narratives a unique double vantage point of looking forward and backward at the same time. At the beginning of

Bockett's book, as he is making his case for cycling as the true "Gentle Art" and best way to reach "some particular object in view," he proclaims, "What a help a cycle is to the enjoyment of these simple pleasures!"[74] The Pennells would have agreed. The pleasures Bockett is referring to here have to do with nature—heather, sunsets, and pine trees—but he, and the Pennells for that matter, could just as easily be talking about the texts of their favorite authors.

Notes

1. Joseph Pennell and Elizabeth Robins Pennell, *Our Sentimental Journey through France and Italy* (London: T. Fisher Unwin, 1887; rev. ed. with appendix, 1893), x. Citations in this essay refer to the 1893 edition.

2. F. W. Bockett, *Some Literary Landmarks for Pilgrims on Wheels*, with illustrations by J. A. Symington (London: J. M. Dent, 1901), 7.

3. For instance, several early cycling clubs cultivated literary connections. The Pickwick Bicycle Club, founded in 1878, insisted that each member adopt a sobriquet in honor of a character from Charles Dickens's *Pickwick Papers*. Pryor Dodge, *The Bicycle* (Paris: Flammarion, 1996), 50.

4. Other examples of literary cycle-travel texts from this period include Annetta J. Halliday, "Wheeling through the Land of Evangeline," *Outing* 15 (December 1889): 197–202; Duncan Moul, *Week-ends in Dickens Land: A Bijou Handbook for the Cyclist and Rambler, with Map* (London: Homeland Association, 1901); Hermann Lea, *A Handbook to the Wessex Country of Thomas Hardy's Novels and Poems* (London: Paul, Trench, Trubner, 1912); Hermann Lea, *Thomas Hardy's Wessex* (London: Macmillan, 1913); Edward Thomas, *In Pursuit of Spring* (London: Thomas Nelson and Sons, 1914).

5. Nicola J. Watson, *The Literary Tourist: Readers and Places in Romantic and Victorian Britain* (London: Palgrave Macmillan, 2006), 1.

6. The Victorian era is known for remarkable achievements in industry and technology (modern factories, advances in printing technology, photography, communications) that make it a period associated with innovation and forward thinking. But at the same time, in arts and literature especially, the Victorians were obsessed with matters of the past. As Raymond Chapman has shown, fiction from this period, such as Dickens's novels, is suffused with nostalgia, and the subject matter of so much of the poetry of Tennyson and Browning, for instance, reaches back to the distant past. See Raymond Chapman, *The Sense of the Past in Victorian Literature* (London: Croom Helm, 1986); Jerome Hamilton Buckley, *The Triumph of Time: A Study of Victorian Concepts of Time, History, Progress, and Decadence* (Cambridge MA: Harvard University Press, 1967).

7. Watson, *Literary Tourist*, 1.

8. Ian Ousby, *The Englishman's England: Taste, Travel and the Ride of Tourism* (Cambridge: Cambridge University Press, 1990), 22.

9. See, for instance, William Howitt, *Homes and Haunts of the Most Eminent British Poets*, 2 vols. (London: Richard Bentley, 1847); T. P. Grinsted, *Last Homes of Departed Genius: With Biographical Sketches of Poets, Painters, and Players* (London: Routledge and Sons, 1867). Mrs. S. C. Hall, *Pilgrimages to English Shrines* (London: Hall, Virtue, 1850); Henry C. Shelley, *Literary By-paths in Old England* (Boston: Little, Brown, 1906); Marion Harland, *Where Ghosts Walk: The Haunts of Familiar Characters in History and Literature* (New York: G. P. Putnam's Sons, 1898).

10. Watson, *Literary Tourist*, 13.

11. Watson, *Literary Tourist*, 132.

12. I am concerned with leisure cycling not cycle racing, a crucial distinction. In the 1880s many leisure cyclists drew attention to this distinction between what Karl Kron calls the "quiet tourists" on cycles and the "showy racers." Kron argues that "racers are nothing more than the foam and froth on the surface of Niagara's whirlpool; they are pretty to look at and convenient to chat about; yet, as the real power and mystery of the pool lie hidden in the depths, so the true spirit and permanent charm of cycling are best exemplified by the army of quiet riders who never display themselves upon a racetrack." Karl Kron, *Ten Thousand Miles on a Bicycle* (New York: Karl Kron, 1887; repr. New York: Emil Rosenblatt, 1982), v.

13. Unsigned review of *Cycling Handbook*, by Lord Bury, *Pall Mall Gazette*, May 20, 1886, 5.

14. Dodge, *Bicycle*, 90.

15. The pilgrimage theme is also featured in their second tricycle book, *An Italian Pilgrimage* (London: Seeley, 1887), or *Two Pilgrims' Progress* as it was known in the United States, about a cycling trip from Florence to Rome. In fact, literary pilgrimage continued to be a favorite mode of their travel writing for the next decade. They also used it in a noncycling book, *Our Journey to the Hebrides* (New York: Harper and Brothers, 1889), which traces the route of Johnson and Boswell's famous jaunt in Scotland. And they wrote a nonliterary-pilgrimage travel book, *To Gipsyland* (New York: Century, 1893), about a bicycle trip to Hungary in search of "authentic" gypsies.

16. See A. D. Chandler and J. C. Sharp, *A Bicycle Tour in England and Wales* (Boston: A. Williams; London: Crosby Lockwood, 1881); Nauticus [Charles Edward Reade], *Nauticus on His Hobby Horse; or, The Adventures of a Sailor during a Tricycle Cruise of 1427 Miles* (London: G. Norman and Son, 1880); Nauticus [Charles Edward Reade], *Nauticus in Scotland: A Tricycle Tour of 2446 Miles in Sixty-Eight Days* (Coventry, UK: Forest Publishing, 1883).

17. The Pennells were admirers of Stevenson's early travel writing, especially his *Travels with a Donkey in the Cévennes* (Boston: Roberts Brothers, 1879). In fact, they dedicated *A Canterbury Pilgrimage* to Stevenson. In addition, there are numerous other references to Stevenson's work in the Pennells' magazine articles and books, including three mentions in *A Sentimental Journey through France and Italy*. The Pennells never met Stevenson, though they did receive a short letter of thanks from him, following the appearance of the Canterbury book. In London the Pennells were friends with Stevenson's cousin, the art critic R. A. M. (Bob) Stevenson.

18. John Ruskin, for instance, one of the most outspoken of the Victorian train critics, argued that "travelling becomes dull in exact proportion to its rapidity." Quoted in Wolfgang Shivelbusch, *The Railway Journey: Trains and Travel in the 19th Century*, trans. Anselm Hollo (Oxford, UK: Blackwell, 1979), 60. He much preferred preindustrial modes such as walking and carriage travel, though, curiously, as the Pennells themselves point out, he was skeptical of cycling's ability to replicate the preindustrial pace of travel. Pennell and Robins Pennell, *Our Sentimental Journey*, 69.

19. In the early 1880s, tricycles, although not as fast as the popular high-wheelers, offered obvious advantages to certain cycle travelers (especially to women and the elderly) who found the dominant high-wheel bicycle, or "ordinary," difficult to mount, dangerous to ride, and not amenable to ladies' clothing. The tricycle was much more accessible, safer, and easier to stop and start (for those who wanted to take a break and admire the scenery); and it could accommodate some luggage as well as a second rider, in the case of tandem models like the ones the Pennells used, for those who preferred to travel with company. In his 1887 account of the contemporary cycling scene, Karl Kron lists several instances of married couples, including the Pennells, who travelled extensively by tricycle in the 1880s, though few besides the Pennells had written about their trips. Kron, *Ten Thousand Miles*, 530.

20. "Pilgrims' Progresses" refers to the Pennells' second tricycle-travel book, *An Italian Pilgrimage*.

21. I am using the terms "sentiment" and "sentimental" here not in the pejorative sense we tend to hold today but rather in the more positive eighteenth-century sense of literature that evokes an excess of sympathetic emotion and pathos. In the second half of the eighteenth century, works such as Jean-Jacques Rousseau's *Julie; or, The New Héloise* (1761), Sterne's *A Sentimental Journey through France and Italy* (1768), and Henry Mackenzie's *The Man of Feeling* (1771) helped popularize this notion that virtue was associated with an individual's ability to feel deeply and exhibit sympathy for the suffering of others. In the nineteenth century, sentimentalism lived on in a slightly different form and was often seen in novels that emphasize the suffering—and especially the

deaths—of children. See, for instance, Fred Kaplan, *Sacred Tears: Sentimentalism in Victorian Literature* (Princeton NJ: Princeton University Press, 1987).

22. Joseph Pennell and Elizabeth Robins Pennell, *A Canterbury Pilgrimage* (London: Seeley, 1885), 20.

23. Pennell and Robins Pennell, *Canterbury Pilgrimage*, 77.

24. In *Our Sentimental Journey*, Elizabeth trains her satirical eye on a French dandy riding a shiny tricycle in Neuvy. At meeting a fellow tricyclist, they expect a certain fellowship, "proof of the freemasonry of the wheel"; but they're disappointed when all the dandy wants to do is boast of the superiority of the "nickel-plated glory of his three wheels" compared to their mud-covered machine. Pennell and Robins Pennell, *Our Sentimental Journey*, 160.

25. Pennell and Robins Pennell, *Canterbury Pilgrimage*, 50–51.

26. Pennell and Robins Pennell, *Canterbury Pilgrimage*, 17, 35, 40.

27. Pennell and Robins Pennell, *Canterbury Pilgrimage*, 35.

28. Elizabeth Robins Pennell, *Life and Letters of Joseph Pennell* (Boston: Little, Brown, 1929), 1:149.

29. For instance, Roger Allbut, *London Rambles "en Zig-Zag" with Charles Dickens* (London: Edward Curtice, 1886); Henry Snowden Ward and Katherine B. Ward, *The Real Dickens Land* (London: Chapman, 1904).

30. Pennell and Robins Pennell, *Canterbury Pilgrimage*, 21, 22. See, for instance, the discussion of Dickens's blend of sentimentality and satire, in James Sutherland, *English Satire* (Cambridge: Cambridge University Press, 1958), 123–25.

31. Pennell and Robins Pennell, *Our Sentimental Journey*, v.

32. Thomas Cook (1808–92) founded one of the first travel agencies in Great Britain and began offering excursions in the 1840s. He later introduced a system of coupons, known as "Cook's tickets," that were valid for restaurant meals and overnight stays at establishments on Cook's list. Pennell and Robins Pennell, *Our Sentimental Journey*, x.

33. Pennell and Robins Pennell, *Our Sentimental Journey*, 54.

34. Laurence Sterne, *A Sentimental Journey and Other Writings*, ed. Ian Jack and Tim Parnell (Oxford: Oxford University Press, 2003), 34.

35. Sterne, *Sentimental Journey*, 35.

36. Pennell and Robins Pennell, *Our Sentimental Journey*, 55.

37. For instance, Watson tells the story of Nathaniel Hawthorne's disappointment at visiting the home of Robbie Burns at Alloway. Hawthorne was devastated to find that it was dirty and smelled bad. Watson, *Literary Tourist*, 88.

38. Pennell and Robins Pennell, *Our Sentimental Journey*, 56.

39. Pennell and Robins Pennell, *Our Sentimental Journey*, 52, 56.

40. Sterne, *Sentimental Journey*, 30; Pennell and Robins Pennell, *Our Sentimental Journey*, 53.

41. Pennell and Robins Pennell, *Our Sentimental Journey*, 53.

42. Pennell and Robins Pennell, *Our Sentimental Journey*, 53.

43. Pennell and Robins Pennell, *Our Sentimental Journey*, 162.

44. Elizabeth Robins Pennell, unpublished London diary, February 8, 1888, Pennell Collection, Harry Ransom Center, University of Texas, Austin.

45. Interestingly, *A Canterbury Pilgrimage* was reissued numerous times in the decade after its original publication. It seemed to retain its appeal for readers in a way that *Our Sentimental Journey* did not. On March 8, 1890, the Pennells, writing anonymously in their "Cycle and Camera" column in the *Penny Illustrated Paper* and noting that the book was being reissued yet again, describe it as "one of the first accounts of a cycling tour which seemed to catch on, and apparently is still catching on with the general as well as the cycling public." "Cycle and Camera," *Penny Illustrated Paper*, March 8, 1890, 154.

46. Bockett, *Some Literary Landmarks*, 8–9.

47. Bockett, *Some Literary Landmarks*, 8.

48. Bockett, *Some Literary Landmarks*, 9.

49. Bockett, *Some Literary Landmarks*, v.

50. Bockett, *Some Literary Landmarks*, vi.

51. Bockett, *Some Literary Landmarks*, 5.

52. Izaak Walton. *The Compleat Angler; or, The Contemplative Man's Recreation*, 5th ed. (1676; repr., London: Bloomsbury, 1988), 39. Originally published in 1655; all citations refer to the 1988 Bloomsbury edition.

53. Walton, *Compleat Angler*, 42.

54. Bockett, *Some Literary Landmarks*, 4.

55. Bockett, *Some Literary Landmarks*, 18.

56. Bockett, *Some Literary Landmarks*, 6.

57. Watson, *Literary Tourist*, 132.

58. Watson, *Literary Tourist*, 13.

59. Bockett, *Some Literary Landmarks*, 245.

60. Bockett, *Some Literary Landmarks*, 233.

61. Bockett, *Some Literary Landmarks*, 235, 262.

62. Bockett, *Some Literary Landmarks*, 262.

63. Bockett, *Some Literary Landmarks*, 117.

64. Bockett, *Some Literary Landmarks*, 117, 265.

65. Bockett, *Some Literary Landmarks*, 137.

66. Bockett, *Some Literary Landmarks*, 140.

67. Bockett, *Some Literary Landmarks*, 28.

68. Bockett, *Some Literary Landmarks*, 28.

69. Bockett, *Some Literary Landmarks*, 9.

70. This particular tablet is not a memorial to a writer but rather tells of "a foul and treacherous murder committed there by night." Charles Dickens, *The Life and Adventures of Nicholas Nickleby*, 3rd ed. (New York: J. Van Amringe, 1840), 207.

71. Bockett, *Some Literary Landmarks*, 228.

72. Newman went on to pen several more cycle-travel books, many of them literary to some extent, if not actual literary pilgrimages like his first book. See Duncan R. Jamieson, "The Cycle Writings of Bernard Newman," *Aethelon* 25, no. 2 (Spring/Summer 2008): 117–30.

73. In his *Natural History and Antiquities of Selbourne* (London: Benjamin White, 1788), which both Bockett and Brooks write about extensively, Gilbert White writes at length about his beloved pet tortoise Timothy.

74. Bockett, *Some Literary Landmarks*, 8.

2 From Charles Pratt to Mark Twain to Frank Norris

Horse versus Bicycle, Man versus Machine

PETER KRATZKE

On the edge of a large park in Hartford, Connecticut, stands a monument with a bronze profile of the park's benefactor and namesake, Col. Albert A. Pope. Though the inscription is a little weathered, its faded words announce the monument's intention: "To commemorate the industrial activities and public benefactions from 1880 to 1905 [of Pope]." In what activities, exactly, Pope succeeded, the inscription leaves unexplained, an odd omission given that Pope has become known as the father of the American bicycle industry. In contrast to the Ozymandias-like effect of the Pope Park monument, a lovingly maintained place not far away is known by every Hartford citizen: the Mark Twain House, in which the high-profile author of *Huckleberry Finn* resided from 1874 to 1891. Despite the two men's eventual positions in America's cultural memory, suffice it to say that Twain's level of success was the opposite of Pope's when the question turned to investing in technologies, and the resulting contrast in biography as well as legacy leads in a variety of ways to the age-old question (usually framed in gendered diction), "Which is to be the master: man or machine?" If the feeling of flying and the fear of crashing when riding a bicycle teach anything, it is that no answer is possible.

Before the development of the bicycle (or "wheel," as it was affectionately called) during the second half of the nineteenth century, the horse was part and parcel of America's personal transportation. Never one to settle on modest goals, Pope introduced his Columbia-model high-wheel "ordinary" (so labeled during the 1880s to distinguish them as the standard type) as nothing short of a replacement for the horse in physical, economic, and social terms. Bruce Epperson summarizes, "The story of this revolution—from the bicycle as a stable-mate to the horse, a play-toy of the rich, to the liberator of everyman—is the story of the Pope Manufacturing Company in its second decade. The allure and popularity of the bicycle did not just happen. It was a deliberately crafted and stage-managed creation, and the Colonel was its impresario."[1] Indeed, evidence of Pope's use of the horse-versus-bicycle topic surfaces almost immediately in Herlihy's story of how, with an illustration of himself atop a Columbia, Pope promoted the ordinary in an 1879 advertisement as "An ever saddled horse which eats nothing."[2] The machine could be made subservient to man, and, for a time, the public bought both the ordinary and the idea.

To convince people that the ordinary should replace the horse, Pope needed to show how the machine functioned. One of Pope's responses was close at hand with his friend and patent attorney, Charles Pratt, whom Pope assisted by publishing Pratt's *The American Bicycler: A Manual for the Observer, the Learner, and the Expert* (1879), an operations manual for the *what, where, why, when, how*, and even *who* about all things related to the ordinary. The personable manual had its day—Stephen Goddard comments that it "would excite laypeople's imaginations in much the same way as *The Joy of Running* would a century later"—and quickly passed into the fog of history, the specific machine central to the text and the memory of Pope going with it.[3] The importance of Pratt's creative spirit to the nation's literary culture, though, can be felt in how authors of fiction used the horse-versus-bicycle topic for thematically responding to the related man-versus-machine question. Twain's *A Connecticut Yankee in King Arthur's Court* (1889) is by far the most famous example of this topic in relationship to the ordinary; and in the following generation of naturalists, which included figures such as Stephen Crane and Jack London, Frank Norris's *The Octopus* (1901) is the best example of this topic in connection with the more familiar safety bicycle, the precursor of modern bicycles with their equally sized wheels and diamond-shaped frame.

Seen through the wide lens of nineteenth-century American culture, the ordinary and the safety may be fairly categorized as a single technology. From this historical viewpoint, the bicycle's emergence across the last three decades of the century was to the public as much a radical *concept* about personal transportation as it was a matter of frame design or gear ratios. David V. Herlihy comments about the era, "For the first time, people could truly imagine a world in which the horse—a beloved but demanding creature—no longer bore the brunt of personal transportation. An exciting new era of road travel loomed ahead, one that would enable even a poor man or woman to travel afar and at will."[4] Considering the bicycle from this overall perspective, too, reveals a logical sequence for any machine that moves from market introduction to physical implementation to technological obsolescence. Just as logically, this sequence—typified in *The American Bicycler*, *A Connecticut Yankee*, and *The Octopus*—begins thematically in the promotion of and belief in man over machine, dwindles to disappointment in machine over man, and culminates in disinterest toward both man and machine.

Charles Pratt and the Introduction of the Bicycle: Promotion of Man over Machine

Vastly different from the earlier fad of the straight-angled machine with steel wheels called a "boneshaker," due to the rough ride when ridden on cobblestone or poorly maintained roads, the ordinary had to be marketed as something lasting. Every picture tells a story: most cycle historians know the photograph lineup of wheelmen ready for a ride on September 11, 1879, in Readville, Massachusetts. Among the figures are Pratt and Pope, their delight in the day almost palpable. Some words in Pratt's manual could just as well provide a caption for the photograph: "There is the charm of mastery and of motion for the rider, and there is the charm of mystery and surprise for the looker-on."[5] Shaping what people saw exactly was Pratt's principal challenge for composing *The American Bicycler*. In his article for an 1883 issue of *Outing* tracing the rise of the bicycle market, Pratt commented, "In 1878 this public hardly knew what to do with the bicycle except to suppress it. Horses are sometimes frightened, and people oftener."[6] Worse, Pratt faced a harsh reality: riding an ordinary was anything but ordinary. Pope himself had reportedly observed when he first saw an ordinary at the 1876 Centennial Exposition in Philadelphia, "One must be an acrobat or a gymnast to ride such a steed."[7] With his manual, Pratt aimed to settle everyone's nerves by demystifying the ordinary's form and function.

Pratt's career was, in the terminology of lawyers, a "difficult case." Goddard provides some insight: "Intense, with wireless glasses, a bushy dark mustache, and a receding hairline, Pratt was a morose man who could speak ten languages and 'desperately needed exercise.'"[8] "He was," Epperson adds, "a better writer and advocate than a litigator. . . . Pratt wasn't good in high-conflict situations; he couldn't depersonalize."[9] At the same time, Pratt embraced the unfettered emotions felt with outdoor activities. Pratt was a hard man to pin down, and his public stringency collided with his private passions in the occasion of *The American Bicycler*. Pratt was probably acutely aware of this polemical problem and addresses it in his manual almost immediately. At a short two pages, Pratt's introductory chapter, titled "Greetings," stutteringly sets a conciliatory tone: "To the public, divided, as he sees it, into two great classes, bicyclers and non-bicyclers, the author would very deferentially raise his cap."[10] His cap doffed, Pratt proceeds down his promotional road.

In writing his manual, Pratt knew that he needed to counter the exaggerations of how many technologies are promoted, for the ordinary was not immune to sensationalism. Most notably, the cover of Charles Spencer's *The Modern Bicycle* (1876)—a book that Pratt dismisses as "meagre, and relates to the 'bone-shaker'"[11]—pictures on its cover a rider atop an ordinary who, in chasing a hare, outpaces a rider on horse.[12] Pratt's manual provides no similar over-the-top drama, the principle of moderation informing just about every aspect of Pratt's approach to the ordinary's mechanics, manner of riding, use as transportation, and cultural position. Pratt's efforts in cofounding the League of American Wheelmen were still a year away (he went on to serve for two years as the organization's first president); and through all the advice Pratt offers, one feels an author rehearsing his theme: "the Observer, the Learner, and the Expert" are all to be included.

Social harmony is a noble goal, and a closer reading of *The American Bicycler* shows that Pratt does not neglect to offer specific tactics toward achieving it. Most conspicuously, Pratt reminds bicyclers that they should err on the side of caution when meeting horses on the road: "It is a courtesy of the road to turn out more than the law requires, to dismount rather than force out a loaded team, to avoid riding at and through a herd of live animals driven on the road."[13] Such courtesy, Pratt explains, stems from how education produces congeniality: "The popular apprehension in advance, that the bicycle would frighten horses, has been practically overcome and proved groundless. The intelligent public has recognized the fact that drivers and riders of horses have, neither by law nor reason, any exclusive rights in the highways, and that this danger, which is of very small proportions, is to be averted by the education of horses, and by mutual care and courtesy on the part of drivers and riders of horses on the one hand, and of bicyclers on the other."[14] For Pratt, the goal is that all parties should come to understand that using the roads is a fundamental right; and given whatever exchanges might ensue on the roadway, all modes of transportation should be mutually accommodated.

Once he places the ordinary on its rightful and, so, righteous road, Pratt attends to the machine's form. Pratt begins his discussion through metaphor that meshes horses with bicycles: "It [the bicycle] runs, it leaps, it rears and writhes, and shies and kicks; it is in infinite restless motion, like a bundle of sensitive nerves; it is beneath its rider like a thing of life, without the uncertainty and resistance of an uncontrolled will."[15] The ordinary had all the advantages of the horse but without any of the problems, and it was much easier to master. Pratt even echoes Pope's earlier advertisement for the Columbia, celebrating, "It is an always-bridled horse; it costs nearly as much in the first place, perhaps, as either a horse or a carriage, but it saves one of them; its feed is a pint of oil a year, and its grooming a handful and ten minutes' attention now and then. It never runs away, requires no harness, and breaks no carriages."[16] Those "handful and ten minutes," though, are not to be underestimated in man's mastery of machine. "It is said," Pratt writes, in appealing to the ordinary's transportation lineage, "that a good horseman is known by the care he takes of his horse;

and this is in some sense true of a bicycler: a good rider will not use a machine in bad condition."[17] As such, "On a tour," Pratt advises, in a similarly characteristic comment, "the machine should be well take care of,—indeed, very much as a horse would under similar circumstances."[18] Beyond considering form, Pratt had much more to say about the ordinary's potentially larger function in transcending the horse.

Despite its genre as an operations manual, weaving through *The American Bicycler* is the promotion of the ordinary's cultural effect. Ever the attorney, Pratt knew the power of language; and in a later section of his manual devoted to organizing clubs and club riding, he outlines various terminology for the task, most of it borrowed from the cavalry: *gallop, walk, halt, ride at ease*, and so forth.[19] Discipline fosters humility, and Pratt demonstrates the resulting moderate spirit in bicyclers. "The ability to ride the bicycle easily and gracefully on occasion," he writes, in connecting bicycling to a sense of "nature's nobility," "is already an accomplishment which no gentleman can afford to be without, even if he be not an habitual devotee."[20] This quality of artful artlessness also explains Pratt's preference for amateurs over professionals, "for the non-professional bicycler ... takes to the roads as a bird to the tree-tops, and there he has his practice."[21] The same tree-top spirit is reflected in the seal Pratt includes for bicycle clubs: beneath a star is the Pegasus-like motto, *Pedibus Bicyclus Addidit Alas* (translated as "The bicycle has added wings to its feet").[22] However, the bicycle's wings, represented in such literary works as *A Connecticut Yankee* and *The Octopus*, would prove as waxen as Icarus's; and for his part, Pratt gave up cycling when his health began to fail in 1885, instead concentrating on sailing.[23]

Mark Twain and the Implementation of the Bicycle: Disappointment in Machine over Man

Because polemical tension all but defined almost every corner of American culture during the final three decades of the nineteenth century—debates simmered between rich and poor, urban and rural, modern and traditional—the distant mirror of medieval hierarchies touched a nerve in popular culture. Armored knights, in particular, featured prominently when the topic turned to technology. For example, a cartoon by Friedrich Graetz for the August 1, 1883, issue of *Puck* depicts a heavily armored knight atop a locomotive that is emblazoned with the word "Monopoly." The knight lowers his spear at the throat of an unarmored, barefooted, and undersized worker on a horse with the word "Poverty" on its neck. The worker's only defense is his hammer, which is inscribed with the word "Strike."[24] Clearly, the common man needed some kind of meaningful response to large-scale industry, and the bicycle offered, at the least, a symbolic tool for the task. Perhaps most famously, Thomas Stevens toured around the world from 1884 to 1887, recounting his sensational adventures in the pages of Pope's *Outing* magazine.[25] To ride around the world meant, surely, that man could control his machines. Mark Twain, however, had his doubts.

During the 1880s, knights were often depicted astride ordinaries instead of horses. Man would seem in such imagery to control machine. For instance, the *Wheel*, published by the Bicycle Touring Club in America, featured in an 1883 issue a cartoon of a knight on an ordinary equipped with nothing less than a Gatling gun. The image creates a kind of "future shock," as the drawing is titled "Nineteen Eighty-Three."[26] More typically, knights on ordinaries were less aggressive. In 1885 Joseph G. Dalton published a second edition of his 1880 collection of bicycle poetry, in which one poem begins,

> Bicycle knights I often spy,
> On horse uncarnate riding by;
> Nimbly they scale his vaulty back,
> And spin along the travelled track.[27]

Although no direct proof is available about Twain's knowledge of this kind of imagery, he would have been hard-pressed to miss it. One way or the other, what can be said with conviction is that, with *A Connecticut Yankee*, Twain all but immortalized the knight-on-bicycle image by turning it on its literal as well as its figurative head.

The physical implementation of the ordinary for Twain came from firsthand experience. Years prior to writing *A Connecticut Yankee*, Twain walked the few blocks from his house to Pope's factory and bought a Columbia Expert Ordinary for the then-princely price of

$142.50.[28] His actual use of the machine was less optimistic than his purchase. Sometime during the 1880s, Twain wrote a short essay titled "Taming the Bicycle," about learning to ride, an essay in which he jokes about dismounting an ordinary, "Try as you may, you don't get down as you would from a horse, you get down as you would from a house afire. You make a spectacle of yourself every time."[29] Coincidentally, Twain, like Pope, saw the bicycle at the 1876 Centennial Exposition; so for no other reason than this crossing of paths, Twain might have found Pope's magazine the *Wheelman* a suitable publication site for his essay.[30] However, according to Jay Pridmore and Jim Hurd, "Pope did not pay for Twain's article and may not have approved of it, entirely."[31] Pope's hesitation is understandable. Twain's essay expresses a thorough (albeit humorous) disappointment in the ordinary's limitations, and the feeling of disappointment has never been effective for marketing purposes. Sooner rather than later, Twain stopped trying to master the ordinary and, in 1886, shopped for a tricycle instead.[32]

Diametrically opposed to Pratt's stance on the man-versus-machine question in his *The American Bicycler* is Twain's *A Connecticut Yankee*; where the former text is promotional and optimistic, the latter is critical and realistic. The authorial reasons are not hard to conjecture; for if ever an American literary author were stung by poor money management, it was Twain. The Hartford-based successes of both the Colt Arms and Pope factories must have been only salt in the wound of Twain's disastrous investment in James Paige's hopelessly complicated typesetter; and *A Connecticut Yankee*, while not quite written with "a pen warmed up in hell" (as Twain suggested in a letter to William Dean Howells), is plenty trenchant.[33] Technology, at once, fascinated and depressed Twain, and the literary result is that the use of machinery by Hank Morgan (the titular character of that novel) is as myopic as Twain's assessment of Paige's contraption.

The horse-versus-bicycle topic in *A Connecticut Yankee* occurs in chapter 38. Hank and King Arthur ready themselves to be hanged, their rescue impossible given the slowness of the knights' horses. Hank stands nearly speechless at what happens next:

But when I saw them put the noose around his [Arthur's] neck, then everything let go in me and I made a spring to the rescue—and as I made it I shot one glance abroad—by George, here they came, atilting—five hundred mailed and belted knights on bicycles!

The grandest sight that ever was seen. Lord, how the plumes streamed, how the sun flamed and flashed from the endless procession of webby wheels!"[34]

Hank's epiphany, though, is far from spontaneous: he had earlier noted that pedal movement such as that of the monk who continuously bows at the Valley of Holiness is "one of the most useful motions in mechanics."[35] On a more interpretive level, Philip L. Leon parses that, because the exclamation point that follows "on bicycles" includes the entire sentence and not just the prepositional phrase, the bicycles are of no more particular interest than any other of the narrative's nineteenth-century technologies that "do not move us to mirth."[36] Humor is a matter of taste, but Leon's observation about Twain's disappointment is well-taken.

As if emphasizing the intellectual and physical process whereby man cannot ultimately master machine, chapter 38 features no fewer than three of Dan Beard's illustrations. The ordinary, which Beard copied from Twain's own Columbia, is seen from three perspectives.[37] The illustration with the caption "Launcelot swept in" celebrates the machine's potential application and depicts a knight resplendent with streamers sweeping backward in a posture very similar to Howard's cartoon for the *Wheel*.[38] "Sir Galahad takes a header" shows the machine's literal pitfalls, especially when an ordinary's front end stops short on a rock.[39] And "Knights practicing on the quiet" depicts man and machine in negotiation as four knights ride in single file in the shadowy distance.[40] Taken together, the chapter's three illustrations emphasize that machines, although empowering for occasional uses, are limited by the limitations of their creators; the ordinary was not only difficult to ride but dangerous when the rider went heels over head. The theme reflects that of the whole novel, which ends with a fearsome spectacle of the machine's domination of man, when the stench of thirty thousand dead knights, killed by

Hank's explosive mines, electrified wire, and line of Gatling guns, chokes Hank's fifty-two young trainees. As Clarence comments in his postscript, "We had conquered; in turn we were conquered."[41] The moment is gut-wrenching and embodies a keen disappointment in the machine's dominance over man. In the novel's wake, authors such as Norris were left to ponder still-deeper questions about man and machine.

Frank Norris and the Obsolescence of the Bicycle: Disinterest toward Man or Machine

The decade of the 1890s has many historical labels, but the "age of the safety bicycle" perhaps best encompasses the various conflicting interests associated with the period. With its design vastly more user-friendly than the ordinary's, the safety sparked a socioeconomic boom during the decade. "By the 1890s," Gilbert King describes, "it was difficult to make any social assumptions about cyclists. They ran the gamut, from academics to laborers to millionaires. While John D. Rockefeller toured the great universities on a bicycle, delivery boys in Chinatown were already making their rounds atop two-wheeled cycles."[42] Elsewhere, the geographical gamut ran from a special bicycle devised for the Klondike gold rush to Twain's observation in recounting his travels from 1896–97 in *Following the Equator* that the inhabitants of Fiji "only sixty years ago . . . were sunk in darkness; now they have the bicycle."[43] This kind of democratization appealed to naturalist authors and their concerns about social policy, and Frank Norris was no exception.

In the transition from the ordinary to the safety, the horse-versus-bicycle topic became less about arguing pedal over hoof power than about using the safety as a way for man to rebalance himself with, if not regain control over, the machine, in an increasingly industrialized America. By 1893, Boston's Lovell Cycles would begin its annual sales catalog with the following: "The bicycle and the horse differ in this respect, that if the latter possesses the swiftness of an arrow, he need not have great endurance to maintain his value. The bicycle, however, must possess both speed and strength, for the former without the latter may end its existence in a day. Strength in construction means continued pleasure to the rider, and speed a heightening of that pleasure. Speed aside from strength is as useless as knowledge without wisdom; but when combined they are perfection."[44]

Lovell's "doth protest too much" sense of the safety bicycle as a perfected technology surfaced in other corners of culture. For example, in an 1896 cover for *Collier's Weekly*, a safety-riding police officer seizes a horse that has overwhelmed a carriage driver, the machine at man's service.[45] Regardless of this promise, naturalist authors were not convinced that this situation was immutable or even socially beneficial. Of course, they were only too correct about the immutability part, for the bicycle quickly reached a condition of *obsolescence*—a word defined as involving "a thing which is out of date or has fallen into disuse." While still in working order, the bicycle, to press the definition of *obsolete* to its Latin root, had simply "grown old."[46]

Although *The Octopus* is loosely based on the 1880 Mussel Slough Affair, critical to the novel's theme is that Norris, writing two decades after the bloody encounter, envisioned Presley's bicycle as a safety. This newer model of bicycle certainly must have been in Norris's thoughts. Norris published in 1897 a short piece for the *Wave* titled "A Bicycle Gymkhana," in which he describes a safety-riding Bloomer bicycle club; and he knew Frederic Remington, who published in 1895 a short story titled "The Colonel of the First Cycle Infantry," which proposed replacing the horse with the safety bicycle for military purposes.[47] *The Octopus* itself also contains several changes that Norris made while composing the novel, changes that increasingly conjure up the safety bicycle.[48] For example, Norris notes that Presley's bicycle features cork grips, an upgrade that was one of the boom's many "sundries."[49] Additionally, Presley "tighten[s] a loose nut on his forward wheel," a clarification that would make little sense were his bicycle an ordinary.[50] At another moment, Presley "push[es] his bicycle in front of him," and Annixter later does the same.[51] To push an ordinary from the back is illogical, but it is common practice with a safety. Finally, Norris depicts Bonneville as a place where "here and there on the edge of the sidewalk were bicycles, wedged into bicycle racks painted with cigar advertisements."[52] Not only would the very size of ordinaries make such a scene unlikely, but the number of bicycles in California (or anywhere else) was not nearly so great during the early 1880s as it would be a decade later.

In *The Octopus*, the symbolism of horses, both those of flesh and blood and of iron (i.e., trains), versus the bicycle is most evident in Presley's "little turn through the country," central to the novel's long first chapter.[53] Early on, Presley's "bicycle flew" while he traversed Los Muertos, the safety bicycle resonant of his centrist position between man and machine, between horse-riding ranchers and steam-powered trains.[54] Reuben J. Ellis argues, "Presley's bicycle serves as a device to emphasize the ideological organization of the land. Presley's bicycle route is neat and linear, following the boundaries imposed by ownership and control."[55] This neatness proves all too spurious, and Ellis continues that Presley's "haste is in effect the desire to terminate the bicycle ride, to use the device of the modern world to obtain an experience that predates it.[56] Just how cutting-edge is this "device," though, is dubious given the rest of the chapter.

The unbalancing of Presley's centrist position concludes *The Octopus*'s first chapter, thus serving to set in motion his long descent to a kind of socioprofessional obsolescence. Near the end of his "little turn," Presley encounters the engineer Dyke, whose train is being held up so that a delayed "crack passenger" train can have an open track: "Presley, after leaning his bicycle against the tender, climbed to the fireman's seat of the worn green leather."[57] For a rare moment, man and machine—large and small—are in harmony. Too soon, however, this delicate harmony is obliterated when Vanamee's sheep find their way onto the railroad tracks, and the passenger train responsible for holding Dyke and his train up becomes an instrument of slaughter. The chapter ends with Presley's awful recollection: "Abruptly Presley saw again, in his imagination, the galloping monster, the terror of steel and steam with its single eye, cyclopean, red, shooting from horizon to horizon; but saw it now as the symbol of a vast power, huge, terrible, flinging the echo of its thunder over the reaches of the valley, leaving blood and destruction in its path; the leviathan with tentacles of steel clutching into the solid, the soulless force, the iron-hearted Power, the monster, the Colossus, the Octopus."[58] After this "massacre of innocents," Presley next appears in the ensuing chapter when he "potter[s] with a new bicycle lamp, filling it with oil, adjusting the wicks."[59] Presley's calmed demeanor suggests that he accepts what has happened, the lamp grotesquely mimicking the iron horse's "single eye" and, as a result, foreshadowing Presley's ineffectualness as a voice of the people.

Obsolescence, as *The Octopus* demonstrates, is only the end to a gradual process. After the incident with Vanamee's sheep, Presley tries mightily to regain his balance. When Phelps and Annixter set out on horse from Magnus's ranch, Presley accompanies them on bicycle.[60] But the mixing of the three characters is slightly awkward, especially when one remembers that the cigar-chomping Annixter will later tell the cigarette-smoking Presley not to fight the railroad because it is "no business of yours."[61] Presley's social role gets only more strained. When he goes into town to obtain some "black lead" for his bicycle, he listens as Caraher provokes the shattered Dyke.[62] In departing, Presley "went away without a word, his head bent, his hands clutched tightly on the cork grips of the handlebars of his bicycle. His lips were white. In his heart a blind demon of revolt raged tumultuous, shrieking blasphemies."[63] Presley's anger is without concrete consequence—he ultimately sees himself as "'a clock with a broken spring'"—and Norris's theme thus emerges: *neither* man nor machine triumphs in a world driven by inexorable forces far beyond human understanding.[64] After he leaves Caraher's, in fact, Presley rides not a bicycle but a pony, a less-than-the-norm horse indicative of Presley's status as an outsider and of his increasing disinterest toward the question of who conquers whom.

The Bicycle's Persistence in Place and Space

Viewed from almost any perspective, the bicycle's appeal fell sharply as America moved into the new century. The reasons were complex and probably unavoidable, and so the short-lived American Bicycle Company, incorporated in 1898 as a last-ditch effort by Pope and others to consolidate the market for safety bicycles, failed quickly when prices spiked downward. By 1902 a company such as Philadelphia's Hart Cycle and Automobile Company listed their "New Century" bicycle for a scant $17.50.[65] Pope had already moved to producing electric automobiles; and Henry Ford, a former bicycle mechanic, envisioned a gasoline-powered future.[66] Still, the bicycle as a technology persisted because, although typical of the way machines moved from promotion to disappointment to obsolescence, the bicycle itself retained an elusive, beautiful balance between man and machine. Nothing has changed. David B. Perry offers this paean to the bicycle's continuing magic: "On a bicycle your destination is where you are. Cycling brings an expanded sense of *place* while traveling through *space*. Through the powerful experience of the journey, cycling opens up the body and mind to the surrounding landscape, the elements of nature, and the whole feeling of being there."[67] In their uses of the horse-versus-bicycle topic, Pratt, Twain, and Norris responded to this "powerful experience of journey," and how each saw the man-or-machine question casts an important light on America's transportation and literary histories.

Notes

1. Bruce D. Epperson, *Peddling Bicycles to America: The Rise of an Industry* (Jefferson NC: McFarland, 2010), 55–56.
2. David V. Herlihy, *Bicycle: The History* (New Haven CT: Yale University Press, 2004), 191.
3. Stephen B. Goddard, *Colonel Albert Pope and His American Dream Machines: The Life and Times of a Bicycle Tycoon Turned Automotive Pioneer* (Jefferson NC: McFarland, 2000), 82.
4. Herlihy, *Bicycle*, 3.
5. Charles E. Pratt, *The American Bicycler: A Manual for the Learner, the Observer, and the Expert* (Boston: Houghton, Osgood, 1879), 74.
6. Charles E. Pratt, "A Sketch of American Bicycling and Its Founder," *Outing*, July 1891, 344.
7. Jay Pridmore and Jim Hurd, *The American Bicycle* (Osceola WI: Motorbooks, 1995), 26.
8. Goddard, *Colonel Albert Pope*, 82.
9. Bruce Epperson, letter to the author, March 10, 2010.
10. Pratt, *American Bicycler*, 1.
11. Pratt, *American Bicycler*, 202.
12. See Herlihy, *Bicycle*, 183.
13. Pratt, *American Bicycler*, 125.
14. Pratt, *American Bicycler*, 192.
15. Pratt, *American Bicycler*, 3.

16. Pratt, *American Bicycler*, 30–31.

17. Pratt, *American Bicycler*, 102.

18. Pratt, *American Bicycler*, 113.

19. Pratt, *American Bicycler*, 177.

20. Pratt, *American Bicycler*, 32.

21. Pratt, *American Bicycler*, 114.

22. Pratt, *American Bicycler*, 170.

23. Epperson, letter.

24. Friedrich Graetz, "The Tournament of Today: A Set-to between Labor and Monopoly," *Puck* 13, no. 334 (August 1, 1883): centerfold, Library of Congress, accessed February 16, 2014, http://www.loc.gov/pictures /item/2012645501/.

25. Thomas Stevens, *Around the World on a Bicycle*, with an introduction by Thomas Pauly (Mechanicsburg PA: Stackpole Books, 2011).

26. C. J. Howard, "Nineteen Eighty-Three," *Wheel*, March 7, 1883, 1.

27. Joseph. G. Dalton, "Initial and Celestial Cycling: A Parody-Mosaic," in *Lyra Bicyclica: Sixty Poets on the Wheel*, ed. Joseph G. Dalton, 2nd ed. (Boston: E. C. Hodges, 1885), 16.

28. Goddard, *Colonel Albert Pope*, 9.

29. Mark Twain, "Taming the Bicycle," in *What Is Man? and Other Essays*, ed. Albert Bigelow Paine (New York: Harper and Brothers, 1917), 290.

30. Philip W. Leon, "'Here They Came!' The Bicycle Rescue in *A Connecticut Yankee*," *Mark Twain Journal* 32, no. 1 (Spring 1994): 29.

31. Pridmore and Hurd, *American Bicycle*, 32.

32. Epperson, *Peddling Bicycles to America*, 56.

33. Mark Twain to William Dean Howells, September 22, 1889, in *A Connecticut Yankee in King Arthur's Court: An Authoritative Text, Backgrounds, and Sources: Composition Publication Criticism*, ed. Allison R. Ensor (New York: W. W. Norton, 1982), 301.

34. Mark Twain, *A Connecticut Yankee in King Arthur's Court*, vol. 9 of *The Works of Mark Twain*, ed. Bernard L. Stein (Berkeley: University of California Press, 1979), 425–26. All citations refer to this edition.

35. Twain, *Connecticut Yankee*, 260.

36. Leon, "'Here They Came!'" 27.

37. Leon, "'Here They Came!'" 29.

38. Twain, *Connecticut Yankee*, 421, 422, 424.

39. Twain, *Connecticut Yankee*, 422.

40. Twain, *Connecticut Yankee*, 424.

41. Twain, *Connecticut Yankee*, 489.

42. Gilbert King, *The Bicycle: Boneshakers, Highwheelers, and Other Celebrated Cycles* (Philadelphia: Running Press, 2002), 75.

43. Mark Twain, *Following the Equator*, in *The Complete Travel Books of Mark Twain: The Later Works; A Tramp Abroad, Life on the Mississippi, Following the Equator*, ed. Charles Neider (New York: Doubleday, 1967), 725. See also Lisa Mighetto and Marcia Babcock Montgomery, "Hard Drive to the Klondike: Promoting Seattle during the Gold Rush; A Historic Resource Study for the Seattle Unit of the Klondike Gold Rush National Historical Park," National Parks Service, November 1998, http://files.eric.ed.gov/fulltext/ED437334.pdf.

44. *Lovell Diamond Cycles* (Boston: Lovell, 1893), 3.

45. Herlihy, *Bicycle*, 624.

46. *Shorter Oxford Dictionary on Historical Principles*, 5th ed., s.v. "obsolete."

47. Reuben J. Ellis, "'A Little Turn through the Country': Presley's Bicycle Ride in Frank Norris' *The Octopus*," *Journal of American Culture* 17, no. 3 (Fall 1994): 19.

48. Joseph R. McElrath Jr. *Frank Norris Revisited* (New York: Twayne Publishers, 1992), 92.

49. Frank Norris, *The Octopus* (1901; repr., New York: Penguin Books, 1986), 9; Pridmore and Hurd, *American Bicycle*, 52.

50. Norris, *Octopus*, 10.

51. Norris, *Octopus*, 28, 89.

52. Norris, *Octopus*, 191.

53. Norris, *Octopus*, 23.

54. Norris, *Octopus*, 15.

55. Ellis, "'Little Turn through the Country,'" 19.

56. Ellis, "'Little Turn through the Country,'" 20.

57. Norris, *Octopus*, 17.

58. Norris, *Octopus*, 51.

59. Norris, *Octopus*, 50, 58.

60. Norris, *Octopus*, 186.

61. Norris, *Octopus*, 513.

62. Norris, *Octopus*, 356.

63. Norris, *Octopus*, 358.

64. Norris, *Octopus*, 565.

65. *New Century* (Philadelphia: Hart Cycle and Automobile Company, 1902), 9.

66. Pridmore and Hurd, *American Bicycle*, 98–99.

67. David Perry, *Bike Cult: The Ultimate Guide to Human-Powered Vehicles* (New York: Four Walls Eight Windows, 1995), 433.

3 "The Face of the Bicyclist"

Women's Cycling and the Altered
Body in *The Type-Writer Girl*

ALYSSA STRAIGHT

A London lady, who teaches a Sunday-school class, and who has recently
become an accomplished bicyclist, was seen riding by her scholars, who
taxed her with it upon the next Sunday. She quietly admitted the fact,
to their great edification. Whereupon one small girl eyed her with some
gravity, and asked with becoming solemnity, "But, Miss, is it quite perlite
to ride the bicycle?"

EVELYN EVERETT GREEN, "Cycling for Ladies"

Alice Meynell, in her short, observational essay "The Woman in Grey"
(1896), asserts that "the figure of a woman on a bicycle in Oxford Street"
reveals the problematic logic of late nineteenth-century hereditary
theory.[1] The scientific thought of the time limited the possibilities
of women's improvement by invoking the "influence of heredity,"
a term Meynell borrows from an unnamed source. Meynell points
out that "professors take it for granted" by their own "slow process
of reason" that "women derive from their mothers and grandmoth-
ers, and men from their fathers and grandfathers."[2] As a result, these
hereditary theorists believe, women continue to pass down their
physical weakness and domestic instincts to their female children,
who inherit none of their fathers' logic or strength. For Meynell, the
woman in gray contradicted the basic biological theory that women
had inherited limited physical and mental capabilities; the woman
in gray had a "watchful confidence" and "was immediately dependent

on no nerves, but her own."[3] Inspired by the cycling woman in gray, Meynell indulges in her feminist critique, turning these unnamed professors' understanding of women's lack of physical strength and mental acuity against them. Furthermore, she suggests that it is the professors' reasoning skills that were lacking when they developed a faulty theory that "fosters the ignorance of women" and justifies and excuses women's subjection.[4]

Meynell concludes her essay by suggesting not only that women are capable of developing exceptional skills (like confidently and independently riding a bicycle) but that their sons and their daughters can benefit from the liberated woman's positive experiences and education.[5] "From the lessons of an unlessoned mind," she writes, "a woman's heirs-male are not cut off in the Common Law of the generations of mankind. Brutus knew the valour of Portia was settled upon his sons."[6] The qualities of the cycling woman in gray—her "watchful confidence" and "common security," as well as "the judgment, the temper, the skill, the perception, the strength of men and horses" she acquires and utilizes in her riding—become qualities for future generations to admire and emulate.[7] The woman on the wheel demonstrates that women's abilities are not curtailed by their contemporaries' deterministic and oversimplified theories of heredity. Through her ability to ride a bicycle, the woman in gray, who had been "educated to sit still," shows that any woman is capable of "doing what nothing in her youth could well have prepared her for."[8] Thus, the lady bicyclist allows Meynell to rewrite hereditary and biological theory and woman's role in it as well as to advocate for the "unsure condition of liberty and content[ment]" that women were clamoring for.[9] The bicycle, the inspirational technology of movement through which Meynell makes her feminist argument, became the impetus that provided women with access to freedom, education, and public spaces.

Meynell's "The Woman in Grey" is just one example of the late nineteenth- and early twentieth-century discourse on the relationship between women's rights, the bicycle, and medicine and biology. While the bicycle became a springboard for early feminist thinking, not just for Meynell, but for New Women in general who "signaled new, or newly perceived forms of femininity" and advocated "women's right to education, employment, and full citizenship," women cyclists also garnered much ill attention.[10] Prior to and during the bicycle boom in the 1890s, a lady who cycled was a threat to late-Victorian masculinity and physical ability and was said to have "hopelessly unsexed herself."[11] As Lillias Campbell Davidson notes in her *Handbook for Lady Cyclists* (1896), "It was supposed that no woman would take to so masculine an amusement unless she was fast, unwomanly, and desirous of making herself conspicuous; and accordingly all cycling women had to suffer from this supposition."[12] These depictions of lady cyclists "embodied hopes and fears about racial development," resulting in much study of the health and bodies of women cyclists and of cycling's overall influence on women's reproductive organs, looks, and dress.[13] Women cyclists were often criticized because of the bodily alterations created by physical exercise, even as the improved muscle tone developed from cycling was praised for improving the constitution and the delicacy of women's nerves. On the one hand, critics discouraged women from cycling because of their perceived natural feminine weakness, or because it was deemed unladylike; on the other hand, proponents of the bicycle credited it as the "rescuer of woman from her special ills: oppressive clothing, inactivity and nervous-reproductive weakness."[14]

Juxtaposing literary texts that incorporate cycling women, like Grant Allen's *The Type-Writer Girl* (1897), with these various conversations on women's cycling, specifically the scientific and medical discourses about women's loss of femininity and physical deterioration, and with firsthand accounts on cycling by lady cyclists, this chapter explores how nineteenth-century physicians read evidence of the bodily changes women experienced as a result of their cycling and argues that ideological assumptions about bicycle riding affected their interpretations of that evidence. These late-Victorian physicians' interpretations also impacted how most contemporaries understood and evaluated the bicycle's social and political impact. Though the lady cyclist's health and body was up for debate regularly in medical journals and pamphlets, some literary texts sought to transform the negative medical discourses about female cyclists' bodies. For example, in Allen's *The Type-Writer Girl*, the body of the protagonist, Juliet, and her cycle are intrinsically connected. Allen's depictions of the bicycle and of the female cyclist repurpose popular discourses on cycling, demonstrating instead that the woman's body is made better and more powerful as a result of her bicycling.

That technology can alter and improve the body is not an unusual concept for the late nineteenth and early twentieth centuries. As Tim Armstrong explains, "At the end of the nineteenth century, it could still be said that many technological developments were modelled on the body—particularly the deficient body, the telephone emerging from research on the mechanism of the ear; the typewriter from a desire to let the blind write by touch; film from persistence of vision."[15] For the turn of the century, technology offered "a re-formed body, more powerful and capable, producing . . . a fascination . . . with the interface between the body and the machine."[16] The distance between the human body and technology collapses. The body is mechanical, and the mechanical is an "extension or development of the body within an evolutionary perspective."[17] As Armstrong so eloquently puts it, "We are not only inventing new machines, but our new machines have turned upon us and are creating new men."[18] Considering technology like the bicycle within this "evolutionary perspective," this chapter tells a revised history of the bicycle and its impact on women. Examining the interaction between Juliet and her bicycle, alongside both positive and negative medical discourses on the lady cyclist, reveals a model of bodily agency, one that illustrates a female body that is powerful, rather than fragile, and one that allows women to rewrite the limiting medical and evolutionary arguments about women's bodies in more positive terms. These positive depictions of the female bicyclist, as seen in Allen's and Meynell's work, ultimately influenced discourses on women's rights, employment, and mobility.[19]

Cultural and Scientific Debates on Female Cycling

The *Times* claimed on August 15, 1898, that the bicycle was "a social boon" and, in some respects, a "social revolution," causing quite a stir, especially where women were concerned.[20] There was much discussion about the bicycle and the newfound freedoms it afforded women. While Lillias Campbell Davidson, a cyclist and promoter of women's cycling, suggested that "cycling for women will not only become a national, but a universal institution; and women all over the world are going to be the better for it, both in mind and body, not only in their generation, but in the generation to come," a number of men and women were reluctant to agree.[21] Some, like Eliza Lynn Linton, argued against female cycling altogether, claiming it was a dangerous freedom, an "intoxication which comes with unfettered liberty."[22] This debate was encoded in the dichotomy of the New Woman versus the Angel in the House. New Women wanted to cycle because it afforded them freedom and opportunity; however, women's cycling also ruffled the feathers of the more traditional men and women because it displaced the socially constructed and internalized ideology of women as submissive, "self-sacrificing and self-regulating ... radiating morality and love."[23] Debates of this nature led some women who cycled to be cautious riders by, for example, resisting the two-wheeler on a principle of conservative modesty. The tricycle was considered more appropriate for ladies, because it did not require them to vault, indecorously, onto the high mount; women could also more safely ride the tricycle in their skirts and dresses.[24] As Robins Pennell noted, "Women . . . have seemed absurdly conservative [when it comes to cycling]; they cling to the three wheels, as if to do so were the concession that made their cycling proper."[25]

Women's mannish and unladylike behavior and dress were most commonly invoked in debates about the propriety of cycling. Most late-Victorian writers on cycling (whether male or female) engaged in conversation about the fashion best suited to riding and the controversy surrounding rational dress.[26] While most writers encouraged the wearing of divided skirts, they also promoted knickerbockers as ideal for cycling because they prevented women's long skirts and dresses from getting caught in the wheels, gears, and chain while pedaling. In addition, the lighter and looser material associated with divided skirts and blouses, and the removal of the tightly laced corset, enabled an easier and healthier riding experience. Robins Pennell explained that "of the greater comfort and safety secured" by adopting what came to be known as rational dress, "there can be no question; the chief drawback to this costume . . . is its conspicuousness."[27] Indeed,

women cycling publicly in rational dress were often subjected to ridicule, hostility, and even violence.[28]

Perhaps because of the strong reactions to women in knickerbockers, women cyclists became especially concerned with the ways in
which they represented themselves publicly. It became important
that the lady cyclist be "at all times," as Miss F. J. Erskine makes clear
in *Lady Cycling* (1897), "neat, smart, and in harmony with her workmanlike machine."[29] This harmony meant that the lady cyclist should
avoid wearing unfashionable riding clothing like "ridiculous blouses
and flower-garden hats" or big skirts that made her look the "balloon
jib of a yacht."[30] Likewise, Campbell Davidson attempts to distance
the lady cyclists of the boom era from their predecessors by accus-
ing those pioneer women of having "cast aside all feminine charm of
looks" in their need to ride as fast and as far as men.[31] Lady cyclists
"are wiser nowadays," she argues, and have discovered that cycling
can "be made graceful, pretty, and charming, as well as enjoyable";
women of the wheel now "know how to ride well, and to look well
in whatever they do."[32] Evelyn Everett Green, in "Cycling for Ladies"
(1896), assures her readers that women "sit up remarkably straight and
carry themselves well."[33] By suggesting that women riders are good
cyclists, Erskine, Campbell Davidson, and Everett Green assure their
detractors that women cyclists aren't masculine in form, feature, and
movement; rather, elegant cycling enhances their feminine grace and
looks. Everett Green, Campbell Davidson, and Erskine are clearly writing in response to a critique not only of women's fashion but also of
their ability to remain "feminine" in the pursuit of exercise and when
infiltrating the male public domain.

The controversy surrounding women's cycling and its accompanying emancipation was perhaps most popularly addressed in the medical field and in relation to women's sexualized bodies. Indeed, public
discussions regarding the lady cyclists' charm and clothing were heavily predicated on medical ideologies about women's cycling bodies,
primarily the notion that cycling contributed to a lack of feminine
physique, beauty, and reproductive abilities. Medical discourse was
sought as a method of containment for women who were too public
or too outspoken or who operated outside the "conventional" model

of femininity.[34] As a result, much deliberation ensued in the medical field about whether or not it was healthy for women to ride bicycles and about what larger impact women's cycling would have on the British nation and its future generations.

Perhaps the most aggressively outspoken opponent to female bicycling (and sports altogether) was Arabella Kenealy. Kenealy was a practicing physician from 1888 to 1894, as well as a journalist and a novelist. In "Woman as Athlete" (1899), Kenealy puts a scientific spin on the public accusations that women cyclists are unfeminine and immodest, ultimately arguing that the new muscles gained through exercising on the bike alter women's personalities. "Woman as Athlete" sets up these larger arguments about women's reproduction and its impact on evolution by scientifically suggesting that the new-found energy and strength cycling women experience is merely the result of hypertrophied muscles and is consequently a disruption of "mental, emotional, and physical" well-being.[35] Though her medical theories are outdated now, Kenealy firmly believed that "the power of a healthy adult can be increased only at the expense of some other power" and that since the "modern woman has inordinately added to her muscle-power" through bicycling, the body must compensate with the loss of "human capability."[36] The cycling woman, by becoming active, is "deifying muscle" over feminine nature; by gaining muscle, the modern woman sacrifices important "womanly faculties."[37]

Kenealy demonstrates these lost "womanly faculties" to the reader through a characterization of her patient Clara's behaviors after taking up cycling. After cycling, Clara's physical beauty has been altered from "suggestive," "elusive," and "charming" to "defined," "unwavering," and "direct."[38] Likewise, her bodily movements, tone of voice, and physical shape are transformed. As Kenealy notes, "Her movements are muscular and less womanly. Where they had been quiet and graceful, now they are abrupt and direct. Her voice is louder, her tones are assertive. She says everything—leaves nothing to the imagination."[39] For Kenealy, Clara's body and its "natural" balance have been disrupted through cycling. The added muscle and lean figure represent a threat to Clara's overall attractiveness and feminine temperament. As Kenealy relates, Clara's new energies are redirected. Now instead of participating in the more "feminine" pursuits of caregiver, comforter, and nurse, she is consumed only with a "pursuit of pleasure."[40] With these arguments, Kenealy makes a distinction between an illusory health characterized by increased muscles, motor capability, and energy on the one hand and actual improved health on the other hand. According to Kenealy, increased muscularity and the resulting loss of sympathetic faculties in women are actually representative of diseased nerves and degeneration.[41]

Clara's body further deteriorates by a disease of the nerves, which Kenealy attributes to cycling. According to Kenealy, "the greatest charm of Clara's face" was "lost in the suspicion of a 'bicycle face' (the face of muscular tension)."[42] A certain Dr. A. Shadwell first diagnosed this malady, defining it as "the peculiar strained, set look" caused by the "double strain—a general one on the nerves and a particular one on the balancing centre" for keeping the cycle upright and avoiding spills.[43] Because "bicycle face" was caused by the "double strain" of the rider attempting to keep her balance, it was classified during the time as a nervous disease and one that often led to dementia, insomnia, or headaches.

While all cyclists were at risk for acquiring bicycle face (along with its associated diseases: "Cyclist's Figure," "Bicycle Hernia," "Cyclist's sore-throat," "Bicycle Fright," "Bicycle Hand," and "Bicycle Foot"), once women began cycling, these potential injuries were reintroduced and discussed in relation to women's bodies with, as James Whorton suggests, "greater urgency, since women were by nature more delicate."[44] These other diseases, especially those that contorted parts of the body like bicycle face and cyclist's figure (a curvature of the spine caused by bending over the handlebars), were taken up as threatening to the future health of the race because they were thought to be transmissible through heredity.[45] Kenealy's concern that "the greatest charm of Clara's face" was lost to bicycle face is directly tied to her fear of women's evolutionary degeneration. Bicycle face is not only a visible representation of the physical and mental distress biking can cause the female body; for Kenealy it also symbolically represents the end of women's natural feminine sympathies.[46] Kenealy ends her essay by calling for ladies like Clara to "retain [their] womanhood" and the "beautiful achievement of evolution" by presumably avoiding exercise, specifically in the form of bicycle riding.[47]

Despite Kenealy's "scientific" study, many women cyclists and writers as well as medical professionals encouraged and promoted bicycle riding for women's health. In direct response to "Woman as Athlete," L. Ormistan Chant mockingly suggests that it is "somewhat premature to accuse Clara of 'squandering the potentiality of the race'... in view of the fact that the first ladies' cycle was put on the market... so few years ago."[48] She asks her readers to let "natural selection" decide what is preferred in women, arguing that it can "be trusted to decide" in favor of the muscular or unmuscular.[49] Similarly, Dr. Oscar Jennings makes it clear that bicycling can only advance the human race. There is nothing, Jennings asserts, that is not "absolutely and wholly curable" by cycling, including rheumatism, gout, obesity, asthma, constipation, diabetes, varicose veins, hernias, hemorrhoids, nervous affections, dyspepsia, and liver disorders (to name a few).[50] Jennings also contends that without sufficient muscular activity, the human race "vegetates and wastes away."[51] Lack of exercise not only "benumbs the intelligence," it also "obscures the moral sense" and produces unhappy, obese, and neurotic people. For Jennings, the cycle in particular "is calculated to banish all kinds of nervous maladies" in women.[52]

Alice Meynell's "The Woman in Grey" aligns well with Dr. Jennings's arguments and stands in direct contrast to the evolutionary arguments made by Kenealy. Meynell is not limited by a misconception about woman's true "nature," as is clear by her overall contention that women are capable of developing into more intelligent and physically healthy versions of themselves. As she notes, "A woman, long educated to sit still, does not suddenly learn to live a momentary life without strong momentary resolution."[53] Rather, the "vibrating pause of perpetual change" that the bicycle makes as the woman in gray pedals onward suggests the development of women toward something better through cycling.[54] For Meynell, the woman in gray is an example of an exceptional modern woman because of the qualities and freedoms bicycling affords her. The language of freedom and equality surrounding the woman as she cycles makes this clear; she is described as "taking her equal risk."[55] In addition, her muscular body is described, not as diseased or as missing a certain mysterious grace, but rather as charm itself. Where Clara, Kenealy's patient, is no longer charming because she has lost that elusive quality of movement, the woman in gray, "seated upon a place of detachment between earth and air," is the embodiment of charm and grace.[56] By existing in a perfectly balanced space, both physically and mentally, she is able to claim an independence, self-assurance, and fearlessness that eludes most of her noncycling contemporaries.

Bicycling Bodies in Grant Allen's *Type-Writer Girl*

The evolutionary narrative in "The Woman in Grey" is further developed in Grant Allen's *The Type-Writer Girl*. This short, first-person novel follows the typewriting adventures of Juliet Appleton, as she describes her social and political philosophies regarding capitalism, evolution, and women's independence; the treatment she receives as a typist at various places of employment; and the love triangle between her, her employer, and his fiancée. Throughout Juliet's narrative, it becomes clear that as a single, twenty-two-year-old woman, she values and craves independence, freedom of movement, and access to the public world. These values are written across the story in a number of ways, but primarily through the technologies (the bicycle and the typewriter) that Juliet uses to secure her independence and employment. Juliet romanticizes these technologies, writing them into mythical narratives of freedom, justice, and even danger. She also relates herself to these technologies on a more physical level, embodying their functions, movements, and qualities as part of her own persona. This embodiment provides Juliet with a language through which she can better express not only her relationship with these technologies but also her value as a woman and laborer within the social and political system of late-Victorian England.

In *The Type-Writer Girl*, Juliet represents a more evolved working woman than other literary representations of typewriting girls. As Clarissa Suranyi explains, where other textual representations of the typewriter girl "humanized and feminized" the workplace and sent the message that "the Victorian angel in the house could be successfully transplanted into the business world and could exert a positive influence on it," Juliet is neither overly feminine nor "self-sacrificing."[57] While she does hold to some gendered stereotypes, Juliet's primary objective is to break open the boundaries of traditional womanhood. As a New Woman, the college-educated Juliet smokes, wears rational dress, and rides her bicycle. Furthermore, she writes her story in evolutionary discourse, narrating herself in a struggle of self versus environment. Juliet utilizes the struggle-for-existence ideology to affirm her rights as a woman to pursue a career, behave as she chooses, and experience adventures. As she states, "In this age the struggle for existence has become one of the rights of woman."[58] Her take on evolutionary theory rests primarily on her self-perception as someone struggling to succeed in a male-dominated environment. For example, upon receiving her first job as a typist at Flor and Fingleman's law offices, she writes, "I have proved myself fittest by the mere fact of survival.... The sole remaining question was, Could I adapt myself to my environment? If so, I had fulfilled the whole gospel of Darwinism."[59] Though she takes some liberties with Darwin, this adaptability to environment and pursuit of personal growth guides Juliet's adventures. The advantages that help Juliet move toward her evolutionary destiny are her typewriter and bicycle, both of which turn out to be more than just technological resources. Rather, they become representatives of the advanced characteristics of the modern womanhood that Juliet values: assertiveness, liberty, and adventure.[60]

Throughout the novel, Juliet's bicycle riding is directly associated with her freedom. For example, Juliet proclaims once while riding, "I rode on, glad to be free once more."[61] As she relates her bicycling experiences, descriptions of her riding are tied to women's freedom from traditional patriarchal roles: "How light and free I felt! When man first set woman on two wheels with a pair of pedals, did he know, I wonder, that he had rent the veil of the harem in twain? I doubt it, but so it was. A woman on a bicycle has all the world before her where to choose; she can go where she will, no man hindering."[62] Juliet's desire for freedom and her attempts to achieve it are represented by the bicycle. Just as the cycling body of Meynell's woman in gray represents the advancement of women through "the vibrating pause of perpetual change," so Juliet's cycle propels her upward on the evolutionary chain of survival in a capitalist and patriarchal world. The bicycle literally moves her from one location to another and from one job to the next, onward through her adventure of self-realization. The sense of freedom Juliet receives from cycling is most fully achieved by Juliet's collapsing of her physical body and identity into the cycle. In the novel, Juliet's connection to the bicycle operates on two levels: one where others lower her and her body to the mechanical and objectified level of the machine and one where she creates and repurposes this body-bicycle relationship for her own advanced sense of self, as well as for monetary and social gain.

Most notably, the merging of Juliet with her bicycle becomes apparent during her visit to and escape from the anarchist commune. In the anarchist commune, the bicycle becomes a symbol of Juliet herself. Here, Juliet provides more description of the anarchists' reaction to her bicycle than to her, which is strange given that Juliet is a single, educated, middle-class Englishwoman seeking to join a ragtag group of immigrant laborers. Though he is surprised to learn Juliet is an anarchist, Rothenberg, the leader of the commune, is more interested in her bicycling clothes. "My costume took his fancy," writes Juliet.[63] His and his comrades' interest does not end here, as Juliet winds up giving the comrades cycling lessons every evening because of their devotion "in equal parts to myself and my bicycle."[64] Juliet gives the readers the impression that, much like at Flor and Fingleman's, she is offered employment at the commune only because of her attractive figure. When Juliet first tells the commune her name, "each man drew himself up and stroked his chin with the very air of a Romeo," and she describes having "resisted the temptations" of the comrades "who would fain have discoursed to me the words of love in many uncouth languages."[65] Their reactions to Juliet ultimately become the source of tension between her and the male comrades, who complain that Juliet "takes no notice of them," despite giving them nightly cycling lessons.[66] When pressured to give them more of her attention, Juliet refuses and threatens to leave the commune. As recompense, the anarchists attempt to keep her bicycle in exchange for the loss of her physical body and its labor. Leon, one of the comrades, argues, "This machine is ours. . . . Whatever any comrade brings into the Community is common property. We will give you your dividend and let you go; but this you must leave with us."[67]

Juliet understands this claim on her bicycle as a claim on her own person and refuses to accept it. She angrily rejects their alleged ownership of her bicycle. "'Sir,'" she says "in [her] most commanding voice, 'you shall not touch my machine. If you venture to detain it . . . I will move for a mandamus to compel you to show cause why you should escape the penalties of praemunire.'"[68] Though appropriating the masculine, legal language learned at Flor and Fingleman's, language whose exact meaning Juliet is somewhat uncertain of, she successfully argues that they have no legal right of supremacy over her or her bicycle. At her refusal, they again try to bargain for her labor at the commune, entreating her to stay on, in hopes of maintaining ownership of her and her bicycle. Juliet, with her hand "laid firmly" on her machine, leaves immediately, retaining her bicycle, her body, and compensation for her labor, and heads to London to "be once more a type-writer."[69] While the anarchists sought to relegate Juliet and her bicycle to the realm of group property, wherein Juliet's body is merely another mechanized cog at work for the function of the community, Juliet sees this arrangement as a form of "coercion" that subjects her to the "tyranny of public opinion."[70] She declares herself an "individual" and rides her bicycle literally to freedom from social, political, and gendered constraints.[71]

Juliet's ride to freedom reiterates the language of freedom she uses elsewhere while cycling. As she moves "into the open air of Banded Despotism," the very act of cycling becomes indistinct from what the cycle represents: her complete authority over self and machine.[72] Thus Juliet repurposes the demeaning relationship of herself and her bicycle as mechanical property to be utilized by others into a complete mastering of her identity and body. This blurring of machine and Juliet is continued as she cycles away from the commune. Though proud of her escape from the comrades, Juliet is left feeling nervous. She is worried that the comrades will overtake her cycling body and limit her newfound self-control. In order to reassert her ownership, she dismounts the bike and begins tinkering with its mechanics; she "called a halt and dismounted for a moment to tighten my loose joints, metaphorically and literally."[73] The parts of the bike and the body become intertwined here: Juliet imagines tightening her trembling limbs, much as she tightens the screws of her bicycle. Putting the bike in perfect order and function also means returning her own body to perfect composure.

When Juliet later crashes her bicycle into the "foreign body" of fellow cyclist Michaela, this body-cycle union is further developed.[74] In the spill, the impact itself injures Juliet's body and bicycle; "I suppose," she says, that "the spill had shattered my nerves."[75] The speed at which she flew down the hill and the result of the impact all register the effects of the bicycle on the human body. Her description of the accident suggests an overall confusion about what damage she is looking at (damage to body or to cycle parts); for though she says she "enquire[d] which of her limbs is broken" before assessing the damage to her wheel, she doesn't notice until much later that her hands are bleeding, while she immediately registers the pain of having "twisted" the "front wheel . . . out of human recognition" and having punctured a tire.[76] Though she mentions her nerves are "shattered," her attention is mostly fixed on the destruction of the bike rather than on her own wounds. And it becomes clear that the tears Juliet cries are over the destruction of the combined assemblage of bike and rider. She admits no real separation between her own body and that of her bike: "I burst into tears outright and sank down on the ground by my broken cycle."[77] The broken cycle and shattered nerves recall that moment when Juliet "tighten[ed] [her] loose joints, metaphorically and literally," signaling that Juliet's shattered nerves are both literal and metaphorical symbols of her bike's damaged frame.[78] Juliet's language of union with her cycle is tied to her desire to take control of her surroundings and to establish herself as a powerful woman. With the blending of her body with the bicycle, Juliet's body is stronger, faster, and more valuable than before, economically, socially, and even (as we see at the commune) sexually. She is able to adopt a more dominant and commanding presence, as is illustrated in her refusal to hand over her bicycle to the commune and in her response to the bicycle crash. Though she bursts into tears, she also retains her "dignity" by "tak[ing] the aggressive first," as is "always a good plan, in [the] case of collision."[79]

Juliet's body is further united with the mechanics of the bicycle through a repurposing of the medical discourses surrounding women's bicycling and nervous systems. On her ride to freedom from the anarchist commune, Juliet references Shadwell's bicycle face. She suggests that the malady represents the rider's thoughtfulness while riding, rather than a nervous condition of her body. While admitting that the "bicycle in full swing ... is not an ideal place for calm reflection," Juliet is able to overcome the "face of the bicyclist" by meditating on her previous troubles and experiences as well as on her future goals and resolutions.[80] Bicycle face loses its destructive intent; Juliet's nerves and physique are not diseased or deformed by her cycling. Furthermore, bicycle face gets redefined as an antidote to nervous disorder: the bicycle has a calming and productive effect on her mental well-being. As her bicycle propels her forward and onward toward better things, she contemplates, once again, the evolutionary journey she has undertaken. Though she determines that "environment was triumphing all along the line," her readers recognize that her very act of cycling is an evolutionary triumph.[81] The bicycle face she suffers from is not the bicycle face of Kenealy or Shadwell. It does not mean a nervous collapse or the end of the human race; rather, it represents strength of will, mental capability, and physical strength.

As witnessed by her bicycle crash, Juliet does not ride with the ideal charm of Meynell's woman in gray or in "harmony with her workmanlike machine," as Erskine and Campbell Davidson recommended. Juliet is still evolving, something that is made clear compared to the woman whom she crashes into. This girl, Michaela, is an inexperienced cyclist and is described as "a wisp of a figure" and a "timid small atomy" compared to Juliet, who is described later by Michaela's fiancé as being "full of intrepid self-reliance; a woman with nerve, audacity, spirit."[82] While Juliet does experience a bit of shock from the collision, Michaela is inconsolable. As Juliet explains, she was "nervously shaken" and "would have fainted ... if ... she was injured."[83] The comparison Allen makes between these two characters only increases the reader's belief that Juliet is a much more evolved, independent, and admirable character. Juliet has nerve; she doesn't suffer from nerves.

Conclusion

The Type-Writer Girl incorporates the discourses surrounding women's bodies and bicycle technology by repurposing them in order to emphasize the importance the machine has for women like Juliet in the period. Though Juliet contracts bicycle face, we find that the putative ailment represents nothing more than Juliet's ability to ride the cycle while thinking profound thoughts and ideas. The bicycle is written onto and as part of Juliet's own body and identity, as a way of representing how women can use technology for their freedom, adventure, and financial independence. Allen's novel also reaffirms the positive impact cycling could have for women's health, nervous systems, and independence. In this way, Allen repurposes the discourses surrounding women's bodies and technologies, arguing instead for the evolutionary improvements technology can offer to women. As Frances E. Willard makes clear, "We [women] rejoiced together greatly in perceiving the impetus that this uncompromising but fascinating and illimitably capable machine would give to that blessed 'woman question' to which we were . . . devoted. . . . We saw that the physical development of humanity's mother-half would be wonderfully advanced by that universal introduction of the bicycle."[84] Willard, like Meynell and Juliet, sees the bicycle and the discourses surrounding women cyclists as influencing and shaping evolution. Rather than damaging women's ability to be capable mothers and wives, the bicycle can develop in women physical and mental qualities that can only improve the future of humanity.

Notes

1. Alice Meynell, "The Woman in Grey," in *Literature and Culture at the Fin de Siècle*, ed. Talia Schaffer (New York: Pearson Education, 2007), 239.
2. Meynell, "Woman in Grey," 236.
3. Meynell, "Woman in Grey," 239.
4. Meynell, "Woman in Grey," 237.
5. In *The Descent of Man* (1871), for example, Darwin theorizes that secondary sex characteristics "are present in both sexes," with each transmitting "the characters proper to its own male and female sex to the hybrid offspring of either sex." Darwin believed, similarly to Meynell, that "equal transmission of characters to both sexes is the commonest form of inheritance." Charles Dar-

win, *The Descent of Man, and Selection in Relation to Sex* (London: Penguin, 2004), 263, 266.

6. Meynell, "Woman in Grey," 239.
7. Meynell, "Woman in Grey," 238.
8. Meynell, "Woman in Grey," 238–39.
9. Meynell, "Woman in Grey," 239.
10. Angelique Richardson and Chris Willis, introduction to *The New Woman in Fiction and in Fact: Fin-De-Siècle Feminisms*, ed. Angelique Richardson and Chris Willis (Basingstoke, UK: Palgrave, 2001), 1.
11. Lillias Campbell Davidson, *Handbook for Lady Cyclists* (London: Hay Nisbet, 1896), 10.
12. Campbell Davidson, *Handbook for Lady Cyclists*, 10.
13. Richardson and Willis, introduction, 13.
14. James C. Whorton, "The Hygiene of the Wheel: An Episode in Victorian Sanitary Science," *Bulletin of the History of Medicine* 52, no. 1 (1978): 80.
15. Tim Armstrong, *Modernism, Technology, and the Body: A Cultural Study* (Cambridge: Cambridge University Press, 1998), 81.
16. Armstrong, *Modernism, Technology, and the Body*, 78.
17. Armstrong, *Modernism, Technology, and the Body*, 80.
18. Armstrong, *Modernism, Technology, and the Body*, 83.
19. Much like the bicycle, communication technologies impacted the way in which women considered their bodies. In fact, Herlihy points out that the "modern-style two-wheeler triggered revolutions both social and technological." David V. Herlihy, *Bicycle: The History* (New Haven CT: Yale University Press, 2004), 3. The bicycle was viewed in similar terms as other technological advancements like the telephone, typewriter, and telegraph, as can be seen by comparing Juliet's use of the typewriter and the bicycle.
20. Quoted in David Rubenstein, "Cycling in the 1890s," *Victorian Studies* 21, no.1 (1977): 71.
21. Campbell Davidson, *Handbook for Lady Cyclists*, 1.
22. Mrs. Lynn Linton, "The Cycling Craze for Ladies," *Lady's Realm* 1 (November 1896–April 1897): 177.
23. Mary Poovey, *Uneven Developments: The Ideological Works of Gender in Mid-Victorian England* (Chicago: University of Chicago Press, 1988), 8.
24. Herlihy, *Bicycle*, 200.
25. Elizabeth Robins Pennell, "Cycling," in *Ladies in the Field: Sketches of Sport*, ed. Violet Greville (London: Ward and Downey, 1894), 252.
26. Many current historians (including David Rubenstein) focus their attention on how bicycling heralded greater freedom of dress for women in the nineteenth century, since women of the time formed societies for national dress reform, such as the Rational Dress Society (1881), the Health and Artistic

Dress Union (1890), and the Rational Dress League (1898). David Rubenstein, *Before the Suffragettes: Women's Emancipation in the 1890s* (New York: St. Martin's Press, 1986), 219.

27. Robins Pennell, "Cycling," 261.

28. Rubenstein, *Before the Suffragettes*, 218. Rubenstein describes the violence enacted against women cycling in rational dress: "The editor of the *Rational Dress Gazette* was struck by a meat hook while cycling in Kilburn.... The hazards involved were summed up by Kitty Jane Buckman in a letter written in August 1897 to her brother S.S. Buckman, geologist and cyclist: 'It certainly can't be worse to ride in Oxford than in London, especially London suburbs. It's awful. One wants nerves of iron, & I don't wonder now in the least so many women having given up the R.D. Costume & returned to skirts. The shouts & yells of the children deafen one, the women shriek with laughter or groan & hiss & all sorts of remarks are shouted at one, occasionally [*sic*] some not fit for publication. One needs to be very brave to stand all that.'"

29. F. J. Erskine, *Lady Cycling* (London: Walter Scott, 1897), 25.

30. Erskine, *Lady Cycling*, 25.

31. Campbell Davidson, *Handbook for Lady Cyclists*, 22.

32. Campbell Davidson, *Handbook for Lady Cyclists*, 22.

33. Evelyn Everett Green, "Cycling for Ladies," in *All Round Cycling* (London: Walter Scott, 1896), 51.

34. Mary Poovey explains that "women's reproductive function defined her character, position, and value, and this function was only one sign of an innate periodicity, and that this biological periodicity influenced and was influenced by an array of nervous disorders—constructed the woman as essentially different from man and, because of the quasi-pathological nature of this difference, as a creature who needed constant and expert superintendence by medical men." Poovey, *Uneven Developments*, 37.

35. Arabella Kenealy, "Woman as Athlete," *Nineteenth Century* 45 (1899): 638.

36. Kenealy, "Woman as Athlete," 639.

37. Kenealy, "Woman as Athlete," 638.

38. Kenealy, "Woman as Athlete," 639.

39. Kenealy, "Woman as Athlete," 640.

40. Kenealy, "Woman as Athlete," 640.

41. Kenealy, "Woman as Athlete," 641.

42. Kenealy, "Woman as Athlete," 641.

43. A. Shadwell, "Hidden Dangers of Cycling," *Living Age* 212, no. 2750 (1897): 833.

44. Whorton, "Hygiene of the Wheel," 82.

45. Whorton, "Hygiene of the Wheel," 71.

46. The disease of athleticism in women contributes directly to the evolution and reproduction of the British race, not just in that these diseases could be transmitted from mother to child, but because of their impact on women's child-rearing capabilities in general. A number of doctors conceded that women's cycling was damaging to their reproductive health. Dr. J. Beresford Ryley advised women to quit cycling during menstruation or while pregnant, because as a woman and possible mother, she should be careful to manage her own reproductive health. J. Beresford Ryley, *The Dangers of Cycling for Women and Children* (London: Ballantyne, Hanson, 1899), 11–12. Others, as Whorton chronicles, raised concerns about women's physical placement on the bike, arguing that the bike's saddle could contract the birth canal, hypertrophy the reproductive muscles (through pedaling), displace the uterus, distort the pelvic bones, or cause general bruising and discomfort. Whorton, "Hygiene of the Wheel," 83. Similarly, Kenealy claimed that athletic women and their diseased bodies inhibit childbearing or lead to degenerate offspring. While women are exerting their muscles by cycling, those muscles can't be used for reproduction, and babies born to bicycling women will be "poor creature[s]" because the muscles that should have been spent fashioning well-formed children are being wasted on the bicycle. Kenealy, "Woman as Athlete," 643.

47. Kenealy, "Woman as Athlete," 641.

48. L. Ormistan Chant, "Woman as Athlete: A Reply to Dr. Arabella Kenealy," *Nineteenth Century* 45 (1899): 746.

49. Chant, "Woman as Athlete," 746.

50. Oscar Jennings, *Cycling and Health . . . Revised and Enlarged Edition* (London: Illiffe and Sons, 1893), 18.

51. Jennings, *Cycling and Health*, 22.

52. Jennings, *Cycling and Health*, 295.

53. Meynell, "Woman in Grey," 239.

54. Meynell, "Woman in Grey," 239.

55. Meynell, "Woman in Grey," 238.

56. Meynell, "Woman in Grey," 239.

57. Clarissa J. Suranyi, introduction to *The Type-Writer Girl*, by Grant Allen, ed. Clarissa J. Suranyi (Peterborough ON: Broadview Press, 2004), 9. Mina Harker in Bram Stoker's *Dracula* (1897) and Bella Thorn in Tom Gallon's *The Girl behind the Keys* (1903) are good examples of typists who "humanized and feminized" the workspace despite being strong, independent women. Mina uses her typewritten documents to aid in the defeat of Dracula, while maintaining her Angel in the House persona. She describes herself as having a "woman's nature" and is declared to have a "woman's heart" by Van Helsing. See Bram Stoker, *Dracula*, ed. Nina Auerbach (New York: W. W. Norton,

1997), 203, 207. Even though she describes herself as "only a weak woman," Bella uses her skills as a typist to thwart her boss's criminal activities. Ultimately, she retires from her typewriting profession in order to take on a more domestic position: she marries Philip Esdaile, a young journalist who aids her throughout her adventures, at the end of the novel. See Tom Gallon, *The Girl behind the Keys*, ed. Arlene Young (Peterborough ON: Broadview Press, 2003), 110.

58. Grant Allen, *The Type-Writer Girl*, ed. Clarissa J. Suranyi (Peterborough ON: Broadview Press, 2004), 28.

59. Allen, *Type-Writer Girl*, 32.

60. Allen himself was a biologist specifically interested in Darwinism. In 1893 he wrote *Charles Darwin*, a book on the life and work of the naturalist. In his assessment of Darwin's work, he notes that the principles of Darwin have been and no doubt will be misunderstood and "tacked on to what are in reality the principles of Lamarck." Grant Allen, *Charles Darwin* (New York: D. Appleton, 1893), 199. In addition, Allen has written a few essays on evolution and women in which he suggests that he supports the "modern woman's demand for emancipation" and is an "enthusiast of the Woman Question." However, Allen insists that women must, for the evolution and continuance of the race of mankind, mother children, "whether [they are] wives or not." Grant Allen, "Plain Words on the Woman Question," in *A New Woman Reader: Fiction, Articles, and Drama of the 1890s*, ed. Carolyn Christensen Nelson (Peterborough ON: Broadview Press, 2001), 212, 220. Thus in *The Type-Writer Girl*, Juliet represents an evolved (intellectually and physically healthy) New Woman despite the fact that she herself does not marry or produce children by the end of the novel.

61. Allen, *Type-Writer Girl*, 87.

62. Allen, *Type-Writer Girl*, 42–43. Juliet's descriptions aren't dissimilar to other descriptions of the cycle by women at the time. The novelist and columnist Lady Violet Greville explains that "women who prefer exercise and liberty, who revel in the cool sea breeze, and love to feel the fresh mountain air fanning their cheeks" are the "better, the truer, and the healthier" for cycling. Violet Greville, preface to Greville, *Ladies in the Field*, iv. Likewise, Robins Pennell argues that the lady cyclist is granted "all the joy of motion ... and of long days in the open air; all the joy of adventure and change. Hers is the delightful sense of independence and power." Robins Pennell, "Cycling," 264–65.

63. Allen, *Type-Writer Girl*, 46.

64. Allen, *Type-Writer Girl*, 57.

65. Allen, *Type-Writer Girl*, 48, 56.

66. Allen, *Type-Writer Girl*, 56.

67. Allen, *Type-Writer Girl*, 56.

68. Allen, *Type-Writer Girl*, 58.

69. Allen, *Type-Writer Girl*, 58.

70. Allen, *Type-Writer Girl*, 57.

71. Allen, *Type-Writer Girl*, 58.

72. Allen, *Type-Writer Girl*, 59.

73. Allen, *Type-Writer Girl*, 59.

74. Allen, *Type-Writer Girl*, 61.

75. Allen, *Type-Writer Girl*, 62.

76. Allen, *Type-Writer Girl*, 62.

77. Allen, *Type-Writer Girl*, 62.

78. Allen, *Type-Writer Girl*, 61.

79. Allen, *Type-Writer Girl*, 61.

80. Allen, *Type-Writer Girl*, 59.

81. Allen, *Type-Writer Girl*, 60.

82. Allen, *Type-Writer Girl*, 61, 119.

83. Allen, *Type-Writer Girl*, 63.

84. Frances E. Willard, *How I Learned to Ride the Bicycle: Reflections of an Influential 19th Century Woman*, ed. Carol O'Hare (Sunnyvale CA: Fair Oaks, 1991), 43.

4 Bicycles and Warfare: The Effects of Excessive Mobility in H. G. Wells's *The War in the Air*

JEREMY WITHERS

In a memorandum composed in 1907, the assistant undersecretary of the British Foreign Office, Sir Eyre Crowe, attempts to take a step back and evaluate impartially the German expansion that was happening at that time. Crowe proclaims: "A healthy and powerful State like Germany, with its 60 million inhabitants, must expand, it cannot stand still. . . . [I]t would be neither just nor politic to ignore the claims to a healthy expansion which a vigorous and growing country like Germany has a natural right to assert."[1] As Crowe's language illustrates, he was clearly sympathetic toward the expansionist tendencies of a major world power like Germany; furthermore, he perceived such expansion as nothing less than a "healthy" endeavor and something to which countries have "natural rights." In his analysis of this important historical document by Crowe, Stephen Kern deems it "one of the most lucid analyses of the imperialistic impulse of all nations at that time and of their commitment to a body of ideas that led them into continual conflict."[2] Of course, Crowe's memorandum is tragically ironic given the fact that the scramble for more territory by countries like Germany would soon lead to the outbreak of the Great War, the devastating conflict that from 1914–18 scattered millions of dead across Europe and left it in ruins.

At the time in which Crowe was writing, expansion was certainly not limited to what the major imperial powers of Europe were doing in Africa and other colonies. Rather, spatial expansion and the collapsing of distance was something carried out by a throng of new technologies: telegraphs and telephones, automobiles, railroads, streetcars, trams, passenger liners, airships. All these technologies played a role in the *zeitgeist* that Crowe's memorandum taps into and that sees the conquering of space and the annihilation of distance as a wholly positive thing. For example, Alfred Harmsworth celebrates how, with the arrival of the motorcar, you can now "lunch with your neighbor five-and-twenty miles off as easily in 1904 as in 1892 you could meet your friend living seven miles from your door," an overcoming of distance that translates to "a better knowledge of your county, and less boredom with your parish."[3]

And it was not just early car enthusiasts like Harmsworth and politicians like Crowe who defended the new capabilities of nations and of technologies to collapse space. Avant-garde artists such as the futurists in Italy also added their voice to the chorus that was enthusiastically celebrating technology, speed, and expansionism. For example, Marinetti, the Italian poet and founder of the futurist movement, declares in 1909, "We [the futurists] say that the world's magnificence has been enriched by a new beauty; the beauty of speed. A racing car whose hood is adorned with great pipes, like serpents of explosive breath ... is more beautiful than the *Victory of Samothrace*."[4] For artists like Marinetti, distance exists as an enemy to be slain by the increased speeds made available through new inventions such as the automobile.

However, one author who voiced concerns about the costs involved in this rampant collapsing of distance is H. G. Wells. In his novel *The War in the Air* (1908), Wells gives us a powerful vision of a world that has become dangerously intoxicated by the project of conquering distance at all costs. Although typically read as a novel prophesying a horrific future state of warfare defined by airplanes and airships raining down destruction from the skies, as well as by a newfound ability to bring devastation into the heart of civilian centers, *The War in the Air* is also a meditation on transportation in general and on technology's redefining of space and distance. This is because in addition to airplanes and airships, the novel's pages brim with references to trains, automobiles, trams, monorails, submarines, motorcycles, and (most importantly for this chapter's focus) bicycles.

In this chapter, I examine Wells's thinking on issues of transportation at this crucial juncture in the development of transportation technologies—a time when motorized vehicles like motorcars and motorbikes are eclipsing earlier modes of transport like bicycles and a time when the skies are being conquered by mechanical flight as the land previously has been by trains and automobiles. In *The War in the Air*, we perceive an author who is deeply anxious about the ways in which the newest modes of transport of the early twentieth century, such as automobiles and airplanes, threaten to make distant places all too accessible. Wells foresees how these new modes of transport can bring far-off people increasingly in contact with one another in ways that foster outbreaks of war. However, throughout the novel, Wells repeatedly returns to the bicycle as an image of an ideal piece of technology that stalwartly outlasts all the others.[5] The bicycle is depicted as a mode of transport that allows its users just enough mastery over space and distance without leading to the conflagration of worldwide warfare that Wells envisions the flying technologies of the future igniting and that Sir Eyre Crowe failed to see as the likely outcome of unchecked expansion such as Germany's.

Since Wells's *The War in the Air* is not as well-known today as the scientific romances he wrote in the 1890s, such as *The Time Machine*, *The War of the Worlds*, or *The Invisible Man*, a brief overview of the novel's plot seems in order. The book can be roughly divided into three sections. What I will call part 1 of the novel details the life of Bert Smallways, a man who lives in the fictional Kentish village of Bun Hill and who eventually becomes co-owner of a bicycle shop. When bankruptcy threatens, Bert and his partner abandon the shop and start a travelling song-and-dance act called the Desert Dervishes. It is while performing this act one day at a seaside resort that Bert accidentally falls into the passenger car of a hot air balloon being piloted by Butteridge, a man now famous for having recently invented an aircraft that is now coveted by various militaries around the world. Bert accidentally falls into the balloon's car at the same time Butteridge falls out. Part 2 begins with Bert floating aimlessly in the balloon; he eventually lands in a secret German airfield and is mistaken for the inventor Butteridge. Going along momentarily with this case of mistaken identity, Bert is forced to accompany the German fleet as it attacks the United States, and his true identity is discovered en route. Narrowly escaping execution, Bert is now forced to be a witness to the horrors of modern, airborne warfare as Germany attacks New York City and then as a second front opens up when a combined Asian fleet also attacks the United States. Part 3 takes place after the war has been raging for some time and Bert finds himself in a world crumbling under the strain of prolonged, all-out warfare. The last few chapters of the book depict a postapocalyptic future in which global society has collapsed and in which, due to a global communications breakdown, people aren't even sure if the war is still going on elsewhere.

From its opening chapter, it is clear that a primary concern of the novel will be the dizzying pace at which new transportation technologies can overtake society and the disconcerting rate at which those technologies can collapse distances. The elderly father of Bert Smallways can still remember the town he lives in, Bun Hill, as "an idyllic Kentish village."[6] But within the father's own lifetime, Bun Hill has seen the arrival of "the railway ... and then a second railway station ... omnibuses, tramcars—going right away into London itself—bicycles, motor-cars, and then more motor-cars."[7] When we first meet old Smallways's son, Bert, he is a character who straddles (literally and figuratively) both the newer and the older forms of technology, for one of the earliest references to Bert in the novel is to him acquiring a "motor-bicycle."[8] However, it is only one page later that we hear of Bert taking a job at a bicycle shop owned by a man named Grubb, a job that leads to Bert becoming "almost a trick rider—he could ride bicycles for miles that would have come to pieces instantly under you or me."[9] In these early chapters, Bert divides his allegiance between newfangled technologies like motorcycles and increasingly unfashionable but still viable technologies like bicycles.[10] However, it is not long before Bert appears to commit himself wholly to motorized forms of travel by preferring to go "teuf-teuff[ing] off into the haze of the traffic-tortured high road."[11]

To explore in greater depth this issue that is of central importance to the novel—the issue of how new transportation technologies collapse space and distance at an alarming, and possibly even dangerous, rate—we turn to a scene in which Bert, Grub, and two ladies decide one holiday afternoon to put together a "cheerful little cyclist party." This group decides to go "picnic and spend an indolent afternoon and evening among the trees and bracken" of the Kentish countryside.[12] "Cyclist party" might be a little misleading here, for Bert actually insists on riding his motorcycle while towing in a trailer a certain Edna Bunthorne, who, we are told, "could not ride" a bike. Grub and his "date," Miss Flossie Bright, ride bicycles borrowed from Bert and Grub's shop. En route to Kent, the cycling party becomes caught up in the congested traffic on the road, traffic that consists of such diverse modes of transport as "bicycles and motor-bicycles," "gyroscopic motor-cars running bicycle-fashion on two wheels," "old fashioned four-wheeled traffic," "tricars," "electric broughams," and "dilapidated old racing motors." In the skies overhead, there are even "several navigable gas airships, not to mention balloons."[13] In short, the whole range of possible modes of transport that exists in the world of the novel is clogging the roads and even the skies. It is a world overrun with transportation, with people frantically going hither and thither and seemingly without purpose but just because they can.

Despite the dizzying assortment of transportation that people are relying on in this scene, Wells suggests that the lowly bicycles of Grub and Flossie are as effective (if not more so) than those other, seemingly more impressive motorbicycles, tricars, electric broughams, and gyroscopic motorcars. The effectiveness of the simple bicycle is shown by the fact that the cycling party (accompanied by Bert on his motorbike) makes it to Kent just as successfully as any of those other vehicles. And the description of their idyllic afternoon spent in Kent suggests that one need not go any farther than this location and this distance to find happiness and rejuvenation: "Our four young people picnicked cheerfully, and were happy in the manner of a happiness that was an ancient mode in Nineveh. . . . [T]he hedges were full of honeysuckle and dog-roses; in the woods the distant toot-toot-toot of the traffic on the dust-hazy high road might have been no more than the horns of elf-land. They laughed and gossiped and picked flowers and made love and talked."[14]

This ability of bicycles to help their riders connect with nature in profound ways is something Wells had been interested in since his 1896 novel *The Wheels of Chance*, in which he describes the main character, Mr. Hoopdriver, an overworked Londoner, as suddenly able to experience nature while on a ten-day cycling holiday into the countryside. One day while riding, Hoopdriver almost hits an animal with his bike, and the narrator informs us, "It was the first weasel [Hoopdriver] had ever seen in his cockney life. There were miles of this, scores of miles of this before him, pinewood and oak forest, purple, heathery moorland and grassy down, lush meadows, where shining rivers wound their lazy way."[15] Like the cycling party discovers in *The War in the Air*, bicycles are more than capable of supplying the necessary amount of access to nature, and at just the right speed for an appreciation of its delights. In this pastoral interlude that precedes the outbreak of war, a war eventually made possible by far-ranging transportations such as the airships unleashed on the world, the novel early on suggests that perhaps you only need to go as far as just outside your town or city to find contentment. And a bicycle can take you there just as well as any of the fancy and complex "gyroscopic motor-cars running bicycle-fashion on two wheels."

In scenes like the restrained ride of the cycling party, Wells anticipates figures like Ivan Illich, the Austrian priest and strident critic of Western modernity who defined "technological maturity" as "the world of those who have tripled the extent of their daily horizon by lifting themselves onto their bicycles."[16] However, to go beyond that "tripling of one's horizon" represents for Illich (and for Wells, I am arguing) technological excess and folly. Similarly, Dave Horton asserts that in contemporary political movements like environmentalism and anarchism, "riding a bicycle becomes less a continuation of the search for modern freedoms [as it was for late-Victorian feminists], and more a critique of the negative social and environmental effects of too much 'freedom' in mobility."[17] In short, Wells prefigures important political figures and movements of the 1970s and later that saw bicycling as a way to reject excessive mobility, that is, to reject people "moving around too much and too quickly."[18]

In fact, the bicycle might take you to Kent and back *even more effectively* than many of those other modes of transport. Wells gestures toward such an idea when, as the cycling party is heading home at twilight, they pass "a four-wheeled motor-car of the old style lamed by a deflated tyre."[19] Despite its motorized sophistication, the automobile is here depicted as still being vulnerable to basic technological failures such as a flat tire. Additionally, and more dramatically, Bert experiences the complete technological breakdown of his motorbike when it suddenly catches fire. As Bert frantically tries to put out the fire and save his cherished machine, "other cyclists arrived, dismounted and stood about, and their flame-lit faces expressed satisfaction."[20] The satisfied faces, it would seem, come from knowing that the technologically simpler bicycle is not vulnerable to these traumatic, unexpected gasoline fires and therefore is not likely to reduce its rider to the comically helpless state Bert finds himself in as he struggles to find wet sand or a blanket with which to put out the fire. As Bert stands over the "blackened ruins" and "ashes of his vanished motor-bicycle" and as Grub and Flossie continue on homeward atop their bicycles, it is clear that the advanced technology of Bert's motorcycle has been more of a liability than an asset for him and that its speed and greater ability to conquer distances has not, in the end, made that motorized machine any more advantageous than the nonmotorized bicycle.[21]

In fact, the motorized machine has an element of danger lurking at its core. This danger comes about because, for Wells, an ability to traverse vast distances correlates with a surge in violent confrontations between people and nations. The most prominent expression of Wells's equating of an ability to conquer space with political instability occurs at the beginning of chapter 4. In this chapter, titled "The German Air Fleet," Wells advances the narrative toward its focus on military technology and on the brutal realities of all-out war in an age of advanced global transportation. But before that war breaks out, Wells first muses for several pages about why transportation technologies in general make military technologies like bombs, guns, and swords so dangerous. It is because transportation brings people who don't (or won't) get along into dangerously close proximity with one another. As the narrator opines, it appears to be a lamentable and rather unchangeable fact of human nature that we all have a "liking for kind, a pride in one's own atmosphere, a tenderness for one's mother speech and one's familiar land."[22] Of course, the frequent result of mixing this "pride" and "tenderness" toward one's own people with a collapsing of space through enhanced modes of transport is, unfortunately, war. The narrator compares these various nations and cultures coming into more frequent contact with one another with "ill-bred people in a crowded public car" who have begun to "squeeze against one another, elbow, thrust, dispute, and quarrel."[23] And whereas quite recently the English had to concern themselves only with their contempt for the French, who resided just across the English Channel, now Bert and people of his generation must contend with the Germans, Asians, and Africans, as well as with "the naturally very muddled politics of the entirely similar little cads to [themselves] (except for a smear of brown) who smoked cigarettes and rode bicycles in Buluwayo, Kingston (Jamaica), or Bombay."[24]

It is, of course, striking that the narrator here associates the bicycle with the dark-skinned people of Zimbabwe, Jamaica, and India; for it gestures toward how (then, as well as now) England and Europe by and large only want to be associated with the most recent and cutting-edge technologies like automobiles and airplanes and not with "backward" technology like the bicycle. But one of the underlying arguments of the novel is that bicycles are a more benign, peaceful, and humane piece of technology because they don't lead to the rampant invasion of each other's space that those other, more recent modes of transport give rise to. The novel suggests that if Europe and England could only have continued to embrace the bicycle in the early twentieth century and not dismissed it as some kind of mere child's toy for the "little cads" of Africa and Asia, then perhaps the devastating, all-out warfare about to be unleashed in the novel might never have occurred.

One other thing that makes Wells's suspicions of the collapsing of space and of the annihilation of distance due to new transportation technologies so interesting is that in published work leading up *The*

War in the Air, most notably *A Modern Utopia* (1905), Wells celebrates the overcoming of distance as a defining characteristic of his imagined utopian world state.[25] Even if *A Modern Utopia* is not a text that is often read, this didactic work has bequeathed to the world a quote cherished by many cycling enthusiasts: "Cycle tracks will abound in Utopia."[26] Bicycles are, significantly, present in this richly imagined utopia, yet we must keep in mind that Wells embeds this well-known line glorifying bicycles in a section of his text that also promotes an array of other modes of transport such as airplanes, trains, trams, monorails, and motorcars. Each of these transportation technologies is seen as playing its part in the hypermobility of the Utopians. For example, when discussing the abundant transportation options available in the world state, the narrator of *A Modern Utopia* proclaims, "No doubt the Utopians will travel in many ways.... [They] will travel about the earth from one chief point to another at a speed of two or three hundred miles or more an hour. *That will abolish the greater distances*."[27] Only a page earlier, the narrator informs the reader, "Utopia will have, of course, faultless roads and beautifully arranged interurban communications, swift trains or motor services or what not, *to diffuse its population*."[28] In sum, in *A Modern Utopia*, published only three years prior to *The War in the Air*, Wells defends having a diversity of transportation technologies and sounds much more optimistic that these various modes of transportation, which put far-flung people repeatedly into contact with one another, can help a society flourish.

However, in the world of *The War in the Air*, most advanced forms of transport instead instigate confrontations between people and those that they deem other. Even in *A Modern Utopia*, Wells gestures toward the idea that, outside of utopia, advances in transportation possess an ominous potential. Wells writes, "On the modern earth ... contact provokes aggressions, comparisons, and persecutions and discomforts."[29] Additionally, when Wells is trying to figure out very early on in *A Modern Utopia* where to even place his perfect society, he expresses anxiety that the world in which he is writing is already shrinking too much and that places aren't feeling sufficiently far away from each other any longer. Ultimately, Wells decides to place his utopia on a completely different planet due to the rampant annihilation of distance happening in his own time. By way of referencing the older utopias of Plato and Sir Thomas More, Wells writes, "Time was when a mountain valley or an island seemed to promise sufficient isolation for a polity to maintain itself intact from outside force," but such physical isolation means next to nothing anymore, because he knows that soon "the flying machine [will soar] overhead, free to descend" wherever it chooses.[30] Until the utopian world state comes into existence and makes people identify with a larger geopolitical entity than just their respective countries or regions, neither *The War in the Air* nor *A Modern Utopia* hold out much hope that peace and contentment will be possible in people's lives if transportation technologies more advanced than bicycles are allowed to proliferate.

Of course, by the early twentieth century, when *The War in the Air* is published, the fervor for and fascination with bicycles has largely subsided. Yet one of the significant ways in which Wells references the now-ignored technological sophistication of the bicycle is to periodically gesture toward how some basic elements of bicycle design lurk at the core of the more "sophisticated" machines that so dazzle people in this novel. That is, even though the bicycle seems by and large a forgettable machine to people in the world of *The War in the Air*, Wells suggests to his readers that the more impressive technologies the novel depicts, such as aircraft, owe their origins (at least in part) to the lowly bicycle. The novel, therefore, looks ahead to work by scholars such as Glen Norcliffe, Fred Fiske, and Marlin Todd— work that highlights the debt that the airplane and the automobile owe the bicycle.[31] For example, Fiske and Marlin poetically describe the bicycle "as a springboard to the heavens."[32] And they provide the following summary of the technological relationship between the bicycle and other transportation technologies like automobiles and airplanes: "Bicycle makers invented many items that were first applied to the bicycle and then later to the motorcar. The differential gear, variable speed transmission, chain drive, ball bearings, wire spokes, tubular steel frames, tubeless tires, and driveshaft are examples. This is true for the aeroplane [as well].... The oversized bicycle chain, and sprockets to help run the propellers, bicycle spoke wire, tubular steel, ball bearings in the sprockets and the modified bicycle hubs, used on the launching skid for takeoff, and later, bicycle wheels—were all used on Wright [brothers] planes."[33]

Wells's novel periodically gestures toward the debt that airplanes owe earlier, more "primitive" forms of transportation technology. For example, the strength of the Asiatic force is affirmed by our narrator to lie "not in their airships but ... in their flying machines proper"; however, the narrator then proceeds to give a quick genealogy of these flying machines, tracing their origins back to the motorbicycle and, ultimately, I would argue, to bicycles themselves.[34] The rider of the flying machine is said to sit "between the wings above ... an explosive engine that differed in no essential particular from those in use in the light motor-bicycles of the period. Below was a single large wheel. The rider sat astride a saddle."[35] The plane's engine is clearly related here to that used on a motorcycle, but the reference to the rider sitting on a saddle atop a large wheel sounds reminiscent of the so-called "ordinary" (or high-wheeler) bicycles that were popular throughout the 1880s and the early 1890s. Put simply, the narrator suggests that the devastatingly effective Asiatic flying machines owe their technological success to the engine design of the motorbike, which in turn gets many of its design elements from nonmotorized vehicles like the ordinary bicycle.[36] Another suggestion of continuity between bicycles and flying machines occurs ten or so pages later when Bert observes Asiatic pilots "wheeling undamaged aeroplanes upon their wheels as men might wheel bicycles, and [springing] into the saddles and [flapping] into the air."[37] In addition to the overt reference to wheeling the plane like one does a bicycle, the reference to springing into the saddle again echoes descriptions of the high-wheeled ordinary bicycle and of the typically athletic manner in which such machines were mounted in their heyday.

Yet even though Wells suggests that the sophisticated Asiatic flying machines share more continuities with the bicycle than might at first be apparent, he still invites the reader to acknowledge the greater simplicity and elegance of the bicycle. This preference for the bicycle appears in the text when Bert first climbs into the crashed Asiatic flying machine that he found on Goat Island and the narrator describes the aircraft as a "big, clumsy thing ... not a bit like a bicycle."[38] In this scene, Bert learns a lesson in the superiority of a bicycle's simplicity once he eventually repairs the flying machine and gets it airborne, for it is in this moment that he finds himself "rushing down at a head-long pace" an experience that gives him "the ineffectual sensations of one whose bicycle bolts downhill."[39]

But as we saw early on in the novel's reference to Bert becoming "almost a trick rider" who "could ride bicycles for miles that would have come to pieces instantly under you or me," Bert was never "inef-fectual" at controlling a bicycle.[40] When he crashes the flying machine into a tree after struggling to gain control over it, it is clear that the simpler design and easier controllability of the bicycle have their advantages. In sum, even though inventions like the motorcycle, the automobile, and the airplane greatly complicate and greatly enhance the design elements that they have appropriated from the bicycle, the overall simplicity of the bicycle, Wells suggests, should still be favored.

The War in the Air foregrounds the myriad advantages of the bicy-cle's simpler (yet more durable and resilient) design most prominently during the apocalyptic final sections of the novel, sections in which Wells begins to depict the war as consuming the entire world and as causing entire societies to collapse. These apocalyptic final sections of the novel showcase Wells's thinking that the bicycle is an ideal piece of technology and of transportation that stalwartly outlasts all the others. For example, as the world is falling to pieces due to the raging war, formerly reliable communications technologies such as "old-fashioned cables" and "Marconi stations across the ocean and along the Atlantic" have all been destroyed or fallen into disrepair.[41] However, news still travels in this war-ravaged landscape via bicycles, for we are told about how "presently came a man on a bicycle with an ill-printed newspaper of a single sheet" to visit Bert and some local Americans Bert has met after escaping Goat Island.[42]

Additionally, in a desperate attempt to turn the tide of the war and to help the United States beat back the Asian invaders, Bert and his new American friends decide it is imperative they deliver Butteridge's plans for building a sophisticated flying machine to the American president. But the problem is they don't know exactly where the pres-ident is, and to find him they will have to cross a war-ravaged landscape without any up-and-running modes of transport such as trains, automobiles, or monorails. Because all other forms of transportation have been paralyzed, the bicycle is the only option left. It is on this journey by Bert and the American militia leader named Laurier to find the president that Wells shows the bicycle's advantages for such a dangerous and grueling ride.

For example, at one point while riding, Bert and Laurier notice that some "Asiatic flying-ships passed overhead," aircraft surely looking to attack people like the two cyclists if they were to be spotted.[43] These aircraft flying overhead could have meant certain death for Bert and Laurier if they had been on a train unable to venture off its track or in a car that had to stick to roads. But Wells tells us that in this situation, where hostile flying ships are coming toward them, the two cyclists simply "made a dash for cover until the sky was clear."[44] The seriousness of their mission means that Bert and Laurier must keep riding at all costs. Thus, after Bert's bicycle at one point suffers a flat tire, Wells informs us, "still he rode," and eventually "at one peaceful village . . . they stopped off to get Bert's tyre mended."[45] Even though bicycles possess that vulnerability of all machines utilizing pneumatic tires, a flat, they still prove reliable enough to allow Bert and Laurier to continue on their mission, and bicycles still provide optimal freedom and maneuverability for evading threats in the sky.[46]

The fortitude and flexibility of the bicycle when dealing with things like flat tires and bellicose Asiatic airships are made all the more clear when readers are told that while travelling to find the president, Bert and Laurier stumble upon both a "monorail train standing in the track" where it had been stranded for six days and a "motor-car with a tyre burst" and with an "old man under the car trying to effect some impossible repairs."[47] Put simply, both the car and the monorail appear as overly complicated machines that can't endure the hardships of this postapocalyptic world. The bicycle, on the other hand, rides on, and Bert and Laurier eventually succeed in their mission to find the president. Having traversed the entirety of the state of New York on bicycles, they successfully turn over Butteridge's plans to the American leader.

Near the end of *The War in the Air*, Wells depicts the bicycle as being a stalwart enough piece of technology to rise to a challenge when needed but with a technological simplicity that might actually work in its favor. Furthermore, throughout the novel, Wells never associates bicycles with an unhealthy mastery of space or a dangerous shrinking of distance. The bicycle is, instead, an ideal form of transportation that provides its users with enough access to places like the restorative countryside surrounding cities but that does not promote people of different nationalities and regions coming into excessive, dangerous contact with one another. As Ivan Illich famously declared, "Free people must travel the road to productive social relations at the speed of a bicycle."[48] H. G. Wells would likely agree with Illich, for *The War in the Air* brims with depictions of catastrophic social relations brought on by the fast-moving speed of airships and other machines.

Notes

1. Crowe's memorandum is excerpted in Imanuel Geiss, ed., *July 1914: The Outbreak of the First World War; Selected Documents* (New York: Charles Scribner's Sons, 1975), 29–31.
2. Stephen Kern, *The Culture of Time and Space: 1880–1918* (Cambridge: Harvard University Press, 2003), 236.
3. Alfred C. Harmsworth, *Motors and Motor-Driving*, 3rd ed. (London: Longmans, Green, 1904), 28. Earlier in his book, Harmsworth also celebrates some of the car races being held at this time that showcased the car's dazzling abilities to shrink distances. See, for example, Harmsworth's discussion of the 732-mile race from Paris to Bordeaux and back (11–12).
4. Filippo Marinetti, "The Founding and Manifesto of Futurism," in *Marinetti: Selected Writings*, ed. R. W. Flint (New York: Farrar, Straus, and Giroux, 1971), 41.
5. For an essay that argues how Wells does not always celebrate the bicycle in his fiction, see Jeremy Withers, "Bicycles, Tricycles, and Tripods: Late Victorian Cycling and Wells's *The War of the Worlds*," *Wellsian*, no. 36 (2013): 39–51.
6. H. G. Wells, *The War in the Air*, ed. Patrick Parrinder (London: Penguin, 2005), 6. All quotations will be from this edition.
7. Wells, *War in the Air*, 7.
8. Wells, *War in the Air*, 7.
9. Wells, *War in the Air*, 8.
10. On the early history of motorcycles, see Mick Walker, *Motorcycle: Evolution, Design, Passion* (Baltimore: Johns Hopkins University Press, 2006), 14–25;

Derek Roberts, *The Invention of Bicycles and Motorcycles* (London: Usborne, 1975), 34–39.

11. Wells, *War in the Air*, 10. "Teuf-teuff" is most likely Wells's onomatopoeic imitation of the sound of a motorcycle's engine. See Wells, *War in the Air*, 282n17.

12. Wells, *War in the Air*, 32.

13. Wells, *War in the Air*, 33.

14. Wells, *War in the Air*, 34.

15. H. G. Wells, *The Wheels of Chance: A Holiday Adventure* (London: J. M. Dent, 1896), 48.

16. Ivan Illich, *Energy and Equity* (London: Calder and Boyars, 1974), 86.

17. Dave Horton, "Social Movements and the Bicycle," *Thinking about Cycling* (blog), November 25, 2009, https://thinkingaboutcycling.files.wordpress .com/2009/11/social-movements-and-the-bicycle.pdf, 11.

18. Horton, "Social Movements and the Bicycle," 11. Anarchist and environmentalist groups criticize moving around "too much and too quickly" due to excessive mobility's connections to such things as the following: skyrocketing energy prices and notions that "peak oil" has been reached; suburban sprawl and its perceived weakening of healthy, lively communities; the role of transportation-caused greenhouse gases in our deepening climate-change crisis; and so forth.

19. Wells, *War in the Air*, 35.

20. Wells, *War in the Air*, 35.

21. Wells, *War in the Air*, 39.

22. Wells, *War in the Air*, 72.

23. Wells, *War in the Air*, 74.

24. Wells, *War in the Air*, 73.

25. The world state is an idea that Wells developed and revisited throughout much of his writing career. For two in-depth studies of Wells's political thought that discuss his various writings on the world state, see John S. Partington, *Building Cosmopolis: The Political Thought of H. G. Wells* (Aldershot: Ashgate, 2003); W. Warren Wagar, *H. G. Wells and the World State* (New Haven CT: Yale University Press, 1961).

26. H. G. Wells, *A Modern Utopia*, ed. Gregory Claeys and Patrick Parrinder (London: Penguin, 2005), 38. All quotations will be from this edition. As an example of the popularity of the "Cycle tracks will abound in Utopia" quote, my own town of Ames, Iowa, has that quote adorning an artist-created bike rack that currently resides outside City Hall.

27. Wells, *Modern Utopia*, 37, my emphasis.

28. Wells, *Modern Utopia*, 35, my emphasis.

29. Wells, *Modern Utopia*, 34.

30. Wells, *Modern Utopia*, 15.

31. See Glen Norcliffe, "From Popeism to Fordism: Examining the Roots of Mass Production," *Regional Studies* 31, no. 3 (1997): 267–80; Fred C. Fiske and Marlin W. Todd, *The Wright Brothers from Bicycle to Biplane* (West Milton OH: Miami Graphics, 1990).

32. Fiske and Marlin, *Wright Brothers*, 34.

33. Fiske and Marlin, *Wright Brothers*, 24.

34. Wells, *War in the Air*, 182.

35. Wells, *War in the Air*, 183.

36. Although Wells doesn't make this connection in the novel, scholars have pointed out how even the earliest airplanes' mechanical engines owe a small debt to bicycles. As Fiske and Marlin write in their study of the Wright brothers' experiments in flight, "With drawings that the Wrights made of a four cylinder engine, Charles E. Taylor, chief mechanic at the [Wrights'] bicycle shop, did most of the work making an engine." Fiske and Marlin, *Wright Brothers*, 33.

37. Wells, *War in the Air*, 198.

38. Wells, *War in the Air*, 228.

39. Wells, *War in the Air*, 230.

40. Wells, *War in the Air*, 8.

41. Wells, *War in the Air*, 238.

42. Wells, *War in the Air*, 238.

43. Wells, *War in the Air*, 244.

44. Wells, *War in the Air*, 244.

45. Wells, *War in the Air*, 244. It is quite possible to ride a bicycle on the rims if necessary, particularly if the terrain is favorable to it. For example, as one scholar informs us, during the infamous attack on Singapore by bicycle-riding Japanese troops during World War II, "heat contributed to numerous leaks and punctures"; consequently, "flat tires were often discarded and the troops rode on rims. On hard dirt and sealed surfaces it was quite practical." Jim Fitzpatrick, *The Bicycle in Wartime: An Illustrated History*, rev. ed. (Kilcoy QLD: Star Hill Studio, 2011), 150.

46. The admirable performance of the bicycle here resembles two long-distance relay races carried out in early twentieth-century Australia. These races pitted automobiles, motorcycles, and bicycles against one another. Fitzpatrick writes of one such race held in 1912 that was analyzed by Australian military officers who "judged the bicycles the most reliable, and least likely to be put out of action by road, weather, mechanical or tire troubles." See Fitzpatrick, *Bicycle in Wartime*, 82.

47. Wells, *War in the Air*, 244, 245.

48. Illich, *Energy and Equity*, 24.

5 Like a Furnace

Alfred Jarry's *The Supermale*, Doping, and the Limits of Positivism

CORRY CROPPER

Le vélo en soi est une forme de dopage.
PAUL FOURNEL, *Besoin de vélo*

Like the Tour de France, French literature has, from its beginnings, tested positive for performance-enhancing drugs. One of the oldest French literary texts, the twelfth-century *Lays* by Marie de France, includes "The Two Lovers," the tale of a young knight who must complete a daunting mountain ascent in order to win the kingdom. To be more precise, the king will only let his daughter and sole heir marry a man who can carry her in his arms to the top of a nearby mountain without stopping. Marie describes the young suitor as being too weak to accomplish such an arduous task, a challenge that the strongest men in the land had unsuccessfully attempted.[1] But the princess, in love with this particular suitor, has another strategy and tells her beloved about someone who can help: "I have a wealthy relative, a woman, who lives in Salerno.... She has practiced the art of medicine for so long that she is an expert in remedies and knows everything about herbs and roots."[2] Salerno, located in modern-day Italy, enjoyed a reputation as a center for medical knowledge in the Middle Ages. So while the princess fasts to lose weight, her true love travels to visit this woman, who examines him and provides "electuaries" and "medicines" with steroid-like potency that do indeed "strengthen him."[3] She also gives him a special endurance drink that, no matter how tired he may become, "will reinvigorate his whole body, including veins and bones, and will fill him with energy as soon as he drinks it."[4] Upon his return, he confidently asks the king for the princess's hand in marriage; but the king, perhaps smelling a rat (or a *pot belge*), invites everyone in the kingdom to turn out for the event. With spectators lining the route to the summit, the young knight realizes that he will be unable to stop in order to drink. As he climbs, the princess feels him weaken and pleads with him to drink the elixir, but he protests: "These people will cry out . . . they would quickly stop me!"[5] Without his potion, the effort proves too much, and he dies of a ruptured heart on the mountaintop. Stricken with grief, the young princess tragically dies by his side, and the king lives out his life in mourning. The involvement of an Italian doctor, doping products, death, and a mountain ascension makes this story eerily prophetic of the modern Tour de France.[6] Herbal brews; magic potions; and strength-giving, life-extending, or love-inspiring elixirs have remained regular features of French literature throughout the centuries. By the twentieth century, the panoply of products includes magic worms that increase endurance, a special herbal wine that aids in climbing, and pharmacist-prepared elixirs that help overcome fatigue.[7]

Alfred Jarry's final novel, *The Supermale*, published in 1902, is the first French novel to bring doping and cycling together.[8] Critics primarily read this novel from a psychoanalytic perspective, first because the protagonist struggles to fit in socially given his large and permanently erect phallus and second because it includes a protracted scene where the protagonist "beats the record" by making love eighty-two times in a single twenty-four-hour period.[9] Others have read *The Supermale* as caricature and comedy: "Like the Greek *Comus*, the central image in *The Supermale* is the phallus and everything associated with it."[10]

I will instead read it primarily as a cycling novel that takes as its theme the relationship between man and machine. Critics have noted Jarry's admiration for machines and, as biographer Alastair Brotchie has described it, his admiration for "the technological perfectibility of man."[11] On the contrary, I argue that Jarry's novel offers a warning against machines and a cynical analysis of positivism and its attendant scientific optimism regarding human perfectibility. To lay the groundwork for my reading of *The Supermale*, I will first trace the attitudes toward doping and human performance in nineteenth-century France. Additionally, I will examine the role the bicycle plays in scientific studies on human performance during the Belle Époque. After examining Jarry's novel within these contexts, I will argue that although Jarry criticizes the ideology of nineteenth-century French positivism, it would remain entrenched in cycling culture only to manifest itself in real-life and fictional doping scandals a century later.

In the several decades before Jarry wrote *The Supermale*, numerous guidebooks, newspapers, travel narratives, and healer's manuals outlined a variety of products designed to help professionals in need of endurance. Travel guides, mule drivers, farmers, and loggers had preceded cycling professionals in arduous ascensions and long journeys. In fact, a 1901 reference manual with tariffs and stopping points for guides, porters, and mule drivers lists many places that the Tour de France would later make famous: the Col d'Izoard, the Alpe d'Huez, and the Col du Galibier, to name a few.[12]

In the Vosges Mountains, nineteenth-century *schlitteurs* (woodcutters), whose death-defying descents with log-laden sleds anticipated the cyclist's dangerous rides, drank a "magical elixir" (usually wine, kirsch, or schnapps) to give themselves strength and to numb the physical pain from their arduous labor.[13] In the Rouergue (a former French province), farmers, usually for breakfast, would drink a bowl of *chabrot*, a mix of bouillon and red wine, to keep up their strength.[14] Climbers in the Alps in the 1850s would often drink *kirschwasser*, a sort of cherry brandy or cognac for "strengthening and refreshing, when the body was unusually weary with a long day's walking or climbing."[15] Still others would mix wine with mineral waters that climbers and guides in both the Alps and the Pyrenees believed had miraculous strengthening powers.[16] In fact, minerals from spring waters would be transformed into tablets in the nineteenth century and marketed throughout France as a digestive aid. And in a hugely popular textbook significantly entitled *The Tour of France by Two Children* (1877), school children were taught that "the various mineral waters are among France's principal riches: no other country counts as many springs famous for healing sicknesses."[17]

As cycling began developing into an organized sport, a new brand of medicine, inspired by positivist philosophy, would appear alongside the spells, potions, and elixirs that had been used for centuries. Positivism, as articulated by Auguste Comte in his *Course in Positive Philosophy* (1830–42), united all "positive" sciences in order to "facilitate useful, constructive activity that would improve the human condition."[18] Positivism held that as science replaced superstition, "industrialists [and not priests and kings] would represent the new temporal power," and "conquest would be replaced by industrial production as the goal of society."[19] It should come as no surprise that organized sport would develop and flourish during the positivist era. As Christian Messenger has recently written, "Sport is the religion of the Positivists in investing selves in the development and the setting of goals."[20] The philosophy of positivist progress extended to include the industrialization of the human body through attempts to medicinally unlock its potential and push its natural physical limits. In his book *The Human Motor*, Anson Rabinbach writes that, by the late nineteenth century, "for young French republican intellectuals, French medicine embodied the insurgent mood of anticlerical and positivist ideas."[21] This was in large part thanks to Claude Bernard's *Study of Experimental Medicine* (1865), a text that, in addition to inspiring Emile Zola's *The Experimental Novel* (1880), promoted positivist medical approaches throughout France.

Dr. Louis Querton's 1905 treatise, *Increasing Output of the Human Machine*, explains that human productivity depends not only on the machines with which they work but also on "the perfecting of the worker himself."[22] The author first explains the composition of human cells, describing the role of oxygen and carbon in powering the "human machine" and providing a review of hematocrit and red blood cells. Dr. Querton then delineates the types of meals that workers should eat in order to get the most out of their bodies. In the book's final chapter, the author concludes, "In the course of this brief study of the diverse means society may use to increase the output of the human machine, we have often pointed out the importance of the role the medical doctor must play in the multiple organizations destined to produce an increase in man's productivity."[23] Here Dr.

Querton equates the human body with machines and outlines how scientists, the high priests of the new positivist faith, can increase "human output."

Other studies from the period explicitly link positivist medical philosophy with improved athletic performance and, more specifically, with cycling. For example, Dr. Fernand Lagrange's 1897 treatise on exercise for adults offers nutritional counsel, including the following metaphor: "We know that one supplies a locomotive's boiler with coal and we commonly say that food is 'the coal of the human machine.'"[24] Dr. Lagrange continues by noting that the amount of "fuel" consumed must equal the amount burned. He then alerts his readers to the benefits of cycling: "The velocipede [a forerunner to the bicycle] perfectly suits all subjects whose blood is impoverished and needs to be enriched by oxygen."[25]

Dr. Lagrange's contemporary Dr. Philippe Tissié wrote books including *Hygiene of the Velocipedist* (1888) and *Fatigue and Physical Training* (1897), as well as articles on gymnastics, cycling, and physiology.[26] His work on fatigue and physical training lists numerous exercises for maintaining health and improving fitness. While discussing cycling and the twenty-four-hour cycling races popular at the time, he notes the positive effects of "stimulants on the speed and cadence of cyclists."[27] These "stimulants" include "alcohol, quina [a plant used to make quinine], kola, coca, and mate [a caffeine-rich South American tea]."[28] Tissié had also studied cyclists and their fatigue and suggested that muscles become weary before cyclists are aware of it; therefore, he says, they should eat food or take stimulants before feeling tired. He also offers the following advice: "The best drink would be a sugar solution corresponding to six times more water than sugar.... Consuming large quantities of sugar increases muscular power from 26% to 33%, and, by slowing fatigue, the increase for a day can reach 61% to 76%."[29] Besides inadvertently inventing the modern sports drink, Tissié here sets out a mathematical, scientific method for improving cycling performance.[30]

Tissié's extensive work with cyclists may stem from the fact that he already sees the bicycle as a metaphor for national character. He writes, "Our French race, like the bicycle, is made of steel and rubber, perhaps more rubber than steel; that is, more elasticity than endurance."[31] This statement is remarkable firstly because, six years before the inauguration of the Tour de France, Tissié views the bicycle as the embodiment of French character. Secondly, he, too, equates the body with a machine, and Tissié's simile implies that the French must strengthen their bodies through rigorous training and the use of stimulants in order to become faster, stronger, more efficient, and more resilient.

Naturally, those looking to ride faster turned to the growing medical establishment for help. An 1894 book entitled *The Art of Winning at Cycling* contains a chapter entitled "Advice from a Doctor," which recommends popular homeopathic treatments and traditional behavioral practices along with more potent modern medicinal options.[32] The chapter recommends purging at the beginning of a training period, rinsing the mouth with water but not swallowing (to avoid gaining weight), sleeping on the right side so as not to "compress the heart," and scrubbing one's skin with a brush to improve circulation.[33] It further recommends drinking coffee only on race days to maximize its effectiveness and taking the following pills: extract of kola (a stimulant), tannin (to ward off diarrhea), quinine extract (an anti-inflammatory), and ratanhia extract (which homeopaths now use to treat dry and cracked skin). In all, the book recommends taking twenty-four pills on race day.

Three years later, a different cycling guide recommends fighting pain and fatigue with laudanum (a tincture of opium) every fifteen minutes and treating colic with drops of chlorodyne (a combination of laudanum, tincture of cannabis, and chloroform) in water.[34] More significantly, the small guide also contains numerous pharmaceutical ads, including the following one for Duffour Kola:

Duffour Kola in concentrated pills is indispensable for cyclists, mountain climbers, hunters, and soldiers.

Duffour Kola knocks out thirst, relieves muscle fatigue, stops shortness of breath.

A box of Duffour Kola takes up very little space, only weighs 50 grams; it is the most portable and least expensive kola brand.

Every cyclist wanting to ride without getting tired will take Duffour Kola.

Each box of Duffour Kola contains 30 doses; good for a long
ride.[35]

The length of many nineteenth-century bike races undoubtedly
drove the need for this type of medicinal assistance. The Bordeaux–
Paris bike race, first run in 1891, was 577 kilometers long; and the
Paris–Brest–Paris, created the same year, was 1,196 kilometers long.
After winning the first Paris–Brest–Paris race, Charles Terront rode
the more than 3,000 kilometers from St. Petersburg to Paris in just
over fourteen days. His manager, H. O. Duncan, writes that Terront's accomplishment proves that "man is still a powerful motor"
and that "the word 'distance' is only a word."[36] Cycling historian
Andrew Ritchie situates this event, and other races like it, within the
context of "Gigantism," which he defines as the "pursuit of super-
lative records" in sport and in "the development of technology,"
such as "the building of the Eiffel Tower [and] the undertaking
of record-setting attempts in cars, motor-cycles, motor-boats, and
airplanes."[37] Given these distances, cyclists undoubtedly embraced
laudanum, morphine, and kola to transform themselves into the
"machines" required to finish these races. These examples suggest
that, for the early professional and amateur cyclist, pharmacologi-
cal assistance would have been ubiquitous to help push the limits
of human endurance.

It is against this backdrop—the rise of positivism, an increase in
experimentation on the human body, a fetishization of machines, and
an increase in the potency of doping products available to cyclists—
that the cyclist-author Alfred Jarry (1873–1907) would write perhaps
the most important French literary work on human athletic performance, cycling, and doping: *The Supermale*. Published in 1902, a
year before the first Tour de France, this novel can be read as a tragic
allegory of positivism taken to its logical extreme. Through the eyes
of the protagonist, André Marcueil, the novel explores the limits of
human performance and draws parallels between sexual and cycling
endurance.

5.1. Alfred Jarry leaving his house in Corbeil to travel to Paris by bicycle in 1898. © Collection Harlingue / Roger-Viollet.

André Marcueil's opening comment in *The Supermale* stimulates conversation among his guests and sets the stage for the rest of the novel: "Love is an act of no significance since one can perform it indefinitely."[38] Instead of viewing love as an emotion, Marcueil considers it a physiological act accomplished by "the human motor"; as such, love is an act, like any other, for which one can prepare through training. When the narrator's friend Dr. Bathybius objects, saying that repetition leads to fatigue, Marcueil maintains that "repetition leads to stamina and skill," adding, "Human strength has no limits."[39] He theorizes, "Complex systems of muscles and nerves enjoy absolute repose, it seems to me, while their symmetrical partner works. We know that each leg of a cyclist rests and even benefits from an automatic massage as restoring as any embrocation while the other works."[40] In other words, he views man as a perpetual motion machine.

The central and longest chapter in the book features a ten thousand–mile race between a locomotive and a team of cyclists riding a five-person bicycle. In a nutshell, the race is set up as a competition between the might of chemistry and the might of engineering. The cyclists are fed a steady supply of a "medicine" that American chemist William Elson created and dubbed the "perpetual motion food," composed primarily of strychnine and alcohol. An engineer and industrialist, Arthur Gough, also an American, challenges the all-star team of cyclists, with the most advanced locomotive ever. The cyclists are locked into the bike, their legs linked together by a metal rod and their heads locked into helmets to keep them facing forward in the most aerodynamic position possible. What's more, they have cars to pace them—though these cars are eventually unable to keep up with the cyclists' pace. The cyclists and the locomotive race at breakneck speed in a dead heat for much of the race, going progressively faster and faster until at over three hundred kilometers an hour the speedometer can no longer register the cyclists' speed. At this point, the cyclist Jewey Jacobs dies (the others know he has died because of the smell). The cyclists fall behind. But after a moment, the body of Jewey Jacobs, thanks to the perpetual-motion food still in his system, seems to work through its rigor mortis and pedals again, even faster than before. The cyclists are able to catch up to the train. Soon, the passengers on the locomotive begin to toss furniture and other parts of the railcars into the boiler in order to keep up.

Yet a strange shadow has been following both the cycling quintuplet and the locomotive from the beginning. Since the cyclists are unable to turn their heads, they cannot see the source of the shadow and so are not sure if it is anything but their imaginations playing tricks on them. But the shadow (which we later learn is Marcueil, the supermale, who has entered the race without an invitation) ultimately overtakes both the locomotive and the quintuplet to win the race. A member of the quintuplet team, Ted Oxborrow, describes Marcueil as a complete master of the bike: "Another cyclist was in front of the locomotive.... His shorts were split at his thighs from the flexing of his extensor muscles! His bike was a racing model unlike any I had seen, with microscopic tires, a better design than the quintuplet; he pedaled as if there were absolutely no resistance."[41]

5.2. Cyclists on a quintuplet around the time Jarry authored *The Supermale*.
Courtesy of Gallica, Bibliothèque Nationale Française.

The work of French cultural theorist Paul Virilio provides a theoretical framework that helps explain Jarry's presentation of man and machine. Virilio writes, "The accident is an inverted miracle, a secular miracle, a revelation. When you invent the ship, you also invent the shipwreck; when you invent the plane you also invent the plane crash; and when you invent electricity, you invent electrocution. . . . Every technology carries its own negativity, which is invented at the same time as technical progress."[42] Elsewhere, Virilio links the accident explicitly with speed: "'One feature, the most distinctive of all, pits contemporary civilization against those that have preceded it: *speed*. The metamorphosis occurred in the space of a single generation,' the historian, Marc Bloch, noted in the 1930s. This situation involves a second feature in turn: *the accident*. The gradual spread of catastrophic events not only affects the reality of the moment but causes anxiety and anguish for generations to come."[43]

Jarry's text intuits similar conclusions. The death of Jewey Jacobs suggests the dangerous limits of medicinal attempts to increase stamina and speed; additionally, the fact that the locomotive essentially devours itself before the race's end posits the limits of and the danger inherent in mechanical attempts to go faster and farther. But an "accident," or flaw, is inscribed within the supermale, Marcueil, too. He is incapable of human affection; and while preparing to demonstrate his (and the book's) initial thesis—that "love" can be repeated indefinitely—he rapes women to death outside his chateau and along the route of the ten thousand–mile race.

It is not until the novel's conclusion that we learn *why* Marcueil was able to outperform both the locomotive and the cyclists who had been taking regular doses of the perpetual-motion food. After a chapter in which the supermale makes love eighty-two times in twenty-four hours (this time with a willing partner), thereby setting yet another record, Dr. Bathybius cannot believe what he has just witnessed. The doctor tells the chemist Elson, "This is not a man, this is a machine."[44] However, as Elson and the engineer Gough remark, Marcueil is incapable of forming an emotional attachment with another person. Hopeful that the impressive Marcueil will marry Elson's daughter, Gough and Elson think of ways to stimulate him to experience real love. Elson exclaims, "Antiquity had its love potions, thought the chemist. We must be able to rediscover the methods, as old as human superstition, that will constrain a soul to love!"[45] But Gough intervenes and instead creates a machine designed to make Marcueil fall in love. This "love-inspiring machine" will shock Marcueil's body with eleven thousand volts of electricity. When he is attached to the machine, though, a surprising thing happens. Instead of the machine filling Marcueil with love, Marcueil reveals himself to be stronger than the machine and instead fills *it* with love. The novel's omniscient narrator expresses it this way, in all caps: "THE MACHINE FELL IN LOVE WITH THE MAN."[46] Dr. Bathybius stammers, "I would have never thought this possible . . . never . . . but it is so natural, in fact! . . . In this era when metal and mechanics are all-powerful, in order to keep up, man must become stronger than machines, like he was stronger than wild beasts. . . . [It is a] simple process of adapting to his environment. . . . But this man is the first man of the future."[47] Humanity's drive to go ever faster, to mechanize, has led to a fundamental and dangerous change in humanity itself.

While the suggestion that humans would evolve in response to machines strikes us today as standing squarely in the realm of contemporary science fiction, during the Belle Époque in France, such thinking was commonplace. Guy de Maupassant's well-known short story "Le horla" (1887) can be read as a depiction of this type of human evolution, portraying the public's fear of what modern medicine's new generation of superhumans could unleash on France and the world.[48] More closely related to the theme of Jarry's novel, Louis Baudry de Saunier's 1894 cycling guide theorizes "the birth of a new human type, the cyclist," and describes him in these terms: "The cyclist is a man made half of flesh and half of steel that only our century of science and iron could have spawned."[49] In short, Dr. Bathybius's conviction that Marcueil had evolved to keep up with machines aligns with popular beliefs of the period.

The above passage further implies that Marcueil has evolved beyond an ability to create emotional attachments. In a 1995 analysis of sex and technology, Virilio explores the connection between technology and the loss of emotional intimacy resulting from a world where everything can be done quickly and remotely. "Whether steam engine (train) or combustion engine (automobile, aeroplane)," Virilio writes, "the acceleration of techniques of propulsion will have caused us to lose touch with tangible reality."[50] The machine era, and the move to reach ever-increasing speeds, put humanity on the path to living lives without the need for human interaction. While Marcueil can have sexual intercourse in a machinelike fashion (notably, Ellen, his female partner on the record-setting night, wears driving goggles, thereby evoking the machinery of the automobile in order to incite Marcueil's desire), he is incapable of feeling love. Jarry's novel posits that when a body becomes a machine, human relationships fail, accidents and crimes result, and love is reduced to one more area in which limits can be tested and records set. The cyclist, part man and part machine, is capable of superhuman feats and records. But the cyclist–speed machine is also preprogrammed with its own accidents: death from crashing at high speeds, from overdosing on doping products—death, that is, from crossing thresholds. Set in 1920, approximately twenty years after its composition, Jarry's *Supermale* is a cautionary prophecy about the negative consequences of speed and technology, a warning of positivism's hubris.

Indeed, Jarry's novel is not unlike a classical tragedy designed to slow society's headlong rush to find answers. Philosopher Simon Critchley has argued that classical Greek tragedy functions as an "emergency brake" on the "relentless speed and the unending acceleration of information flows that cultivate amnesia and an endless thirst for the short-term future."[51] Gough, Elson, and Bathybius each believe in their own gods from positivism's pantheon: engineering, chemistry, and medicine, respectively. But like Oedipus, they are blind to the consequences (i.e., the flaw embedded in their certainty), and they fail to apply the brakes. The novel's final scene depicts Marcueil breaking free from the love-inspiring machine.

> In a paroxysm of painful effort, Marcueil broke free from the straps holding his arms and lifted his hands to his head. . . . Marcueil rushed down the stairs . . . the three men understood how lamentably tragic a dog with a pot tied to its tail can be. When they arrived at the chateau's exit, they could only see a grimacing silhouette that pain caused to dart about the avenue with superhuman speed; who grasped the gate with a steel fist with no other thought than to flee and to fight, and who had broken two rods of this monumental gate. . . . And the body of André Marcueil, nude and plated in spots with reddish gold, remained enmeshed with the bars. . . . The Supermale died there, twisted in iron.[52]

Jarry's protagonist ends his life as the tragic victim of his own arrogance and physical strength—a victim of positivist experimentation in a society driven to make humans evolve in order to keep up with their mechanized environment. Marcueil's death—a death that notably occurs as he is melded with iron, the industrial symbol of the era—figures as the novel's final accident, as the catharsis of this machine-age tragedy.[53]

Following the French defeat to Prussia in 1870 (the symbolic beginning of the machine age in France), there was much hand-wringing about the perceived weakness of French men who spent too much time studying and not enough time exercising. Consequently, government-sponsored gymnastics programs were put in place to improve the physical health and strength of French schoolboys. This perception of weakness became something of a cliché that persisted well into the twentieth century. As late as the 1960s, French statesman and general Charles de Gaulle tasked Maurice Herzog, a French mountaineer and administrator, with developing France's sporting culture. Herzog complained, "There is an old prejudice against sports in this country, a prejudice that goes back to the intellectual man who was pale, a poor physical specimen, a Rimbaud, a Verlaine, a Proust. Sports were for the man who was not clever."[54] Here Herzog traces the origins of a crisis in masculinity back to the nineteenth century and, significantly, back to poets and novelists. Literature, it would seem, makes men weak. Jarry's text offers a counterexample via a protagonist who embodies strength and masculinity; but at the same time, the novel thematizes the consequences of a political imperative to improve the nation's men, to make them stronger, faster, and more virile. Jarry's novel suggests that this type of engineering has unforeseeable consequences and that inevitable accidents are inscribed in the very theories that positivists and politicians alike had promoted at the turn of the last century.

Jarry's novel also underscores the theological consequences of transforming man into motor. After witnessing the supermale's sexual exploits, Dr. Bathybius writes, "God is infinitely small."[55] He later adds that man will "crush the gods, this vermin."[56] Similarly, when writing about the Tour de France in his *Mythologies* (1957), Roland Barthes expresses fear of a superhuman replacing God: "Doping a cyclist is as criminal, as sacrilegious as wanting to imitate God; it amounts to stealing the privilege of the spark from God."[57] In the same vein, Virilio reminds us of the aphorism that Karl Kraus had penned after World War I: "The machine has declared war on God."[58] For Virilio, the warnings of Kraus—or of Jarry for that matter—have gone unheeded. The quest for speed led to tragedies such as the sinking of the *Titanic*; the carnage of World Wars I and II; and, more recently, the radioactive meltdown of Chernobyl. It has displaced God with the new transcendence of progress, and the need to shatter records has required even more human sacrifice than religions of the past.

Jarry underscores this displacement in "Christ's Passion Considered as an Uphill Bicycle Race," a short parody published in 1903 just three months before the inaugural Tour de France.[59] The story features Jesus Christ as a cyclist who competes against other riders in a fourteen-turn climb up Golgotha, each turn calling to mind a station of the cross. The sports journalist Saint Matthew describes a prerace flagellation designed to get the riders' blood moving and to serve as a "hygienic massage."[60] Once Pilate gives the signal to start, Jesus shoots off the starting line but is soon stalled by a flat tire caused, of course, by a patch of thorns that "punctured the whole circumference of his front tire."[61] The two thieves-turned-cyclists pull ahead while Jesus receives help from his trainer, Simon of Cyrene, who carries his bike up the hill for part of the course. But most importantly, the cross is transformed into the frame of a bike, and Jesus reclines on this cross-shaped frame, hands spread wide over the wooden handlebars in order to reduce wind resistance.[62] In other words, Jarry once again satirically places the machine in a divine role, while portraying Christ as a sort of man-machine destined to fail. In fact, Christ crashes out of the race in the twelfth turn, the twelfth station of the cross. The anticlericalism of late nineteenth-century France, spurred on by the Dreyfus affair, is, of course, evident in this story. But when this story is coupled with *The Supermale*, it becomes clear that Jarry is again condemning any system that claims ultimate truth or that posits itself as a supreme solution to society's ills. I agree with Marieke Dubbelboer, who writes, "Jarry mocks all who would replace religion with a naïve belief in technology . . . [and] rejects any doctrine that attempts to provide explanations and absolute truths, be it science or religion."[63]

A year after the publication of *The Supermale*, the Tour de France was launched and sponsored, not by the cycling newspaper *Le Vélo*, but by its competitor, a sporting newspaper called *L'Auto*—a title that implied that the machine (bicycles along with the motorcycles and automobiles that accompanied them) would be the race's defining feature.[64] Despite what Lance Armstrong has written—"It's not about the bike"—bicycle racing *is* about the human-machine partnership.[65] Jarry's novel prefigures the tour in its depiction of this partnership: the supermale Marcueil evolves to compete with machines, the cyclists

5.3. Maurice Garin at the conclusion of the first Tour de France. Courtesy of Harold B. Lee Library, Brigham Young University.

on the five-seater bike have their legs connected like the wheels of a locomotive, machines have "organs," and the chemist who feeds cyclists the perpetual-motion food uses the same fuel for vehicles.[66]

In a famous photo of Maurice Garin, winner of the first Tour de France, the cyclist stands facing the camera holding his bike in front of him.[67] The bike occupies the most space in the photo. Also, to Garin's right stands his masseur (or *soigneur*) examining him, perhaps looking for a vein. Whether he is doing this in order to administer an injection from whatever menacing tool is in his right hand or to assess the cyclist's heart rate remains a mystery. But it is clear that Garin did not try to hide the *soigneur*, demonstrating the banality of medical intervention for professional riders. If man is a machine, or nothing more than an extension of one, then improving his performance via injections, doping, or perpetual-motion food is to be expected as a matter of course. Doping a cyclist in 1903 had been as natural as fine-tuning a locomotive or improving an automobile. Garin is a superhuman, an example of the ultimate positivist endurance machine, the result of technologically advanced equipment, training, and medical intervention.

Despite Jarry's warnings, an underlying acceptance of the cyclist as machine—and the accompanying acceptance of doping—has continued from the positivist era and the days of Garin through today.[68] Television commentators routinely refer to cyclists' legs as "pistons" and speak of cyclists "getting their engines going." Pearl Izumi's Winter 2008 cycling catalog features the title "The Superiority of the Human Machine." The cover explains, "It's the most perfectly designed machine the world has ever known. It can turn pizza and powdered donuts into massive kilowatts of mountain-eating horsepower. Its gas pedal is sheer will. The harder you push it, the stronger it becomes. . . . *You're born with the greatest engine the world has ever known*" (original emphasis). Similarly, a 2009 article in the *Boulder Report* describes research linking calcium transfer to endurance in these terms: "Think of the muscle as a piston in an engine—fuel and oxygen enter the combustion chamber and, under pressure, are ignited to provide energy. But if the system isn't tightly sealed and unburned fuel remains after the spark plug ignites at the peak of the piston cycle, the engine doesn't run as efficiently. . . . In this scenario, the experimental benzothiazepines act as a kind of biochemical ignition timing system."[69]

If advertisers and analysts use this language, it may be because professional cyclists and trainers do the same. Eddie Borysewicz, the former U.S. cycling team coach who had signed Armstrong to his first professional cycling contract, responds to criticisms that his team had engaged in illegal blood boosting during the 1984 Olympics in this way: "If we pump tires with helium [instead of regular air], wear our new helmets, [and] use new wheels, are we immoral because everyone does not have them?"[70] Borysewicz argues that since equipment is not the same for each team, cyclists themselves need not be expected to prepare with the same training regimen as their competitors. But more perniciously, Borysewicz's comment echoes nineteenth-century positivist thinking, implying that riders themselves are one more piece of cycling equipment and should be refined through injections or transfusions and improved just like wheels, helmets, or tires.

Lance Armstrong himself had commissioned his suppliers to make his equipment more aerodynamic so that he could be faster for the Tour de France. Journalists Reed Albergotti and Vanessa O'Connell write that "the program was dubbed F-One, to reflect Lance's intention for cycling to have access to high-tech equipment that was as outstandingly excellent as that used by a sport like Formula One."[71] While the F-One initiative may have been a reference to Armstrong's equipment, Willy Voet, one-time *soigneur* of the Festina team (not Armstrong's team), suggests that riders themselves are referred to as Formula One cars. In his memoir, Voet writes, "When you are tuning up a Formula One car, you deal with the tyres, the engine, and the aerodynamics one by one. Every parameter has to be just perfect. *It's the same with a cyclist.* You can work out after every stage of a race what state the rider is in, depending on his blood-test readings and the graph traced by the heart-rate monitor which he wears during the race."[72] Instead of comparing Formula One cars to bikes, Voet compares the cars to the cyclists themselves. Hence, Voet and countless others see cyclists as machines that must be finely tuned.[73]

Finally, cyclists who use doping products are frequently called *chaudières* by other cyclists. It is a French word that means a boiler, heater, furnace, or cauldron. This slang term seems to have foreshadowed the doom of Saunier Duval's sponsorship of a professional cycling team. Saunier Duval is a French heating and boiler company; indeed, in their first year of sponsorship, the entire team withdrew from the tour after two of their riders tested positive. But the term again underscores that cyclists are machines, like the locomotive in Jarry's *Supermale*. In short, calling a cyclist a *chaudière* emphasizes the cyclist's identity as a dehumanized machine and represents the continued acceptance of enhancing human performance via technological means that dates back to the French Belle Époque and even, as we saw, back to the medieval poems of Marie de France.

Notes

The epigraph reads, "The bike itself is a form of doping." Paul Fournel, *Besoin de vélo* (Paris: Seuil, 2001), 30. Unless otherwise noted, all French translations in this essay are my own.

1. "N'estes mie si vertuus." Marie de France, "Les deux amants," in *Lais* (Paris: GF Flammarion, 1994), 182.
2. Marie de France, *Lais*, 182, 184.
3. Marie de France, *Lais*, 184, 186.
4. Marie de France, *Lais*, 186.
5. Marie de France, *Lais*, 188.

6. The theme of ancient strength-giving plants persists in popular modern representations. In René Goscinny and Albert Uderzo's popular French comic-book series *Astérix*, a magic potion made from mistletoe and other plants gives the Gauls a superhuman strength, allowing them to regularly defeat the numerically and organizationally superior Roman armies. The volume *Astérix in Switzerland* (*Astérix chez les Helvètes* [Paris: Hachette, 1970]) features a search through the Swiss hills for edelweiss, prized for its curative powers.

7. Prosper Mérimée's *Lettres d'Espagne* (1833) features a porter who "lost his wind" but recovers it by eating magic beasts fed on unbaptized children's flesh (in *Carmen et treize autres nouvelles* [Paris: Gallimard, 1965], 427). Peasants in Honoré de Balzac's *Les paysans* drink a special *vin cuit* to help them in their mountain ascensions ([Paris: Furne, Dubochet et Cie / Hetzel et Paulin, 1846], 525). And the narrator of Charles Baudelaire's prose poem "Le Gâteau" pauses in his mountaineering expedition to drink from "a flask of a certain elixir that pharmacists sold to tourists in those days" (in *Le spleen de Paris* [Paris: GF Flammarion, 1987], 103).

8. A special thank you to Jean-Christophe Valtat both for pointing this novel out to me some years ago and for the reference to Tissié's work (cited below). Valtat's excellent article on *The Supermale* historically contextualizes Jarry's theories on fatigue and the machine. Jean-Christophe Valtat, "Le dynamomètre, la bicyclette et la chaise électrique: Théories énergétiques et psychologies de la fatigue dans *Le Surmâle* d'Alfred Jarry," *L'Etoile-Absinthe*, nos. 103–4 (2003): 65–74.

9. Alfred Jarry, *Le surmâle: Roman moderne* (Paris: Mille et Une Nuits, 1996), 19. See also the excellent articles by Michel Pierssens, "Les savoirs du surmâle," *Revue des sciences humaines* 74, no. 203 (1986): 129–39; and Philip Hadlock, "Men, Machines, and the Modernity of Knowledge in Alfred Jarry's *Le Surmâle*," *SubStance* 35, no. 3 (2006): 131–48.

10. Bettina Knapp, "Jarry's *The Supermale*: The Sex Machine, the Food Machine, and the Bicycle Race; Is It a Question of Adaptation?" *Nineteenth-Century French Studies* 18, nos. 3–4 (1990): 492.

11. Alastair Brotchie, *Alfred Jarry: A Pataphysical Life* (Cambridge MA: MIT Press, 2011), 251.

12. Société des touristes du Dauphiné. *Guides, porteurs et muletiers de la société: règlements et tarifs, chalets et refuges* (Grenoble, France: Société des Touristes du Daupiné, 1901), 24, 32.

13. Alfred Michiels, *Les bûcherons, les schlitteurs des Vosges* (Paris: Berger-Levrault, 1878).

14. Patricia Auger-Holderbach, *La cuisine paysanne en Rouergue: Tradition et vie quotidienne* (Rodez, France: Editions du Rouergue, 1992), 30–31.

15. J. Bayard Taylor, *Views A-foot; or, Europe Seen with Knapsack and Staff* (New York: George P. Putnam, 1852), 399. See also John Ball, *Peaks, Passes, and Glaciers* (London: Longman, Green, Longman and Roberts, 1860), 167.

16. Jean-François Soulet, *La vie quotidienne dans les Pyrénées sous l'ancien régime du XVIe au XVIIIe siècles* (Paris: Librairie Hachette, 1974), 175.

17. G. Bruno [Augustine Fouillée], *Le tour de la France par deux enfants* (Paris: Belin Frères, 1895), 121.

18. Mary Pickering, "Auguste Comte," in *The Literary Encyclopedia*, June 25, 2010, http://www.litencyc.com/php/speople.php?rec=true&UID=977 (accessed April 2, 2014). Note, too, that Comte's philosophy directly inspired the motto "Order and Progress" on Brazil's flag.

19. Pickering, "Auguste Comte."

20. Christian Messenger, *Sport and the Spirit of Play in Contemporary American Fiction* (New York: Columbia University Press, 1990), xiv.

21. Anson Rabinbach, *The Human Motor: Energy, Fatigue, and the Origins of Modernity* (New York: Basic Books, 1990), 88.

22. Louis Querton, *L'augmentation du rendement de la machine humaine* (Paris: V. Giard and E. Brière, 1905), 2.

23. Querton, *Augmentation*, 211.

24. Fernand Lagrange, *De l'exercice chez les adultes* (Paris: Félix Alcan, 1897), 19.

25. Lagrange, *De l'exercice*, 317.

26. Philippe Tissié, *La fatigue et l'entraînement physique* (Paris: Félix Alcan, 1897); Philippe Tissié, *Hygiene du vélocipediste* (Paris: Doin, 1888).

27. Tissié, *Fatigue*, 23.

28. Tissié, *Fatigue*, 166.

29. Tissié, *Fatigue*, 22–23.

30. In one of his more bizarre studies, Tissié sought to demonstrate the importance of drinking plenty of sugar water by injecting a rabbit with the urine of a cyclist who had consumed only milk during a twenty-four-hour race. The urine was so concentrated that it took only ten cubic centimeters to kill the one-kilogram rabbit. See Tissié, *Fatigue*, 6.

31. Tissié, *Fatigue*, xvi.

32. Antony Fauveau and F. Fauveau, *L'art de vaincre à vélo* (Paris: Imprimerie F. Cassegrain, 1894).

33. Fauveau and Fauveau, *Art de vaincre à vélo*, 54, 66.

34. F. P. D., *Guide cycliste* (Toulouse, France: Labouche Frères, 1897), 18.

35. F. P. D., *Guide cycliste*, 23–28.

36. H. O. Duncan, quoted in Andrew Ritchie, *Quest for Speed: A History of Early Bicycle Racing, 1868–1903* (El Cerrito CA: privately printed, 2011), 333.

37. Ritchie, *Quest for Speed*, 351.

38. Jarry, *Surmâle*, 7.

39. Jarry, *Surmâle*, 11.
40. Jarry, *Surmâle*, 13.
41. Jarry, *Surmâle*, 74–75.
42. Paul Virilio, *Politics of the Very Worst* (New York: Semiotext[e], 1999), 89.
43. Paul Virilio, *The Original Accident*, trans. Julie Rose (Cambridge: Polity Press, 2007), 3.
44. Jarry, *Surmâle*, 127.
45. Jarry, *Surmâle*, 127.
46. Jarry, *Surmâle*, 132.
47. Jarry, *Surmâle*, 132.
48. Guy de Maupassant, *Le horla* (Paris: Paul Ollendorff, 1887).
49. Louis Baudry de Saunier, *L'art de bien monter la bicyclette* (Paris, 1894), 23, 25, quoted and translated in Christopher S. Thompson, *The Tour de France: A Cultural History* (Berkeley: University of California Press, 2008), 27.
50. Paul Virilio, *Paul Virilio Reader*, ed. Steve Redhead (New York: Columbia University Press, 2004), 177. This passage is from Paul Virilio, *Open Sky*, trans. Julie Rose (London: Verso, 2008). This is a translation of Virilio's 1995 book *La vitesse de libération*.
51. Simon Critchley, "Tragedy's Philosophy" (lecture, Radboud University, Nijmegen, Netherlands, 2011), http://www.ru.nl/soeterbeeckprogramma /terugblik/terugblik-2011/terugblik-per/tragedy'-philosophy/teksten/lezing -simon/ (accessed February 22, 2014; site discontinued).
52. Jarry, *Surmâle*, 133–34.
53. In an essay on masculinity in Jarry's works, Sylvie Young discusses Virilio and *The Supermale*, noting that the machine's failure in the final scene leads to Marcueil's death. See Sylvie Young, "Smiting Masculinity: From Jarry's *Surmâle* to Cendrars' *Confessions*," in *Masculinities in Twentieth- and Twenty-First-Century French and Francophone Literature*, ed. Edith Biegler Vandervoort (Cambridge: Cambridge Scholars Publishing, 2011), 14. I would argue that for Jarry the larger problem is that as humans *become* machines, particularly in the form of cyclists, they themselves become scapegoats of the positivist era.
54. Maurice Herzog, quoted in Lindsay Sarah Krasnoff, *The Making of Les Bleus: Sport in France, 1958–2010* (Lanham MD: Lexington Books, 2013), 41.
55. Jarry, *Surmâle*, 94.
56. Jarry, *Surmâle*, 96.
57. Roland Barthes, *Mythologies* (Paris: Edition du Seuil, 1957), 115.
58. Virlio, *Original Accident*, 33.
59. Alfred Jarry, "Christ's Passion Considered as an Uphill Bicycle Race," in *Selected Works of Alfred Jarry*, ed. Roger Shattuck and Simon Watson Taylor (New York: Grove Press, 1965).
60. Jarry, "Christ's Passion," 122.

61. Jarry, "Christ's Passion," 122.

62. Jarry, "Christ's Passion," 123.

63. Marieke Dubbelboer, "Un univers mécanique: La machine chez Alfred Jarry," *French Studies* 58, no. 4 (2004): 480.

64. On the topic of machines and the first Tour de France, see Philippe Gaboriau, "The Tour de France and Cycling's Belle Epoque," in *The Tour de France, 1903–2003: A Century of Sporting Structures, Meanings and Values*, ed. Hugh Dauncey and Geoff Hare (London: Frank Cass, 2003), 57–78.

65. Lance Armstrong, *It's Not about the Bike: My Journey back to Life* (New York: Putnam, 2000).

66. Describing a car, Jarry's narrator remarks, "The machine shamelessly exposed . . . its *organs* of propulsion." Jarry, *Surmâle*, 51, my emphasis.

67. The photo first appeared on the cover page of *La Vie au Grand Air*, no. 254 (July 24, 1903). It is titled *Le Portrait de Garin*. The caption reads, "The Tour de France, the most gigantic cycling race ever organized, just concluded with the victory of Maurice Garin who covered the 2,400 kilometers of the route in 94 hours 33 minutes. Our photograph was taken at the moment Brillouet, well-known as a masseur in sporting circles, had just taken hold of Garin to give him a shower and a well-deserved massage. Next to Garin is his youngest son, a future champion of the road!" Surprisingly, Brillouet looks more like a butcher than a masseur. His posture implies that he is going beyond the role one would typically expect a simple masseur to play.

68. For a summary of doping in the Tour de France from its beginnings to the present, see Thompson, *Tour de France*, 225–55.

69. Joe Lindsey, "Study Unveils Newest Front in Doping Fight," *Boulder Report*, January 14, 2009, http://blogs.bicycling.com/blogs/boulderreport/2009/01/14/study-unveils-newest-front-in-doping-fight/ (accessed February 25, 2014; site discontinued).

70. Eddie Borysewicz, quoted in Reed Albergotti and Vanessa O'Connell, *Wheelmen: Lance Armstrong, the Tour de France, and the Greatest Sports Conspiracy Ever* (New York: Gotham Books, 2013), 32.

71. Albergotti and O'Connell, *Wheelmen*, 178.

72. Willy Voet, *Breaking the Chain: Drugs and Cycling, the True Story*, trans. William Fotheringham (London: Yellow Jersey Press, 2001), 65, my emphasis.

73. One further note on (the now-disgraced) Armstrong as a machine: After retiring from cycling in 2005, Armstrong returned to the Tour de France in 2009. With photographer Elizabeth Kreutz, he published a book about his comeback and the entire 2009 season and titled it *Comeback 2.0: Up Close and Personal* (New York: Touchstone, 2009). The "2.0" is certainly a nod to a computer operating system or software that is enhanced and rereleased. But it also stands as a reminder that cyclists are performance machines to be enhanced and fine-tuned.

6   Albertine the Cyclist

A Queer Feminist Bicycle Ride through
Proust's *In Search of Lost Time*

UNA BROGAN

The period that saw the first boom in the bicycle's popularity in France corresponds chronologically with the events of Proust's *In Search of Lost Time* (*À la recherche du temps perdu*, published 1913–27). The seven novels are set in the time period spanning roughly from 1879 to 1919; and given Proust's commitment to reviving every detail of a lost world, it comes as little surprise that the then hugely popular machine—the bicycle—features in his universe.[1] The bicycle makes its first appearance in a scene toward the end of the second volume, *Within a Budding Grove* (*À l'ombre de jeunes filles en fleurs*, 1919), along with the cyclist who will remain central to much of the rest of the work, Albertine. This emblematic scene has been examined by several critics, but until now little attention has been given to subsequent appearances of Albertine the cyclist.[2] By following the bicycle's complex itinerary through the universe of *In Search of Lost Time*, I will unravel the machine's rich contribution to the ever-shifting portrait of the novel's heroine, a young woman who dares to challenge the strict moral codes of bourgeois society. Albertine's bicycle, I argue, is mobilized in order to trace the outlines of a radical new social order, one that would embrace not only new gender identities but also subversive sexual orientations.

Wheels of Change

Specific dates are rare in Proust, but certain details in *Within a Budding Grove*, such as the hotel manager Aimé's mention of the beginning of the Dreyfus affair, allow us to situate the events of the novel in the mid-1890s.[3] This period witnessed the widespread adoption of the bicycle in the midst of a raging debate about its place in society.[4] Initially an aristocratic pursuit, cycling became more widely accessible at the end of the century, largely thanks to the invention of the safety bicycle in 1884 and its subsequent mass production.[5] As Eugen Weber notes, taxation figures for 1898 indicate 375,000 bicycles in France; by 1914 this number had swollen to 3.5 million.[6]

The turn-of-the-century society that Proust masterfully portrays was one that was undergoing profound change, while parts of it remained firmly anchored in tradition. According to Hartmut Rosa, the fin de siècle was an era defined by acceleration, in which technological and social transformations were perceived to occur at an increasingly rapid pace. Rosa characterizes Proust as an author who responded to the acute social change happening around him by seeking to bring alive a recent and static past.[7] By reviving a world that was definitively swept away by the First World War, Proust breathes life into "frames of institutions, ways of life and mind, that had long been crumbling," as Eugen Weber puts it.[8] The sedate society of Proust's youth provided the prelude to the profound changes and destruction that occurred after 1914. The bicycle—a thoroughly modern instrument that was nonetheless noted for its "primitivism" from its very beginnings—is a striking symbol of the dual need for a connection to the past alongside ever faster (and potentially destructive) movement into the future. Rosa points to an acceleration threshold beyond which social integration becomes impossible, and Ivan Illich before him argues that "free people must travel the road to productive social relations at the speed of a bicycle."[9] Poised on the cusp of modernity, the bicycle allows us to conceptualize a unique window in time— before the invention of motorcars and airplanes—when an efficient, individualist, and modern means of transportation accelerated social relations, while respecting the social "speed limit" and thus ensuring an essential link to the past was retained.[10]

It is one of the great achievements of Proust's work to have managed to re-create in literature this sense of cohabiting development and stasis in fin de siècle France. Proust willingly cut himself off from the realities of postwar Paris, devoting all his time to writing in a cork-lined room in order to revive the memory of a world on the brink of extinction. We journey with him to the final years of the nineteenth century, when France experienced a period of political calm and the bicycle's popularity boomed. Following a hundred years of turmoil, during which empires, constitutional monarchies, and republics all took their turn in government, the establishment of the long-lived Third Republic (1870–1940) heralded a period of relative stability. For the first time, many of the laws established by the Napoleonic Code of 1804 were revised, laying the foundations for much of modern French legislature. Notably, in the case of women, this meant better access to education and freedom to work, to own property, and to ask for divorce.[11] These small but significant legal gains were accompanied by a growing women's movement, which demanded complete social equality for women, including the right to vote. As was the case in Great Britain, the United States, and elsewhere, the bicycle played a crucial role in the struggle of these early feminists in France, who saw in the bicycle both the symbolic and the actual means to achieving freedom in clothing, movement, and lifestyle.[12]

These transformations were not viewed with optimism by all. The Third Republic was founded as a result of a humiliating political defeat in 1871, when, with the Prussians at the gates of Paris, workers of the capital had joined together to form the Paris Commune, celebrated by Marx as the first true manifestation of a proletarian government.[13] The repression of the Commune soon after its creation, when approximately twenty thousand civilians were executed in the space of a week, acted as a bloody reminder of the deep inequalities persisting within French society. The swelling and increasingly wealthy bourgeois class was vividly aware not only of the menace of foreign powers (Germany's military prowess continued to escalate following its victory in the Franco-Prussian war) but also of the domestic threat from the downtrodden lower classes. Within this context, the rapidly evolving position of women was interpreted by many as a sign of social decay, with traditional family and societal values being dangerously eroded. Detractors of the bicycle railed against women's newly discovered freedom to roam; deplored their adoption of the bloomers (*culottes*) required to ride the machine comfortably; and vociferated in articles about the supposed health dangers posed to women cyclists, claiming for example that bicycle saddles afforded women masturbatory pleasures or reduced their fertility.[14] In a society that still considered the main function of women to be reproductive, female cycling habits were partly held responsible for the falling birthrate, which decreased by 27.4 percent in the period between 1870 and 1914.[15] Theories of social degeneration (*dégénérescence*), influenced by social Darwinism and eugenics, helped spread the fear that the decadent bourgeois nation was on the decline.[16] As Christopher Thompson and Fiona Ratkoff have convincingly argued, the degeneration debate "became focused on the female cyclist," an emblematic figure whose unexpected arrival in urban and rural France was indeed a striking symbol of the new zeitgeist.[17]

The Apparition of a Cyclist

There is no doubt in Proust's young narrator's mind, as he stands before the Grand Hôtel in the stylish French seaside resort of Balbec, that the young women he suddenly beholds striding across the beach are an entirely unknown phenomenon. In this masterful sequence resembling an impressionist painting, the group first appears as a moving blur and gradually acquires detail as the narrative progresses, as though the viewer were slowly stepping back from a canvas. One of the first observations the narrator makes about the indistinct group is that "one of these strangers was pushing in front of her, with one hand, her bicycle."[18] The anonymous cyclist is Albertine, and it is her bicycle that will repeatedly be used to identify her, until her name is learned some time later. As Marie-Agnès Barathieu notes, Proust constitutes "a metalanguage around and starting from the bicycle" in the characterization of Albertine.[19] The bicycle stands defiantly at the end of the first sentence describing the heroine and will return in each new layer added to her portrait. As we shall see, her unconventional clothing, rough language, and robust body are all emanations of her identity as a cyclist.

The young women make their dramatic entry at the moment of the day when the bourgeois hotel guests are taking their daily stroll on the beach, and the awkward, "unharmonious" gestures of the latter could not stand in greater contrast to the graceful, purposeful movement of the youthful "flock of seagulls" clothed in "special outfits" designed for playing sports.[20] These women are clearly at ease in their "beautiful bodies with beautiful legs, beautiful hips, healthy and calm faces, which looked agile and clever" as they move effortlessly across the beach.[21] Though they are walking, their bold movements recall those of the reckless cyclists termed *vélocipédards* (a near equivalent of the English "scorchers") in the 1890s. The young women overtake and avoid the stuffy bourgeois walkers, and one of them even leaps over a "horrified old man" as he sits on his deck chair.[22] The first words that reach the narrator's ears are "slang words which were so uncouth and cried so loudly ... (among which I nonetheless made out the unpleasant phrase of 'live my own life')."[23] This battle cry of young womanhood instantly convinces the narrator that these women must have an even deeper involvement in the world of cycling than he had previously imagined. Abandoning the hypothesis that they are of high social class, he remarks, "I concluded rather that all these young women belonged to the population which frequents velodromes, and must be the very young mistresses of racing cyclists."[24] As it turns out, they belong to "the very wealthy petite bourgeoisie, from the world of business and industry," and it is the precarious position of their own social class that their audacious actions are challenging.[25]

This memorable sequence, central to the rest of the work since it introduces Albertine, provides a compelling portrait of the changes being wrought in contemporary French society, and it is fitting that Proust should place "the young woman with the bicycle" at its center.[26] Siân Reynolds points to the British affectations in the speech and manners of Albertine and her friends to argue that the "New Woman" was chiefly a cultural construct in the United States and Great Britain, maintaining that attempts to import her to France were forced and unsuccessful.[27] However, I would argue that such behavior was typical of the climate of anglomania in fin de siècle France and does not necessarily imply that the French inherited only a watered-down version of feminism. Albertine's bicycle, pushed in front of the group, acts as a banner brandished to announce the birth of a new society.

Françoise Gaillard points out that "the young woman with the bicycle is an unstoppable force that not only shakes up strolling holidaymakers, but also social barriers, cultural codes, and generational relations."[28] Through their daring behavior, dress, and language, the figures on the beach "make a social space for themselves as women and as young people" and provide a triumphant portrait of *la femme nouvelle*, a figure alternatively respected or reviled but in all events recognized as a major presence in turn-of-the-century France.[29]

While certain contemporary commentators held that the bicycle contributed to biological degeneration through its adverse effects on fertility and social degeneration by facilitating women's freedom of movement, others such as Dr. Juste Lucas-Championnière argued that this new technology could play an important role in the regeneration of the declining nation through physical activity: "The bicycle represents *women's accession to physical exercise*; and physical exercise for women means the future regeneration of that part of the nation doomed to degeneration."[30] The supreme feats of physical endurance accomplished by early racing cyclists even led some to imagine that a new race of superhumans would result from the invention of the bicycle, a concept that Alfred Jarry humorously explored in his 1902 novel *Le surmâle*.[31] Though Albertine does not win a ten thousand–mile race against a steam train, as Jarry's hero does, she boasts she can ride to the races at la Sogne three times faster than the tram.[32] In a rare manifestation of physical vigor, even the sickly narrator finds the energy to accompany the young women on their bicycling day trips.[33] Thus, while presenting a challenge to conservative bourgeois society, Albertine and her friends also reflect the contemporary view that physical exercise and greater independence for women were part of the solution to preventing the decline of the privileged social classes.[34]

Bicycles: Perception and Desire

Albertine's refusal of the bourgeois patriarchal order runs much deeper than it appears in this initial sequence, as will become clear from an examination of relevant passages from *The Captive* (*La prisonnière*, 1923). However, before pedaling forward, I would like to take a detour that will provide us with an insight into Proust's semantic and aesthetic mobilization of the bicycle. In *Within a Budding Grove*, the machine is first glimpsed by the narrator from the seat of Madame de Villeparisis's carriage as it is being ridden by an anonymous, desirable "farm girl, shopkeeper's daughter," or an "elegant young lady."[35] These initial evocations of the object simply bring it into the narrator's field of vision, associating it with desire and fleeting visions of beauty but attributing it to no one character in particular. Its specific role becomes more concrete in the passage just examined, where we saw how the bicycle serves as a point of reference in a moving mass, and is subsequently used to identify Albertine in her different degrees of individualization. As Barathieu observes in her meticulous study of the semantics of journeys in Proust, "The label of cyclist is a practical means of differentiating [Albertine] from the others, and at the same time, this entirely metonymic designation confirms the characteristic element pointed to by the dynamics of the text."[36] Indeed, the metonymic identification of Albertine as "cyclist" provides us with a microcosmic example of Proust's aesthetics of perception, in which phenomena are first apprehended by their outward features, before gradually acquiring definition and meaning. Proust's writing seeks to mirror this accumulative and deceptive process of perception that constantly presents us with "optical errors," since the object itself is ever changing: "We think we are catching up on it, it moves again."[37] This description of perception itself vividly recalls the fragmentary way we perceive a passing cyclist.[38]

It is within this moving field of perception that desire takes root. Albertine's identity as a fleeting, unattainable cyclist is key to her attraction. When she is finally introduced to her admirer in the painter Elstir's studio, seated in a "silk dress," the narrator finds her merely "mediocre and touching," compared with the ravishing "bicycling bacchante" he had glimpsed on several occasions in Balbec.[39] Later, in *The Captive*, the narrator will characterize Albertine as "a being of flight" and repeatedly recall her "flying by on her bicycle," when trying to get to the root of his desperate jealousy and desire for her.[40] Thus, an appreciation of her beauty cannot simply rely on the fact of her physical attractiveness but must also take into account her movement through space, her dynamism and speed.

The connection between desire and flight is recalled in a further portrait of bicyclists in *The Captive* when the narrator and Albertine make an outing to the fashionable park the Bois de Boulogne. In a portrait reminiscent of Jean Béraud's painting *Le chalet du cycle* (1900), Proust depicts "three young women sitting beside the immense arch of their bicycles which stood next to them, like three immortals leaning on a cloud or on a fabulous steed on which they made their mythological journeys."[41] These "Goddesses" provide their admiring onlookers with a glimpse into another realm, and the classical imagery suggests a fascination with a mythical past that is also reflected in the images used in contemporary bicycle advertisements.[42] Observing these beings, the narrator reflects on "the similarities between desire and travel," two themes wonderfully represented by the bicycles against which the women are leaning.[43] Elsewhere in the park, we are provided with a rare portrait of a cyclist in movement: "Farther along another young girl was kneeling near her bicycle, fixing it. Once the repair was finished, the young racer got on her bicycle, but without straddling it as a man would have done. For an instant the bicycle swayed, the young body seemed to have grown a sail, an immense wing; and soon we saw the young creature, half-human, half-winged, angel or peri, disappearing at full speed, continuing her voyage."[44] This glimpse of a self-sufficient cyclist who repairs and then mounts her bicycle before disappearing into the distance provides an evocative illustration of women's new social horizons. The flight and bird metaphors used in this passage also echo turn-of-the-century literature and advertising posters, which frequently likened cycling to flight, often through images of winged young women, as in the well-known "Gladiator" poster.[45] One contemporary literary example of the tendency to associate cycling with flight is Maurice Leblanc's *Voici des ailes* (Here are wings, 1898), a novel in which the liberating experience of cycling leads two young couples to cast off their tight clothes and marital bonds, pedaling in free love into the horizon.

Androgynous Cyclists

Leblanc's novel is a euphoric celebration of the social, spatial, and sexual liberation brought about by the bicycle. This liberation operated on a practical level, since cycling allowed couples to meet unsupervised; but it also had an aesthetic dimension. Leblanc explicitly compared the bicycle to the human body and admired the openness and visibility of its simple mechanism. The "sincerity" of the machine (which he opposed to the hidden engine of the motorcar) was something he hoped to see mirrored in people's renewed relationship to bodies and sex.[46] The bicycle plays a role in awaking desire, since, as Rosemary Lloyd notes in her examination of the bicycle in Leblanc's novel, "its wheels act like a pair of magic spectacles to reveal both its own desires and those of everything around it."[47] I would argue, however, that *Voici des ailes* remains essentially a male-centered fantasy that leads to nothing more radical than the formation of two new heterosexual couples. At a time when, according to Michel Foucault, medical authorities were attempting to rigidly classify sexuality according to fixed categories, Proust's narrative provides a subtle, subversive, and very modern portrait of a fluid spectrum of gender and sexual identities.[48] Rather than attempting to establish boundaries, Proust carefully points to new identities made possible through the intermingling of various characters and objects, including Albertine and her bicycle.

However, in the early days of cycling, the object of the bicycle aroused fears of gender blurring. It is interesting to note that in French there are at least two words for "bicycle," one of which is feminine, *bicyclette*, and the other, *vélo*, masculine.[49] Although there are historical reasons for this and some variation in their meaning (for example, the former often alludes to old-fashioned town bikes, while the latter is used more generally and also applies to racers), they are essentially interchangeable and refer to the same object. Yet the bicycle's lack of gender specificity is more than just a linguistic peculiarity. Some nineteenth-century observers were particularly alarmed by the degendering of female cyclists. Sarah Bernhardt and Stéphane Mallarmé, for example, both deplored the adoption of bloomers by women cyclists, claiming that such a practice necessarily entailed a loss of femininity.[50] An article in the newspaper *L'Auto-Vélo* in 1897 satirically announced the birth of a new species: "the bicycle-woman ... who seems to have both male and female traits, without having any clearly defined sex."[51]

Albertine offers us a vision of a character who adopts "both male and female traits." Writing in the 1920s, when communities of cross-dressing women, or "inverts," had, according to gender theorist Judith Halberstam, "developed into visible and elaborate subcultures," Proust looks back to the world in which such identities began to crystallize.[52] His narrative takes place amid what Halberstam terms "the momentous negotiations about gender that took place at and around the turn of the century … [and which] played a part in untangling once and for all the knots that appeared to bind gender to sex and sexuality in some mysterious and organic way."[53] Albertine represents for the narrator "a new variety of female beauty," but one that goes beyond the boundaries of the conventionally feminine and is instead one of the myriad manifestations of what Halberstam calls "female masculinity."[54]

References to Albertine's masculinity are already present when we first encounter the young woman using slang, wearing unusual clothing, and "pushing a bicycle and walking with a swagger" along the beach in Balbec.[55] In the painter Elstir's studio, when the narrator catches a glimpse of "the young cyclist" framed in the window like one of the impressionist paintings hanging on the walls, she greets the painter midride, "without stopping," provoking a flurry of desire in the narrator.[56] Burning to follow Albertine but waiting for Elstir to accompany him outside, the young hero paces impatiently around the studio until he discovers a portrait of "a young actress from another time half-dressed as a man."[57] The pleasure the narrator derives from looking at this portrait is a result of the subject's fluid gender: "The gender seemed to be on the point of admitting that it belonged to a slightly boyish girl, then it evaporated and appeared again later, giving the impression of a depraved, pensive, and effeminate young man, then fleeing again, it remained elusive."[58]

This association between mobile cyclists and fluctuating gender reoccurs in *The Captive*. The narrator, watching the morning traffic from his window, first mistakes a male pedestrian for "an inelegant woman."[59] This instance of gender confusion is immediately followed by a description of speeding, blurred, sexless cyclists, at one with their machines: "The winged hunters, in changing hues, sped toward the stations, their bodies hugging their bicycles."[60] This image is in turn reflected in *The Fugitive* (*Albertine disparue*, 1925) when the narrator recalls a memory of Albertine as an androgynous cyclist warrior: "leaning over her mythological bicycle wheel, on wet days shrouded in her warrior's tunic made of rubber that defined the curve of her breasts."[61] The ambiguity surrounding cyclists' gender is one of the reasons why the bicycle is such a productive image for Proust, a writer for whom an individual's gender is not a fixed state but a constant flux. It is as elusive as any of our impressions and as fleeting as a passing cyclist.

Queer Bicyclists

In addition to contributing to the destabilization of gender divisions, the bicycle plays an important role in expressing queer desire.[62] In Balbec the narrator is jealous of Albertine's visits to female friends and associates his own suspicions with her incessant bicycle riding. It is only after her death that he receives evidence of her sexual encounters with women, in the form of a letter from the Balbec hotel manager, Aimé. He confirms that Albertine bribed staff so that she could bring many different women with her into the shower.[63] In the confusion that follows this discovery, the narrator tortuously imagines her walking and cycling from one lover's house to the next: "Albertine had lived in one place, walked to the next, and ridden her bicycle to the next."[64] While the narrator and Albertine are living together in *The Captive*, the narrator recounts how Albertine "would tell me in the vaguest of terms, as though it were a secret, about her bicycle rides in Balbec."[65] Though she does not share what was "secret" about her bicycle rides, she goes on to admit being propositioned in a carriage by the narrator's former lover, Gilberte, and clandestinely staying at a female friend's house for three days, only emerging onto the street once, "disguised as a man, just for fun."[66] In this rare moment of openness between the narrator and Albertine, we are provided with a glimpse of the lives of turn-of-the-century, cross-dressing, cycling lesbians—a lively portrait that may also have drawn on the female cross-dressers visible in Europe by the early 1920s. Living in a society that shunned queer desire, Proust's characters must come up with their own lifestyles and languages to express it. When referring to desire between women, the narrator employs the term *gomorrhéen* (from the biblical city Gomorrah, destroyed by God for its sinfulness), while Albertine uses the euphemism *mauvais genre* ("bad taste").[67] Along with this coded language and cross-dressing, the bicycle plays a key role in Albertine's attempts to explore and communicate her sexuality.

The bicycle is also used to point to this inexpressible sexuality in the depiction of the novel's other queer hero, baron de Charlus. The violent dispute overheard by the narrator between Charlus and his lover Jupien that opens the fourth volume, *Sodom and Gomorrah* (*Sodome et Gomorrhe*, 1921–22), contains a telling mention of "a very nice cyclist" who makes deliveries for the pharmacist.[68] In his biography of Proust, Ghislain de Diesbach explains with reference to the author's correspondence that male delivery cyclists acquired an unexpected role at this time, occasionally solicited to meet the sexual demands of rich men: "A new speciality appeared, thanks to technological progress, a speciality which was particularly appreciated by gentlemen of a certain age: telegram delivery boys. Cycling gave them muscles, they were fresh from the outside air. These young men, who could easily climb five floors to deliver a telegram, were in general very well received and one only had to slip a large tip into their hands to discreetly let them know that an additional service was expected of them."[69] We may therefore safely presume that Charlus's reference to a nice delivery cyclist is an attempt to arouse Jupien's jealousy. In *The Captive* a young dairywoman's offhand reference to her plans to go cycling that afternoon acts as a trigger for the narrator's fit of jealously about Albertine's desire for women. Upon the mention of cycling, he suddenly catches sight of a newspaper advertisement that informs him that the actress Léa (known to be queer) is performing at the play that Albertine has gone to see that morning.[70] In the panic that follows this discovery, the narrator sends his servant to retrieve her from the theater, and a bicycle once again plays a role in carrying a message from Albertine to her jealous lover: "I am on my way, though slower than this cyclist whose bike I would gladly take so I could be at your side sooner."[71] Although in this second instance the cyclist is carrying an apparently devoted message, the context of the bicycle's two appearances here—framing the jealous outburst— reveals its symbolic role as a vehicle for the expression of Albertine's unutterable sexuality. It is significant that while Albertine pedaled freely to see women in Balbec, she cannot, in her performed role of a bourgeois heterosexual woman in Paris, ride a bicycle back to her lover's house and is instead confined to a carriage.

The narrator appears to be appalled by Albertine's queer desire. However, it is thanks to his recognition of the slippage between queer and straight relationships that the artist comes to an appreciation of the variegated continuums that exist in human experience and that are reflected in art. The fluctuating spectrum of sexuality is clearly evoked in the scene where the narrator recounts Charlus's discovery of the actress Léa's sexually explicit letter to his lover, Morel. This letter undermines Charlus's preconceptions on strictly defined sexualities, as he realizes that his potential rivals for Morel's love include "not just those he had thought, but an entire, huge part of the planet, made up of women as well as men, of men who loved not only men but also women."[72] In this way, Charlus comes face-to-face with "the sudden insufficiency of a definition" when it comes to attempting to characterize sexuality or indeed any aspect of human nature.[73] Attending Madame Verdurin's salon, the narrator is racked by jealousy over Albertine's potential desire for Mademoiselle Vinteuil's lover, the woman who has brought to life the unfinished last work of the great composer Vinteuil. As the narrator is transported by the septet he is hearing for the first time performed by the violinist Morel, Charlus's lover and protégé, he gains a crucial insight: it is thanks to two queer relationships, characterized as "impure elements," that this major work has at last seen the light of day.[74]

Death of a Cyclist

Albertine is ultimately too radical for the society in which she lives. Indeed, the second time the narrator catches sight of her at the seaside, it is as she is being marched home by her English governess, "her head bent like an animal being made to go back into the stable against its will."[75] It is only thanks to her trademark machine ("She was pushing the same bicycle") that the narrator is able to recognize the independent young woman he beheld on the beach, now under the yoke of "an authoritarian person."[76] This scene prefigures the narrator's own sequestration of Albertine in his Paris home in *The Captive*. It is the narrator, as a representative of the conservative bourgeois class the young woman is challenging, who is responsible for the tragic transformation of his lover. He himself notes the striking contrast between "this Albertine shut up in my house" and the young woman whom "everybody used to follow, whom I had such difficulty catching up on, flying by on her bicycle."[77] In Judith Butler's terms, he actively encourages her, once under his roof, to perform "proper" femininity—that is, to dress and behave in the manner expected of well-to-do young women.[78] Rejecting her bloomers of old, he goes to great lengths and expense to acquire fashionable new dresses for Albertine. He seeks very precise advice from his aristocrat neighbor, the duchesse de Guermantes, on the most appropriate styles and materials in which to clothe his captive.[79]

Albertine's new status as a "domesticated wild animal" is brought vividly to life in a scene in the narrator's bedroom where, asked to play the pianola, the movements of her limbs recall those that previously she had employed to ride her bicycle.[80] The pianola is described as "a magic scientific lantern," whose music, like the bicycle, allows its listeners to be transported in space and time.[81] This instrument, however, is firstly a symbol of her sequestration. Her legs, which had "turned the pedals of a bicycle all through her adolescence," now "moved up and down in turn on those of the pianola."[82] Examining her hands, the narrator is once again reminded of a cyclist's pose: "Her fingers, which had previously been familiar with handlebars, now lay on the *keys* like the fingers of a Saint Cecilia."[83] The narrator and the society in which he lives have broken this once vigorously independent cyclist. She has become an incarnation of the virgin patron saint of music, constrained to perform and to conform to Christian, bourgeois norms.

On the final page of *The Captive*, the narrator discovers Albertine has disappeared. His desperate attempts to win her back at the start of the sixth volume, *The Fugitive*, are in vain, as she is soon thrown from a horse and dies. Some critics have pointed out that this death mirrors that of Alfred Agostinelli, Proust's driver and secretary, who died in a plane crash in 1914.[84] It is significant that it is a horse and not a modern vehicle, such as a bicycle, a car, or a plane, that is to blame for Albertine's death. A symbol of the old world, of both the aristocracy and the wealthy and aspiring bourgeoisie, the horse comes to deal the coup de grâce (after the blows dealt by the narrator himself) to this radical new cyclist who dared to challenge distinctions of gender, sexuality, and class. Yet the society that destroys her will itself perish in the trenches of the First World War, and Albertine's challenge will not be forgotten in the postwar reexploration of identities she helped pioneer.

Conclusion

In turn-of-the-century France, the bicycle—and more specifically the female cyclist—was intimately tied to contemporary debates. Cycling was attacked and praised with equal fervor and held up alternately as a symbol of social progress or decay. Just as a spinning bicycle wheel gives the illusion of remaining static, radical change was occurring beneath a veneer of stasis in France during the Belle Époque. In Proust's evocation of a lost world, the bicycle proves to be an extremely productive metaphor, not only thanks to its incarnation of the conflicting forces shaping modernity, but also because of the way in which it reflects fragmentary perception and evokes the fluctuating nature of desire. For Proust's contemporary Leblanc, the bicycle had a "double destiny," uniting in a single object opposed elements such as the exact dimensions of the human body and the infinite sensations of speed and liberty.[85] It is an invention that brings together opposed poles in the perfect machine, evoking "extreme harmony and grace made from strength and lightness."[86] Poised between two centuries, the bicycle allows us to conceptualize the "double diversity"[87] of an era on the brink of extinction.

Notes

1. On the history of bicycling in turn-of-the-century France, see Eugen Weber, *France, fin de siècle* (Cambridge MA: Harvard University Press, 1986), 195–212; Ronald Hubscher, ed., *L'histoire en mouvements: Le sport dans la société française (XIXe–XXe)* (Paris: Armand Colin, 1992).
2. See Marie-Agnès Barathieu, *Les mobiles de Marcel Proust: Une sémantique du déplacement* (Villeneuve-d'Ascq, France: Presses Universitaires du Sep-

tentrion, 2002); Anne-Marie Clais, "Portrait de femmes en cyclistes ou l'invention du féminin pluriel," *Cahiers de Médiologie*, no. 5 (1998): 69–79; Siân Reynolds, "Albertine's Bicycle; or, Women and French Identity during the Belle Epoque," *Literature and History* 10, no. 1 (2001): 28–41.

3. Marcel Proust, *À la recherche du temps perdu*, ed. Jean-Yves Tadié, vol. 2, *À l'ombre de jeunes filles en fleurs (II)*, *Le côté de Guermantes* (Paris: Bibliothèque de la Pléiade, 1988), 164. Unless otherwise noted, all French translations are my own.

4. See Pierre Thiesset and Quentin Thomasset, eds., *Les bienfaits de la vélocipédie* (Paris: Pas de côté, 2013).

5. Weber, *France, fin de siècle*, 195–97.

6. Weber, *France, fin de siècle*, 200.

7. Hartmut Rosa, *Accélération: Une critique sociale du temps*, trans. Didier Renault (Paris: Découverte, 2010), 58.

8. Weber, *France, fin de siècle*, 2.

9. Ivan Illich, *Energy and Equity*, in *Toward a History of Needs* (New York: Pantheon, 1978), Ivan Illich Archive, last modified July 15, 1995, http://www.ecotopia.com/webpress/energyEquity/.

10. The automobile and the airplane also feature in *À la recherche*. See Barathieu, *Les mobiles*, for an extended discussion of their role.

11. Christopher Thompson and Fiona Ratkoff, "Un troisième sexe? Les bourgeois et la bicyclette dans la France fin de siècle," *Le Mouvement Social*, no. 192 (2000): 12.

12. Reynolds, "Albertine's Bicycle," 31.

13. Karl Marx and Friedrich Engels, *Writings on the Paris Commune*, ed. Hal Draper (New York: Monthly Review Press, 1971).

14. Ludovic O'Followell, *Bicyclettes et organes génitaux* (Paris: J.-B. Baillière et fils, 1900), 63–64.

15. Thompson and Ratkoff, "Un troisième sexe?" 13.

16. Daniel Pick, *Faces of Degeneration: A European Disorder, c. 1848–1918* (Cambridge: Cambridge University Press, 1989), 37–59; Christopher Thompson, "Regeneration, *Dégénérescence*, and the Medical Debate about Bicycling in Fin-de-Siècle France," in *Sport et santé dans l'histoire*, ed. Thierry Terret (Sankt Augustin, Germany: Academia Verlag, 1999), 339–46.

17. "s'est focalisée sur la femme cyclist"; Thompson and Ratkoff, "Un troisième sexe?" 10.

18. "Une de ces inconnues poussait devant elle, de la main, sa bicyclette"; Proust, *À la recherche*, 2:146.

19. "pour constituer un métalangage autour et à partir de la bicyclette"; Barathieu, *Les mobiles*, 174.

20. "peu harmonieuses"; "bande de mouettes"; "une tenue spéciale"; Proust, *À la recherche*, 2:146–47.

21. "beaux corps aux belles jambes, aux belles hanches, aux visages sains et repo-sés, avec un air d'agilité et de ruse"; Proust, *À la recherche*, 2:149.

22. "vieillard épouvanté"; Proust, *À la recherche*, 2:150. See Thiesset and Thomas-set, *Les bienfaits*, 161–65, for some contemporary portraits of and reactions to vélocipédards.

23. "des termes d'argot si voyous et criés si fort … (parmi lesquelles je distinguai cependant la phrase fâcheuse de 'vivre sa vie')"; Proust, *À la recherche*, 2:151.

24. "je conclus plutôt que toutes ces filles appartenaient à la population qui fréquente les vélodromes, et devaient être les très jeunes maîtresses de cou-reurs cyclistes"; Proust, *À la recherche*, 2:151. Thompson ("Un troisième sexe?" 32) and Weber (*France, fin de siècle*, 200) both point out that cycling clubs and velodrome racing were increasingly the reserve of the working classes in the 1890s.

25. "une petite bourgeoisie fort riche, du monde de l'industrie et des affaires"; Proust, *À la recherche*, 2:200.

26. "la jeune fille à la bicyclette"; Proust, *À la recherche*, 2:186.

27. Reynolds, "Albertine's Bicycle," 36.

28. "la jeune fille à bicyclette est une force qui va, et qui ne bouscule pas seule-ment des estivants en promenade, mais des barrières sociales, des codes mon-dains, des rapports générationnels"; Françoise Gaillard, "À l'ombre de jeunes filles en vélo ou l'invention de la jeunesse," *Cahiers de Médiologie*, no. 5 (1998): 84.

29. "se font un espace social en tant que filles en en tant que jeunes"; Gaillard, "À l'ombre de jeunes filles en vélo," 84.

30. "La bicyclette, *c'est l'avenement de la femme aux exercices du corps*; et la pra-tique des exercices du corps pour la femme, c'est pour l'avenir la regen-eration de la part de la nation appelée fatalement à dégénérer"; Juste Lucas-Championniere, *La bicyclette* (Paris: Léon Chailley, 1894), 47, my emphasis.

31. See Corry Cropper's essay in this collection for more on Alfred Jarry.

32. Proust, *À la recherche*, 2:231.

33. Proust, *À la recherche*, 2:251.

34. For more on this debate, see Thompson, "Medical Debate about Bicycling in Fin-de-Siècle France."

35. "fille de ferme … fille de boutiquier"; "élégante demoiselle"; Proust, *À la recherche*, 2:71.

36. "Létiquette de cycliste est un moyen pratique de la différencier des autres, et en même temps, cette désignation toute métonymique confirme l'élément car-actéristique distingué par le dynamique du texte"; Barathieu, *Les mobiles*, 126.

37. "des erreurs d'optique"; "nous pensons le rattraper, il se déplace"; Proust, *À la recherche*, 2:229.

38. In addition to impressionist painting, the fragmentary representation of bicycles, cars, and machines also recalls the work of futurist artists such as Natalia Goncharova.

39. "robe de soie"; "médiocre et touchante"; "bacchante à bicyclette"; Proust, *À la recherche*, 2:228.

40. "un être de fuite"; "filant sur sa bicyclette"; Marcel Proust, *À la recherche du temps perdu*, ed. Jean-Yves Tadié, vol. 3, *Sodome et Gomorrhe, La prisonnière* (Paris: Bibliothèque de la Pléiade Gallimard, 1988), 600, 576.

41. "trois jeunes filles étaient assises à côté de l'arc immense de leurs bicyclettes posées à côté d'elles, comme trois immortelles accoudées au nuage ou au coursier fabuleux sur lesquels elles accomplissent leurs voyages mythologiques"; Proust, *À la recherche*, 3:675.

42. "Déesses"; Proust, *À la recherche*, 3:675.

43. "les similitudes même du désir et du voyage"; Proust, *À la recherche*, 3:677.

44. "Plus loin une autre fillette était agenouillée près de sa bicyclette qu'elle arrangeait. Une fois la réparation faite, la jeune coureuse monta sur sa bicyclette, mais sans l'enfourcher comme eût fait un homme. Pendant un instant la bicyclette tangua, et le jeune corps semblait s'être accru d'une voile, d'une aile immense; et bientôt nous vîmes s'éloigner à toute vitesse la jeune créature mi-humaine, mi-ailée, ange ou péri, poursuivant son voyage"; Proust, *À la recherche*, 3:677–78.

45. See Nadine Besse and André Vant, "A New View of Late 19th Century Cycle Publicity Posters," in *Cycle History 5: Proceedings of the 5th International Cycle History Conference*, ed. Rob Van der Plas (San Francisco: Cycle Publishing, 1994).

46. "sincerité"; Maurice Leblanc, *Voici des ailes* (Vierzon, France: Pas de côté, 2012), 12.

47. Rosemary Lloyd, "Reinventing Pegasus: Bicycles and the Fin-de-Siècle Imagination," *Journal of the Society of Dix-Neuviémistes* 4 (2005): 56.

48. Michel Foucault, *The History of Sexuality*, vol. 1, *An Introduction*, trans. Robert Hurley (New York: Vintage, 1980).

49. There are also several informal words for the bicycle, including *bécane* (feminine), *biclou* (masculine), and *petite reine* (feminine). See Odon Vallet, "Vélo, bicyclette, histoire des mots," *Cahiers de Médiologie*, no. 5 (1998): 15–18, for an etymological consideration of the various words for bicycle; and Philippe Delerm, *La première gorgée de bière et autres plaisirs minuscules* (Paris: Gallimard, 1997), 88–89, for a philosophical reflection on the difference between *bicyclette* and *vélo*.

50. Thiesset and Thomasset, *Les bienfaits*, 110, 114.

51. "la femme-vélo . . . qui paraît tenir à la fois du mâle et de la femelle sans sexe bien défini"; Thiesset and Thomasset, *Les bienfaits*, 105–6.

52. Judith Halberstam, *Female Masculinity* (Durham NC: Duke University Press, 1998), 75.

53. Halberstam, *Female Masculinity*, 48.

54. "une nouvelle variété de la beauté féminine"; Proust, *À la recherche*, 2:165; Halberstam, *Female Masculinity*, 1–43.

55. "qui poussait une bicyclette avec un dandinement des hanches"; Proust, *À la recherche*, 2:151.

56. "la jeune cycliste"; "sans s'arrêter"; Proust, *À la recherche*, 2:199–200.

57. "une jeune actrice d'autrefois en demi-travesti"; Proust, *À la recherche*, 2:204. The portrait is of Odette de Crécy, later to become Madame Swann, who is an object of the narrator's desire in the first part of *Within a Budding Grove*.

58. "le sexe avait l'air d'être sur le point d'avouer qu'il était celui d'une fille un peu garçonnière, s'évanouissait, et plus loin se retrouvait, suggérant plutôt l'idée d'un jeune efféminé vicieux et songeur, puis fuyant encore, restait insaisissable"; Proust, *À la recherche*, 2:205.

59. "une femme peu élégante"; Proust, *À la recherche*, 3:643.

60. "les chasseurs ailés, aux teintes changeantes, filaient vers les gares, au ras de leur bicyclette"; Proust, *À la recherche*, 3:644.

61. "penchée sur la roue mythologique de sa bicyclette, sanglée les jours de pluie sous la tunique guerrière de caoutchouc qui faisait bomber ses seins"; Marcel Proust, *À la recherche du temps perdu*, vol. 4, *Albertine disparue, Le temps retrouvé* (Paris: Bibliothèque de la Pléiade, 1989), 70.

62. It is interesting to note that in French *pédale* is not only part of a bicycle but also a slang term for a queer person.

63. Proust, *À la recherche*, 4:97.

64. "Les noms de ces stations . . . Albertine avait habité l'une, s'était promenée jusqu'à l'autre, avait pu aller souvent en bicyclette à la troisième"; Proust, *À la recherche*, 4:99–100.

65. "me racontait sans précision aucune, en de sortes de fausses confidences, des promenades en bicyclette qu'elle faisait à Balbec"; Proust, *À la recherche*, 3:886.

66. "déguisée en homme, histoire de rigoler plutôt"; Proust, *À la recherche*, 3:878, 838.

67. Proust, *À la recherche*, 3:592, 878.

68. "un cycliste très gentil"; Proust, *À la recherche*, 3:11.

69. "Une spécialité nouvelle est apparue, grâce aux progrès de la technique, spécialité particulièrement appréciée des messieurs d'un certain âge: les petits télégraphistes. La pratique de la bicyclette leur donne du muscle, le vent de la course de la fraîcheur. Ces tout jeunes gens, qui n'hésitent pas à monter cinq étages pour délivrer un 'petit bleu,' sont en général bien reçus et le seul fait de leur glisser dans la main un gros pourboire est une façon discrète de leur faire comprendre que l'on attend d'eux un service supplémentaire"; Ghislain de Diesbach, *Proust* (Paris: Editions Perrin, 1991), 418.

70. Proust, *À la recherche*, 3:651.

71. "j'arrive moins vite que ce cycliste dont je voudrais bien prendre la bécane pour être plus tôt près de vous"; Proust, *À la recherche*, 3:663.

72. "pas seulement ceux qu'il avait crus, mais toute une immense partie de la planète, composée aussi bien de femmes que d'hommes, d'hommes aimant non seulement les hommes mais les femmes"; Proust, *À la recherche*, 3:720–21.

73. "l'insuffisance soudaine d'une définition"; Proust, *À la recherche*, 3:721.

74. "des éléments impurs"; Proust, *À la recherche*, 3:769.

75. "tête basse comme un animal qu'on fait rentrer malgré lui dans l'étable"; Proust, *À la recherche*, 2:185.

76. "elle poussait une bicyclette pareille"; "une personne autoritaire"; Proust, *À la recherche*, 2:185.

77. "cette Albertine cloîtrée dans ma maison"; "jadis tout le monde suivait, que j'avais tant de peine à rattraper, filant sur sa bicyclette"; Proust, *À la recherche*, 3:576.

78. Judith Butler, "Performative Acts and Gender Constitution: An Essay in Phenomenology and Feminist Theory," *Theatre Journal* 40, no. 4 (1988): 519–31.

79. Proust, *À la recherche*, 3:541.

80. "bête sauvage domestiquée"; Proust, *À la recherche*, 3:884.

81. "une laterne magique scientifique"; Proust, *À la recherche*, 3:883.

82. "manoeuvré pendant toute son adolescence les pédales d'une bicyclette"; "montaient et descendaient tour à tour sur celles du pianola"; Proust, *À la recherche*, 3:884.

83. "Ses doigts, jadis familiers du guidon, se posaient maintenant sur les *touches* comme ceux d'une sainte Cécile"; Proust, *À la recherche*, 3:884, original emphasis.

84. Barathieu, *Les mobiles*, 192.

85. "double déstinée"; Leblanc, *Voici des ailes*, 8.

86. "une harmonie extrême, une grâce faite de force et de légèrté"; Leblanc, *Voici des ailes*, 8.

87. "diversité double"; Proust, *À la recherche*, 2:665.

7 The Existential Cyclist

Bicycles and Personal Responsibility in
Simone de Beauvoir's *The Blood of Others*

NANCI J. ADLER

Simone de Beauvoir is widely recognized as an author, philosopher, and feminist; but she was also a wildly enthusiastic bicyclist. Forbidden to ride a bike as a child, she learned how to cycle as an adult, and it quickly became a passion. In a 1976 interview with John Gerassi, Beauvoir discussed apprehensions about aging, looked back at her life, and mused, "I know today that I shall never be able to go wandering through the hills on foot, that I shall never again ride a bicycle, that I shall never again have relations with a man."[1] This statement reveals the level of importance cycling had for her. Like other author-cyclists, Beauvoir employed bicycles in fiction as both literal means of transportation and as literary symbols. In her early novel of personal existential challenges, *The Blood of Others* (*Le sang des autres*, 1945), her characters ride bicycles throughout Nazi-occupied Paris; but more significantly, Beauvoir uses a single bicycle as a symbol of the existential transformation of protagonist Hélène Bertrand. This existential transformation, one defined by Hélène learning to examine her life and take full responsibility for her decisions and actions, is the fundamental theme of the work.

Today, the streets of Paris teem with automobiles, motorcycles, taxis, buses, and bicycles. It is a pedestrian-friendly city in which these multiple modes of transportation, as well as the famed art nouveau–styled underground Métro system, are readily embraced. Like many Western cities, these Parisian streets were first traversed for centuries by foot or by horse.[2] But the refinement of the bicycle in the nineteenth century dramatically changed the street environment. By the 1890s, dirt roads became busy with bicycles, which were equally fashionable and practical, for purposes of both leisure and commerce. This period of the bicycle's lofty stature as the de rigueur method of personal transport was short lived, however. With the invention and proliferation of the automobile in the early twentieth century, motorized vehicles took over the road, and infrastructure and usage became focused on motorized transport.[3]

The Parisian progression of urban transportation from foot to horse to bicycle and then to automobiles (a progression typical of Western cities) was interrupted briefly yet notably during a somber episode: the Nazi occupation of the city. World War II, and its accompanying fuel and material shortages, created a resurgence of bicycle use in much of Europe and even North America but especially in Paris.[4] Out of necessity, Parisian civilians took to their bicycles, and bicycles regained their position as an important transportation option as well as a means of escape—literally and figuratively—from physical danger and emotional troubles.[5]

It was in this historical setting of occupied Paris that Simone de Beauvoir set her third published work, *The Blood of Others*. Although Beauvoir is perhaps best known for *The Second Sex* (*Le deuxième sexe*), her 1949 nonfiction work of feminist philosophy, she published numerous novels over a half century. *The Blood of Others* integrates Beauvoir's existentialist philosophy in its emphasis on personal action and responsibility. The novel follows several characters in their twenties and thirties as they struggle with personal and moral decisions. Terry Keefe maintains that *The Blood of Others* is Beauvoir's most explicitly moral novel, to the extent that it may be viewed as "over-stuffed with moral matter" of life choices regarding relationships, the use of people as the means to an end, the significance of art, dilemmas of violence, and the possibility of moral abstention.[6] Told through a series of nonsequential flashbacks framed with opening and closing scenes at Hélène's deathbed, the novel centers on protagonists Jean Blomart and Hélène Bertrand as they wrestle with the constraints of their upbringings and with decisions regarding careers, lovers, politics, and the Nazi occupation. Beauvoir gestures toward the novel's existential agenda of examining individual responsibility with her book's epigraph quoting the sagacious Father Zossima from Dostoyevsky's *The Brothers Karamazov*, who espouses the philosophy "each of us is responsible for everything and to every human being."[7]

Throughout its pages, *The Blood of Others* depicts the wartime resurgence of bicycle use by civilians; however, a bicycle is not just a means of transportation for Hélène but a symbol of her transformation.[8] The bicycle as symbol is not an afterthought in the work. For example, scenes in the second chapter of the novel focus exclusively on three major characters—Hélène; Hélène's fiancé, Paul; and Jean Blomart—and their interactions with a sparkling pale-blue bicycle, providing a direct material link between her relationship with the bicycle and her relationships with the two men and their influence on her life.[9] Hélène's actions relating to this beautiful bicycle also reveal her childlike selfishness and illustrate her lack of self-understanding and lack of purpose in her life. While some bicycles in the novel are used for quotidian transport, it is the single, shiny, pale-blue bicycle that represents Hélène's existential transformation. When the bicycle eventually fades and changes from an object of beauty into a utilitarian vehicle, Hélène likewise leaves her frivolous self behind and finds her own utility and purpose.

Just as an individual may value a bicycle for either its beauty or its usefulness, cultural trends similarly reveal disparate reasons for appreciating bicycles. During the bicycle boom of the 1890s, brought on by the invention of the easily mastered safety bicycle, bicycles were both fashion statements and practical vehicles.[10] During this time, they were not children's toys but innovative machines used by adults. This distinction is evident in contemporary literature, in which bicycles are commonly referred to as "machines." Arthur Conan Doyle, H. G. Wells, and Émile Zola were, like Beauvoir, all bicycle enthusiasts as well as authors, and they often refer to bicycles as machines in their turn-of-the-century novels and short stories. The word "machine" stresses the bicycle's value as a tool of progress and of power.[11] In *The Blood of Others*, set a half century after the invention of the safety bicycle, bicycles return to a position of power as an effective machine for civilians and the French Resistance, which is significant as it relates to the bicycle's use as a transformational symbol. For wartime civilians, cycling was a matter of necessity. Under Nazi occupation during World War II, the Paris street scene changed radically. According to Julian Jackson, in *France: The Dark Years, 1940–1944*, these years were the new "heyday of the bicycle" due to fuel shortages.[12] With little fuel available to civilians, motorized transport was unreliable. Scenes in *The Blood of Others* reflect this reality—civilians sit by the road with empty petrol cans and seek news of available fuel supplies; Parisians flee the Nazi invasion in cars, carts, and bicycles; civilians use bicycles for routine travel; and resistance fighters glide quietly through the dark streets of Paris on bicycle to throw homemade bombs into Nazi-occupied buildings.[13] During the war, the bicycle is restored to its preautomobile status as a purposeful, useful machine.

Beauvoir's own appreciation of bicycles, her relationship with cycling, and her use of bicycles in *The Blood of Others* are informed by the historical context of cycling as it evolved during her lifetime. Beauvoir was born in 1908, after the fin de siècle bicycle boom, just as the bicycle's glory days were cut short by the introduction of the automobile. Automobiles quickly made bicycles less important as transportation and diminished their status as a fashion statement. According to David V. Herlihy, the advent of the automobile relegated the bicycle to the status of a toy or a "poor man's carriage."[14] Although bicycles continued to be used by some as utilitarian vehicles or for exercise, they were no longer emblems of fashion or emancipation.[15] By the early twentieth century, social status and progressive thinking were denoted not by bicycles but by the newly invented automobile.[16]

It is noteworthy that bicycles were absent from Beauvoir's childhood. For her family, bicycles were neither a necessity nor a fashion statement. Beauvoir's parents raised her in a strict, protected environment. According to Deidre Bair, young Beauvoir was not permitted experiences that encouraged pleasurable sensations, because her mother felt that sensual experiences could lead to sexual feelings, something that the mother discouraged. For this reason, Beauvoir was forbidden to ride a bicycle or to visit a public beach or swimming pool.[17] It is possible that the fact she was prohibited from riding a bike as a child increased the joy that Beauvoir experienced when she cycled as an adult. The freedoms and pleasures granted by bicycles to Beauvoir in defiance of her parents parallel the freedoms bestowed on progressive women of the 1890s who dared to flout convention by donning bloomers, straddling a bicycle seat, and riding unchaperoned in the streets.[18] With the advent of war, the adult Beauvoir took to cycling enthusiastically, learning to ride in 1940 at the age of thirty-two and riding for daily transportation as well as for recreation, including several weeklong cycling vacations. Beauvoir reported that cycling improved her state of mind and provided a "delicious sense of freedom."[19] Her letters to Jean-Paul Sartre written in the summer of 1940 exude enthusiasm for her newfound joy, as she describes her adventures in learning to ride and the thrill of mastering the bicycle, even describing herself cycling like a "lusty wench."[20] Beauvoir's mother must have been appalled.

In *The Blood of Others*, Hélène Bertrand's first revealing encounter with a bicycle occurs when she is a young adult, in a scene set in Paris in 1934 before the start of World War II. Young Hélène lives in a sheltered world that recalls Beauvoir's own childhood, but Hélène's constraints are created not by her parents but by her own unwillingness and inability to engage in the adult world of personal responsibility and accountability. Hélène's life revolves around her family's sweetshop, where she decorates and sells chocolates, and around her boyfriend of three years, Paul. Hélène does not feel passionately about Paul; she simply needs a boyfriend and wants him to stand beside her "nice, and snug and faithful."[21] She is bored with her life yet lacks ambition or insight to make meaningful changes. "Her boredom," we are told, "sour and insipid as curdled milk, was part and parcel of her own flesh."[22]

When Hélène observes a beautiful new bicycle through the sweetshop window, she is captivated by its sleek elegance and immediately wishes it were hers. She covets the bicycle not for its usefulness but for its sparkling handlebars, pale-blue frame, beautiful yellow seat, and slender profile.[23] Thinking of it as a "splendid prize," she never considers purchasing a similar bicycle or asking permission to borrow it; instead, her childish impulse is to steal it, simply because she wants it "and must have it."[24] This impulsive, self-indulgent behavior defines young Hélène. She is unable to see the value of her life in the same way she is unable to recognize the value or purpose of a bicycle and admires one only for its superficial beauty. It is only after her existential transformation, years later, with her progression into adulthood, that she rides a bicycle with purposefulness, at which point the outward appearance of the bicycle no longer matters to her.

Young Hélène's lack of existential purpose is exemplified by her decision to live in a childlike state similar to that which Beauvoir describes in her work *The Ethics of Ambiguity* (*Pour une morale de l'ambiguité*, 1947). The immature Hélène has yet to understand her role in the world and chooses to live as a child, a condition that Beauvoir describes as a life of submission to an external authority, a submission that absolves one from responsibility. Beauvoir wrote in *The Ethics of Ambiguity* that a child can choose to be recalcitrant and lazy because his "whims and faults concern only him. They do not weigh upon the earth."[25] The child lives in a state of security because she is insignificant and can act with impunity because her actions engage nothing. This is the immature Hélène before her existential transformation—a person of childish and selfish impulses willing to steal a pretty bicycle without thinking about the consequences of her actions and simply because she wants it.

Beauvoir's existentialist philosophy is woven throughout the work, as Hélène and her friends Jean, Paul, Denise, Jacques, and Marcel struggle with questions about the meaning, purpose, and value of life. Beauvoir herself declared that this novel was written during her literary "moral period" brought on by the war, during which she personally came to understand human solidarity and personal responsibility; and she concluded that "it was possible to accept death in order that life might keep its meaning."[26] Beauvoir's existential philosophy centers both on an individual's freedom of choice and personal responsibility and on the necessity of engaging with the world. Eleanore Holveck contends that the experiences of Hélène express Beauvoir's philosophical ideas, specifically that there are no absolute values, that actions form values, and that the freedom to act is authentic only when one accepts full responsibility for one's own actions, because accepting responsibility establishes one's freedom.[27] An individual's reason for existence is created by his or her existence; actions therefore both create and define one's purpose in life.[28] This concept that one's actions (or inactions) create the essence of a person is a critical element of Beauvoir's philosophy and permeates *The Blood of Others*. Hélène's existential transformation will occur only when she is willing to engage in the world, act freely, and take responsibility for her actions.

This existential viewpoint of the necessity of action is illustrated in an early scene in which a character, Jacques, decides to join and become an active member of the Communist Party. Young Jacques, struggling with his life path, states, "Suddenly I felt that I could no longer bear to be alive, unless my life were to serve some purpose."[29] From an existential perspective, finding and acting on a purpose creates meaning for his life. Jean Blomart has already found his purpose, first as a Communist and then as a resistance fighter, although he struggles with his position of protection and privilege arising from his family's status and wealth. He is also troubled by his responsibility for shedding the blood of other resistance fighters (hence the title of the novel) in his role as a leader. While arguing that he and his colleagues must perform public acts of violence in the fight against the Nazis, his comment is quintessentially existential: "We only exist if we act."[30] But the young Hélène struggles with her place in the world as a shopgirl without aspirations and wonders: "Why does one live at all?"[31] Hélène has yet to find a purpose for her life and is as yet unable to connect her own actions (or inactions) with her lack of purpose.

In the prewar setting, Hélène is absorbed in her own needs and sulks when her desires are not met. Carolle Gagnon argues that Beauvoir's use of food throughout the work, specifically Hélène's early love of chocolate and sweets and her subsequent rejection of them, symbolizes Hélène's transformation from child to purposeful adult and Nazi resister, but the bicycle is an equally significant symbol of this transformation.[32] As a young woman, Hélène responds to an inquiry about what she wants in life with "I like chocolate and beautiful bicycles."[33] Later, as a resistance leader, Jean Blomart agonizes over Hélène's suffering after an abortion and thinks, "My poor child, my poor little child. How young she was! She liked chocolate and bicycles and went forward into life with the boldness of a child."[34] Hélène's desires are the longings of a juvenile who needs protection and lacks self-knowledge or purpose. At this point in her life, Hélène perceives bicycles as extravagant objects, something that she wants merely because they are pretty and she thinks she should possess one. Like her, a bicycle at this point in the novel is an attractive decoration without utilitarian purpose.

The immature Hélène does not perceive the bicycle as the useful machine of commerce and social change that it was characterized as a half century earlier. Instead, her early relationship to bicycles echoes general perceptions of the bicycle during the 1920s and 1930s. According to bicycle historian Pryor Dodge, the bicycle in France during the late 1930s symbolized the leisure and newly created era of paid holidays; it was a recreational toy.[35] Hélène's initial desire for a bicycle in this prewar scene is simply a whim; she wants a bicycle for its beauty and because it symbolizes material wealth and leisure. The chapter's opening sentences describe her intense desire for the machine sitting unattended near her shop: "The bicycle was still there, brand new, with its pale-blue frame and its plated handlebars which sparkled against the dull stone of the wall. It was so lissome, so slender, that even when not in use it seemed to cut through the air. Hélène had never seen such an elegant bicycle. 'I'll repaint it dark green, it'll be even more beautiful,' she thought."[36]

She admires it and decides, like a spoiled child, that she simply must have it. Its importance to Hélène is exaggerated far beyond its actual value, as if it could provide the purpose or meaning that she lacks in her life. Her desire for the bicycle is so intense that her lips and hands tremble as she contemplates theft.[37] She wonders whether she can steal the bicycle but is uncertain of her resolve: "'Have I become such a coward?' How she wanted that bicycle! It had become a symbol of her earthy lot, and if she did not find out a way of making it hers, all hope was lost."[38] Touching the handlebars and admiring it with increasing desire, she is prevented from acting by telling herself that she would be easily recognized in her neighborhood as the bicycle thief and that it would simply be taken from her and returned to the owner.

Afraid to commit the actual theft herself (yet another example of her inability to take responsibility for her choices), she contrives to have a new acquaintance, Jean Blomart, a friend of her fiancé's and a Communist, steal it for her later that evening. Hélène lies to Jean, telling him that the bicycle is hers, and asks him to retrieve it from the courtyard, which he does. Hélène feels momentarily satisfied and rejoices: "'My bicycle, it is really mine! By and by I'll go through the streets, I'll go right across Paris. I'm sure it runs perfectly.' It seemed to her that her whole life was transfigured."[39] But the joy derived by the theft and acquisition of the bicycle, the satisfaction of her childish desire, is short lived. Paul is angry and uncomfortable with Hélène's behavior and with her trickery. As the three start to discuss the theft in terms of private property and the furthering of personal interest, Hélène notices Jean's reluctance to engage her in the conversation, and she realizes that he "took her for a child."[40] She is insulted further when she recognizes that Jean's indulgence for the escapade is due to the fact that he considered it to be a childish prank. Hélène's actions and the reaction of those around her emphasize her self-imposed position as a child, unwilling to shoulder adult responsibilities. Exasperated by their conversation that touches on politics and philosophy, Hélène accuses the two men of "strutting about self-importantly" as if they held the fate of mankind in their hands. She is unable to fathom their concern for the world at large, the world beyond her narrow, personal sphere, and claims she can care only for those she personally knows.[41] Leaving the two men, she storms away in a fury on the stolen bicycle. For the immature Hélène, the bicycle provides a means of retreat from an uncomfortable situation, and she avoids having to further examine or defend her self-centered perception of the world.

A few hours later that same evening, her attitude toward the bicycle has completely changed. The night air is cold, and riding the bicycle feels unpleasant to her. Stopping at a café and parking the bicycle, she feels burdened by it and then bored by its faithful obedience when she returns to it after having a drink: "She looked at the bicycle in disgust: just where she had left it, like a patient and unwelcome dog."[42] The momentary passion of heartfelt desire quickly faded. Alone, Hélène despairs as she wonders, "Why should I be here? I, who am I?"[43] Even when riding the bicycle or while walking, she recognizes that she is aimless. The theft of the bicycle and its hasty rejection emphasizes both her childish demeanor and her lack of commitment or purpose. Although the bicycle provides a means of moving ahead physically, there is no goal; and likewise, Hélène is not yet able to progress emotionally or philosophically. Her existential plight overwhelms her, but she begins to wonder if Jean might prove to be a source of understanding.

As Europe marches toward war, Hélène and Paul end their engagement, and Hélène eventually becomes romantically attached to Jean, who is increasingly active in politics and as a trade union organizer. But Hélène remains emotionally and philosophically immature. She is described by Jean as an "aimless little girl" and by Paul as a "hysterical little girl."[44] Hélène and Jean argue about personal responsibility toward others; and though Hélène tries to persuade Jean that he is not responsible for everyone, her own lack of responsibility leads her to feelings of uselessness.[45] As her relationship with Jean grows, Hélène continues to question the purposelessness of her life, wondering whether having Jean is enough to fulfill her.[46]

After the Nazi invasion of Paris in 1940, Hélène and her contemporaries continue to struggle with their personal lives and must deal with the turmoil of war and political change. As the war progresses and Jean and Paul choose to fight the Nazis as members of the French military and later with the civilian resistance, Jean is continually conflicted by his bourgeois upbringing, his Communist ideals, his loathing of violence, and his role as a leader among resistance fighters. Paul is active in the resistance but is later captured and detained by the Nazis. Jean and Hélène break off their relationship after Hélène manages to have Jean reassigned to a safer military post in Paris and Jean is infuriated with her intervention. Both men, in any case, firmly believe that one's actions create one's essence, and their beliefs are evidenced by their actions against the Nazis. Jean believes that "we only exist if we act," while Paul asserts that the only form of resistance possible is deeds, not words.[47] Although conflicted about the use of violence, they believe they must act on behalf of others. Hélène, however, feels no responsibility toward the world at large or the French people. She even befriends a Nazi official, is seduced by the fine dinners and material goods he can provide, and contemplates leaving France and traveling to Germany with him. Her small sphere of personal comfort is still her greatest concern.

However, after having been continually exposed to the ideas of her more purposeful friends and parents, Hélène slowly begins to recognize the significance of her actions (and inactions) and begins to contemplate personal accountability. Although she has not yet committed herself to the resistance, her self-centered nature is challenged. The war not only changes Hélène's frivolous and thoughtless ways but also transforms the bicycle that had been an object of Hélène's childish desire only a few years before. Whereas it was once merely a fanciful indulgence, the bicycle becomes a useful tool to her during the occupation. For Hélène and the Parisian population at large, bicycles find renewed utility due to the scarcity of gasoline and automobile parts.[48] Both Hélène and the bicycle she once coveted have aged and become worn, but both have also become more valuable and substantial through the passage of time. When Hélène pedals her bicycle for her final meeting with Herr Bergmann, the Nazi officer she has befriended, the bicycle's durability symbolizes her own emerging inner strength and usefulness. Hélène reflects on the bicycle thusly as she rides it swiftly along the boulevard Saint-Michel: "It was dirty and rusty; the layers of blue and green paint were coming through the black varnish, but it was still a good machine."[49]

At this pivotal meeting with Herr Bergmann, Hélène's transformation is strengthened; with newfound self-understanding, she assesses her situation honestly and resolves to stay in Paris and cut her ties with the Nazis. Refusing chocolate from Herr Bergmann, she claims, "I loathe chocolate," and thereby rejects her childish self.[50] By declining the offer of chocolates, Hélène actively rejects Bergmann and the offers of material comfort that come with friendship with the Nazis. Hélène, however, does not reject her other childhood love: the bicycle. The worn and rusty bicycle has evolved much as Hélène has evolved. It is no longer a whimsical object; it is a useful machine. Hélène is on her way to becoming, like the worn but trustworthy bicycle she now rides out of necessity, part of the machinery of the resistance.

Hélène's sense of responsibility for others develops slowly during the occupation and is solidified when she is unable to escape disturbing encounters with the Nazis. In particular, Hélène witnesses a young Jewish girl, Ruth, being separated from her mother and detained by the Nazis for deportation. Hélène's slow maturation finally enables her to feel compassion for the child Ruth even though the child is not known to her personally. Hélène watches with despair as Ruth, screaming frantically, is torn from her mother. Standing nearby, Hélène "remained motionless like the others," aware that "her presence made no difference." But soon afterward, she bursts with understanding: "I was watching the March of History! It was my personal history. All that is happening to me."[51] Once able to care only about those close to her, without regard to a broader concept of humanity, Hélène expands her capacity for self-understanding, through her personal experiences in occupied Paris. With new insight, she begins to recognize that everything that transpires around her—regardless of how it affected her as an individual—is her personal history.

This realization rouses Hélène to act, and she rides her bicycle with a fresh sense of purpose. In one of the last flashbacks of the novel, Hélène visits her Jewish friend, Yvonne, who is hiding from the Nazis in a church. Hélène promises Yvonne that she will meet with and enlist the assistance of her former lover, the resistance leader Jean Blomart, to plan an escape route for her. After making her promises, Hélène mounts her bicycle to find Jean. This, Hélène's decisive moment of commitment to the resistance, occurs while on a bicycle, as she rides with newfound commitment and conviction.[52] Upon meeting Jean, she tells him not only that she wants to help Yvonne escape but that she also wants to work with his resistance group. Hélène implores, "I know you help people. I know you're doing something. Give me something to do!"[53] Hélène recognizes the need to act and, in an existential realization, knows that her actions will give meaning to her life.

Hélène's purposeful life is brief. Soon after joining the resistance, she dies of wounds suffered during a dangerous nighttime raid to free her former fiancé Paul from a detention camp. Even though the raid is conducted under Jean's leadership, he tries at the last minute to dissuade Hélène from going. But the transformed Hélène insists on making her own decisions and taking responsibility for them. According to Holveck, "Hélène has learned that acting freely in this world means taking responsibility for her past, her body, her situation. She makes it clear that she is not acting for Jean's sake. She chooses freely and accepts full responsibility."[54] Bicycles appear one last time in the narrative as one of the resistance fighters rides a bike as a signalman during this raid. Hélène's role in the mission is not as a cyclist but as an automobile driver.[55] Once Hélène finds a meaningful path for her life, the bicycle loses its symbolic function. Cars, in short, are now free to replace bikes in the novel. Contemplating her final act as a member of the resistance, Hélène knows that she has made her life meaningful and valuable: "Now she was no longer alone, no longer useless and lost under an empty sky."[56] The narrative ends where it began, with Hélène dying in a small room, under the care of Jean.

Simone de Beauvoir, a passionate cyclist herself, understood the power of bicycles. She integrated bicycles throughout *The Blood of Others* in ways that reflect Parisian life in the 1930s and 1940s and her personal experience of cycling in Nazi-occupied France. Resistance fighters indeed put bicycles to use in their efforts. Nathalie Sorokine, a close, longtime friend of Beauvoir's, rode through Paris flinging pamphlets from her bicycle basket in support of resistance efforts.[57] Many of Beauvoir's scenes in *The Blood of Others* reflect this historical reality. But the bicycle is also a symbol of the existential transformation of Hélène from a self-absorbed, childlike adult to an adult with a meaningful and purposeful life. The young Hélène has a selfish and whimsical desire for a pretty bicycle, which quickly bores her and is carelessly cast aside. Her early life, like her desire for the bicycle, is frivolous and lacks intent and commitment. Nearly a decade later, the mature Hélène rides a worn but reliable bicycle, a useful machine, when she commits to joining the Nazi resistance. By this act, Hélène resolves anxieties about her value as a person and creates a life, however brief, that provides her with both meaning and purpose.

Notes

1. Simone de Beauvoir, interview by John Gerassi, *Society*, January–February 1976, accessed with corrections by Andy Blunden online at "*The Second Sex* 25

Years Later," Marxists Internet Archive, February 2005, http://www.marxists .org/reference/subject/ethics/de-beauvoir/1976/interview.htm.

2. H. Sutherland Edwards, *Old and New Paris* (London: Cassell, 1894), 30.

3. David V. Herlihy, *Bicycle: The History* (New Haven CT: Yale University Press, 2004), 5, 251, 298; Andrew Ritchie, *King of the Road* (London: Wildwood House, 1975), 168, 174.

4. Julian Jackson, *France: The Dark Years, 1940–1944* (Oxford: Oxford University Press, 2001), 251; James Laux, *The European Automotive Industry* (New York: Twayne Publishers, 1992), 148.

5. Simone de Beauvoir, *Letters to Sartre*, trans. and ed. Quintin Hoare (New York: Arcade Publishing, 2012), 330, 340. Beauvoir herself found cycling in Paris to be "absolutely delightful" even while Nazis occupied the city and wrote that by learning to ride a bike, she had found a "new joy." For others, bicycles provided the means to flee invading and occupying troops. See, for example, Alan J. Levine, *Flight and Survival in World War II* (Westport CT: Greenwood Press, 2000), 5, 117; Rachel G. Fuchs, "Crossing Borders in Love, War and History: French Families during World War II," *Pacific Historical Review* 79, no. 1 (2010): 9.

6. Terry Keefe, "Literature and Existentialist Ethics in Simone de Beauvoir's 'Moral Period,'" in *The Ethics in Literature*, ed. Andrew Hadfield, Dominic Rainsford, and Tim Woods (Basingstoke, UK: Macmillan, 1998), 255.

7. Fyodor Dostoyevsky, *The Brothers Karamozov*, trans. Constance Garnett (New York: Lowell Press, 2009), 177, 318, 335.

8. Beauvoir is not unique as a novelist in her use of bicycles. Twentieth-century works of fiction that use bicycles in meaningful ways include Dorothy Richardson's *The Pilgrimage*, Ernest Hemingway's *The Sun Also Rises*, F. Scott Fizgerald's *Tender Is the Night*, Samuel Beckett's *Molloy*, Luigi Bartolini's *Bicycle Thieves*, Flann O'Brien's *The Third Policeman*, and Frank Stockton's *A Bicycle of Cathay*.

9. Margaret Burrell, "The Problem of Individual Responsibility in *Le sang des autres*," *New Zealand Journal of French Studies* 16, no. 2 (November 1995): 30. According to Burrell, in one scene, the intriguing Jean Blomart is represented by the bicycle that belongs to someone else. Hélène's fiancé, Paul, is represented by the bicycle after she comes to despise it, faithful and dull.

10. Ritchie, *King of the Road*, 160–62, 167–68. The term "safety bicycle" refers to the design of the modern bicycle, with two equivalent-sized wheels and a geared pedal-and-chain system, unlike the earlier high-wheeled bicycles that were difficult to mount and on which riders sat high off the ground. Herlihy, *Bicycle*, 235, 241.

11. Ritchie, *King of the Road*, 136–41; Herlihy, *Bicycle*, 258, 264.

12. Jackson, *France*, 251.

13. Simone de Beauvoir, *The Blood of Others*, trans. Yvonne Moyse and Roger Senhouse (London: Penguin Books, 1964), 163, 196, 199–201, 205–6, 208, 221–22. The scenes of fleeing Parisians reflect Beauvoir's personal experience.

14. Herlihy, *Bicycle*, 7–8.

15. Bicycling continued to appeal to athletes. The Tour de France was established in 1903 and continues to this day, interrupted only by two world wars.

16. Sidney H. Aronson, "The Sociology of the Bicycle," *Social Forces* 30, no. 3 (March 1952): 312; Herlihy, *Bicycle*, 343. European automobile giant Renault was established in 1899 and began manufacturing its own automobiles in 1903.

17. Deirdre Bair, *Simone de Beauvoir: A Biography* (New York: Touchstone, 1990), 85.

18. Aronson, "Sociology of the Bicycle," 308; David Rubinstein, "Cycling in the 1890s," *Victorian Studies* 21, no. 1 (Autumn 1977): 61, 66–68.

19. Beauvoir, *Letters to Sartre*, 312, 314, 328, 333, 340; Simone de Beauvoir, *The Prime of Life*, trans. Peter Green (Cleveland: World Publishing, 1962), 390; Bair, *Simone de Beauvoir*, 257, 265–66.

20. Beauvoir, *Letters to Sartre*, 312, 314, 328, 333, 339–40.

21. Beauvoir, *Blood of Others*, 86.

22. Beauvoir, *Blood of Others*, 43.

23. Beauvoir, *Blood of Others*, 36–37.

24. Beauvoir, *Blood of Others*, 37.

25. Simone de Beauvoir, *The Ethics of Ambiguity*, trans. Bernard Frechtmam (Secaucus NJ: Citadel Press, 1948), 35.

26. Beauvoir, *Prime of Life*, 547.

27. Eleanore Holveck, "*The Blood of Others*: A Novel Approach," *Hypatia* 14, no. 4 (Fall 1999): 4.

28. See part 2, "Personal Freedom and Others," in Beauvoir, *Ethics of Ambiguity*.

29. Beauvoir, *Blood of Others*, 29.

30. Beauvoir, *Blood of Others*, 189.

31. Beauvoir, *Blood of Others*, 71.

32. Carolle Gagnon, "Resistance and Rescue in Beauvoir's *The Blood of Others* and *The Mandarins*," *Semiotica* 172 (2008): 247.

33. Beauvoir, *Blood of Others*, 71.

34. Beauvoir, *Blood of Others*, 100.

35. Pryor Dodge, *The Bicycle* (New York: Flammarion, 1996), 178. Even in the mid-twentieth century, however, bicycles in Europe remained in use as practical transportation, more so than in the United States.

36. Beauvoir, *Blood of Others*, 36.

37. Beauvoir, *Blood of Others*, 37. Beauvoir's pupil and friend, Nathalie Sorokine, stole, repainted, and then sold bicycles to make money during the war.

According to Deirdre Bair, Beauvoir's fictional character Hélène is partly based on Sorokine. Bair, *Simone de Beauvoir*, 237.

38. Beauvoir, *Blood of Others*, 44.
39. Beauvoir, *Blood of Others*, 46.
40. Beauvoir, *Blood of Others*, 49.
41. Beauvoir, *Blood of Others*, 49–50.
42. Beauvoir, *Blood of Others*, 51–52.
43. Beauvoir, *Blood of Others*, 52.
44. Beauvoir, *Blood of Others*, 56, 84.
45. Beauvoir, *Blood of Others*, 121–23.
46. Beauvoir, *Blood of Others*, 145.
47. Beauvoir, *Blood of Others*, 161, 189.
48. Jackson, *France*, 251; Tania Long, "It's Still the Same Glowing Paris," *New York Times*, September 10, 1944, sm8; Kathleen Cannell, "Parisians Returf Air Raid Trenches," *New York Times*, July 14, 1940, 18.
49. Beauvoir, *Blood of Others*, 209.
50. Beauvoir, *Blood of Others*, 213.
51. Beauvoir, *Blood of Others*, 230.
52. Beauvoir, *Blood of Others*, 231.
53. Beauvoir, *Blood of Others*, 232.
54. Holveck, *"Blood of Others,"* 13.
55. Beauvoir, *Blood of Others*, 233. Jean Blomart's initial thought about how Hélène could be useful to his organization concerns her ability to drive an automobile.
56. Beauvoir, *Blood of Others*, 235.
57. Kate Fullbrook and Edward Fullbrook, *Simone de Beauvoir and Jean-Paul Sartre: The Remaking of a Twentieth-Century Legend* (New York: BasicBooks, 1994), 134.

8   Communing with Machines

The Bicycle as a Figure of Symbolic
Transgression in the Posthumanist Novels
of Samuel Beckett and Flann O'Brien

AMANDA DUNCAN

> The bicycle itself seemed to have some peculiar quality of shape or person-
> ality which gave it distinction and importance far beyond that usually pos-
> sessed by such machines.... I realized that I had been communing with this
> strange companion and—not only that—conspiring with her ... both knew
> that the hope of each lay in the other, that we would not succeed unless we
> went together, assisting each other with sympathy and quiet love.
>
> FLANN O'BRIEN, *The Third Policeman*

Samuel Beckett's *Molloy* and Flann O'Brien's *The Third Policeman*, two
texts central to the radical formal reevaluation of the novel that is post-
modernism, both reject the expressive or mimetic model of language
in favor of a literary style that foregrounds movement, play, and the
indeterminacy of meaning. Just as apparent with these novels, however, is their shared interest in bicycles. Itself a kind of literary *vehicle*
for the author, the bicycle embodies, in part, the cyclical structure
of these works, which, by beginning with their end, undermines the
sense of formal progress implicit in the traditional narrative of the
novel. As the novels' bicycles traverse geographic boundaries only to
question the very idea of movement or progress, they also engage the
idea of human and text as a collection of impersonal forces, of circuits and moving parts whose goal is no longer to reach an end but

to map and survey new semantic fields and to pave the way for new narrative potentials.

O'Brien, like Beckett, was born in Ireland as a colonial subject of the British Empire, although unlike Beckett, he grew up speaking Irish and was quite young at the founding of the Irish Free State. For both writers, formal English was linked to an oppressive power that, as a part of a globalizing imperial movement, stressed economic efficiency and representational clarity and that used language as a tool to categorize people according to racial status. The authors' rejection of formal English, however, corresponded with a mutual aversion to the language of Irish cultural nationalism, which imposed on its intellectuals an idealized use of Irish Gaelic and which, as a result, only reproduced what was for Beckett and O'Brien the oppressive logic of the colonial symbolic: its tendency to hegemonize and homogenize language. Neil Murphy and Keith Hopper thus accurately describe O'Brien's short 1941 novel, *An Bèal Bocht* (from the Irish phrase "putting on the Poor Mouth," meaning to exacerbate one's own misery), "as both a celebration of the Irish language and a slaying of sacred national cows."[1] As O'Brien wrote to Sean O'Casey, "It is an honest attempt to get under the skin of a certain type of 'Gael,' which I find to be the most nauseating phenomenon in Europe. I mean the baby-brained dawnburst brigade who are ignorant of everything, including the Irish language itself."[2]

Similarly, Beckett's own letters and essays on art communicate his endeavor to dismantle the means-to-ends characteristics of formal English and to "drill holes" in the ideology implicit in all realist or idealized forms of representation. His 1937 letter to Axel Kaun (sent from Nazi Germany, where Beckett was visiting to study art) offers what is perhaps one of the most succinct articulations of this desire. "More and more my language appears to me like a veil," he writes, "which one has to tear apart in order to get to those things (or the nothingness) lying behind it. . . . To drill one hole after another into it until that which lurks behind, be it something or nothing, starts seeping through—I cannot imagine a higher goal for today's writer."[3] This attention to the nonrelational possibilities of the linguistic vehicle as opposed to its function as an expressive means to an end is a defining feature of Beckett's and O'Brien's literary works. In what follows, I show how Beckett and O'Brien foreground the figure of the bicycle as a special kind of sign whose function is not to signify but to expose important dynamic textual processes (like contingency, displacement, and the autonomy of the signifier) that, according to them, remain elided by the realist representational modes valorized by hegemonic, imperialistic discourses.[4]

Beckett and Nonrelation

In Beckett's essays on aesthetics, two works stand out in his treatment of the notion of nonrelation: his 1927 essay on Joyce's *Work in Progress*, "Dante ... Bruno.Vico ... Joyce," and his 1949 postwar "Three Dialogues" on the painted image, cowritten with the artist and art critic Georges Duthuit.[5] In "Dante ... Bruno.Vico ... Joyce," Beckett identifies the power and uniqueness of Joyce's language in terms of his use of "primitive metaphors," a phrase Beckett uses, unconventionally, to indicate the way Joyce's language isolates the literary vehicle from its absorption in a means-to-ends arrangement, such that it no longer signifies in the usual sense but appears to us as an image or "thing." To use Beckett's words, the primitive metaphor always involves force or movement; it insists in language or is produced physically, as a result of a particular kind of surface movement or combination of signs. Such is why, he continues, "[Joyce's] writing is not about something; it is that something itself."[6] Having moved beyond the controlling oppositions of form and content, subject and object, Joyce's nonrelational metaphors emerge as an immanent figure for what Beckett calls (quoting Vico) "the exteriorization of thought" on the word surface.[7]

"Dante ... Bruno.Vico ... Joyce" gives us a definition of literary language in terms of what Beckett will later call its "impossibility"— the literary sign comes forward as the negation of the object and points to the disappearance of immobile conditions upon which knowledge (or representation) rests. In Beckett's words, the sign communicates a contradiction or difference that is at odds with the expressive exigencies of human meaning. Beckett's 1949 "Three Dialogues," a work written with Duthuit on the subject of the painted image in the work of Bram van Velde (among other painters), describes this impossibility as the absent origin, or occasion, of all aesthetic creation.

DUTHUIT: Would it be too much to ask you to state again, as simply as possible, the situation and act that you conceive to be [the artist's]?

BECKETT: The situation is that of him who is helpless, cannot act, in the event cannot paint, since he is obliged to paint.... I suggest that van Velde is the first whose hands have not been tied by the certitude that expression is an impossible act.... My case, since I am in the dock, is that van Velde is the first to submit wholly to the incoercible absence of relation, the absence of terms ... the first to admit that to be an artist is to fail.... This fidelity to failure [he makes] a new occasion, a new term of relation ... unable to act, obliged to act, he makes, an expressive act, even if only of itself, of its impossibility, of its obligation.[8]

Beckett thus consistently testifies to the nature of the aesthetic work as something that abandons or destroys the ties that connect the vehicle for meaning to a fixed idea. In this way, the aesthetic vehicle appears as an absence of relation—as an aporia or impasse that announces what Roland Barthes famously calls the "death of the author" as a coherent and unified subject.[9] In opposition, then, to what Beckett conceives as the ideological representation of reality (the characteristic feature of which is to secure the end of what language has to reveal in advance of its revealing), the imaginative representation takes nonknowing, or ignorance, as its point of departure. Deprived of the ability to express, the modern author has a responsibility that now lies in his or her "obligation," as Beckett later puts it, to refuse the impulse to master or appropriate the movement of signification and to remain faithful to the nonhuman force it gathers from the mechanical or autonomous associations of signs, which are internal to the work itself. In this way, the linguistic vehicle acquires a life and an independence of its own. This circular, immanent approach to the generation of meaning in language will heavily inform Beckett's postwar novels and short prose works.

Beckett's Bicycle as a (Non)representational Vehicle

Published only two years after "Three Dialogues," Beckett's *Molloy* is famous for its characters' failure of to use language as a tool that structures or gives meaning to events in the novel. Like the speaker's narrative in O'Brien's *The Third Policeman* (which begins only after the narrator's death), Molloy's narrative unfolds in an elliptical manner, as a frustrated attempt to compile a report of the series of events that led him to commence writing. The novel begins, then, at the very moment at which the subject merges with the movement of his own language and where what is written becomes its own object. The effect, notes Molloy, is the strange creation "of a world at an end ... its end brought it forth, ending it began ... and I too am at an end, when I am there."[10]

Finding it impossible (or simply refusing) to "tell his story," Molloy instead wanders on his bicycle, taking circular paths that mirror the nonprogressive structure of the novel. Less concerned with the meaning and value of its symbols than with the processes or movement of writing itself, Beckett's *Molloy* thus opens up with a series of ontological questions—questions that were central to Beckett's "Three Dialogues"—concerning the way literary meaning is said to be supported, transported, or displaced by the linguistic sign. As Molloy, immobilized by his stiff leg, sets off on his bicycle, he describes his mode of transport in the same terms that Beckett used three years before in the "Dialogues" to articulate the literary imagination's encounter with its "vehicle" of expression as an experience of silence, impossibility, and the failure to express.[11] Itself a metaphor for this generative process in which the author joins with the sometimes uncontrollable, or autonomous, textual production of meaning, the bicycle is the means by which the author is transported through a blank surface and by which he is driven to abandon his epistemological and ontological bearings. "I went," he tells us, "I had forgotten where I was going. ... It is difficult to think riding, for me. When I try and think riding I lose my balance and fall. ... I went on my way, the way of which I knew nothing, qua way, which was nothing more to me than a surface, bright or dark, and always dear to me."[12] And it is with this same sense of ignorance and disorientation—the sense of working with and moving through nothing—that Molloy then turns to reflect on the abyssal nature of his own writing: "Not to want to say, not to know what you want to say, not to be able to say what you think you want to say, and never to stop saying, or hardly ever, that is the thing to keep in mind, right in the heart of composition."[13] Whether he speaks of the impossibility of voluntarily directing the movement of his bicycle or of the impossibility of directing the movement of signification in writing, Molloy's discourse signals the rejection of the notion of the author as a ruling presence that would remain in total freedom of linguistic contingency, such that he or she may be said to transport meaning by means of the vehicle at will.

Together with his constant, almost bemused, interest in the infirmity of his body, Molloy's continuous complaints in the novel therefore revolve around his inability to master the voices or significations that break into his own discourse. As a figure who is constituted by the movement of writing, formed and transformed by an agency that exists outside himself, Molloy expresses his feeling of passivity and powerlessness in terms of being ventriloquized, like a puppet, by a radical other: "Saying is inventing. Wrong, very rightly wrong. You invent nothing . . . all you do is stammer out your lesson, the remnants of a pensum one day got by heart and long forgotten."[14] Condemned to show himself, while hiding himself, in words and voices that can never be assumed, Molloy begins to refer to himself as a "Chameleon," or as a nonhuman "creature" who possesses no localizable essence. In a hilarious but touching image, he realizes this epithet by covering himself in a coat made from strips of paper that he gathers from the *Literary Times Supplement*. Dressed in this way, he withdraws, while riding his bicycle—a figure that suggests activity and passivity, as well as the indeterminacy of agency or progress—into a sea of textuality, himself a mobilization of the words of others, a collection of literary refuse that (in a very Joycean manner) he later uses as toilet paper. As a subject of language, Molloy can only bear witness to himself as a being that constantly disappears into the language of the other.

"The most you can hope," he reflects, finally, while riding his bicycle, "is to be a little less, in the end, the creature you were in the beginning, and the middle."[15]

What is at stake in this generative process that is so characteristic of Beckett's bicycles and the texts they traverse is precisely a transgressive practice, a movement of negation that passes to the outer boundaries of the subject and destabilizes the identity logic on which language establishes itself as law. In *Molloy*, as in *The Third Policeman*, it is thus only a matter of time before characters on their bicycles, crossing geographical and ontological borders, find themselves caught up in painful, life-threatening confrontations with policemen, whose function is to establish these boundaries and to control the movement of bodies and significations across them. In *The Third Policeman*, for example, their obsession with bicycles is so profound that the police spend most of the time tracking their courses, and to encounter an officer of the law is to run up against the ever-present question, "Is it about a bicycle?" In *Molloy* the passage in which our narrator rides his bicycle across the border of his town, only to be accosted by the police, is one of the most poignant and comical in the novel.

Having resolved to go see his mother (a perpetual figure of circularity, generation, and decay), Molloy takes his bicycle through the outer threshold of his town, speaking affectionately of his machine all the while: "Thus we cleared these difficult straights, my bicycle and I, together."[16] But a little farther on, Molloy is hailed by a policeman who takes him to the barracks and tells him that, as Molloy says, "my way of riding, my attitude while at rest, astride my bicycle, my arms on the handle bars, my head on my arms, was a violation of I don't know what, public order, public decency." He continues:

> Modestly I pointed to my crutches and ventured one or two noises regarding my infirmity, which required me to rest as I could, rather than as I should. But there are not two laws, one for the healthy, another for the sick, but one only to which all must bow, rich and poor, young and old, happy and sad. He was eloquent. Your papers! [the sergeant] cried. . . . Now the only papers I carry with me are bits of newspaper to wipe myself, you understand, when I have a

stool.... Now the sergeant, content to threaten me with a cylindrical ruler, was little by little rewarded for his pains by the discovery that I had no papers in the sense this word had a sense for him, nor any occupation, nor any domicile, that my surname escaped me for the moment and that I was on my way to my mother, whose charity kept me dying.[17]

Since Beckett's critical essays consistently depict colonialist and nationalist discourses as hostile to the primary processes pervading the subject and textual play, it is only natural that his literature should depict writing as a crossing of boundaries and a gesture of transgression, here envisioned in the wandering of the "vehicle" and its confrontation with the law. As a self-reflexive staging of the movement of signification itself, Molloy's encounter with the policeman is characteristic of the oppressive, social, and symbolic function of the law, which demands from its subjects a fixed identity (your papers?) and a fixed origin (your mother?), not to mention a certain level of social decorum (especially while riding bicycles, apparently) that remains characteristic, according to Molloy, of colonial education: "To apply the letter of the law to a creature like me is not an easy matter.... And if I have always behaved like a pig, the fault lies not with me but with my superiors, who corrected me only on points of detail instead of showing me the essence of the system, after the manner of the great English schools."[18] On an ontological level, that is, the image of Molloy and his bicycle (or even the image of Molloy resting, passively on his vehicle) would constitute, as Beckett writes, a kind of degeneracy or transgressive sickness of language, since it points to a movement of signification that has broken with its lawful ties to authorial meaning and begun to wander like a defective force; for the "authorities," it appears to be a violation that linguistic identity cannot be traced to a proper origin.

Accordingly, we might say that the transgressive image of Molloy and his bicycle bears witness to what Joyce calls a "desophistication" of language, something that can be seen in Beckett's literature in terms of its obscene "worklessness," its refusal to be useful or to work toward a specific goal, a refusal that destabilizes the traditional distinctions between means and ends and, in doing so, destroys the significations that provide the foundations for culture. Set free of these significations, and left to its own wandering, the vehicle acquires a validity and life of its own. To borrow from Beckett's words on the subject of Joyce's *Work in Progress*, in *Molloy*, "words are not the polite contortions of the 20th Century's printer's ink. They are alive. They elbow their way onto the page and disappear."[19] In *Molloy*, the narrator describes precisely this transgressive process, by which the vehicle manages to exceed the limits of language and acquire its own life, to play: "A confused shadow was east. It was I and my bicycle. I began to play, gesticulating, waving my hat, moving my bicycle to and fro before me, blowing my horn, watching the wall. They [the policemen] were watching me through the bars, I felt their eyes upon me. The policeman on guard told me to go away. He needn't have, I was calm again. The shadow in the end is no better than substance."[20]

In "Structure, Sign, and Play in the Discourse of the Human Sciences," Jacques Derrida defines "play" as a movement in writing that exiles its origin into its substitute, such that there remains no transcendental signified to ground the work in a fundamental immobility.[21] This dynamic, poststructuralist approach to the generation of meaning comes very close to the kind of textual operations that we have seen in Beckett's language, whose playfulness is so beautifully captured above in the loving intimacy and confusion that is Molloy, his vehicle, and his shadow. For much like the novel as a whole, this image works relentlessly to put into play those boundaries that traditionally work in language to separate the subject and the object, human and nonhuman, "substance" (or being) and "shadow" (or nonbeing), in order to guarantee the static determinacy of meaning. Beckett's way of writing sets the work (or the vehicle) in motion, as it were, and thereby engenders in language a complex structure of interlacing or intertwining—a temporization that, as Derrida says, passes "beyond man and humanism."[22]

Beckett's own interest in the philosophical notion of play, however, likely finds its origin in Kant's theory of aesthetics and teleology in the *Critique of Judgment*. Indeed, Beckett's letters and notebooks show that he was a rigorous reader of Kant, and critics argue that Kant can provide an entry point for a philosophically inflected reading of Beckett's work. In "Beckett's Three Critiques: Kant's Bathos and the Irish Chandos," for example, Jean-Michel Rabeté suggests that the establishment of a movement without object or end in Beckett's literature implies a consideration of the beautiful as defined by Kant's aesthetics, which attributes to the work a "purposiveness without a purpose," and that Kant associates with the free play of the imagination.[23] What the phrase "purposiveness without a purpose" implies, as Kant himself writes, is the way in which artistic genius cannot describe or comprehend how it brings about its products, since the function of the aesthetic work is precisely to pass beyond human reason and to "set the concept in motion," adding to the concept that which is ineffable.[24]

In the trilogy (*Molloy, Malone Dies, The Unnamable*), references to this kind of double movement—a movement through which language acquires a purpose that has no teleological direction or end—are often expressed by Beckett via a confused and playful overlapping of activity and passivity, movement and nonmovement. When, for instance, the creature that speaks in *The Unnamable* considers the impossibility of appropriating the movement of his own discourse, he does so with reference to the same terms of ignorance or passivity that Molloy uses to describe the involuntary motion imparted to him by the writing machine that is his bicycle:

> The only problem for me was how to continue since I could not do otherwise, to the best of my declining powers, in the motion which had been imparted to me. This obligation, and the quasi-impossibility of fulfilling it, engrossed me in a purely mechanical way, excluding notably the free play of the intelligence and sensibility so that my situation rather resembled that of an old broken-down cart or bat-horse, unable to receive the least information either from its instinct or from its observation as to whether it is moving towards the stable or away from it, and not greatly caring either way.[25]

Common to Beckett's literature and Kant's philosophy on aesthetics is thus an essential element of blindness or powerlessness: the artist encounters the vehicle—his own language—as a machine that insists on playing its own game. In Beckett's literature, as in Kant's aesthetics, both reason and meaning break down while something else continues, without purpose or human intention. For Beckett, then, the very possibility of literature would take root in the fact that the imagination is forced to ground itself on a linguistic vehicle—a vehicle that is imagined in Molloy in the figure of the bicycle—whose "transport" is nonidentical to its own aims.

Literary language is not, for Beckett, a vehicle of human significance; indeed, it is useless in this respect. To write is to become a machine, to transform oneself into a collection of parts, speeds, movements, to reduce oneself to speechlessness and immobility, to become other, to disappear. By joining with the movements of his bicycle in each of its unforeseen stages or shifts, Molloy thus puts his own humanity into play in writing and survives passively in his creation as a silent witness to the fact that the literary vehicle has carried him beyond the limits of what can be articulated by signification. This intimately interlocking double movement embodied in the image of the bicycle in *Molloy* will later constitute the force that propels *The Unnamable*: "I'm still in it . . . all words, there's nothing else. . . . I can feel it, they're going to abandon me . . . perhaps they have said me already, perhaps they have carried me to the threshold of my story, before the door that opens on my story . . . if it opens, it will be I . . . it will be the silence."[26]

And thus we might say, finally, that the principle function of the bicycle in Beckett's work is to emblematize or embody the trajectory of the subject and its meaning toward the point of disappearance in language. This way in which Beckett's bicycles bear witness to a metonymic slippage in literary language—a wandering of the signifier that displaces its author (or passenger) as the prime mover of his or her own narrative progress—is also what connects Beckett's *Molloy* thematically to Flann O'Brien's novel *The Third Policeman*.

O'Brien's "Desiring Machines"

In O'Brien's *The Third Policeman*, the bicycle invokes the Platonic figure of desire as a form of delirium that breaks with human reason.

As figures of both sexual and symbolic transgression, bicycles are the single consuming interest of the law in the novel—bicycles must be policed, their movements carefully documented in surveillance note-books, the behavior of their cyclists obsessively monitored. Bicycles, moreover, have genders and are intimately connected to human sexuality. Men usually do not ride female bicycles, and individuals must be careful not to ride bicycles too often, lest their "particles get too mixed up" with that of the bicycle—a confusion of substances that Sergeant Pluck associates with the "Atomic Theory."[27] This theory, which is closely associated with the spinning or whirling effect of bicycles, consists of the belief that everything is composed of minute atoms "flying around in concentric circles, arcs, and geometrical fig-ures," the end result being that people who spend most of their lives riding bicycles "get their personalities mixed up with the personali-ties of their bicycle," on account of the interchanging of atoms. "You would be flabbergasted," says Sergeant Pluck, "at the number of peo-ple in these parts who nearly are half people and half bicycles ... [or] at the number of bicycles that are half-human almost half-man, half-partaking of humanity."[28] As the machine's association with transgres-sion indicates, to become a cyclist in O'Brien's novel—"to let things get so far that [one] is half or more than half bicycle"—elicits a break with the set of Cartesian dualisms between the subject and its object that traditionally function to establish man's privileged position at the center of things and his self-present relation to meaning. Similar to its treatment in *Molloy*, the function of the bicycle in *The Third Police-man* is to inaugurate a movement of desire in language according to which the conscious subject and its meaning break down, disappear, and pass entirely into the object or into the movement of significa-tion itself. Thus for O'Brien the bicycle is not a simple machine but a model of the destructive and generative mechanisms through which desire expresses, or deploys itself, in language.

To adopt a term that Deleuze and Guattari often use in *Anti-Oedipus*, O'Brien's bicycles present themselves as "desiring machines"—a phrase that designates the way that desire functions in language to fragment the reified, immobile relations between word and thing, subject and object, which ground the powers of state, police, and law in order to produce new, subversive flows, or mobile relations.[29] To be sure, in *The Third Policeman*, O'Brien's bicycles, with all their chains, turnings, and gears, produce atomizations, or indeterminacies, between human and machine, subject and object, that his language registers on an ontological level in terms of a series of circuits, or signifying chains, that shatter and disperse the linear movement of narrative progress. More specifically, these circuits, or signifying chains, operate by juxtaposing meaningful signifiers with certain inhuman or absurd potentials for nonmeaning that are internal to the metonymic or associative machinery of the text.[30]

A simple but illustrative example of this kind of metonymic machinery appears in a short scene in which our narrator, having been detained by the police and sentenced to death for murder, falls asleep in his cell only to be awakened by the sound of hammering on his coffin. This dreamlike sound persists in the novel for a couple of pages by way of its metonymic associations and, refusing to be dropped by expressive ends of narrative organization, loses its ties to an original, signified content. Eventually, an extended chain of associations works to produce a hilarious but meaningless semantic proliferation, complete with footnotes and commentary, concerning the "importance of percussion" in the "de Selby dialectic"—a manuscript containing theories to which our narrator remains dedicated, despite the fact that (like Joyce's *Finnegans Wake*) they remain both meaningless and forged. Consequently, at the very moment in which narrative action is escalated to its highest point (the potential death of our narrator), O'Brien draws the reader's attention away from plot and toward the impossibility of grounding meaning internally, in a single authorial agent. In this way, he points to the book as a machine shot through with autonomous and impersonal forces, which dissolve both story and meaning into a never-ending movement of intertextuality and play.

Commentators on O'Brien's works have not failed to appreciate the decidedly postmodernist way in which *The Third Policeman* joyously defies meaning through the perpetual use of digression and circularity of plot. Maciej Ruczai, for example, describes the novel as a *Divine Comedy*–like work, but one that is "decapitated, lacking the necessary component of upward progression" characteristic of Dante's two poems that follow the *Inferno*, the *Purgatorio* and the *Paradiso*. In Ruczai's words, *The Third Policeman* "never arrives at the final union of Being and knowing but moves in circles"; "it stays within the infernal zone of fragmentation, angry incomprehension and distortion."[31] Ruczai does well to recognize in O'Brien's novel a critique of epistemology that prevents its readers, and its characters, from attaining anything like unmediated knowledge. What is of even more interest in this context, however, is the way in which this critique of epistemology often surfaces in *The Third Policeman*, in terms of a kind of radical play that undermines characters' access to a stable knowledge of objects in the phenomenal world. Accounting for some of the stranger visual metaphors in the novel, this play opens up what might be called a negative perception on the part of its characters, a destabilizing nothingness or loss, which intervenes between subjects and their perception of reality.

For example, in one of the most baffling of these scenes, Sergeant MacCruiskeen performs an intricate procedure involving the manufacture of an infinite series of wooden chests, each successively smaller though similar in dimension, until it becomes impossible to perceive the objects produced in the series, there being "no glass strong enough, to make them big enough to be regarded truly as the smallest things ever made." Describing the possible endlessness of the series, MacCruiskeen remarks, "The one I am making now is nearly as small as nothing. Number One would hold a million of them at the same time.... The dear knows where it will stop and terminate."[32] Likewise, in a characteristic turn, MacCruiskeen refuses to use his magnifying glass as a tool to bring imperceptible objects into a visual field commensurate with the scale of human perception. Instead, he uses it to make things disappear by magnifying "everything so big that there is room in the glass for only the smallest particle ... not enough of it to make it different from any other thing that is dissimilar."[33] In this way, he uses his magnifying glass in the same way as the novel's bicyclists use their "desiring machines," for what begins as a human-prosthetic technology quickly plunges the human being into an unrelenting play, until being disappears or withdrawals into a never-ending series.

O'Brien's characters in *The Third Policeman* remain absorbed in the unsettling task of plunging objects, things, and even themselves into a ceaseless symbolic displacement, since as elements of autonomous series these objects become more like words than things; but in doing so they also realize a certain posthumanist play best illustrated in the image of the bicycle. That is, just as the bicycle appears as a supplement that gives expression to human mobility only to conceal a more unsettling ontological decentering of human autonomy, postmodern literary language appears to give expression to human intention only to enact a mobilization of signifying chains that engages its user in a never-ending series of ellipses, frames, and frames within frames.

This radical rethinking of the relation between the subject and language, or humans and (representational) technology, precisely reflects the radical transformation that Beckett and O'Brien brought to the novel form: whereas language is typically a vehicle for subjective interiority and self-presence for the traditional novel, for Beckett and O'Brien it is no less a communing with machines, a transformation of the subject into a nameless link on a symbolic chain. Consider, for example, the key moment when O'Brien's nameless narrator finally reflects on the nature of his inner voice, or soul, named Joe, who accompanies and comforts him throughout the novel; and he turns out, upon closer scrutiny, to be another one of the many endless series in the novel. If the narrator has an inner voice, does the inner voice have an inner voice? Is the narrator himself, in turn, only the inner voice of another creature? This ontological play opens to an unlimited series of vertiginous reframing: "Was I merely a link in a vast sequence of imponderable beings, the world I knew merely the interior of the being whose inner voice I myself was? Who or what was the core?"[34] The same phenomenon can be observed in Beckett's radical experimentation with language, as in *The Unnamable*, where the close investigation of both a subjective core, or innerness, and an objective world of things only reveals a vertiginous chain of signifiers in motion: "I'm in words, made of words, others' words, what others, the place too, the air, the walls, the floor, the ceiling, all words, the whole world is here with me, I'm the air, the walls, the walls ... this dust of words, with no ground for their settling."[35]

Endless mobility, or linguistic movement, in the place of stable essence is an essential quality of the revolution that Beckett and O'Brien made in literary form, a quality that *The Third Policeman* captures in the image of the perfect and graceful union of the human with the movements of the bicycle. Toward the end of the novel, for instance, O'Brien gives us the metaphor of bicycle and rider as ballet dancers, suggesting we should envision this union of human innerness and externalized symbolic chains captured in the bicycle in terms of music or dance, where words operate like a temporal rhythm or propulsive impulse, expressive of their own unfolding: "[The bicycle and I] had traveled the passage . . . with the grace of ballet dancers, silent, swift and faultless in our movements, united in the acuteness of our conspiracy. . . . [S]he moved away eagerly under me in her own time."[36]

This movement of writing might explain how Beckett's own wish to drill holes, as he says, into the logic of relation led him to a mature style that, like O'Brien's, rigorously challenged a concept of authorship that subordinates literary language to human knowledge with its illusion of stable ground. Beckett and O'Brien's revolutions in the novel form would have us rethink the abyssal nature of this ground as the temporality of the literary vehicle itself.

Notes

1. Neil Murphy and Keith Hopper, "Editor's Introduction: A(nother) Bash in the Tunnel," special issue, *Review of Contemporary Fiction* 31, no. 3 (Fall 2011): 11.
2. Murphy and Hopper, "Editor's Introduction," 11.
3. Samuel Beckett to Axel Kaun, 1937, in *The Letters of Samuel Beckett*, ed. Martha Dow Fehsenfeld and Lois More Overbeck, vol. 1, *1929–1940* (Cambridge: Cambridge University Press, 2009), 518.
4. While readers have not failed to take notice of the figure of the bicycle in *Molloy*, few studies have seriously addressed the important relationship between this theme and the ontological, epistemological, or political elements of the work. One of the most interesting among these is Hugh Kenner's 1968 article, "The Cartesian Centaur," which approaches the figure of the bicycle in Beckett's work as a metaphor for the Cartesian ideal of a body that would operate like a machine, in perfect unison with the mind. For Kenner, in other words, Molloy's bicycle would represent the Cartesian dream of "knowing and moving like a god," a dream that is successively

denied to each one of Beckett's later characters. See Hugh Kenner, *Samuel Beckett: A Critical Study* (Berkley: University of California Press, 1968), 132. Similarly, Janet Menzies's "Beckett's Bicycles" argues that the bicycle motif in Beckett's literature represents the aspiration for Cartisian unity and ease of progress, the achievement of which would only coincide with death or the end of the "life struggle." See Janet Menzies, "Beckett's Bicycles," *Journal of Beckett Studies*, no. 6 (1980): 97–105. On the other hand, Deleuze and Guattari open their work *Anti-Oedipus: Capitalism and Schizophrenia* with an image of Molloy and his bicycle to illustrate a movement of desire that is directed against Cartesian man, his knowledge, and his position at the center of things. "Beckett characters are cut differently," they write, "here the subject is produced as a residuum along side the desiring machine [the bicycle] . . . the subject itself is not at the center, which is occupied by the machine, but at the periphery, with no fixed identity, forever decentered, defined by the states through which it passes." See Gilles Deleuze and Felix Guattari, *Anti-Oedipus: Capitalism and Schizophrenia*, trans. Robert Hurley, Seem Mark, and Helen R. Lane (Minneapolis: University of Minnesota Press, 1983), 20.

5. Beckett's interest in what I have described above as nonrelational aesthetics is well documented by a number of critical studies. Dearlove's *Accommodating the Chaos: Samuel Beckett's Nonrelational Art*, for example, argues that the rationale behind Beckett's style was an unremitting search to find a "literary shape" for the proposition that "perhaps no relationships exist between or among the artist, his art, and an external reality." See J. D. Dearlove, *Accommodating the Chaos: Samuel Beckett's Nonrelational Art* (Durham NC: Duke University Press, 1982), 2. Begam's *Samuel Beckett and the End of Modernity* argues that Beckett's language represents a cutting of the Cartesian ties between word and thing, subject and object, that had for centuries made up the rational basis for the realist novel. See Richard Begam, *Samuel Beckett and the End of Modernity* (Stanford CA: Stanford University Press, 1996).

6. Samuel Beckett, *Disjecta: Miscellaneous Writings and a Dramatic Fragment*, ed. Ruby Cohn (New York: Grove Press, 1984), 27.

7. Beckett, *Disjecta*, 29.

8. *Samuel Beckett: The Grove Centenary Edition*, vol. 4, *Poems, Short Fiction, Criticism*, ed. Paul Auster (New York: Grove Press, 2006), 560–63.

9. Roland Barthes, "The Death of the Author," in *Image, Music, Text*, trans. Stephen Heath (New York: Hill and Wang, 1977).

10. Samuel Beckett, *Molloy*, trans. Patrick Bowles, in *Three Novels*: Molloy, Malone Dies, The Unnamable (New York: Grove Press, 1958), 40.

11. Janet Menzies's "Beckett's Bicycles" also associates the figure of the bicycle in *Molloy* with the expression of the failure to express. "In the trilogy," she writes, "the picture of a real man on a real bicycle provides Beckett with

an image of the method by which he may come nearest to confronting his problems of self-expression. The tension between a constant awareness of the ideal vision of unity [of intellect and bicycle] and the impossibility of its realization by humanity is the source of the humour, the optimism and the positive effect of Beckett's writing." Menzies, "Beckett's Bicycles," 103.

12. Beckett, *Molloy*, 26.
13. Beckett, *Molloy*, 28.
14. Beckett, *Molloy*, 32.
15. Beckett, *Molloy*, 32.
16. Beckett, *Molloy*, 19.
17. Beckett, *Molloy*, 20–22.
18. Beckett, *Molloy*, 25.
19. Beckett, *Disjecta*, 29.
20. Beckett, *Molloy*, 23–24.
21. Jacques Derrida, "Structure, Sign, and Play in the Discourse of the Human Sciences," in *Writing and Difference*, trans. Alan Bass (Chicago: University of Chicago Press, 1982), 280–81.
22. Derrida, "Structure, Sign, and Play," 292. The radicalization of the notion of a coherent subjectivity in writing, in addition to the persistent of use of movement and play as opposed to the logical determinacy of meaning, connects Beckett's works to the poststructuralism of Jacques Derrida (1930–2004), French philosopher and founder of deconstructionism. When Derek Attridge in 1989 asked Derrida why he had never written on Beckett, Derrida agreed that the author's works are, in Attridge's words, "self-deconstructive." Derrida responded, "[Beckett] is an author to whom I feel very close, or to whom I would like to feel myself very close; but also too close. Precisely because of this proximity, it is too hard for me, too easy and too hard." See Derek Attridge, "'This Strange Institution Called Literature': An Interview with Jacques Derrida," in *Acts of Literature*, ed. Derek Attridge (New York: Routledge, 1992), 60–61.
23. Jean-Michel Rabeté, "Beckett's Three Critiques: Kant's Bathos and the Irish Chandos," in "Samuel Beckett: Out of the Archive," special issue, *Modernism/Modernity* 18, no. 4 (November 2011): 699–719. See also Immanuel Kant, *Critique of Judgment* (Indianapolis: Hackett Publishing, 1987), 715.
24. Kant, *Critique of Judgment*, 175.
25. Samuel Beckett, *The Unnamable*, in *Three Novels:* Molloy, Malone Dies, The Unnamable (New York: Grove Press, 1958), 320.
26. Beckett, *Unnamable*, 414.
27. Flann O'Brien, *The Third Policeman* (Champaign: Dalkey Archive Press, 1999), 83–85.
28. O'Brien, *Third Policeman*, 85–86.

29. Deleuze and Guattari, *Anti-Oedipus*, 36–39.

30. The process by which O'Brien's novel (and the bicycle that inhabits it) forms circuits that introduce indeterminacy, or nonmeaning, into the narrative progression of events resonates in many ways with Beckett's prose. In *Molloy*, for example, Beckett often replaces story, or meaning, with the exploration of various mathematical combinatorials, as in the absurd sucking-stones episode, which details Molloy's attempt to circulate an equally distributed number of stones from jacket pocket to jacket pocket until he finally abandons all order of preference. In Beckett's late prose and films for television (like *Quad* or *All Strange Away*), story, or plot, is rejected entirely in favor of the development of various combinations of bodily positions or attitudes.

31. Maciej Ruczaj, "Infernal Poetics / Infernal Ethics: *The Third Policeman* between Medieval and (Post)modern Netherworlds," *Review of Contemporary Fiction* 31, no. 3 (Fall 2011): 100.

32. O'Brien, *Third Policeman*, 74.

33. O'Brien, *Third Policeman*, 137.

34. O'Brien, *Third Policeman*, 118.

35. Beckett, *Unnamable*, 386.

36. O'Brien, *Third Policeman*, 173.

9 "Hi-Yo, Silver"

The Bicycle in the Fiction of Stephen King

DON TRESCA

In March 1979 Stephen King was invited to participate in a panel discussion on horror sponsored by a Manhattan bookstore. During the question-and-answer period at the end of the discussion, an audience member asked the writers if they could remember anything from childhood that was "particularly terrible." In his response, King told what he calls a "train story" so that the questioner would not feel "totally disappointed" by the fact that the other two panelists, Janet Jeppson and Robert Marasco, could not recall any traumatic childhood experiences. King stated that, according to his mother,

> I had gone off to play at a neighbor's house—a house that was near
> a railroad line. About an hour after I left I came back (she said), as
> white as a ghost. I would not speak for the rest of that day; I would
> not tell her . . . why my chum's mom hadn't walked me back, but
> allowed me to come home alone. It turned out that the kid I had
> been playing with had been run over by a freight train while play-
> ing on or crossing the tracks (years later, my mother told me they
> had picked up the pieces in a wicker basket).[1]

When King informed the audience that he could not actually recall the childhood incident himself, Jeppson, a psychiatrist as well as a novelist, remarked, "But you've been writing about it ever since."[2] Jeppson's comment points out that King has been writing about fatal accidents his entire career and specifically about the destructive power of adult forms of mechanical transportation. Looking at his body of work, one sees that there is a death in nearly every one of King's novels that is caused by either a car or a train.[3] Even when they are not causing death, cars and trains are frequently seen in King's fiction as vehicles of evil and destruction. However, there are vehicles in his work that do not hold the same destructive value and that are actually seen as symbols of the innocence and imaginative magic of childhood. Those vehicles are bicycles.[4] Bicycles (or references to bicycles) are relatively infrequent in King's work; but when they do appear, they have a tremendous effect on the narrative, carrying great symbolic weight within the text. In this chapter, I focus on some of the more significant references to bicycles in King's work and demonstrate that bicycles can be seen as symbols of almost magical regeneration as opposed to the degenerative power of cars and trains.

Stephen King sees childhood as a time when human beings are most innocent because of their ignorance of worldly evil. This ignorance is most frequently manifested in King's fiction by the presence of a bicycle, a vehicle that serves largely as the child's method of navigating the world in which he or she lives. The moment when the bicycle is destroyed, abandoned, or otherwise separated from the child becomes the moment at which worldly evil makes itself known to the child, causing elements of corruption to seep into the child's life, elements that can be best understood and dealt with only years later from the point of view of adulthood. Throughout his work, King laments this separation of childhood and innocence, which he addresses from the viewpoint of an adult man seeking to deal with these issues while living in an America that attempts to desensitize its young by exposing them continuously to violence and sex in both the entertainment and news media, forcing children to mature at too early an age. This all too early maturity is symbolized in King's work by an initial earth-shattering traumatic discovery that causes the child to recognize the imperfections of the world and the inherent corruption just below its surface, a discovery made by a wide variety of his underage characters, ranging from young children like Mark Petrie in 'Salem's Lot (1975), Danny Torrance in

The Shining (1977), Abra Stone in *Doctor Sleep* (2013), and the Losers Club in *It* (1986) to teenagers like Carrie White in *Carrie* (1974), Arnie Cunningham in *Christine* (1983), and Alice Maxwell in *Cell* (2006). While these young characters possess the weapons for survival in King's hostile universe—a productive imagination, a love for simple things, a gentle nature—they are often made vulnerable by an adult society that teaches them violence, hostility, and greed, which for some, such as Brian Rusk in *Needful Things* (1991), leads to their ultimate destruction.

Adults in King's world, on the other hand, must actively seek to escape the corrupt world by venturing into a realm of imagination first experienced in childhood. Unless they can approach the oncoming evil with a child's mentality, they are doomed to adult reasoning, an insistence on literalizing reality that can lead to catastrophe. Alexander Nenilin states that King's ideal character integrates both adulthood and childhood in order "to cope with irrational chaos rushing into everyday life because he doesn't suffer from the gap separating rational and irrational. Therefore, he is the first to discover the presence of chaos. He manages to understand its essence and he knows how to handle it."[5] In King's work, this embracing of childhood trauma and this attempt to cope with it through an adult mindset are often symbolized by adults retaking possession of a bicycle from their childhood that they then use to bridge the gap between knowing adulthood and innocent childhood.

King's first real use of the bicycle in this manner occurs in his early novel *The Shining*. This novel details the mental disintegration of Jack Torrance, an alcoholic and unsuccessful writer, as he is manipulated by the evil spirits inhabiting the Overlook Hotel, where he serves as the winter caretaker. The malevolent hotel is attempting to get Jack to murder his wife Wendy and his son Danny because the boy has a remarkable psychic gift, which Danny's friend and mentor Dick Halloran calls "shining" and which the hotel wishes to claim as its own.[6] The bicycle appears as a symbol of Danny's innocence that his father seeks to destroy at the command of the hotel. The bicycle first appears to Jack when he and his friend, Al Shockley, run it over while driving home after a night of drunken carousing:

They came around the last curve before the bridge at seventy, and there was a kid's bike in the road, and then the sharp, hurt squealing as rubber shredded from the Jag's tires. . . . Then the jingling crashing sound as they hit the bike at forty, and it had flown up like a bent and twisted bird, the handle-bars striking the windshield, and then it was in the air again, leaving the starred safety glass in front of Jack's bulging eyes. A moment later he heard the final dreadful smash as it landed on the road behind them. . . . [F]rom far away Jack heard himself saying: "Jesus, Al. We ran him down. I felt it."[7]

After the search for a body produces only the crumpled remains of the bicycle, "Jack thought later that some queer providence, bent on giving them both a last chance, had kept the cops away, had kept any of the passersby from calling them," and had placed a bicycle "with nobody riding it . . . in the middle of the road."[8] Jack interprets the bicycle event optimistically as the work of a divine authority benevolently disposed toward his welfare, sparing him (and Al) the trauma of murdering an innocent child but still giving them enough of a glimpse of what might have happened to shock them both into sobriety. Tony Magistrale claims that Jack's interpretation of the event is wrong and that the providence that placed the bicycle in his path is not a benevolent entity at all but the dark energy of the hotel reaching out to begin its corruption of Jack, suggesting that Jack's corruption began long before the hotel makes itself known to the family.[9] In the novel, this corruption finds its fulfillment once the family enters the Overlook Hotel the following winter and Jack conveniently finds the scrapbook of the Overlook's sordid history, which this malevolent providence has placed in a location within the hotel where Jack is certain to find it.[10]

The connection between the destruction of the bicycle and Jack's attempt to destroy Danny is developed further through King's connection of the bicycle accident with Jack's breaking of Danny's arm in a fit of drunken rage after Danny accidentally spills beer over the pages of Jack's manuscript. The two incidents of innocence destroyed are linked irrevocably in Jack's mind as he looks in on Danny in his bed when he has made it home after the accident. He sees Danny with

"his arm still buried in the cast," which causes him to begin to justify the behavior that led to Danny's condition; "but the last plea was
driven away by the image of that bobbing flashlight as they hunted
through the dry late November weeds, looking for the sprawled body
that by all good rights should have been there, waiting for the police.
It didn't matter that Al had been driving. There had been other nights
when he had been driving."[11] Jack's connection of the two events (and
his realization that the night he broke Danny's arm was one of the
times "he had been driving") convinces him to stop drinking, fulfilling the prophecy that Magistrale claims is made by the malevolent
providence responsible for placing the bicycle in front of the car in
which Jack was a passenger. Jack is so traumatized by the event with
the bicycle that he gives up alcohol entirely, a change that produces
a tremendous psychological strain in Jack that culminates in a full
mental breakdown at the Overlook and that makes him much more
susceptible to the hotel's manipulations.[12] Jack himself even makes
the connection between the destruction of the bicycle and his violent breaking of Danny's arm at the moment when he fully gives in
to the hotel and becomes the monster it wants him to be: "He heard
the hard, horrible snap as Danny's arm broke. He saw the bicycle flying brokenly up over the hood of Al's car, starring the windshield.
He saw a single wheel lying in the road, twisted spokes pointing
into the sky like jags of piano wire."[13] Jack finally sees here, in a final
glimpse of humanity before he is subsumed by the malevolence of
the hotel, that he alone is responsible for the near destruction of his
son's childhood innocence, equating the physical abuse of the arm
breaking with the symbolic destruction of the bicycle.[14]

In a later book, *The Regulators* (1996), published by King under his
pseudonym Richard Bachman, the first killing attributed to the alien
creatures known as the Regulators is of a young boy named Cary
Ripton, a fourteen-year-old riding his bicycle through the neighborhood while delivering newspapers. Although the narrative reveals a
secret sexual fantasy Cary has about one of the neighborhood girls, it
also stresses his childish innocence. Most of the text devoted to Cary
reveals him talking about youthful activities, such as going to school
and playing Little League baseball; and he is directly referred to in

the text as a virgin, further highlighting his innocence.[15] When Cary is killed via shotgun blast by the Regulators as they sit inside a van, it is key that the first indication of his death is that he "flew off the seat of his bike."[16] Similarly, in *'Salem's Lot*, after eleven-year-old Mark Petrie's parents are murdered by the vampire Barlow, Mark is described by one of the other characters as looking "like he fell off his bike."[17] Describing both Cary and Mark as having fallen off or been forced off the bicycle suggests that, for both of these characters, their loss of innocence and introduction to the horrifying world of adult violence is forced upon them. They do not give up their innocence by getting off the bicycle willingly but are instead removed forcefully.[18]

Likewise, in the novel *Needful Things*, Brian Rusk is a middle school boy whose innocence is forcibly taken from him by the villain of the text, Leland Gaunt. As with Cary, Brian's innocence (and his eventual loss of it) is symbolized by his bicycle. He is initially described prior to the opening of the shop as riding on his bike "through downtown right after school"; but on the day he discovers the shop is open and decides to venture inside, Brian "hardly rode his bike at all on his way from school."[19] Instead, Brian is pushing his bike along the road and is nearly run down by a passing pickup truck, symbolizing the ways in which childhood innocence is threatened by the menacing adult world. At the same time as he is pushing his bicycle, he is, we are told, lost in an intense sexual daydream about his teacher, Miss Ratcliffe. Having the daydream interrupted, Brian prepares to return to his state of innocence, suggested by the fact that he is preparing "to mount his bike and pedal the rest of the way home," when he notices the Open sign in the window of the shop.[20] Torn between getting on his bike and entering the store, he ultimately chooses to abandon his bicycle (and his childhood).

Brian's experience within Gaunt's shop cements his corruption, a corruption made further evident by his decision to play a horrible prank on a local neighbor woman. Performing this prank is what he must agree to "pay" Gaunt for a rare autographed 1956 Sandy Koufax baseball card for his collection. After Brian "buys" the card and leaves the shop, having agreed to the terrible trick, he does not immediately mount his bike. Instead, he "leaned the handlebars against his belly while he reached in his pants pocket" for the card.[21] This is a transitional moment, the point at which the material item he gained at the cost of his innocence becomes more important than riding the bike. King emphasizes this loss of innocence with some rather sexually suggestive language. After walking the bike for a brief period and daydreaming about Miss Radcliffe, he leans the bike against his belly and reaches into his pants. Although he is reaching for the card to verify its existence and his possession of it, the sexual connotation of reaching into his pants makes the symbolic value of the movement clear. When Brian finally does get on the bike, his demeanor and attitude toward riding the bike has changed. No longer does Brian leisurely ride through the town on his bike. Now he begins "to pedal ... fast," desperate to get his prize home and into the safety of his bedroom.[22] Michael Collings suggests Brian's brief sexual fantasy and intentional abandonment of the bike to enter the sinister shop are significant because they indicate that within each person, regardless of age or life experience, there exist internal weaknesses by which that person can be trapped and corrupted as well as that innocence and morality are fragile things that can be shattered by external physical desires (such as Brian's obsessive need to possess the baseball card).[23]

Unfortunately, Brian's knowledge of his own self-interest and corruption begins to eat at him almost immediately, seemingly dooming him to destruction. When he awakens the next day after his encounter with Gaunt, his loss of childhood innocence is established both physically ("His penis was a small, hard branch inside his pajama trousers") and mentally ("His first impulse was to open his mouth and yell for his mother, as he had done when he was small and a nightmare invaded his sleep. Then he realized that he *wasn't* small anymore, he was eleven ... and it wasn't exactly the sort of dream you told your mother about").[24] King describes the weather in the scene to accentuate Brian's mental anguish and separation from his childhood innocence: "He could hear the sound of rain, hard now, pelting against his bedroom window, driven by huge, whooping gasps of wind. It sounded almost like sleet."[25] Brian's youthful, trusting nature, evident in the introductory scene with Gaunt in which he walks into the shop boldly and without hesitation, is replaced in this scene with an awful paranoia in which he dreads telling his family or friends about the baseball card for fear that his father will discover he paid next to nothing for it and will force him to return it. Brian's corrupt greed for the card ("He was not going to give it up") trumps his innocent desire to trust and confide in his parents.[26]

When it comes time to perform his prank the next morning, Brian is able to ride his bike, but he again does so "fast" and with "his heart beating hard in his chest."[27] He does not take the time to look around at his surroundings as he does earlier in the book. Instead, "Brian pedaled through the business district without looking across Main Street … pausing briefly at intersections for a perfunctory glance each way before hurrying on again."[28] When he reaches his destination, he immediately abandons his bike, and his mind drifts down a tainted path as he begins to construct a complex lie about his reason for being at the neighbor's house in case he gets caught while sneaking around the house in order to conduct his sinister business. After completing his task, he rinses his hands off using the outside faucet. This cleaning of the hands becomes an inverted baptism—instead of emerging clean and pure, his hands are numb, red, and chapped.[29] When he leaves the house, he does not ride his bike; instead, he "walked it back down the driveway" like he walked it earlier in the book just prior to arriving at Needful Things.[30]

From this point on, Brian's demeanor changes, and he no longer uses the bicycle for enjoyment, for the joy of the ride. Instead, the bicycle merely becomes a conveyance, a way to get from place to place. As he becomes more corrupted, the bicycle becomes more difficult to handle. For example, while riding his bicycle down the street on his way to play another trick Gaunt required of him, Brian discovered that it "was hard to pedal his bike and even harder to keep it balanced."[31] Brian has transformed because of his experiences with Mr. Gaunt, changing from a "sunshiny sort of boy" to one who is "buried behind heavy banks of cloud which were still forming" (yet another connection between bad weather and Brian's loss of innocence).[32] When he learns that Wilma Jerzyck, the woman on whom he played his prank, died as a direct result of it (she is killed by Nellie Cobb, the woman she blames for the incident), he falls into a depression so deep it overwhelms and transforms him. His "summer tan" (a manifestation of his sunshiny-boy appearance) begins to fade, revealing "a complexion [that] was in an unusual state of pre-pubescent revolt ... [with] purplish shadows under his eyes," an indication that leads Sheriff Pangborn to believe Brian "is a long way from right.... There's something badly sprained, maybe even broken here."[33] After this, the readers do not encounter Brian again until he shoots himself in the head with his father's rifle, still clutching desperately the Sandy Koufax baseball card.[34]

Unlike in *Needful Things*, in which the bicycle is merely a symbolic device used to represent the child character's innocence but without any real power of its own, occasionally in King's works the bicycle becomes a magical object imbued with the pure power of childhood innocence. Silver, Bill Denbrough's bicycle in *It*, is just such an object. Silver is key to helping Bill and the rest of the Losers Club, as children in 1958 Derry, Maine, to escape their battle with the monstrous Pennywise the Clown.[35] When it first appears, Silver is a relatively innocuous-looking bike, certainly not suggestive of any of its inherent magical power. Yet at the same time, it is clearly described as a unique bike: "A big Schwinn, twenty-eight inches tall ... [leaning] gloomily on its kickstand, bigger than the biggest of the others on display, dull where they were shiny, straight in places where the others were curved, bent in places where the others were straight.... [I]t looked pretty shoddy, with its old paint and the old-fashioned package carrier mounted above the back wheel and the ancient oogah-horn with its black rubber bulb."[36]

Bill sees such strength and power in the bicycle that he immediately names it Silver after the Lone Ranger's horse, another symbol of purity and trustworthiness, from a time when such traits were highly prized. Thus, Silver itself becomes a member of the Losers Club. Bill buys Silver from the bicycle shop for twenty dollars after his brother, George, is murdered by Pennywise; and while riding the bike after a few false starts, caused by its large size compared to Bill's small body frame, Bill discovers the bike's hidden power. Initially, Bill uses Silver simply as an escape, as a coping mechanism after his brother's death: "Once he was on Silver he became someone else.... It was all behind him now: his stutter, his dad's blank hurt eyes as he puttered around his garage workshop, the terrible sight of the dust on the closed piano cover upstairs—dusty because his mother didn't play anymore. . . . George going out into the rain, wearing his yellow slicker, carrying the newspaper boat with its glaze of paraffin. Mr. Gardener coming up the street twenty minutes later with his body wrapped in a blood-stained quilt; his mother's agonized shriek. All behind him."[37]

Soon, however, Silver reveals its true purpose as an embodiment of childhood innocence that Bill uses to escape the corruption of the murderous Pennywise: "Silver continued to pick up speed. [Bill] was beginning to feel the road now, beginning to fly. Bill could feel him go. . . . Bill Denbrough found himself racing to beat the devil, only now the devil was a hideously grinning clown whose face sweated white greasepaint, whose mouth curved up in a leering red vampire smile, whose eyes were bright silver coins. A clown who was, for some lunatic reason, wearing a Derry High School jacket over its silvery suit with the orange ruff and the orange pompom buttons."[38]

The reference to the Derry High School jacket that Pennywise wears while chasing them (having first disguised himself as the teenage werewolf played by Michael Landon in the 1957 film *I Was a Teenage Werewolf*) suggests that Bill is not just escaping Pennywise the monster but also his fear of maturing, of becoming a teenager with the requisite bodily transformations that take place after puberty.[39] The werewolf, a physical manifestation of the primitive male sexual self, is the very image of a dark, mature masculinity that Bill is attempting to evade.[40] He wants to keep his innocent childhood for as long as possible.

After the Losers Club members manage to defeat Pennywise, they make a pact to return to Derry if the creature ever returns, and then the friends slowly drift apart. Bill eventually leaves Derry behind, moving to the United Kingdom after he becomes a successful novelist and marries the beautiful film star Audra Phillips. However, Bill is summoned back to the town, along with the other members of the Losers Club, when the menace of Pennywise reemerges in 1984. When he arrives, providence allows him to find Silver once more, this time in the window of a local thrift store. Although the bike is much worse for wear than when he had it as a child and Bill contends that his "bike-riding days are over," he buys Silver from the store for twenty dollars and stores it in the garage of Mike Hanlon, the local librarian and the only member of the Losers Club to have remained in Derry.[41] Mike, realizing the power of the bike, helps Bill fix the flat tire (with a tire-patching kit he magically happened to buy despite not having a bike and not knowing why he would need it) and gives him playing cards to place in the spokes as Bill did as a child. Although Bill reiterates to Mike that he has no intention of riding Silver again, he repairs the flat and adds the cards, working with such diligence that "he had nearly forgotten Mike was there; he had become completely absorbed in small yet utterly satisfying acts of maintenance."[42] Bill's discovery and repair of Silver represents his attempt at recovering the faith he had as a child in the talismans of protection (which Silver represented to him). Bill is the one concerned that the Losers Club will not be able to defeat Pennywise as adults, because he believes the only way they were able to defeat the creature before was through their innocent faith in the magic power of childhood fantasy; or as he tells the others, "What it really came down to was we wuh-wuh-wished our way out.... I'm not sure that grownups can do that."[43]

King sees much of his work (and *It* in particular) as a call to adults to redeem themselves by thoughtfully looking back on their youth and remembering the magic of childhood.[44] King stated that he is "interested in the notion of finishing off one's childhood as one completes making a wheel. The idea is to go back and confront your childhood, in a sense relive it if you can, so that you can be whole."[45] The Losers Club members are able to do that as adults by closing what they call their "magic circle" of friendship (through the realization that their experiences in childhood allowed them "to give birth to the people they will become ... [who] must necessarily birth the people they were.... The circle closes; the wheel rolls").[46] This magical circle, or wheel, finds its ultimate expression in Silver when Bill uses the bicycle at the novel's end to miraculously awaken his wife from her living death of catatonia, allowing the power of his childhood belief in magic to empower him with the ability to "beat the devil" one final time. Through the final ride on Silver, Bill achieves an epiphany and learns a valuable lesson about faith and the belief in childhood fantasy.[47] As Bill himself states in the novel's conclusion, "If life teaches anything at all, it teaches that there are so many happy endings that the man who believes there is no God needs his rationality called into serious question."[48]

In direct contrast to the innocent purity of the childhood bicycle, the adult-oriented automobile is seen throughout King's fiction as destructive, as a site of evil more powerful than any haunted house or demonic temple. King himself referred to the automobile as "a symbol for the technological age or the end of innocence [since] it plays such a part in adolescence and growing up."[49] For many of King's characters, the monstrous nature of certain individuals can be viewed through a description of the car they drive. For example, in King's first novel, *Carrie*, Billy Nolan's sinister character is addressed immediately through a description of his car: "Billy's car was old, dark, somehow sinister. The windshield was milky around the edges, as if a cataract was beginning to form. The seats were loose and unanchored. . . . The car smelled of oil and gas. . . . The back wheels were jacked and the hood seemed to point at the road. And of course he drove fast."[50]

Other examples of ominous cars being associated with the corruption of their drivers include George Stark's menacing Toronado with the "HIGH-TONED SON OF A BITCH" bumper sticker that he drives literally out of his burial crypt in *The Dark Half* (1989) and the car that Billy Halleck uses to accidentally run down the old gypsy woman while Billy is distracted by his wife's sexual advances in *Thinner* (1984). The tainted character of all three men (Billy Nolan, George Stark, and Billy Halleck) is mirrored both in the cars they own and the manner in which they drive them (fast, recklessly, irresponsibly). The condition of the car speaks to the condition of the man.[51]

In *Christine* King's readers witness the ultimate corruption of man by automobile. The novel features Arnie Cunningham, a sweet-natured teenage geek who becomes entranced by a 1958 Plymouth Fury named Christine that he believes will be his ticket to popularity and success with girls. Despite his friend Dennis Guilder's assurances that he does not need the car to be empowered, Arnie purchases Christine and soon falls under her fatal spell. The car, it seems, is possessed by the angry spirit of its previous owner, Roland LeBay, who sacrificed his wife and daughter to gain power of his own. Christine initially seems protective of Arnie, willingly destroying his enemies (the local bullies who threaten and intimidate him) and granting him the power he craves. However, Christine is a parasite draining Arnie of his innocence and completely alienating him from his friends and family. Christine becomes all the significant other that Arnie could ever need, a situation that ends up in disaster when Arnie makes the decision to rebel against Christine, leading to his death at the hands of Roland LeBay's dark spirit.[52]

Mary Findley perceives the association between Christine and Roland LeBay (and, by extension, Arnie Cunningham) as a commentary on the detrimental relationship that Americans have with their automobiles. Often unable to pay in full for their cars, Americans become slaves to monthly car payments in addition to the other expenses associated with car ownership: insurance, gasoline, maintenance.[53] Automobile owners are tied to their vehicles through these unseen financial chains to the point that the car becomes emblematic of the kind of adult "responsibility" that children manage to avoid by virtue of their ownership of bicycles. Similarly, for Donna and Tad Trenton in *Cujo* (1981), the car becomes a literal prison from which they are unable to escape, a situation that dooms the innocent child Tad to death by sapping the very vitality he needs to stay alive.

After nearly forty years and over fifty published books, Stephen King continues to expand on his treatment of bicycles and automobiles as symbols of childhood and adulthood, innocence and corruption. His recently released novel *Mr. Mercedes* (2014) focuses on Brady Hartfield, a serial killer who uses a car as his weapon of choice, focusing once more on the use of the automobile as an instrument of death and destruction.[54] The symbolic value of the bicycle and the automobile clearly continue to hold great weight in King's imagination, showing that for him the vehicles serve as much more than simple transportation. They become both backdrop and character, the locus of childhood purity and the sobering introduction to adult codes of behavior that will slowly taint that purity.[55]

Notes

1. Stephen King, *Danse Macabre* (New York: Berkley Books, 1981), 83.
2. Joseph Reino, *Stephen King: The First Decade,* Carrie *to* Pet Sematary (Boston: Twayne, 1988), 4.
3. Fatal or near-fatal automobile accidents occur in *Carrie* (1974), *'Salem's Lot* (1975), *The Shining* (1977), *The Stand* (1978), *The Dead Zone* (1979), *Roadwork* (1981), *Christine* (1982), *Pet Sematary* (1983), *The Talisman* (1984), *Thinner* (1984), *It* (1986), *Misery* (1987), *The Tommyknockers* (1987), *The Dark Half* (1989), *Needful Things* (1991), *Insomnia* (1994), *Desperation* (1996), *Bag of Bones* (1998), *Hearts in Atlantis* (1999), *Dreamcatcher* (2001), *From a Buick 8* (2002), *The Dark Tower VII: The Dark Tower* (2004), *Cell* (2006), *Lisey's Story* (2006), *Duma Key* (2008), *Under the Dome* (2009), *11/22/63* (2011), and *Doctor Sleep* (2013). Trains are associated with death, destruction, and evil in many of King's works. The dead body of a young boy run down by a train becomes the object of fascination in the novella "The Body" (1982). Jack Sawyer and his friend Richard Sloat journey through the radioactive Blasted Lands in a train filled with the weapons their enemy wants to use to decimate two different worlds in *The Talisman*. The gunslinger Roland and his band of allies encounter two different evil trains in *The Dark Tower III: The Waste Lands* (1991): the seemingly innocent but actually deeply malevolent Charley the Choo-Choo and the insane Blaine the Mono. A group of travelers who died in a horrible train wreck find themselves trapped in the limbo of a nightmarish small town while waiting for another train to arrive to take them to their final destination in the short story "Willa" (2006). And a small carnival train is haunted by the ghost of a murdered girl in *Joyland* (2013). The only positive symbol of a train comes late in King's career. In *Doctor Sleep*, Dan Torrance and his allies use the Helen Rivington, a miniature train designed to be a children's ride, as a mode of transportation to help save Abra Stone, a little girl with psychic powers, from the malevolent cabal known as the True Knot. In this situation, the train they use is designed for children and, therefore, has many of the same connotations of innocent play as bicycles do in King's work.
4. Although bicycles have been around since the 1880s, they were not used as a method for youth transportation until the advent of the motorized vehicle in the 1920s. They were eventually mass-produced as a primary youth-oriented product in the 1950s. By the late twentieth and early twenty-first century, bicycles were so well established as a youth item that films of the era presented them exclusively as items of childhood play (e.g., Steven Spielberg's *E.T. the Extra-Terrestrial* [1982] and Jean-Pierre and Luc Dardenne's *The Kid with a Bike* [2011]), while adults who rode bikes in films were frequently seen as perverted (e.g., Todd Field's *Little Children* [2006]) or childlike and immature (e.g., Tim Burton's *Pee-Wee's Big Adventure* [1985]).

5. Alexander Nenilin, "Stephen King and the Theme of Childhood in the Anglo-American Literary Tradition" (thesis abstract, StephenKing.ru, 2006), 23, http://www.stephenking.ru/texts/stiven_king_i_problema_detstva/stephen _king_and_the_theme_of_childhood.pdf.

6. The "shining" is basically Halloran's grandmother's word for the ability to read minds, to see into both the past and the future, and to locate missing items. While Halloran's grandmother characterizes the ability to shine as a gift, she also warns her young grandson of the dangers of shining if the person with the ability misuses it or begins to feel superior to other humans from possession of the ability. See Stephen King, *The Shining* (New York: Doubleday, 1977), 24.

7. King, *Shining*, 38–39.

8. King, *Shining*, 39.

9. Tony Magistrale, *The Moral Voyages of Stephen King* (Mercer Island WA: Starmont House, 1988), 16.

10. King, *Shining*, 154.

11. King, *Shining*, 40–41.

12. Magistrale, *Moral Voyages*, 16.

13. King, *Shining*, 345.

14. In Stanley Kubrick's film adaptation of *The Shining* (1980), Kubrick removes the references to Jack's destruction of the bicycle, but Danny can be seen frequently riding through the halls of the Overlook Hotel on his Big Wheel tricycle. Kubrick inverts King's symbolic use of the bicycle in his work, transforming the Big Wheel as the "epitome of American 1970s childhood; a bastion of good, clean fun and innocence" into "a horrifying symbol of malevolence . . . an inverted image of childhood; a spinner of suspense, a possessed vehicle of ill-intent and a symbol of psychic terror." In Kubrick's filmic universe, the innocence of childhood, a protective buffer in King's fiction, becomes easily corrupted by the evil of the hotel. See Georgina Guthrie, "Screengem: Danny's Tricycle in *The Shining*," *Filmspot* (blog), November 7, 2013, para. 2, http://georginaguthrie.wordpress.com/2013/11/07/screengem -dannys-tricycle-in-the-shining/.

15. Richard Bachman [Stephen King], *The Regulators* (New York: Penguin, 1996), 34.

16. Bachman, *Regulators*, 44.

17. Stephen King, *'Salem's Lot* (New York: Doubleday, 1975), 352.

18. The van the Regulators use as their base of operation (i.e., murder vehicle) stresses the death and destruction associated with those characters and their mode of transportation, as opposed to the youthful innocence that Cary on his bicycle represents.

19. Stephen King, *Needful Things* (New York: Viking, 1991), 15–18.

20. King, *Needful Things*, 20.

21. King, *Needful Things*, 36.

22. King, *Needful Things*, 36.

23. Michael Collings, "The Persistence of Darkness," *StarShine and Shadows*, April 29, 2008, http://www.starshineandshadows.com/essays/2008-04-29.html.

24. King, *Needful Things*, 79, original italics.

25. King, *Needful Things*, 79.

26. King, *Needful Things*, 82.

27. King, *Needful Things*, 102. Alexandra Nagornaya states in her work on Stephen King's "body texts" that King focuses on the movement of the heart when he wants to suggest the emotional turmoil of a character in crisis, creating the sensation of the organ becoming a fully independent living thing that attempts to warn the person to whom it is attached that the action in which they are engaged could lead to their own demise. She specifically references the numerous examples of Brian's heart racing and engaging in "complex acrobatic tricks" as evidence for her thesis. See Alexandra Nagornaya, "Stephen King's Body Worlds: Language Conventions and Creativity in Depicting the Inner Body," *Athens Journal of Humanities and Arts* 1, no. 1 (January 2014): 62–64.

28. King, *Needful Things*, 103.

29. The hand washing could also demonstrate a relation between Brian and another corrupted figure, Pontias Pilate, who attempted to remove the stain of his corruption by saying, "I wash my hands of this" (Matthew 27:24). Equating Brian's perversion with that of the man who sentenced Christ to death suggests how far from his childhood innocence Brian has fallen.

30. King, *Needful Things*, 109.

31. King, *Needful Things*, 244.

32. King, *Needful Things*, 357.

33. King, *Needful Things*, 461.

34. King, *Needful Things*, 519.

35. The Losers Club is the name Bill gives to himself and his small group of friends (which includes Ben Hanscom, Beverly Marsh, Richie Tozier, Mike Hanlon, and Stan Uris). Bill dubs them the Losers Club ironically because, despite the outside community's view of them as weak and worthless, Bill sees great strength and value in all his friends, in much the same way he saw strength and value in the cheap and seemingly worthless silver bike in the window of the bike shop.

36. Stephen King, *It* (New York: Viking, 1986), 220–22.

37. King, *It*, 229–30.

38. King, *It*, 381.

39. The werewolf is frequently seen in scholarly literature as a direct symbolic reference to the onset of puberty and the seemingly magical transformation that takes place as the child's body matures, including developing increased musculature, growing hair in unexpected places all over the body, and falling prey to deep and heretofore unknown sexual desires. See Brian J. Frost, *The Essential Guide to Werewolf Literature* (Madison: University of Wisconsin Press, 2003), 24.

40. Kenneth B. Kidd, *Making American Boys: Boyology and the Feral Tale* (Minneapolis: University of Minnesota Press, 2004), 160.

41. King, *It*, 604.

42. King, *It*, 609.

43. King, *It*, 932. The extreme stutter over the word "wished" symbolizes Bill's reluctance to believe he can recapture that ability as an adult. See Margaret L. Carter, "The Turtle Can't Help Us: The Lovecraft Legacy in Stephen King's *It*," *Strange Horizons*, December 19, 2005, para. 19, http://www.strangehorizons.com/2005/20051219/king-lovecraft-a.shtml. At the same time, the reemergence of Bill's childhood stutter is a tangible suggestion that it is possible for an adult to recapture the nature of the child within him- or herself to allow access to that more innocent power. See Gabriel Rodriguez, *It*: An Annotated Look at Stephen King's Epic Novel, n.d., http://stephenkingsit.weebly.com (accessed December 17, 2013).

44. Jonathan P. Davis, *Stephen King's America* (Bowling Green OH: Bowling Green State University Popular Press, 1994), 63.

45. Douglas Winter, *Stephen King: The Art of Darkness* (New York: New American Library, 1984), 185.

46. King, *It*, 1135.

47. Carter, "Turtle Can't Help Us," 25.

48. King, *It*, 1135.

49. Stephen Jones, *Creepshows: The Illustrated Stephen King Movie Guide* (New York: Billboard Books, 2002), 33.

50. Stephen King, *Carrie* (New York: Doubleday, 1974), 106.

51. Tony Magistrale, *Hollywood's Stephen King* (New York: Palgrave Macmillan, 2003), 158.

52. Stephen King, *Christine* (New York: Viking, 1983), 461–62.

53. Mary Findley, "Stephen King's Vintage Ghost-Cars: A Modern-Day Haunting," in *Spectral America: Phantoms and the National Imagination*, ed. Jeffrey Andrew Weinstock (Madison: University of Wisconsin Press, 2004), 211.

54. King's bicycle-automobile dichotomy has even bled into the fiction of his son Joe Hill. Hill's novel *NOS4A2* focuses on two opposing characters: Charles Manx, a pedophiliac serial killer who abducts children in his vintage 1938 Rolls-Royce Wraith with the NOS4A2 license plate, and Victoria

McQueen, a young woman who can seemingly magically locate things by riding her Raleigh Tuff Burner bicycle through a bridge called the Shorter Way. The central conflict of the narrative is between the one who would destroy the innocence of children (represented by the car) and the one who would rescue those children from him (represented by the bicycle). Hill even intensifies the connection through direct allusions to King's earlier work, such as a map showing the locations of Derry, Maine, and a place called Pennywise's Circus, both references linking Hill's novel to King's *It*, which, as discussed in this essay, also features a character with a magical bicycle. See Joe Hill, *NOS4A2* (New York: HarperCollins, 2013).

55. Magistrale, *Hollywood's Stephen King*, 25.

PART 2 **BIKES IN FILM**

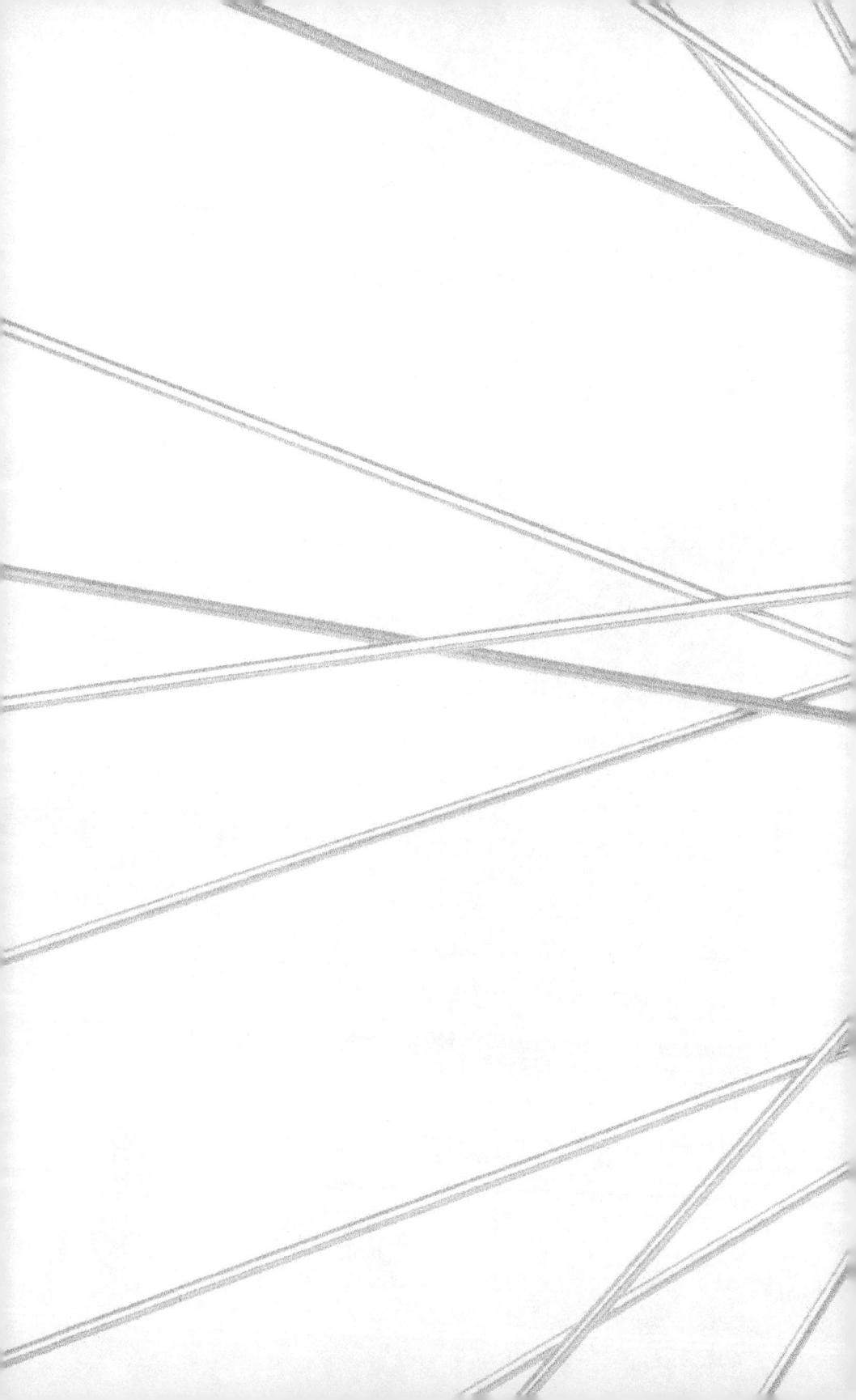

10 "I'll Get You, My Pretty!"

Bicycle Horror and the Abject Cyclicity of History

MATTHEW PANGBORN

In the classic American film *The Wizard of Oz* (1939), the main character, Dorothy Gale, finds herself trapped in her Kansas farmhouse as a tornado lifts it into the air. After a window detaches itself from her bedroom wall and hits her head, she catches glimpses of the familiar figures of her life, flying past outside: a coop full of chickens, a cow, her aunt in a rocking chair, farmhands—and then her busybody neighbor, Miss Gulch, riding on a bicycle that transforms before Dorothy's eyes into a witch's broom. Miss Gulch, now the Wicked Witch of the West, cackles. Dorothy screams. And in that scream, only Dorothy's second in a sequence that has haunted millions of TV-watching children every fall since the late 1950s, may be read not just a character's fear but also a nation's extreme discomfort with the particular kind of transformation the bicycle represents, a horror, properly speaking, still evoked by the bicycle today.[1]

To get at that horror, it is first necessary to acknowledge the importance of the sequence to the film and of the film to the nation. The tornado functions as something of a plot "twister," by which Dorothy may be transported from her aunt and uncle's farm to a child's dreamland of munchkins and flying monkeys, from which she can only return via a heroine's journey, discovering within herself courage, compassion, and intelligence. The film's importance to the nation lies in its depiction of this journey as involving the trade-in of an impoverished, sepia-toned heartland for a Technicolor fantasy of emeralds, rubies, and gold, an exchange the United States was only too eager to make after a decade of the Great Depression. Dorothy, then, serves as representative of a nation desirous not just of the better-off but of the fantabulously wealthy. The film's lesson, delivered as unsubtly as a window upside the head, is that viewers have in themselves the power to reframe the world to effect that change. After all, if a windstorm is all that is needed for our main character to arrive in a brighter, shinier place, isn't she already a Gale?

Since the film's annual TV screenings began in 1959, thereby increasing estimation of the film, critics of *The Wizard of Oz* have tended to read it either as a Joseph Campbell–esque fable on that difficult process of growing into adulthood or as a political allegory on that even more difficult subject of U.S. monetary policy. The former view sees Dorothy as an adolescent Every Girl trying to make sense of the changes that come with adulthood (the ruby slippers standing in, for example, for the red blood of menarches); the latter finds in symbols such as the yellow brick road reference to national debates about the coinage of precious metals. These were in full flush at the time of L. Frank Baum's writing of the source novel for the film, *The Wonderful Wizard of Oz* (1900); but controversy around these policies only persisted through Franklin Delano Roosevelt's repeal of the gold standard six years before the film's release.[2] The latter reading has perhaps had the most staying power, evidenced by the popular nicknaming of recent Federal Reserve chairs Alan Greenspan and Ben Bernanke as the Wizard of Oz by those critical of their policies.[3] But given the film's historical moment, it is easy to combine the two readings.

Reading the film as a national coming-to-riches story, or what he calls a "secular myth of America," Paul Nathanson examines *The Wizard of Oz* as "recapitulat[ing] American history": "It begins in the Munchkin City (actually a village or town not unlike those of an earlier America) and concludes in the Emerald City (a large and impressive metropolis not unlike New York or Hollywood). Linking them all is the Yellow Brick Road (a paved highway through the wilderness in both time and space)."[4]

Central to this reimagined history is the faith that history can only run one way, in the direction of progress. For Nathanson, what undergirds this "civil religion" are "fantasies of technologically advanced urban communities," represented by the Emerald City, whose temple-like structure is marked by "a collection of 'decorative light wheels' . . . and hubcaps" just like those that appear "on a frieze in the Chrysler Building."[5] Oz, then, isn't just any American utopia; its traffic-signal palette of red, yellow, and green riches (i.e., ruby, gold, and emerald) identifies it as that car-centric vision James Howard Kunstler has wryly dubbed the "Era of Happy Motoring." Sociologists call the ideology that has grown around that vision "automobility": the notion that cars are more than just vehicles but carry with them "a politics of freedom and equality," enabling "the 'natural' development of society both to greater mobility and to greater individualization and thus associat[ing] their users, and their corollaries, roads, with modernity itself."[6] The car, in short, is what will reframe Americans' outlook; and after World War II banishes the Depression, it is war-hero president Dwight Eisenhower who literalizes the metaphor of the path of gold with the $25 billion Federal-Aid Highway Act of 1956.[7]

The 1939 audience would have understood the Technicolor of the film's central Oz section to signify unrealistic fantasy (a perception that may have initially lessened serious appreciation of the film); however, with the buildup of colorful advertising around its TV presentations, viewers instead began to ask why Dorothy would ever want to return to the farm.[8] Oz, in other words, begins to look more like home than that stretch of land just north of Oklahoma, reflecting viewers' acculturation to the oddly Oz-like realm of the road-traveling shopper. For there is a lot in *The Wizard of Oz* that anticipates the training that young women of the postwar period especially will undergo to become fully fledged "consumer citizens" of the new advertising age orbiting around the car: the "show windows," the greeters, the errands, the dizzying array of choices, the return to the family with food (even if in Dorothy's case it is only food for thought).[9] The naturalization of Oz's fantasyland as American TV-and-car-culture landscape comes full circle by 1999, when Keanu Reeve's character in *The Matrix*, having chosen to give up the life he has been living in a computer-generated illusion, is told, "Buckle your seatbelt, Dorothy, 'cause Kansas is going bye-bye." Even in *The Matrix*'s futuristic world, trading in the unfulfilling unreality of Kansas is still something one does in the language of the car.[10]

Here we begin to get some hint of why the bicycling Miss Gulch should be read by Dorothy and by the nation as a witch on a broomstick and why the bicycle itself should so appall contemporary America. All the important elements are available in that glimpse outside Dorothy's window: the past technology that must be forgotten, the laboring body that should be hidden, and a temporal-spatial dislocation that threatens to disorient not just Dorothy but also the viewer.

Looking Backward

We thus begin our consideration of bicycle horror with a look backward at an old movie not by accident. As the oft-told bicycle mechanic's joke has it, the answer to the question of when the bicycle was invented is always "Yesterday."[11] Not only does the machine lack a clear origin, but its various innovations are also often proven to be simply reintroductions of past designs.[12] One thing we know for certain, however, is that its first boom in popularity in the United States during the 1890s brought about many of the developments we have come to associate with the automobile. The source of today's demands for more and better roads? The bicycle, whose first enthusiasts lobbied governments to provide safer streets for their new hobby.[13] The original pattern for the mass-manufacturing system often referred to as "Fordism"? The bicycle, one of "the very first—and most expensive— mass-produced luxury durable consumer goods," whose production in the United States "developed into one of the largest industries in the country."[14] And the origin of the discourse of freedom that has come to surround the car? The bicycle, which "to youths . . . gave speed; to women, freedom; and to . . . all . . . exercise and adventure."[15] In every case, where the automobile is supposed to be singular, the height of technology and individual empowerment, the bicycle is there before it, a disavowed origin but also something of a doppelganger, a double that reveals too much about the subject.

The bicycle thus emerges in the language of motorists as both absurdly, shockingly old ("a donkey cart without the cart, where you do the work of the donkey," as P. J. O'Rourke put it) and absurdly, shockingly new (a "spread of dull whirrs, sharp whistles and sanctimonious pedal-pushing," according to the same author).[16] In both cases, however, is found the assumption of an already existing intimacy between the bicycle and the motorist—a refusal by the bicycle to meet the motorist's perceived needs and the expectation of some kind of judgment on the motorist going the other way. That is, to borrow the title of Edward Bellamy's technophilic utopian tale *Looking Backward* (1888), published just before the bicycle's first American boom and Baum's *Oz*, the bicycle seems primitive, something the driver must glance back in time to consider, while at the same time its more progressive response to modern crises makes the car seem regressive, or backward. O'Rourke's motorist does not merely feel guilty about driving, when a healthier, greener alternative exists, after all; nor does he imagine the cyclist scolding him. He feels the bicycle itself casting shame. This image of the bicycle as something of a disapproving origin for modern car culture suggests its power for the contemporary viewer is related to Julia Kristeva's concept of the abject, which finds its source in an original part of the self supposed to be cast off in the psychoanalytic subject's formation but which haunts it as a rejected part of its early development.

According to Kristeva, the classic example of the abject is the mother, with whom the infant identifies before entering into the symbolic world and against whom the infant must imaginatively act in order to take a place as a functioning individual within the symbolic order.[17] The mother is thus "thrown off," and this separation is maintained, even as the subject recognizes a foundational power to a part of him- or herself thrown away with her. Cultures also produce abjects, as anything that threatens to blur the boundaries culture puts in place between self and other must be similarly rejected. Horror arises when people or objects refuse to stay in neat categories or when the subject's recognition of self in the other produces something of a disorienting double vision. The figure of the mother, for example, is often divided into "good" (nurturing and accepted) and "bad" (threatening and rejected). O'Rourke's anticipation of disapproval from the pedal-pushing bicycle suggests it is a "bad" mother; that the car might function as a "good" is supported by every ad extolling a comfortable interior wherein one might be cooed to by the female voice on the GPS. In 1939, at *The Wizard of Oz*'s release, the United States might have wished itself parentless, being pulled into the biggest old-world war of all time; but by the arrival of full-blown "Happy Motoring" in the 1950s, the "good" mother was everywhere, as nearly every car, it seemed, came equipped with Dagmar bumpers, what one admirer describes as resembling a "massive set of chrome breasts."[18]

The bicycle offers none of the externalization of the positively maternal embodied by the car—neither womb-like cuddle nor Oedipal curves—and thus may be identified as "bad" mother, its rider looked on as someone who has not yet mastered the necessary psychical separation of adulthood. The bicycle, signaling the persistence of the primitive or childlike in modernity, thus provides a double source of discomfort: a made object with the power to stunt the "natural growth" of the otherwise adult human riding it yet one with an aura of judgment against the world the car has nurtured. The rider on the bicycle appears not as a powerful human user with an inanimate tool, a familiar subject and object, but as something of an "assemblage," to use the Deleuzo-Guattarian language suggested by Jane Bennett in her recent exploration of "nonhuman forces" in our lives, in which the human is not the only (physical *or* moral) agent or "actant."[19] Even before Miss Gulch on a bicycle turns into a witch on a broom, therefore, and even before her bicycle takes to the air, the partnership of the human and the machine conjures up a magic of hybridization but also critique, whereby both the cyclist and the car-centric world can be made instantly to appear lacking.

The Gasping Body

The blurring of lines between human and thing in the motorist's gasp at the monstrous cyclist—his or her shockingly backward, "over-mothered" appearance, which hints at a critique of modernity but also of assumptions about agency—is not the only abject moment in such a view, however. The cyclist also shocks through a seeming ability to return a reflection of the motorist, an effect available in the film scene, in which bicycle and rider respond to the viewer's wish they go away by becoming a broom and witch, but also an effect evidenced in letters to newspaper editors like the following, in which the solicitude for the safety of those on two wheels regularly becomes an assertion of danger to the driving self: "I came around a blind curve and a cyclist was suddenly only feet away from me in the middle of the road. Two vehicles were directly across from me in the opposite lane. I had no choice but to slam on my brakes. Had a car been behind me, I would have been creamed. Would the biker have been responsible for my rear-end collision? Nope. He would have pedaled along his merry way."[20]

Noncyclists have, from the bicycle's first American boom, been worried about the physical dangers cyclists run: not just of injury but of the "'bicycle stoop' [that] allegedly resulted when racers arched their backs for long periods" or "bicycle face," supposedly brought about by grimacing while keeping one's "vehicle in balance."[21] If these worries seem hyperbolic, one reason could be that they act out a wish fulfillment on the body enjoying a happiness that car culture declares is reserved for the driver. In other words, whatever view one has of the letter writer's sincerity, it is clear the anger directed at the cyclist is shaped at least in part by the shock of having "no choice" in a vehicle supposed to guarantee freedom.

Kristeva's example of the infant who desires to control orally the mother's breast seems apropos here, as the infant generates a masking fear for its own aggressive impulse, an "I am afraid of horses, I am afraid of being bitten," which cloaks the infant's own "I am afraid of biting."[22] Drivers worry for cyclists, in other words, because they feel the desire to run them over. In *The Wizard of Oz*, the bicycling Miss Gulch threatens to take away Dorothy's dog, Toto, because it has bitten her; could it be that orphaned Dorothy's anger at her lack of a mother is played out in that bite against a woman who shows the same dangerous but seductive ability to go where she pleases?[23] Both danger and seduction are apparent in the letter, too. That is, the writer does not merely appropriate the threat to the other as a threat to the self, to mask the threat she herself poses and to suggest some means of control of the other, in the name of safety; she also imagines for the other that happy escape she wants for herself. The blurring of lines between viewer and viewed in this moment has to do not just with resentment but with desire.

That one source of discomfort at the appearance of the cyclist should be an upwelling of desire should not surprise us, because the bicycle is, as Paul Fournel suggestively describes, "the shortest path to the doubling of yourself. Twice as fast, two times less tired, twice as much wind in your face. It's all right always to want more."[24] And since the bicycle's invention, onlookers have felt—if not necessarily understood—this pull. Writers offered advice both medical and aesthetic especially to New Women cyclists garbed in bloomers, recommending, for example, "neat ankle action"; but panic quickly grew that the activity "prevented women from having children . . . and encouraged improper liaisons with the opposite sex. . . . Some even hinted that friction between a woman and her saddle caused illicit sexual arousal."[25] In The Wizard of Oz, Miss Gulch does not wear bloomers, but the film's insistence on her ugliness suggests she functions as a warning for Dorothy not to follow in the pedal-strokes of the suffragettes of an earlier era, lest she grow up to be a spinster—or, even worse, a creature disfigured by her own desire.[26] After all, the swoon Dorothy experiences at the glimpse of the Wicked Witch of the West, the gyrations of the bed Dorothy has collapsed onto, and the witch's later repeated calling out to Dorothy, "I'll get you, my pretty!" all suggest that the witch pursues her for reasons surpassing mere vengeance or greed and that Dorothy somehow feels the power of a desire the film itself dares not name.[27]

The bicycle thus not only blurs the line between human and thing, putting paid to the problematic modern "faith" critiqued by Bruno Latour in his provocatively titled We Have Never Been Modern, which faith holds that humanity may be categorized as entirely separate from nature and things, but it also prompts recognition of the desire of the viewer to cross such lines.[28] That is why Miss Gulch's transformation into witch, which should comfort viewers disturbed by a figure of horror more relevant than that which plagued Salem in the 1690s, actually heightens the scene's disturbance: viewers can recognize the powerful effecting of their desire but also the scene's anticipation of it—its "knowing" of what they want. As for the bicycle, it is only too clearly a hybrid, a "'curious vehicle [whose] passenger is its engine,'" which results in a "relationship, even a temporal fusion or assemblage, between human and machine that is distinctive from other vehicles in what it requires, enables, and effects."[29] And what the bicycle seems to effect, judging from its doubling, its merry way, is pleasure. But it also seems to "know" this. Didn't it appear in front of the writer of the above newspaper letter, after all, right at that moment when she discovered she had "no choice," demonstrating there was indeed a choice, a tempting one, even if it were one she would never consider?[30] The same issue arises on those roadside signs urging drivers to take caution, by picturing a riderless, antiquated bicycle, sometimes accompanied by the caption Watch for Bicycles. That one of these bicycles might be carrying a rider is perhaps too explicit an evocation of pleasure for the sign to suggest. Is the subject of the sign public safety or pornography? Just who is being protected here?

The Wizard of Oz presents Dorothy's all-too-modern desire to escape to a land beyond troubles in a vision of the only independently mobile woman she knows mounted on a bike, a woman who "owns half the county" and thus is exempt from the farm's labor. Dorothy's reaction is disorientation. The scene resembles the dream of Freud's "Wolf Man" of a tree outside his bedroom window filled with staring wolves, which the psychoanalyst concludes references the child's witnessing of the "primal scene" of his parents having sex.[31] Only, in the film, the conjoining has to do with a pleasurable human-machine combination, echoed by the glimpses of the aunt on a rocking chair and the farmhands rowing a boat.[32] Does modernity have its own primal scene between human and machine? The film's reaction is a picture of panic. An outside shot shows the heights to which the house is carried by the tornado; and when we return to the room in which Dorothy is trapped, the confines of the bedroom seem even closer. All of this is commanded by a strangely mesmeric and eyelike stare, outside the window, from an impossibly placed and unrelentingly spinning pair of bicycle wheels.

Cyclicity Now

Everything in the scene of Dorothy gasping in horror at Miss Gulch is moving in circles: the tornado, the spinning house, the gyrating bed, the curve of each moving object in the sky as the windowsill maintains its framing, and, of course, the turning of those bicycle wheels. The entire world seems without direction, except that the witch's orientation from left to right, the direction of reading eye movement and the side of the room with the door, suggests that whichever way Dorothy might try to escape, Miss Gulch is going that way, too. The relationship Americans have had with the bicycle is seemingly one the bicycle does not want to end. Or to speak less extravagantly, one might say that as a partner in the origin of modernity, the bicycle has helped place modern humans on a path that, if it has an end, will have something to do with the bicycle. Among the questions the bicycle forces its viewer to ask, then, are not just "Where did it come from?" and "What is it doing here?" but "Where are we *both* going?"

Much has been written about Americans' disdain for history. While Europeans have been interested for centuries in the ends of history, it is only in the United States, seemingly, that history could be declared ended.[33] The United States has a particular investment in the notion of improvement, a "New World" detached from the "Old," but also an idiosyncratic demand for this history to produce a utopia as soon as possible. As Jon Savage observes, writing about the "new vitalism" of the 1890s that witnessed the rise of mass marketing, "Whereas time for Europeans was seen in a sequence of events, with the present following the past, for more and more Americans time represented a total instantaneity, an infinitely prolongable NOW!"[34] It is this NOW! that is reinforced by the automobile's push-button responsiveness, which allows a driver wishing to turn on the air conditioner or to zoom off at one hundred miles an hour to do so by simply lifting a finger or toe. Cyclists' view of history is necessarily much different, as they must rely on their own strength and judgment—and in a pinch, outside help—because if they want to speed up, there will most definitely be a price to pay.

To mount a bicycle is thus to enter an experience of life with no sure happy ending, a threshold space between the workaday world and pleasurable chaos, which we might equate with carnival—those communal, festive moments outside "real" time and "normal" rules—except that it is in the nature of car culture not to admit such a gray area.[35] "Automobility," as Zygmunt Bauman argues, "fosters individu-

ality, competition, rejection of all collective responsibility, aggressive-
ness, and domination by way of movement, speed, and escape."[36] What
Bauman describes is a war, of course, one that shows in the number
of car-related casualties in the United States, "35,000 to 40,000 deaths
and 2 million injuries each year," which would seem acceptable only
in a struggle of national importance.[37] This is one reason drivers so
often speak about cyclists in terms of warfare. In a couple of 1988 letters to the *New York Times* editor, for example, writers alerted authorities to the "Kamikaze bicyclists upon us."[38] Bicycles and their riders,
seeming to exist in another experience of time, represent a return of
those natural cycles the car is supposed to overcome; they are traitors,
participating in nature's counterattack.

Yet, like Dorothy in her bedroom, the automobile driver glances
out the window to see a world full of circular turnings, a world the
driver has tried violently—but unsuccessfully—to transcend.[39] Even
the economic version of American utopianism, the endless growth
fable that has lulled economists since the United States' founding, has
suffered many boom-and-bust cycles. Indeed, the crash of American
bicycle manufacturing in 1897 is what lured so many of the industry's leaders into automobile production in the first place.[40] But automobile drivers, who cannot see, after all, their own wheels, are like
investors who come to the stock market just as a bubble is about to
pop—sure that they are the exceptions to the cyclical. And thus lowly
reminders of the power the cyclical still has over us appear from the
automobile like pests of an almost supernatural persistence, like the
newspaper boy in *Better Off Dead* (1985), who shows up on his jingling single-speed at the unlikeliest moments to demand from John
Cusack's character an unpaid debt: "Where's my two dollars?"[41]

What emerges, then, from the driver's glance outside the window
at the cyclist is a slow, multistage recognition: First, the rider on the
bicycle is not the only desiring, machine-human hybrid out on the
road. And second, while the car is supposed to act as champion of a
modernity at escape velocity, it has yet to outrun the bicycle's reminder
of human vulnerability to both natural and assembled cycles. Bennett
uses the example of someone riding a bicycle on gravel to illustrate an
assemblage, as in observing the rider's activity of "throw[ing] . . . weight

this way or that, inflect[ing] the bike in one direction," a bystander may find some hint of all of the other actants at work, much like judging the wind from the blowing of the trees.[42] Once that multiplicity of forces is gauged, as Bennett comments, "the ethical responsibility of an individual human now resides in one's response to the assemblages in which one finds oneself participating: Do I attempt to extricate myself from assemblages whose trajectory is likely to do harm? Do I enter into the proximity of assemblages whose conglomerate effectivity tends toward the enactment of nobler ends?"[43]

To even consider the possibility of acting other than according to automobility, however, is to confront the disturbingly anti-Ozian reality of car culture: its pollution, its casualties, its extravagant waste of resources. It means contemplating a destination for the nation that is likely to have very little resemblance to a Bellamy-esque, industrialist utopia in which we all win awards for our courage, brains, and compassion. And it means putting under severe scrutiny the seemingly commonsensical equation of technological development with human progress, because if our machines are our fellow actants, the car at least seems to have a power, like witchcraft, to lead us astray.

Conclusion: What the Bicycle Sees

So where, then, does the bicycle want to lead us? That is, not only does Miss Gulch stare from that place reserved for a higher power, but the bicycle, too, appearing as an original and rejected coagent of sorts, looks back with its two dizzyingly busy wheel-eyes on that modernity we humans had thought was a private, intraspecies affair, casting judgment—and perhaps offering another perspective on our common path. When we survey poor Miss Gulch, we see the figure the bicycle has made of her, a mockery of the main tenets of modernity and automobility, without her seeming to know it. But has not the car made creatures of us, too? Yearning like Dorothy to escape the antiquated, the impoverished, the physically demanding, we have reached repeatedly for the same old story of our separation from and mastery over nature, waiting for that magic moment when the rest of the universe begins to read off the same script.

The bicycle's take on things is that this idea of a separation is mistaken, a judgment Deleuze and Guattari suggest we should not be surprised to receive from it, as "tools exist only in relation to the interminglings they make possible or that make them possible. The stirrup entails a new man-horse symbiosis that at the same time entails new weapons and new instruments. Tools are inseparable from symbioses or amalgamations defining a Nature-Society machinic assemblage ... a society is defined by its amalgamations, not by its tools."[44]

Each tool, car or bicycle, guides our thinking, enabling but also limiting our possibilities; moreover, in the words of Deleuze and Guattari, each tool's vulnerable amalgamation—not mastered object—has the power to define us. Modernity, which Latour reminds us is supposed to be "defined in terms of humanism, either as a way of announcing the birth of 'man' or announcing his death," reveals itself instead as a multiplicity of partnerships announcing neither human triumph nor human tragedy but signaling only the continued efforts of humans to navigate the world.[45] Modernity's grand ambition either for birth or death, the Utopia or Bust slogan of the car, seen in this light, the bicycle's light, becomes something harder, simpler, more humble.

But to think that the horror the bicycle evokes in us can be resolved with such a calm and reasoned recognition is to miss the point of horror, which tells us in its every filmic interpretation that any threat to our sense of well-being is most dangerous when it appears dead or explained away. The bicycle's reflection on modernity is not merely a matter of storytelling critique, of course. The car has spurred us would-be moderns to feed its appetite for fuel and newer and bigger roads just as it has promised to sate our appetite for domination and escape, and the consequences of those enacted desires are all around us. We live, in other words, in a world the car has helped to imagine and build. And if the bicycle is growing in use, for the total number of trips by bicycle in the United States has tripled since the days of the 1970s oil embargo, perhaps the bicycle knows something we are not talking about.[46] Its gearing is a measure of our own strength, its design a reflection of our own desire, its needs proportionate to our own weaknesses. It has emancipated New Women and energized old men; it has taught its own hard lessons about the open road to generations of grimly balancing children. Perhaps, just perhaps, with its disturbing recent reemergence, the bicycle is bringing with it a nature we thought we had put behind us and a future whose shape we never would have chosen for ourselves.

Notes

The author would like to thank Rachel Mairose for her assistance in research.

1. *The Wizard of Oz*, directed by Victor Fleming (1939; Burbank CA: Warner Home Video, 2013), DVD.
2. Paul Nathanson, *Over the Rainbow:* The Wizard of Oz *as a Secular Myth of America* (Albany: State University of New York Press, 1991), 55–95; Ranjit S. Dighe, ed., *The Historian's* Wizard of Oz: *Reading L. Frank Baum's Classic as a Political and Monetary Allegory* (Westport CT: Praeger, 2002), 14, 24.
3. Yves Smith, ECONned: *How Unenlightened Self Interest Undermined Democracy and Corrupted Capitalism* (New York: Palgrave Macmillan, 2010), 199–232.
4. Nathanson, *Over the Rainbow*, 122.
5. Nathanson, *Over the Rainbow*, 133, 227, 38.
6. James Howard Kunstler, *The Geography of Nowhere* (New York: Touchstone, 1993); Steffen Böhm, Campbell Jones, Chris Land, and Matthew Paterson, eds., *Against Automobility* (Malden MA: Blackwell Publishing / Sociological Review, 2006), 7.
7. Richard F. Weingroff, "Federal-Aid Highway Act of 1956: Creating the Interstate System," *Public Roads* 60, no. 1 (Summer 1996), U.S. Department of Transportation, Federal Highway Administration, last modified June 15, 2015, http://www.fhwa.dot.gov/publications/publicroads/96summer/p96su10.cfm.
8. Nathanson, *Over the Rainbow*, 28. Indeed, for at least one critic of the film, the moral of Dorothy's journey is that "the bonds of family are omnipresent and inescapable," as if her Kansas home were a prison. See Andrew Gordon, "You'll Never Get Out of Bedford Falls: The Inescapable Family in American Science Fiction and Fantasy Films," *Journal of Popular Films and Television* 20, no. 2 (1992): 2–8.
9. Joel Spring, *Educating the Consumer-Citizen: A History of the Marriage of Schools, Advertising, and Media* (Mahwah NJ: Lawrence Erlbaum Associates, 2003), 22–26.
10. There is also, of course, the very real, physical trip Neo takes by car in order to meet Morpheus and escape from the matrix; this car ride starts, appropriately enough for the founder of a new world, at the Adams Street Bridge. See *The Matrix*, directed by Andy Wachowski and Lana Wachowski (1999; Burbank CA: Warner Home Video, 2007), DVD.

11. Luis Vivanco, *Reconsidering the Bicycle: An Anthropological Perspective on a New (Old) Thing* (New York: Routledge, 2013), 40.

12. A good example of the phenomenon of the newest thing in cycling also being the oldest is the popularity today of balance bikes for toddlers. Manufacturers' websites tout the model's innovation as allowing children to skip training wheels; and one's marketing of a special Harley Davidson model, encouraging children to equate "freedom and fun" with "feeling the wind in your face on the open road," seems designed for youngsters to skip the bicycle stage of childhood development altogether. Strider Bikes, "Strider Revved for Harley-Strider Bikes," Motorcycle USA, November 8, 2013, http://www.motorcycle-usa.com/568/17384/Motorcycle-Article/Strider-Revved-for-Harley-Strider-Bikes.aspx. Only, the supposedly unique make of the balance bike is almost exactly the same as the very earliest of bicycles, known variously as the "velocipede," the "Draisine," or the "hobbyhorse," unveiled in southern Germany nearly two centuries ago. See also Vivanco, *Reconsidering the Bicycle*, 27.

13. Michael Taylor, "The Bicycle Boom and the Bicycle Bloc: Cycling and Politics in the 1890s," *Indiana Magazine of History* 104 (September 2008): 213–40.

14. Vivanco, *Reconsidering the Bicycle*, 26; David V. Herlihy, *Bicycle: The History* (New Haven CT: Yale University Press, 2004), 278. For a thorough study of Fordism's precursor in bicycle manufacture, see Glen Norcliffe, "Popeism and Fordism," *Regional Studies* 31, no. 3 (1997): 267–80.

15. Herlihy, *Bicycle*, 264.

16. P. J. O'Rourke, "Dear Urban Cyclists: Go Play in Traffic," *Wall Street Journal*, April 2, 2011, http://www.wsj.com/articles/SB10001424052748704050204576218600999993800.

17. Julia Kristeva, *Powers of Horror: An Essay on Abjection*, trans. Leon S. Roudiez (New York: Columbia University Press, 1982), 64–65.

18. Matt Hardigree, "The Ten Best Car Design Elements of All Time," *Jalopnik* (blog), October 28, 2008, http://jalopnik.com/5069475/the-ten-best-car-design-elements-of-all-time; Craig Fitzgerald, "Dagmar Bumpers," *Hemmings Motor News*, October 2006, http://www.hemmings.com/hmn/stories/2006/10/01/hmn_feature21.html.

19. Jane Bennett, *Vibrant Matter: A Political Ecology of Things* (Durham NC: Duke University Press, 2010), 37.

20. Barbara Baker, "Bicyclists Need to Use Common Sense to Assure Safety for All," *Pittsburg Post-Gazette*, August 1, 2013, http://www.post-gazette.com/opinion/letters/2013/08/01/Bicyclists-need-to-use-common-sense-to-assure-safety-for-all/stories/201308010219.

21. Herlihy, *Bicycle*, 271–72.

22. Kristeva, *Powers of Horror*, 38–39.

23. Dorothy herself does not bite the other woman, of course; but she approves of the dog's action and is more willing to give up her home than her pet. The dog's biting of Miss Gulch is also not the last time in the film that Toto will act on Dorothy's own feelings and hunches, such as when the dog pulls aside Oz's curtain and expresses its disapproval of the man's duplicity by barking at him.

24. Paul Fournel, *Need for the Bike*, trans. Allan Stoekl (Lincoln: University of Nebraska Press, 2003), 24.

25. Frederick Alderson, *Bicycling: A History* (New York: Praeger, 1972), 94; Herlihy, *Bicycle*, 271, 266–67.

26. The 1970 British film *And Soon the Darkness* functions as an even more obvious cautionary tale, dealing with the disappearance of a young woman in France on a bicycling tour. *And Soon the Darkness*, directed by Robert Fuest (1970; New York: Thorn EMI / HBO Video, 2002), DVD. The 2010 American remake of the same title moves the scene of the action to Argentina but keeps the framing of the dangerously independent (and sexual?) female tour by bicycle. *And Soon the Darkness*, directed by Marcos Efron (Beverly Hills CA: Anchor Bay Entertainment, 2010), DVD.

27. References to the film both in popular culture and in criticism regularly comment on what seems to be a boundary-crossing sexual subtext. For example, for a reading of *The Wizard of Oz* as a lesbian fantasy, one only strengthened by Judy Garland's gaining status as a gay icon later in her career, see Alexander Doty, "'My Beautiful Wickedness': *The Wizard of Oz* as Lesbian Fantasy," in *Hop on Pop: The Politics and Pleasures of Popular Culture*, ed. Henry Jenkins, Tara McPherson, and Jane Shattuc (Durham NC: Duke University Press, 2002), 138–57. Much could be said as well about the bicycle's own apparent threat to heteronormativity.

28. Bruno Latour, *We Have Never Been Modern*, trans. Catherine Porter (Cambridge MA: Harvard University Press, 1993).

29. Vivanco, *Reconsidering the Bicycle*, 11–12.

30. An 1898 letter to the editor gets to the core of the matter in describing in the view of the bicycle and rider an "impossib[ility] to determine where the intelligence of the thing is." See Q. McAdam, letter to the editor, *New York Times*, June 8, 1898. The question is not merely where control of the thing lies—in other words, with the bicycle or the rider—but whether the steering of this combination is a matter of rationality or desire.

31. Sigmund Freud, *The "Wolfman" and Other Cases*, trans. Louise Adey Huish (New York: Penguin, 2003), 203–319.

32. Freud's explanation is critiqued by Deleuze and Guattari, who instead read the Wolf Man's dream as his recognition of himself as a multiplicity, a "machinic assemblage." See Gilles Deleuze and Felix Guattari, *A Thousand*

Plateaus, trans. Brian Massumi (Minneapolis: University of Minnesota Press, 1987), 26–38.

33. Francis Fukuyama, *The End of History and the Last Man* (New York: Free Press, 1992).

34. Jon Savage, *Teenage: The Creation of Youth Culture* (New York: Penguin, 2007), 55.

35. Mikhail Bakhtin, *Problems of Dostoyevsky's Poetics*, ed. and trans. Caryl Emerson (Minneapolis: University of Minnesota Press, 1984), 122–37.

36. Zygmunt Bauman, *Liquid Modernity* (Cambridge, UK: Polity, 2000), quoted in Vivanco, *Reconsidering the Bicycle*, 5.

37. Vivanco, *Reconsidering the Bicycle*, 5.

38. Peter Forstenzer, letter to the editor, *New York Times*, October 31, 1988; Evelyn Williams, letter to the editor, *New York Times*, November 14, 1988.

39. As Nathanson discusses in relation to the film, the directions of time at work in Dorothy's voyage of self-discovery themselves play out a conflict between the straight line and cycle, which I identify with automobile and bicycle: "Ozian time is linear and future oriented" and could "generally be described in terms of 'progress,'" while "Dorothy's goal in Oz (the future) is nothing more than a return to Kansas (the past)." *The Wizard of Oz*'s mythic power lies, for Nathanson, in its reconciliation of a "progressive, urban utopianism" with the return to an "original garden paradise." See Nathanson, *Over the Rainbow*, 48, 173.

40. Herlihy, *Bicycle*, 282.

41. *Better Off Dead*, directed by Savage Steve Holland (1985; Hollywood CA: Paramount, 2002), DVD.

42. Bennett, *Vibrant Matter*, 38.

43. Bennett, *Vibrant Matter*, 37–38.

44. Deleuze and Guattari, *A Thousand Plateaus*, 90.

45. Latour, *Never Been Modern*, 13.

46. Vivanco, *Reconsidering the Bicycle*, 2.

11 Bicycles in Truffaut's *Jules and Jim*

Images of Emancipation and Repression

CHARLES L. P. SILET

Jules and Jim (1962) was François Truffaut's third feature-length film and his first period one.[1] Set in the years just before and after the First World War, it is a film about love and friendship; connection and loss; and one of Truffaut's most prominent themes, the human cost of social and economic control. This chapter examines some issues raised by the film's depictions of cycling and argues that Truffaut found inspiration for his representations of cycling in the fin de siècle French advertising posters that marketed bicycles to female consumers.

Furthermore, this essay examines how the film draws on two interrelated, turn-of-the-century cultural phenomena, the New Woman and bicycles, in its depiction of Catherine and her unconventional relationship with the film's titular characters. While Truffaut's film is not a documentary (although it does contain documentary elements), it is set in the pre– and post–World War I era, and it depicts that period with a certain attempt at accuracy.[2] The creation of the female lead, Catherine (Jeanne Moreau), depends to a certain extent on characteristics of the New Woman, in dress, behavior, and aspiration. One of the ways Truffaut explores her character is through several scenes involving bicycles and bicycling, an element of the film not yet examined by scholars. Close analysis of these cycling scenes, then, not only reveals connections with the film and the period it depicts but also aids in understanding the trajectory of the character of Catherine.

I

Truffaut's *Jules and Jim* is linked to the historical turn-of-the-century France through the presence of period posters in the film and through the bicycling scenes in the film. Bicycles were often featured on advertising posters of the fin de siècle, posters that were frequently directed at female consumers. As scholars of the period have noticed, these cycling posters reflect changes in the position of women at the time and offer an interesting site for cultural discussion. The presence of the New Woman, with her alterations in female dress, greater freedom of movement, and diminished domestic roles, is among the most obvious gender issues reflected in the bicycle posters. The period setting of *Jules and Jim* and the portrayal of Catherine in Truffaut's film, I argue, draw on the imagery and the social changes of this period that were depicted in these bicycle posters.[3]

As a result of advances in distribution and chromolithography, French posters in the last decade of the nineteenth century became colorful and dramatic and proved to be of considerable importance in the new consumer economy. Along with other goods of the period, bicycles became the subject of graphic advertisements that were decorating the walls, sides of buildings, and kiosks of Paris. Their ubiquitous presence turned the city into a public art gallery, one that helped to shape the aesthetic sensibilities and social attitudes of the inhabitants.[4] As with most advertising, the images on the posters were selling a lifestyle and a set of values, as well as a product. For example, some bicycle posters feature female subjects and, through a variety of visual approaches, promote a sense of freedom, escape, and exhilaration, all feelings that the purchase and riding of a bicycle supposedly offers women.[5]

For example, in a full-color 1895 poster for Gladiator Cycles, by the artist known only by the initials L.W., a young woman and a bicycle appear suspended against a background of a blue starry sky. The name of the cycle brand occupies the upper left, and the name of the shop where it may be purchased occupies the lower right of the poster. The cycle has feathery wings on the pedals, and the body of the woman gripping the handlebars is floating parallel with the

11.1. A bicycle poster for Cycles Gladiator.

bike's frame, her thick, reddish-blonde hair streaming out behind her.
She is completely naked.[6]

It is an arresting image. And although at first blush this may appear
an odd way to sell bicycles, the presence of images of nude women
in publically displayed posters was used to sell a variety of goods.[7]
In any event, the image in the advertisement suggests many things.
The flying, weightless suspension of the elevated woman promotes
a feeling of exhilaration, an escape from the world of the everyday,
of social convention. Her nakedness removes many of the restraints
imposed by the standard female clothing of the end of the nineteenth
century and taps into a growing trend for clothing reform, especially
for cyclists, being promoted by women's organizations at the time.[8]
The association with the bicycle suggests that having a cycle may open
up new ways of living, even of being, for the woman who rides one.
Interestingly enough, it is the sort of imagery that is found (if usually
in somewhat subdued form) in the other bicycle advertisements. But
no matter how the women were dressed (or not dressed), just depicting a woman riding a bicycle could be provocative, because riding a
bicycle in the 1890s was still a daring act for women, one that often

included changing clothing styles to a form of dress that would allow for more vigorous physical movement like that of cycling.

Like other posters of the period, bicycle posters were created by a variety of artists and appear in a variety of styles. For example, there is one by Alphonse Mucha in his usual art nouveau style, all flowing hair and flowing clothing, very feminine and very soft and appealing. Artists Henri Gray and Jean de Paléologue (Pal) both created posters of thinly dressed women holding aloft their cycles in very much the style of the nearly anonymous one described above. In short, the posters reflect the fact that bicycling by the 1890s was more widespread and not just the plaything of cycling clubs or the equipment of professionals for sporting events. The bicycle became associated with individual mobility, with being wheels for the masses, and became an instrument of social leveling and, in general, an instrument of cultural change.[9]

The French advertising posters follow the imagery associating women with bicycles that had proliferated in all sorts of other mass media with the growth of bicycle riding throughout the nineteenth century. In his *Bicycle: The History*, David V. Herlihy analyzes a variety of media depictions of women and bicycles, including cartoons for magazines like the British humor journal *Punch*, drawings for cycling journals, and stories in newspapers.[10] In Herlihy's book there are illustrations depicting women and bicycles, with images ranging from scantily clad women participating in cycle races to women wearing bloomers (the latter being a widespread source of jokes). Both costumes provided enhanced flexibility in women's dress. Women on bicycles also graced the covers of periodicals, including the *Police Gazette*, a magazine that featured an article about a provocatively clad French cyclist, Ernestine Bernard, who competed in a three-mile race against a horse.

To sum up, fin de siècle France was characterized by increasing prosperity, new art styles like art nouveau (called *le style moderne* in France), and broad changes in social and individual morality. It was the end of one era and the beginning of another. There was a general rejection of the restrictions of the past and an emphasis on a more emancipated future. Among the most significant changes was

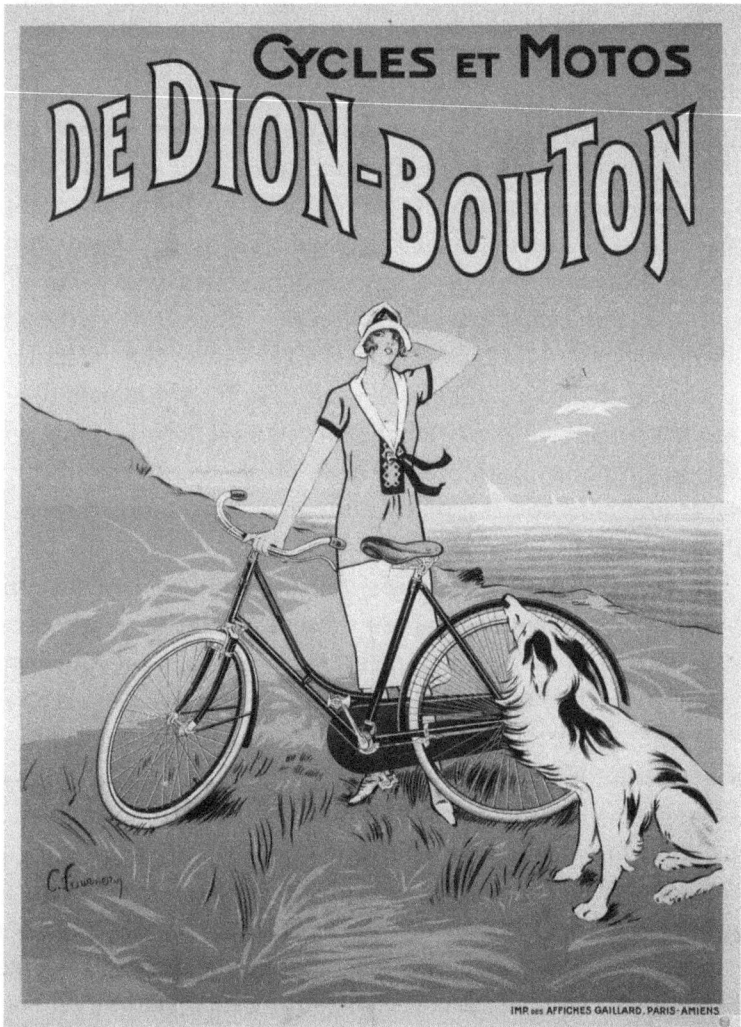

11.2. A bicycle poster for De Dion Bouton.

the emergence of the New Woman, a socially progressive and more sexually liberated female, a figure who therefore became the locus of many of the anxieties of the time.

There was a growing fascination with the mechanical, too, which would have included the bicycle, the emerging automobile, and even the art form that would become the most significant for the new century—film, an art that combined the technology of photography with the traditions of theater, dance, and literature. Such a cultural mix gave to the years before World War I a richness that influenced society and the arts late into the twentieth century. The atmosphere of this period suffuses François Truffaut's *Jules and Jim*, and it permeates details in the film, like the presence of bicycles and of a liberated woman.

II

The screenplay for *Jules and Jim* is based on a novel of the same title by Henri-Pierre Roche, with the adaptation by Truffaut and Jean Gruault.[11] The script for *Jules and Jim* follows quite closely the novel's basic plot, includes many of the specific details of the novel's narrative, and even directly quotes portions of the novel through the use of a voice-over narrator. The screenplay is, of course, much shorter than the novel and by necessity truncates many of the novel's episodes and deletes a number of its characters by combining some of them, particularly in the case of Catherine (called Kate in the book), who is an amalgam of several of the women Jules pursues in the novel. Nevertheless, much of the dialogue and the general scope of the narrative are derived from the novel by Roche.

Given this faithful adaptation, it is, therefore, interesting that there appear scenes of significance in the film involving bicycles even though in the novel Roche never associates his main characters with them. Nonetheless, descriptions of cycling episodes involving the three main characters of the film appear in the published screenplay, an obvious addition inserted by its adaptors, Truffaut and Gruault. As is often true of screenplays, the short descriptions of the bicycling scenes in the script were expanded during the shooting of the film, thus making them even more revelatory. The scenes that feature bicycles prove to be important for the development of character and for introducing cultural connections that link the film with the historical period of the novel. The next section of this essay will demonstrate that the formerly overlooked images of bicycles in the film draw on the cultural significance of bicycles during the historical period in which the film is set, especially as they appeared graphically on turn-of-the-century advertising posters. Furthermore, this next section will demonstrate that Truffaut clearly intended to use the cycling rides to indicate the changing character of Catherine and the changing relationship among the principal characters.

III

The film contains three scenes involving bicycles. In all three scenes, Truffaut expands on the sketchy description of bicycles in the screenplay and uses the scene to illustrate Catherine's state of mind and to explore her relationships with Jules and Jim. Two of these scenes feature a bicycle ride in the country. In the first of these two scenes, the three friends express their joy at the sense of freedom and exuberance provided by the bicycles. Truffaut then uses a second country bicycle ride to reveal the subtle changes time has wrought in Catherine's life and the changes in her personality that mark the beginnings of Catherine's slide into a discontentment that results in her suicide. Although both cycling adventures convey a certain sense of freedom and exuberance, there are differences. The third bicycle scene, which appears between the other two, does two things. First, it looks back on the male camaraderie Jules and Jim experienced before Catherine; and second, it foreshadows the conclusion of the film by connecting the images of the bicycle and the automobile.

In these three scenes, the bicycle and bicycling provide more than just a means of transportation. This is especially true of the two countryside cycling scenes, which come at roughly one-third and two-thirds of the way into the film, providing a certain formal symmetry to the appearances of bicycles. Especially given the historical context of the film (its pre–World War I setting), the bicycle and bicycling offer a connection between the bicycle as a consumer product and the content, particularly visual, in turn-of-the-century advertising posters for bicycles aimed at female consumers. The imagery of these advertisements provides the social context for understanding the bicycle as an instrument of gender reconfiguration at a time of largely repressive and conservative gender roles for women.

The initial bike-riding scene begins in Catherine's apartment and moves to scenes at the beach where the three are going to vacation.

The beach scenes are sun filled and joyous, and they depict Catherine and the men at the happiest they will be in the film. They dress in white, frolic on the beach, and ride bicycles. The sequence begins when Jim stops by Catherine's room to help her deliver her luggage to the train for their outing by the seaside with Jules. Her apartment has appeared in an earlier scene but without a bicycle. This time, however, her bicycle is prominently propped against the iron footboard of her bed. The juxtaposition of the bicycle with the bed suggests a sexual association, one of several references in this scene to her sexuality and its possible connection to Jim, who has come to collect her. Besides, it is Jim who asks Catherine if they are going to take the bicycle to the train and then places it across the threshold of her apartment door. The juxtaposition of the bicycle and the bed has sexual overtones for Jim but may also suggest that Catherine's true love is not Jim or Jules but the bicycle and the independence and freedom associated with it.

She is not dressed for the trip and is still in her nightdress when Jim arrives, and it catches fire as she burns some old love letters, which Jim puts out. (Catherine often tries to begin a new love affair by symbolically ending her old one.) As she is getting ready, she asks Jim to do up the back of her dress, which he does. Later in the film, he will confess to Catherine that looking at her neck was the only way he could express his desire for her without revealing it. This cluster of references to sex and desire will become one of the motifs of the film and will provide much of the tension among the Catherine-Jules-Jim triangle that drives the film's plot. The themes of sex and desire also refer back to those late nineteenth-century advertising posters featuring women and bicycles. Catherine's sexuality is a reminder, too, of the overall theme in the film of unconventional women expressing unconventional mores.

Once at the seaside and out in the open air and sunshine, Catherine appears happy and relaxed. She leads Jim and Jules on a hike through the woods as they look for the "last traces of civilization." As with the race across the footbridge earlier in the film, when Catherine cross-dressed as Thomas, she precedes the two men. On a later day, the three set out from the holiday villa for a bicycle ride to the

11.3. A trip up from the beach by Jim, Catherine, and Jules.

beach. It is a sunny day; and even though trees line the road at times, the scene brims with bright sunshine. At first Jim is in front of the others, but soon Catherine takes the lead. Jules always remains in the rear. The mise-en-scène here not only discloses Catherine's need to be unencumbered by male domination (she leads after all) but also places Jim between her and Jules, one of the main character placements that fluctuates and dominates the film. Catherine continues to lead the men behind as they all cycle back after the excursion to the beach.

In the second half of this first beachside cycling scene, the cyclists are initially shown pushing their bicycles up from the beach and then are shot from a distance, with the camera looking down on them through a line of trees. Catherine again leads, but this time Jules and Jim ride together behind her. There is no sense of exhilaration or of speed, and they cycle slowly off screen. The distance from the camera prevents any recognition of their faces, and the languidness of the ride suggests a shift in mood. The closest the camera gets to the cyclists is when Jules is telling Jim that he is going to marry Catherine, and then the camera pans to film Catherine, who is far ahead. The distance reminds the viewer that she is also far from being the ideal wife or potential mother.

This observation is borne out in the following scene, where we observe Jim and Jules in the foreground playing dominoes, with Catherine in the background positioned between the two players. Clearly, the blocking is meant to show how she is coming between the two friends. In contrast with the white clothing worn earlier during the cycle ride to the beach, an outfit that complimented their joyful excursion, all three now wear dark clothing, indicating a stark change in mood. In all the scenes during the seaside vacation, Jules, Jim, and Catherine wear roughly the same-hued clothing: white on the cycle ride, striped tops at the beach, and darker clothing afterward. At this stage in the film, the three are still connected, even though clearly there are some potential disruptions ahead.[12]

Earlier, Jules had just been talking to Jim about marrying Catherine, to which Jim replied that she is not meant for marriage and motherhood—she is an apparition for men to admire, not to own. The connection of this conversation and the two men's differing perspectives on Catherine with the sense of openness and unrestrained joy associated with the seaside and with bicycles provides a link to the second bicycle ride, when Catherine is both married and a mother.

The second bicycle ride takes place after the war and in Germany (an alien country for Catherine), and it exposes some of the contradictions present in her life. By now the tone of the film has darkened considerably, and the second cycling scene conveys a different sense of the threesome than was conveyed by the first seaside outing. The ride, this time, clearly shows a Catherine whose life has been altered. Now torn between her love for Jim and her lover Albert and with her marriage to Jules in tatters, Catherine's exuberance during the ride seems less joyful than slightly panicked. The speed is faster, the distance between the riders has increased, and the background of the dark wood is more ominous.

The context of this second bike ride is that Jules and Jim have reconnected some time after the armistice, and Jules has invited Jim to visit them. Jim finds the relationship between his two friends strained. Both Jules and Catherine at one time or another confess to him that the marriage is in name only. Catherine has even taken several lovers through the years, and even now she is contemplating leaving Jules for Albert, who will take the young child Sabine as well as Catherine and who wants to marry her and have more children with her. The scenes in the chalet are cramped, claustrophobic, and restrictive, with the actors placed close together amid the furniture and with the camera framing them in tight two shots and three shots. Additionally, Jules and Catherine have separate bedrooms. However, the affair with Albert is giving way to one with Jim. This addition of a new lover for Catherine is visually depicted in the second bicycle ride. In fact, Albert's appearance, pushing his bicycle and with guitar slung over his back, initiates the beginning of the sequences of the second cycling scene.

During this bicycle ride, it is Albert and Catherine in the lead at first, until Catherine pulls ahead and Albert peels off onto a side road, a situation obviously suggesting the end of their affair and the opening of the way for Jim. Catherine is now once again in front, with Jim (who is carrying Sabine on his bicycle) riding behind her and looking at her and with Jules, as always, in the rear. A closer camera shot emphasizes Jim's fascination with the back of Catherine's neck. Catherine once again asserts her independence by taking the lead, but such independence is now complicated by her marriage and motherhood. The ride this time is faster, still exhilarating but a little frantic, as they coast downhill. The ride requires no effort, because the terrain provides the momentum. Since trees hem in the road, it is lacking the bright sunlight of the former ride and the openness of the seaside. Although this is the last time Catherine seems actually happy in the film, the shortness of the ride suggests only a brief period of contentment. The sense of freedom associated with the posters is gone. The independence promised by those advertisements has been darkened by the war, and the demands of domestic life are impinging on Catherine's sense of self, the self she imagined back in Paris when she was single.

Once again costume is noteworthy. During the ride, Albert is in light-colored clothes, but he soon leaves the group. In contrast, Jim wears a dark sweater and light pants; and Jules, a dark top and light pants. As if to announce her ambivalence over her relationships with the two men, Catherine wears a striped pullover, which combines the dark and light connections, with a light skirt. The mixture of light and dark clothing still ties these three together but in a more ambivalent way. As things have changed for Catherine, they also have changed for Jim and Jules. The confusion that besets Catherine about her gender role and the loss of her definition as an independent woman taint the affair she now inaugurates with Jim. Their attempt to have a child and their failure to communicate or articulate their desires dooms the relationship.

The third scene of importance featuring a bicycle comes not long after the seaside episode and between the two riding scenes analyzed

11.4. A last bicycle ride by Jules, Jim, Sabine (on Jim's bike), Catherine, and Albert.

above. The importance of this scene is as a precursor to the ending of the film. It also connects bicycles with cars and with an even earlier mode of transportation, the horse-drawn cart. It is also the scene that most prominently features posters, posters that not only reflect turn-of-the-century Paris but also refer to the melding of the fine and the popular arts. That is, both film and commercial posters were art forms bridging the gap.

The scene is set up when Catherine asks Jim to meet with her at their café, apparently to discuss her decision to marry Jules or perhaps to ask Jim if he loves her too. In the film, cafés are most prominently associated with Jules and Jim in their pre-Catherine friendship. Jim agrees to the meeting and shows up late at the café only to sit, waiting fruitlessly. The interior of the café provides a setting featuring turn-of-the-century posters. There is, for example, an advertisement for a Picasso exhibition and a large (presumably colorful) poster advertising an entertainment venue in Montmartre called "Moulin de Galette." Here Truffaut foregrounds the posters, which clearly provide an important part of the context of the film, if not its actual texture. Truffaut routinely used readable props in his films, such as newspapers, books, signage of all sorts, and, in this scene, posters.[13] These readable details give the film greater cultural breadth, along with the references to sculpture, painting, and drama. In the café scene, the Picasso poster is placed next to one for a popular entertainment. The reference here is to the arts of the early twentieth century, such as film and advertising posters, that were beginning to blur the distinction between popular and fine art.

11.5. Jim at the café with posters on the wall.

Assuming that Catherine is not coming, Jim eventually leaves the café. No sooner is he gone than Catherine shows up, a conventional turn in romantic films. She is dressed fashionably with a hat and carrying a parasol. However, she barely steps into the café, remaining instead in the doorway looking into it. The camera is now positioned inside and cuts to a view looking at her and outside the cafe. As she scans the room for Jim, what is noticeable behind her is a poster on a rather distant fence, its contents undecipherable. It's as if the posters of the past are now only faintly readable but remain a part of the background of the film. While Catherine searches for Jim, three vehicles pass by on a street behind her and in front of the distant poster: first a horse-drawn cart, next an automobile, and then a bicycle. The car's engine is noisy, calling attention to the vehicle's presence. The symbolic gesture is clear. Not only will the automobile replace the bicycle, overtaking the culture of cycling in France; but also it is a precursor of what is to come in the film itself. Catherine will abandon the bicycle for the automobile—the open, expansive mode of transportation of the cycle for the noisy and confining interior of the car. The car also, of course, will become the vehicle of death for Catherine and Jim when she kills both of them by driving off the bridge into the Seine. The compacting of images in the café scene, of tying together posters, bicycles, automobiles, Catherine and Jim, makes this brief moment one of the most significant in the film.

Finally, if there is one overall image associated with Catherine and her doomed attempt to escape the restrictions of convention, it is the gradual compression of her personality, represented visually by the physical restrictions that the film imposes on her. Her environment actually gets smaller as she undergoes a loss of self and a loss of independence. The crowded Parisian cafés of the film's opening seem inviting, but she is not seen there. The positioning of her physically between Jules and Jim, to suggest that she is coming between the friends, is often done with her image being squeezed, being filmed compressed between Jules and Jim. The cycling scenes remove her from her cramped apartment and give her space but only temporarily. As the film progresses, she is accorded little time away from the oppressiveness of the overstuffed rooms of her marriage and from the confinement of her domestic situation. Although at the chalet she can escape temporarily, it is often to the woods, where a forest of trees and its shadows further oppress her. The ultimate confinement is that of the automobile, which becomes her means of suicide, which is appropriate given its dark and confining interior. After death, she is further confined first to a coffin and then after cremation to an urn. And that urn is finally placed into the narrow confines of the columbarium, her wish to free her ashes having been denied.

This final act of suppression, denying even Catherine's last wishes, negates the promise of those long-ago cycling posters with their colorful imagery of free-wheeling women released from many of the historical restrictions imposed on their sex. In fact, the entire trajectory of the film moves from the mostly carefree prewar opening to a darker postwar world of death and loss. By the film's conclusion, both Jules's best friend and his wife are dead, leaving him alone, his life literally turned to ashes. The last image we have of him is of a solitary man walking slowly toward the cemetery exit.

All cultural products are of their time and place; and no matter what the subject matter or style, every painting, every novel or book of poetry, every piece of music, and every film either directly or indirectly reflects the culture of the period from which it arises. There are many ways in which the film *Jules and Jim* is connected with the time in which it was made. The film was shot and released in the early sixties, a period that experienced a new surge of feminism and an accompanying shift in sexual mores, a growing concern with the war in Vietnam, and a proliferation of innovative film styles, of which the New Wave was among the more important. Truffaut's film in various ways deals with such contemporary issues but through its own period focus.

Truffaut's fictional account of the lives of three characters from the First World War allowed him to explore in an oblique way concerns that were central to the 1960s, which constitute a perspective on his own time. The world that *Jules and Jim* inhabits is a sexually liberated one, and Catherine is surely an avatar of feminism. Furthermore, the film takes place against the background of a devastating war; and stylistically, it incorporates some of the advances in cinematic techniques of the late fifties and early sixties.

As the sixties wore on, however, things changed. Protests against the Vietnam War intensified, the birth control pill helped to propel a sexual revolution, feminists became more vocal and confrontational, and filmmakers experimented even more daringly with both the style and content of their films. Now, from the perspective of over half a century later, *Jules and Jim* appears, if not exactly quaint, at least as an artifact from an earlier, more gentle time. It hardly seems like a 1960s film at all. In the world of the film, Jules and Jim argue over philosophy and literature and live in an insular, apolitical bohemian world. Their protests are not confrontational; they do not demonstrate in the streets. By the standards of the 1960s, the film's sexuality is mild, with no nudity, no simulated intercourse, and no sexually explicit language. Although the film features a ménage a trois, it is not sensationalized. The film views World War I from a distance, largely through stock footage, without gore or graphic violence. Even Truffaut's cinematic style owes as much to Hollywood tradition as it does to the innovations of the New Wave. Only with the unconventional character of Catherine and her unexpected suicide does the film actually confront the harsh reality of gender discrimination that feminists challenged as the decade progressed.

However, in the end, *Jules and Jim* remains a charming film full of exuberance and sadness, one that provided a showcase for three young actors and their equally young director. It was also a film that helped to propel a revolution, one that changed the world of cinema and brought to prominence a new generation of filmmakers. The search for a new pictorial vocabulary that the artists of the turn of the century invested in their posters has been the search of modern cinema as well, especially in the groundbreaking work of the French directors of the New Wave.

Notes

1. *Jules et Jim*, directed by François Truffaut (Paris: Les Films du Carrosse / SEDIF, 1962). *Jules et Jim* (*Jules and Jim*) followed Truffaut's films *Les quatre cents coups* (1959) (*The Four Hundred Blows*) and *Tirez sur le pianiste* (1960) (*Shoot the Piano Player*), both of which did much to define the New Wave, an innovative style of film developed by young French filmmakers in the late 1950s and early 1960s. For a good overview of the New Wave, see James Monoco, *The New Wave: Truffaut, Godard, Charbrol, Rohmer, Rivette*, 2nd ed. (New York: Oxford University Press, 1976). Among Truffaut's other period films are *La sirène du Mississippi* (1969) (*Mississippi Mermaid*); *L'enfant sauvage* (1970) (*The Wild Child*); *Les deux Anglaises et le continent* (1971) (*Two English Girls*); *L'histoire d'Adèle H.* (1975) (*The Story of Adele H.*); and *Le dernier metro* (1980) (*The Last Metro*).

2. Truffaut uses stock footage in depicting turn-of-the-century Paris and in a montage sequence of actual film footage from the First World War.

3. See Ruth E. Iskin, "The Pan-European Flâneuse in Fin-de-Siècle Posters: Advertising Modern Women in the City," *Nineteenth-Century Contexts* 25, no. 4 (2003): 333–56; David V. Herlihy, *Bicycle: The History* (New Haven CT: Yale University Press, 2004); and Mary Weaver Chapin, *Posters of Paris: Toulouse-Lautrec and His Contemporaries* (Milwaukee WI: Milwaukee Art Museum; London: Prestel Verlag, 2012). These works all discuss the relationship between the posters and gender.

4. There are numerous books on the posters of the fin de siècle. Some discuss posters in the context of art movements like art nouveau. See, for example, see Robert Schmutzler, *Art Nouveau* (New York: Harry H. Abrams, 1978); Debora Silverman, *Art Nouveau in Fin-de-Siècle France: Politics, Psychology, and Style* (Berkeley: University of California Press, 1989); Ghislaine Wood, *Art Nouveau and the Erotic* (New York: Harry H. Abrams, 2000). Others focus more closely on the production methods and how they shaped the content as well as the style of the posters. See, for example, Fleur Roos Rosa de Carvalho and Marije Vellekoop, *Printmaking in Paris: The Rage for Prints at the Fin de Siècle* (New Haven CT: Yale University Press, 2013). There are also books

that concentrate on the posters themselves. See, for example, Jane Abdy, *The French Poster: Chéret to Cappiello* (London: Studio Vista Limited, 1969); Victor Arwas, *Belle Époque: Posters and Graphics* (New York: Rizzoli, 1978); and Harold F. Hutchison, *The Poster: An Illustrated History from 1860* (New York: Viking Press, 1968). All of these studies discuss the artistic, social, economic, and political impact of posters.

5. Chapin, *Posters of Paris*, includes six full-color plates of bicycle ads featuring women and is one of the more recent collections of fin de siècle posters. For examples of posters of women and bicycles, see also Hutchinson, *The Poster*; Alain Weill, Réjane Bargiel, and Musée de l'Affiche, *Trois siècles d'affiches françaises* (Paris: Musée de l'Affiche, 1978).

6. Chapin, *Posters of Paris*, 152 (plate 104).

7. There does seem to be a penchant for posters selling products with nude women. Chapin's *Posters of Paris* contains plates by Henri Gray for Cycles Sirius and by Pal for Déesse (Goddess) bicycles, both of which feature women swathed only in filmy wraps elevated in the sky with their cycles. That said, Pal also did an ad for a kerosene lamp, and Gray created a poster for Stella Oil, both cases using the similar naked female figures suspended in the air. Herlihy, *Bicycle*, 414, includes an American photograph of a semiclad woman holding a drink aloft while riding a bicycle. The nude impulse apparently knew no boundaries. However, Chapin includes an example of a poster that was modified to cover up the nudity of their subjects. See Chapin, *Posters of Paris*, figs. 46 and 47. How often this censorship occurred is unclear.

8. The influence of the bicycle as part of a broader expansion of athletics for women is explored in Patricia Marx, *Bicycles, Bangs, and Bloomers: The New Woman in the Popular Press* (Lexington: University of Kentucky Press, 1990), see especially chapter 6, "Women's Athletics: A Bicycle Built for One"; in Herlihy, *Bicycle*; in Ruth Calif, *The World on Wheels: An Illustrated History of the Bicycle and Its Relatives* (New York: Cornwall Books, 1983); and in Robert A. Smith, *A Social History of the Bicycle: Its Early Life and Times in America* (New York: American Heritage Press, 1972). Changes in woman's dress are mentioned in all these books, often to highlight the criticism leveled at the clothing or to satirize it. For a broader examination of the cultural significance of clothing in general, one that is not only more comprehensive but also more carefully theorized, see the classic work Anne Hollander, *Seeing through Clothes* (Berkeley: University of California Press, 1993).

9. See Herlihy, *Bicycle*; Smith, *Social History of the Bicycle*; Marx, *Bicycles, Bangs, and Bloomers*.

10. David V. Herlihy includes illustrations from the early years of cycling such as cartoons and advertising pieces that both satirize women and cycling and often make fun of female cyclist's clothing, nevertheless showing that at least

some women were participating in the new sport before the expansion of the popularity of cycling during the later years of the century.

11. Henri-Pierre Roche, *Jules et Jim* (Paris: Editions Gallimard, 1954). This work was reprinted by Marion Boyars Publishers (London) in 1981 in an English translation by Patrick Evans. It is an episodic work, a series of vignettes like movie sequences, following the friendship between Jules and Jim, which becomes a ménage à trois with the addition of Kate (Catherine in the film but still Kate in the English translation). The screenplay for the film, written by François Truffaut and Jean Gruault, was based on the Gallimard edition of the novel. The original French-language edition of the screenplay was titled *Jules et Jim* and published by L'Avant-Scène du Cinéma in 1962; the English language version was published by Simon and Schuster in 1968 in a translation by Nicholas Fry.

12. There is an interesting business with hats. Catherine wears one while they are cycling at the beach and when she goes to meet Jim at the café; but after the war, she seldom wears one. It is an indication of the changing social customs. She does wear a cloche hat on the day she kills herself and Jim, which, along with her glasses, is another sign of her increasing confinement.

13. Posters do appear in the film on the walls of cafes and on board fences (see the photos accompanying the published screenplay). Aside from period posters advertising a Picasso exhibition and the Moulin de Galette, Truffaut also prominently includes a recruiting poster for the war effort, the posters attached to the *pissoir*, and a cover for *Cahiers du cinema*, the cinema journal that published his early film criticism and launched him in the film world. There are some forty-five stills from the film that are printed with the English-language translation of the screenplay. Four of them feature bicycles. One of those four stills is of an interior of Catherine's apartment, another is of the three main characters pushing their bikes up from the beach, and a third is of the ride in Germany after the war. It is clear that the editors of the screenplay felt these scenes were important enough to merit inclusion with the script. The fourth bicycle still is of Jules and Jim riding bicycles in Paris and apparently belongs with the montage at the film's beginning when we are first introduced to the two men. However, this shot was omitted from the completed cut of the movie. It is interesting that in the final version of the film Jules and Jim only ride their bicycles when they are with Catherine.

12 We Hope, and We Lose Hope

The Postman's Bicycle in
Andrei Tarkovsky's *The Sacrifice*

BENJAMIN VAN LOON

The bicycle hasn't always been *just* a bicycle. In its history, the bicycle has been the currency of the afterlife (Flann O'Brien's *The Third Policeman*), an artifact of hell (Samuel Beckett's *More Pricks Than Kicks*), a Proustian shard (Vladimir Nabokov's *Speak, Memory*), a means for survival (Wang Xiaoshuai's *Beijing Bicycle*), a piece of incriminating evidence (Antonio Bardem's *Death of a Cyclist*), and countless other things along the way. But one such entry in this canon of texts provides a uniquely critical, ambiguous, and dynamic take on the definition of "bicycle" as such: *Offret* (*The Sacrifice*), a philosophical, apocalyptic film released in 1986 and directed by the notoriously abstruse Russian director Andrei Tarkovsky (1932–86).

In this essay, I examine the role of the bicycle in Tarkovsky's film and argue that before the bicycle becomes anything (a tool, a toy, a means of transport, etc.), it is first a poetical metaphor. I don't suggest that Tarkovsky exclusively aims to poeticize about bicycles in *The Sacrifice*. Rather, through what film scholar Thomas Redwood calls Tarkovsky's "poetics of cinema," the objects in the film (notably, the bicycle)—and life itself—are elevated into a poetical realm.

According to Redwood, the pacing, editing, landscape, composition, and mise-en-scène are all elements of style in *The Sacrifice*; and style is the preeminent poetical mode for Tarkovsky.[1] No one element in *The Sacrifice* is more or less important than any other element, which reflects Tarkovsky's poetical project and aesthetic philosophy of filmmaking. In his book *Sculpting in Time*, Tarkovsky says poetry is "a particular way of relating to reality," such that "mise-en-scène, rather than illustrating some idea, should follow life."[2] Tarkovsky's films have a poetical logic that aims not to interpret life but to depict it as it is, with all its difficulties, elations, and mysteries. The bicycle thus initially seems incidental in *The Sacrifice*, but its elemental role in crafting the style of the film, which attempts to "follow life," casts the bicycle into the poetical realm.

The Sacrifice is the seventh and final film directed by Tarkovsky, who died of lung cancer a month after the film's American release date in November 1986.[3] *The Sacrifice*, not surprisingly, is a film about a man facing death; it tells the story of Alexander (Erland Josephson)—a solemn and erudite journalist and critic—and his family, who stay together in a humble two-story dacha on a lonely Baltic island off the cost of Sweden. Alexander is joined by his wife, Adelaide (Susan Fleetwood); his teenage stepdaughter, Marta (Fillipa Franzen); his son, pet-named Little Man (Tommy Kjellqvist); and the family's two maids, Julia (Valérie Mairesse) and Maria (Guðrún Gísladóttir), the latter of whom may also be a "witch." We learn through various sonic clues—the roar of military jets, panicked radio announcements, anxious whispers—that the family has fled to the island due to some kind of war or worldwide apocalyptic event. Yet even as it addresses such solemn subjects as death, spirituality, apocalypse, anxiety, self-doubt, and human nature, *The Sacrifice* is an expression of contrition. Its stark and complex textures are steeped in Tarkovsky's mystical, poetical, and penitent aesthetic (the island's rocky shoreline, achromatic horizon, and omnipresent nautical breeze are drawn straight from Ingmar Bergman's filmic palette).[4]

The Sacrifice opens in silence with its title displayed in a simple, white, serif font against a black background. The title fades, and the other opening credits appear over a detail from Leonardo da Vinci's early, unfinished painting *The Adoration of the Magi*. The plaintive aria "Erbarme dich, mein Gott, um meiner Zähren Willen," from Johann Sebastian Bach's Matthäus-Passion, bwv 244, plays over this. The credits orient the viewer to the poetical quality of the film, awash in reverential tones.

In the opening scene, Alexander and Little Man use stones to prop up a leafless tree along the island's craggy shoreline. Alexander tells a story about an old Orthodox monk, and out of the left of the frame comes the postman, Otto (Allan Edwall), riding a bicycle down the dirt road and stopping to wish Alexander good tidings on his birthday. This is our first glimpse of a bicycle in the film. His bicycle is a classic, black, single-speed utility bicycle with front and rear fenders and a front basket that Otto uses to carry his posts.[5] That Otto and his bicycle are introduced in this way—an essential element in the nearly ten-minute-long, single-shot scene—provides an early poetical clue about the bicycle within the fabric of the film.[6] The bicycle's nearly constant movement in this scene—with only a few brief pauses—suggests that the metaphor of the bicycle is dynamic, organically conforming to both the natural contours of the landscape and the unnatural gaze of the camera.

Otto and Alexander exchange greetings, and their conversation turns to God. Alexander walks away from the shoreline as they speak, trailed by Little Man, with Otto riding lazy circles around the two of them. Whereas Alexander seems somber and depressed, Otto seems positive and good-humored. Otto speaks of the dwarf that "paralyzes" Zarathustra in Nietzsche's *Thus Spoke Zarathustra* and of his fascination with the idea of eternal recurrence, which is first articulated by Nietzsche in *Zarathusra* in a section titled "On the Vision and the Riddle." To the dwarf (that "spirit of gravity"), Zarathusra says, "And must we not return and run in that other lane out before us, that long weird lane—must we not eternally return?"[7] Or as Otto puts it, is it not the case that we are born, we hope, we live, we lose hope, we die, and then we are born again and remember nothing. Alexander asks, "Do you really believe in this dwarf?" Otto nods and says, "Yes"; though, instead of continuing to ride his bike in circles, Otto sits on the ground next to the machine.[8] Tarkovsky is perhaps being too obvious with the choreography of the scene and its Nietzschean connotations, though this is also his subtle way of undermining an ever-fashionable Nietzsche with an antimodernist irony, which I'll discuss later.

Beyond this first scene, the plot of *The Sacrifice* unfolds in poetical contrast to the formalist cinematic rules of division between dream and "reality." If not enforced by critics, these rules of division are often imposed by viewers, whose perceptions are informed by formalist standards, which can be problematic for viewings of *The Sacrifice*. In his work *Andrei Tarkovsky: Elements of Cinema*, Robert Bird claims that, of Tarkovsky's films, *The Sacrifice* is "the one most susceptible to allegorical readings," which is a tendency largely engendered by Tarkovsky's own self-assessment in his work of aesthetic philosophy, *Sculpting in Time*, in which he claims outright that the film is a parable.[9] For Bird and other Tarkovsky scholars like Redwood, Le Fanu, Botz-Bornstein, Martin, and Johnson and Petrie, Tarkovsky's assessments of his own work are suspect and may actually contribute to misappropriations of themes in Tarkovsky's films. Johnson and Petrie write, "By means of interviews, talks . . . and his book *Sculpting in Time*, Tarkovsky succeeded to a remarkable extent in creating a framework that ensured his films would be discussed and understood in terms largely established by him."[10] Bird criticizes this view, suggesting that "by adopting a moralizing and often self-important tone, in his printed texts . . . Tarkovsky unwittingly contributed to the tendency of interpreting his films as wooly mystical fables."[11] Tarkovsky has an extensive body of written work that must necessarily be contended with in any serious study of his films, though; following Bird, I also suggest that it is important "not to read Tarkovsky's films through his statements, but to read his statements through his films."[12]

Read in this way, Tarkovsky's assessment of *The Sacrifice* as a parable is far less interesting than some of the film's other clues, which he provides elsewhere in his noncinematic work. In a 1978 interview with Tonino Guerra from *Telerama*, Tarkovsky describes, in response to a question about his earliest memory, an unsettling fragment from his childhood that seems not very distant from the world of *The Sacrifice*:

The first [memory] that I remember happened when I was a year and a half. I remember the house, the open terrace, the stairs from the terrace—only five or six steps—and the railing. Between the staircase and the angle of the house was an enormous lilac bush. It was a cool and sandy place. I would roll an aluminum hoop from the gate to the lilacs. At one point I hear a strange noise coming from the sky. I am seized with a panicked fear of dying, and hide myself beneath the lilacs. I look up at the sky since that's where the noise is coming from. There's a fearsome noise that becomes more and more intense. All of a sudden, between the branches I see an airplane pass. It's 1933. I never thought it might be a bird, but something very terrible.[13]

These are the same intense noises that disrupt Alexander's otherwise simple life on the island, beginning when the roar of fighter jets is heard around the film's forty-five-minute mark. Otto had just used his bike, with the handlebars turned sideward, to deliver a large, framed, original map of Europe from the 1700s to Alexander for his birthday. This is our second glimpse of Otto's bike in the film. Otto balances the framed map on the drive-side pedal of the bike as he pushes it along the road. Julia, the maid, helps Otto remove it from the bicycle, and the two of them let the machine fall to the ground. Stunned at the uniqueness of the gift, Alexander asks how such kindness is possible. "Through sacrifice," Otto answers, adding that no gift is possible without sacrifice. Otto has supposedly sacrificed much in order to attain this extravagant gift that far exceeds his apparent means, and that this extravagance finally finds its way to Alexander by riding sidesaddle on a lowly utility bicycle reinforces the nature of Otto's altruism. And yet this juxtaposition of a working-class tool, the bicycle, with an upper-crust collector's object, the map, provides an early reference to the dynamism of the bicycle as metaphor, insofar as the machine (metaphor) adapts to its environment rather than forcing the environment to adapt to itself (which would be the case if Tarkovsky were ignorant of his poetics).

The bicycle's two appearances in the film thus far have not been without reason, despite appearing otherwise. This is because the bicycle is equal to all other narrative elements, as Redwood suggests when he argues, "Tarkovsky's late films [*Mirror, Stalker, Nostalghia,* and *The Sacrifice*] contradict the formalist insistence on a distinction between *syuzhet* (or 'narrative') materials and stylistic devices."[14] In *The Sacrifice,* these narrative materials include Otto's gift, the map of the Netherlands, because it propels the perceived narrative trajectory, whereas

Tarkovsky's utilization of variegated film stocks might be dismissed as merely stylistic. In contradiction to this distinction, Redwood explains, "in Tarkovsky's late films it is first and foremost through stylistic devices that the spectator can make sense of their narratives."[15]

The bicycle thus becomes an indispensable component of the narrative texture as it is thrust into a cinematic space without any formalistic insistence on the divisions between style and *syuzhet*; it is one of the many threads in Tarkovsky's pied cinematic fabric. As *The Sacrifice* elaborates Tarkovsky's own hermeneutical philosophy (that is, his interpretation of the world), so too do the elements constituting its narrative whole. Tarkovsky writes, "All through the time I was working on the screenplay [for *The Sacrifice*], I was constantly preoccupied with the idea of *equilibrium*, of sacrifice, of the sacrificial act, the *yin* and *yang* of love and personality."[16] Even as the bicycle is woven into the poetical fabric of *The Sacrifice*, it also represents an incarnation of Tarkovsky's preoccupation with equilibrium. Without it, the bicycle can't work. Without it, the poesy of the film itself becomes unbalanced.

If Tarkovsky's poetics are hermeneutical in *The Sacrifice*, it is because the core subject of the film concerns the Apocalypse—a subject that Tarkovsky is ready and willing to engage, especially in the later years of his career and his conflicted relationship with Cold War Soviet politics. In a 1984 lecture given at St. James's Church in Piccadilly, Tarkovsky claims outright, "The Apocalypse is perhaps the greatest poetic work ever created."[17] He's referencing the biblical version of the Apocalypse found in the book of Revelation, though his belief in the poetry of the Apocalypse is based not on theological principles but, rather, on aesthetic conditions. He says, "We are accustomed to the Revelation being interpreted and explained. In my view, this is precisely what should not be done, because the Apocalypse cannot be interpreted."[18] He adds that the Apocalypse "is an image, and if a symbol can be interpreted, an image cannot." Elsewhere, he declares himself an "enemy of symbolism" and thus elevates the superiority of the image in filmic composition.[19] For this reason, the Apocalypse is not an image *merely* but, rather, an "image of the human soul, with all its responsibilities and obligations."[20]

For Tarkovsky, the human soul is "created in the image and like-ness of God," which means that it has been imbued with the will to create.[21] But the human act of creation has become bankrupt in Tar-kovsky's antimodern, antitechnological point of view. He continues, "Artists have come to regard the talent they have been given as their property. . . . This explains the lack of spiritual content in modern art."[22] Tarkovsky upholds film as a prime example of this bankruptcy, positing it as an art that arose "in a market aimed at pure profit."[23] This drive toward commercialization is itself a symptom of increased technological precedence and influence in the creative process.[24] For Tarkovsky, "all the so-called technological progress that accompanies history has essentially created prostheses" and has occurred at such a rapid rate that "we are now victim to an avalanche-like process of technological growth."[25] If this process does not itself proceed toward Apocalypse, the Apocalypse is what renders technological progress absurd. At this point, we can look back to the subtle irony of the first scene with Otto and Alexander's rhetorical sparring over Nietzsche and eternal recurrence. The bicycle lies on the ground, and Otto sits next to it, an image of temporary defeat by the spirit of gravity.

This antitechnology stance and its relationship to Tarkovsky's poet-ical notion of the Apocalypse complicates the role of the bicycle in *The Sacrifice*, because outside the Tarkovskian universe, the bicycle is generally depicted as a simple, unassuming symbol of technologi-cal progress (or, if you prefer, of modernity). Outside Tarkovsky, the bicycle might actually be one of the most perfect symbols for tech-nological progress, because its basic design and functionality has remained essentially unchanged for the last one hundred years of use. Aside from tweaks and slight mechanical improvements, the bicycle is more fully realized than many other similarly ubiquitous techno-logical artifacts. In other words, if the Apocalypse implies a collapse or an undermining of the technological, or entropy of our "civiliza-tion" (as Tarkovsky calls it) induced by the "freedoms" we've sacrificed in the name of technification, the bicycle, despite its simplicity and supposed innocence, becomes a suspicious object and consequently an image that is critical of how "progress" is taken for granted, with-out reserve. With this in mind, the moments in the film in which

Otto's bike is allowed to fall haphazardly to the ground—like when he delivers the map or when he lets Alexander borrow the bicycle later—find new meaning.

Though these scenes might find new meaning in this way, the image of the bicycle in *The Sacrifice* in general is complicated by the other philosophical musings that address Tarkovsky's work. For example, in his essay "The Thing from Inner Space," Slavoj Žižek suggests that Tarkovsky tends toward "religious obscurantism."[26] Furthermore, Mark Le Fanu writes that Tarkovsky is antimodern and idealistic. He argues, "The emphasis on the ideal, as a sort of criticism of reality, is an unmissable thread running through all of Tarkovsky's writings, and as such is inseparable from his sense of the profound wrongness of the regime he was living under."[27] Frederic Jameson claims that Tarkovsky is a "naturalist mystic."[28] Bird writes of Tarkovsky that his "stories and characters sometimes seem like mere occasions for showing earth-stained objects, burning buildings, water-logged landscapes, and, perhaps most fundamentally, an invisible but poignant *atmosphere*."[29] Redwood suggests that Western critics and intellectuals have a difficult time interpreting Tarkovsky's films due to Tarkovsky's insistence that his work be received as a form of "high art," along with all the hermeneutical difficulties this insistence entails, including the accompanying and somewhat "obvious" thematic diagnoses—mysticism, spiritualism, pantheism, naturalism—invited by Tarkovsky's films.[30] Though these criticisms are all relevant, they do not diminish the importance of Tarkovsky's view of the image. The bicycle is an image, though we must also bear in mind Le Fanu's warning that even as Tarkovsky's work is inflected by Russian symbolist aesthetics, there is "a residue of 'pure imagery' that is ultimately 'just there' and beyond interpretation."[31] If the image is "just there" in this sense, it is still significant (if it weren't, then it could easily be replaced by a motorcycle or car without altering the narrative). I venture that the bicycle is an *appropriate* device for being "there," due to its pure simplicity as a technology, though this simplicity is layered in an experiential mystique, reflected by our own day-to-day curiosities about the bicycle—that one never forgets how to ride it, that the memory of learning how to ride always remains, and so forth. This mystique may also support why bicycles are often depicted with an air of whimsy, nostalgia, and—as I've already mentioned—innocence.[32]

The narrative of *The Sacrifice* plays with the bicycle's mystique, but from a vantage point critical of the naïveté that undergirds modern society's appropriation of technology. After the somewhat failed celebration of Alexander's birthday, we enter into a typically Tarkovskian somnambulistic montage: Little Man sleeping in a child's bed next to a window with sensuous white curtains undulating inward and outward like a membrane over an open sill; Alexander and Otto studying a reproduction of *The Adoration of the Magi* on Alexander's wall; Alexander wandering into the main room of the house, where sits his family, the doctor, Julia, and Otto, listening to a governmental radio broadcast portending the end of the world; Alexander's wife having an extended nervous breakdown, only to be given a shot by the doctor; and finally, Alexander's plea to the God he does not believe in. Alexander's plea begins with his recitation of the Lord's Prayer. As he stumbles over the prayer and speaks the words "Deliver us from evil," he kneels to the ground and begins his own prayer:

> Lord, deliver us in this terrible time. Don't let my children die; nor my friends; my wife; Victor; all those who love Thee and believe in Thee; all those who do not believe in Thee, because they are blind; those who haven't given Thee a thought, simply because they haven't yet been truly miserable; all those who in this hour have lost their hope, their future, their lives, and the opportunity to surrender to Thy will. . . . I will give Thee all I have. I'll give up my family, who I love. I'll destroy my home and give up Little Man. I'll be mute and never speak another word to anyone. I will relinquish everything that binds me to life, if only Thou dost restore everything as it was before, as it was this morning and yesterday, and end this sickening, deadly, animal fear. Yes, everything, Lord, help me. I will do everything I have promised Thee.[33]

Alexander lays down on a couch and falls to sleep, and it's at this point we enter the realm of reality-dream ambiguity that complicates *The Sacrifice*. According to Botz-Bornstein, Tarkovsky makes such heavy-handed use of dream narrative because it's a construct that serves both as a rejection of formalism and "as an intermediary between abstractness and concreteness."[34] This mediating role of the dream is important because when the bike makes its third appearance, it is unclear if it is appearing in reality or in fantasy, though for Botz-Bornstein (and also for Redwood), the dream has its own logic (or "time truth," as Tarkovsky suggests in *Sculpting in Time*), such that "the temporal laws of the [dream] scene are absolutely true in the sense that they are absolutely 'necessary' in regard to the material itself."[35] Thus, when Alexander "awakens" from his dream, it is a gesture no more or less abstract than when he is covertly greeted by a whispering Otto knocking on his front door. Is Otto really there? Does the news Otto brings have any bearing on the concrete world? Due to such a complicated logic of "filmdream," as Botz-Bornstein calls it, these questions have no bearing or sense in the world of *The Sacrifice*. What we see is what is there, and that is all the logic necessary. Johnson and Petrie write, "Tarkovsky seems to want us to experience the central 'action' of the film as simultaneously real and not real, just as the images are simultaneously colour and black & white."[36] It is thus not surprising that Otto offers Alexander "one last chance" in an apparent answer to Alexander's desperate prayer, despite Otto's absence during Alexander's moment of reckoning.

Earlier in the film, Otto claims to be a collector of "strange incidents," or what we'd call unexplained events, like a soldier who died in a war appearing in a photograph after his death—a tale he tells with great gravitas. The last chance Otto offers Alexander appears to be from his strange-incident collection: Maria, Alexander's maid from Iceland, lives alone in "a farm on the other side of the bay, behind the old church." Alexander must go to her and sleep with her, and then "all of this" will be over, if that's what he wishes. According to Otto, who has "collected the evidence," Maria is a witch, but "the best kind of witch." Alexander doubts Otto, wondering if Otto has lost his mind or if this is another of the postman's "Nietzschean pranks."[37] Perhaps as an invitation, or a taunt, Otto tells Alexander that he has left his bike by the shed. His only word of warning is to be careful; the bike's front wheel has a few broken spokes.

After Otto leaves, Alexander sneaks out and retrieves the bike, pedaling down a rutted dirt road vaguely reminiscent of the "Starvation Strings" Anna-Maria Rautio and Lars Ostlund write about in their historical examination of bike trail networks in northern Sweden.[38] This is the third and final appearance of Otto's bike in the film. The path Alexander rides on has clearly been ridden on by cars too, but it doubles as a vestigial trace of prevehicular (premodern) transport, itself critically mirroring the "impression of complete emptiness" that initially attracted Tarkovsky to filming on the island.[39] Rautio and Ostlund look to the bicycle for the early development of such trails, though it was later when the automobile proliferated that many of the trails originally plotted and intended for bicycle use were transformed into vehicular roads. The usefulness of these "strings" failed but left a permanent imprint as a cultural legacy as premodern (and essentially pretechnological) symbols.[40] When Alexander tries to avoid a pothole in the road and falls in his attempt to reach Maria, it is thus difficult not to also see this scene as a complicated technological metaphor: the vestigial traces of technological progress are not suited to the act of Alexander's will to redemption and the Apocalypse he wishes to delay.

Alexander arrives at Maria's hovel; and after some pleading, he wins her sympathies. At first, she is resistant to his advances; but when he holds a gun to his head, she has a change of heart and gives him the surety of her love. During copulation, the two of them float above the bed as if in a dream, and we then return to what we presume is a version of Alexander's earlier vision of an apocalyptic street strewn with garbage and wrecked cars. Only this time, instead of desolation, the street is abuzz with panicked people running helter-skelter in tattered clothes. Alexander seems to then awaken back on the same couch where Otto had left him earlier. Robert Bird's description sums up this climactic scene:

> Leonardo's *Adoration of the Magi*, shown in changing light, dissolves into a colour shot of the naked Marta, who chases chickens through the house; the shot tracks right, following Adelaide, who moves along the corridor to the room where Alexander sleeps on

the sofa beneath the Leonardo. He awakens, exclaims "Mama," rises and shuts off the Japanese music, which lingers, however, for a fleeting second. Encouraged, Alexander calls the office of his editor to confirm that the world is still standing; the persistence of material reality is confirmed when Alexander knocks his knee against the table, incurring real pain and a limp that lasts for the remainder of the film. The viewer might be tempted similarly to classify the foregoing sequence as Alexander's dream. However, there are any number of spatial folds that prevent it from being dismissed so easily. As it comes apart the space is suspended as the point of intersection of human gazes, not as a ruin, but as the site of potentiality.[41]

The film ends with Alexander keeping his promise to God. After ensuring that the house is empty, Alexander sets fire to it. His family and the doctor are out for a walk. He acts alone and in silence. It's an arresting and meticulous scene, culminating in a long, fiery, wide-angle tracking shot.[42] Alexander wears a robe and stands outside the burning home, and Victor, the doctor, runs up to him. Alexander begins to talk but then remembers his promise—his sacrifice. An ambulance inexplicably arrives, and two orderlies pack Alexander into the back as the fire rages and reflects off the waterlogged landscape.

After the ambulance drives off, the film ends in the same place it began: at the tree. But this time, Little Man stands alone and watches the ambulance drive past with his father inside. Like Otto on his bicycle at the beginning of the film, the ambulance enters from the left of the frame, though instead of good tidings, there is only the hum of the engine. Little Man lies at the base of the tree and speaks his first and only line in the film: "In the beginning was the Word. Why is that, Papa?"

It's a difficult ending because it can't be read as a resolution. For Redwood, the ending marks finality in "the most consistent of Tarkovsky's mature films, for it integrates the elusiveness of meaning into its very material composition. But for the same reason it is also a tragic and impossible film, a confession of failure in a way, of the model's inability to control reality and of the conceiver's inability to manage the rub."[43] It is, therefore, an immediate poetic expression of reality, because reality has no resolution; it is simply *there*, like an image. That the film ends in the same place it begins implies a certain sense of *revolution* that trumps any formalist intonations of so-called standard storytelling. And it is this concept of revolution over resolution—originally foretold in Otto's remarks (and Tarkovsky's hermeneutical hints) about Zarathustra's dwarf—of which the bicycle ultimately works as a metaphor within the poetic structure of *The Sacrifice*.

It's a happy coincidence that as we discuss bicycles, Zarathustra describes the dwarf as a spirit of gravity. Zarathustra also calls the dwarf his "devil and archenemy" whose paralyzing weight puts "thoughts like drops of lead into my brain" as the two of them traverse up a lifeless mountain.[44] Courage is what empowers Zarathustra to "stand up" to this dwarf and force him to recollect where they are on the path up the mountain, that the path behind and in front of them runs straight from and straight to eternity and that where they stand is at the present. "Everything straight lies," the dwarf says, mockingly. "All truth is crooked, time itself is a circle."[45] Zarathustra is defiant, and he says, "Must not all things that *can* run already have run along that lane? Must not all things that *can* happen already have happened, been done, and passed by?"[46] The dwarf leaves, and Zarathustra hears a dog howl in the distance. The howl seems familiar to him: "Had I ever heard a dog howl thus? . . . Yes! When I was a child, in my most distant childhood."[47] Zarathustra, in a sense, had *returned*.

The idea of eternal recurrence, or revolution, is central to *The Sacrifice* and is likewise mirrored in the metaphor of the bicycle. It's a sound—the arousal of his aural sense—that returns Zarathustra to a moment of his "most distant childhood." Sound functions in a similar way in *The Sacrifice*. There is the roar of the jet; the sparse soundtrack is peppered with the haunting and distant *kulning*, an ancient and atonal form of Swedish folk music primarily sung by women and originally used to call in livestock from the pastures; and we hear Japanese *hotchiko*, or bamboo flute music, which is what Alexander listens to both when he awakens from his night with the witch and then again when he sets his house aflame.[48] All these nonnative sounds serve as points of mediation with the extratemporal, which mirrors Tarkovsky's own views on extratemporality, or eternity: "I am convinced that life is only the beginning. I know that I can't prove it, but instinctively *we know that we are immortal*."[49] Nietzsche describes this cognizance—this suspicion of immortality—as *Das grosste Schwergewicht* (which Walter Kaufmann translates as "the greatest weight") when he more fully expounds on the idea of eternal recurrence in section 341 in *The Gay Science*. In this passage, Zarathustra's dwarf becomes a demon bearing news of the eternal return. This news can be accepted with terror or with praise, much like Alexander's own emotions when facing his death and the possibility of changing fate once and every time after that. It is the bicycle that mobilizes his will. Nietzsche writes, "The question in each and every thing, 'Do you desire this once more and innumerable times more?' would lie upon your actions as the greatest weight. Or how well disposed would you have to become to yourself and to life *to crave nothing more fervently* than this ultimate eternal confirmation and seal?"[50] By sleeping with Maria in an attempt to spare his family the anxiety and pain of the Apocalypse, Alexander was also asking himself, "Do you desire this once more and innumerable times more?" That is, if he saves them once, might they also be (and have been) saved indefinitely, in the recurrence of all eternity? Like the stroke of a bicycle pedal, up and down, Alexander hopes, loses hope, and hopes again.

Because *The Sacrifice* so liberally blends dream and reality, it's useful here to note that there are three distinct times in the film where it's clear we're entering a dream. The bicycle appears in three other distinct scenes. This is a strange parallel; but if we resist the temptation to reduce it to a symbol, the parallelism mirrors Tarkovsky's own mystical-aesthetic view of the image, itself borne by Tarkovsky's awareness of the "philosophical problems linked to the subjectivity of perception."[51] Tarkovsky resolves these problems by making the "real" world "deeply strange."[52] This is itself a poetical tendency, though Tarkovsky adds, "It's impossible to create something unreal. Everything is real and unfortunately we aren't able to abandon reality. We can express ourselves toward the world that exists in a poetic way. . . . Personally, I prefer to express myself in a metaphoric way."[53]

In this "metaphoric way," the bicycle in *The Sacrifice* "follows life." At first it's *just* a bike in a movie. But Tarkovsky's insistence that his films be received as art, rather than entertainment, invites a more far-reaching analysis than this essay can take on by not only looking at the postman's bicycle *as* a bicycle but also by asking what that bicycle *is*. Tarkovsky says, "My objective is to create my own world and these images which we create mean nothing more than the images which they are."[54] This logic is summarized by Tarkovsky's infamous quote about the "meaning" of "the Zone" in his 1979 postapocalyptic film, *Stalker*. In *Sculpting in Time*, he writes, "People have often asked me what the Zone is, and what it symbolizes.... The Zone doesn't symbolize anything, any more than anything else does in my films: *the zone is a zone*."[55] In *The Sacrifice*, this tautology is more concrete—and more abstract: the bike is a bike, as well as everything that the bike is.

Notes

1. Thomas Redwood, *Andrei Tarkovsky's Poetics of Cinema* (Newcastle, UK: Cambridge Scholars Publishing, 2010), 233.

2. Andrei Tarkovsky, *Sculpting in Time* (Austin: University of Texas Press, 1989), 21, 25.

3. Many suspect that Tarkovsky's relatively young death at the age of fifty-four was a result of the toxic pollutants he was exposed to while filming his 1979 film, *Stalker*, which was filmed at a former Estonian hydroelectric plant downriver from a chemical plant. Many production assistants fell ill during filming; Anatoly Solonitsyn, who played the writer in *Stalker*, died of lung cancer in 1982. Larisa Tarkovskaya, assistant director of *Stalker* and Tarkovsky's second wife, also died of a cancer identical to Solonitsyn and Tarkovsky in 1988. For further reading, see Stas Tyrkin, "In *Stalker*, Tarkovsky Foretold Chernobyl," *Komsomolskaya Pravda*, March 23, 2001, trans. and stored on Nostalghia.com, http://people.ucalgary.ca/~tstronds/nostalghia.com/The Topics/Stalker/sharun.html.

4. After a cursory glance at the mise-en-scène in *The Sacrifice*, the viewer can easily confuse it for a Bergman film. Tarkovsky filmed on the Baltic island of Gotland—the larger, brother island of Fårö, which is where Bergman lived and filmed *Hour of the Wolf*, *Through a Glass Darkly*, and many other films. Additionally, Sven Nykvist, best known for his cinematographic work with Bergman, served as the cinematographer for *The Sacrifice*, which also saw Daniel Bergman, Ingmar Bergman's son, serve as a camera assistant for the production. Anna Asp, Academy Award–winning pro-

duction designer for Bergman's *Fanny and Alexander*, served as production designer for *The Sacrifice*; and Erland Josephson, cast here in the lead role, is best known for his Bergman roles, including David in *Cries and Whispers*, Baron von Merkens in *Hour of the Wolf*, Isak Jacobi in *Fanny and Alexander*.

5. Otto's bike is of the type mass-produced across Europe before and during World War II. Because *The Sacrifice* is filmed in Sweden, it's safe to suggest that Otto's bike is of Swedish manufacture, if not a bit antiquated. I posted a few screen captures of the bicycle on various bike-related Internet forums; and though nobody could identify the exact manufacturer (there is no head badge), one user suggested that the bike could possibly be built by Kronan, though this is unverifiable.

6. This is the first of 115 total shots in *The Sacrifice*. At nine minutes and twenty-six seconds, this tracking shot is the longest single-take scene in any Tarkovsky film. See Vita Johnson and Graham Petrie, *The Films of Andrei Tarkovsky: A Visual Fugue* (Bloomington: Indiana University Press, 1994), 195.

7. Friedrich Nietzsche, *Thus Spoke Zarathustra*, trans. Clancy Martin (New York: Barnes and Noble Classics, 2005), 136.

8. In *On the Genealogy of Morals and Ecce Homo*, Nietzsche appropriately quips, "Give no credence to any thought that was not born outdoors while one moved about freely—in which the muscles are not celebrating a feast, too." Friedrich Nietzsche, *On the Genealogy of Morals and Ecce Homo*, trans. Walter Kaufmann (New York: Vintage Books, 1969), 239–40.

9. Robert Bird, *Andrei Tarkovsky: Elements of Cinema* (London: Reaktion Books, 2008), 209; Tarkovsky, *Sculpting in Time*, 218.

10. Johnson and Petrie, *Films of Andrei Tarkovsky*, xiii.

11. Bird, *Andrei Tarkovsky*, 21.

12. Bird, *Andrei Tarkovsky*, 21.

13. John Gianvito, ed., *Andrei Tarkovsky: Interviews* (Jackson: University Press of Mississippi, 2006), 46.

14. Redwood, *Poetics of Cinema*, 12.

15. Redwood, *Poetics of Cinema*, 13.

16. Tarkovsky, *Sculpting in Time*, 218, my emphasis.

17. Andrei Tarkovsky, "On the Apocalypse" (lecture, St. James Church, Piccadilly, London, July 18, 1984).

18. Tarkovsky, "On the Apocalypse."

19. Gianvito, *Andrei Tarkovsky*, 122.

20. Tarkovsky, "On the Apocalypse."

21. Tarkovsky, "On the Apocalypse."

22. Tarkovsky, "On the Apocalypse."

23. Tarkovsky, "On the Apocalypse."

24. See Walter Benjamin, "The Work of Art in the Age of Mechanical Reproduction," in *Illuminations: Essays and Reflections*, ed. Hannah Arendt, trans. Harry Zohn, 217–52 (New York: Schocken Books, 1969).

25. Tarkovsky, "On the Apocalypse."

26. Slavoj Žižek, "The Thing from Inner Space," *Mainview*, September 1999, http://www.lacan.com/zizekthing.htm.

27. Mark Le Fanu, "Christianity, Sacrifice, and Submission: The Social and Philosophical Thought of A. Tarkovsky," *Independent*, December 30, 1986, http://www.andreitarkovski.org/articulos/lefanu2.html (accessed January 1, 2014; site discontinued).

28. Frederic Jameson, *The Geopolitical Aesthetic: Cinema and Space in the World System* (Bloomington: Indiana University Press, 1992), 100.

29. Bird, *Andrei Tarkovsky*, 10, original emphasis.

30. Redwood, *Poetics of Cinema*, 19.

31. Le Fanu, "Christianity, Sacrifice, and Submission."

32. Additionally, there's a sense of mysterious intuitiveness in the idea of riding a bicycle and the idea that once you've learned, you never forget how to ride a bicycle. Thus the mystery is not only empirical but also cognitive.

33. Transcribed from *The Sacrifice*, directed by Andrei Tarkovsky (1986; New York: Kino International, 2011), DVD.

34. Thorsten Botz-Bornstein, *Films and Dreams: Tarkovsky, Bergman, Sokurov, Kubrick, and Wong Kar-Wai* (Lanham MD: Lexington Books, 2007), 6.

35. Botz-Bornstein, *Films and Dreams*, 11.

36. Johnson and Petrie, *Films of Andrei Tarkovsky*, 174.

37. The fiftieth poem in Nietzsche's prelude to *The Gay Science* is a poem titled "Lost His Head" ("Den Kopf verloren"). It reads, "Why is she clever now and so refined? / On her account a man's out of his mind, / His head was good before he took this whirl: / He lost his wits—to the aforesaid girl." Friedrich Nietzsche, *The Gay Science*, trans. Walter Kaufmann (New York: Vintage Books, 1974), 62–63.

38. The Starvation Strings were so named due to the meager wages laborers earned while constructing the trails.

39. Gianvito, *Andrei Tarkovsky*, 160.

40. Anna-Maria Rautio and Lars Ostlund. "'Starvation Strings' and the Public Good: Development of a Swedish Bike Trail Network in the Early Twentieth Century," *Journal of Transport History* 33, no. 1 (June 2012): 43.

41. Bird, *Andrei Tarkovsky*, 220.

42. This scene was actually shot twice. On the first take, only a single camera was used; and after the house was set to flame, the camera jammed. The production crew built a new house in less than two weeks and refilmed the scene. The 1988 film *Directed by Andrei Tarkovsky* (directed by Michal Leszc-

zylowski) is a poetical behind-the-scenes documentary of the filming of *The Sacrifice*, with significant time given to the composition of this penultimate scene.

43. Redwood, *Poetics of Cinema*, 236.

44. Nietzsche, *Zarathustra*, 134.

45. Nietzsche, *Zarathustra*, 136.

46. Nietzsche, *Zarathustra*, 136.

47. Nietzsche, *Zarathustra*, 136.

48. For the kulning, Tarkovsky used selections from Karin Edvards Johansson's album *Locklåtar från Dalarna och Härjedalen* (Sveriges Radio Records, 1963, catalogue no. RELP 5017). The hotchiko songs, "Singetsu," "Nezasa No Shi-rabe," and "Dai-Bosatsu," were performed by Watazumido-Shuso (Everest Records, 1982, group no. 3289).

49. Gianvito, *Andrei Tarkovsky*, 47. This filmic connection is especially true regarding Tarkovsky's use of music, because music, for Tarkovsky, "is the highest form of art, notwithstanding the fact that music is received on an emotional level and presents pure abstraction" (Gianvito, *Andrei Tarkovsky*, 39). That is to say, abstraction from everything, including time itself.

50. Nietzsche, *Gay Science*, 274.

51. Botz-Bornstein, *Films and Dreams*, 88.

52. Botz-Bornstein, *Films and Dreams*, 95.

53. Gianvito, *Andrei Tarkovsky*, 86.

54. Gianvito, *Andrei Tarkovsky*, 67.

55. Tarkovsky, *Sculpting in Time*, 200, my emphasis.

13   Bicycle Borrowers after Neorealism

Global Nou-velo Cinema

ANNE CIECKO

The safety bicycle (a prototype for the modern street bicycle) was invented in the late nineteenth century, at about the same time as the first movie camera. Starting with the first film to be given public exhibition, *Workers Leaving the Factory* (*La sortie des usines Lumière à Lyon*, 1895), protodocumentary *actualités* by the legendary French filmmaking pioneers Auguste and Louis Lumière include images of bicycles. Existing in three similarly structured versions filmed during different seasons, with all containing bicycles, *Workers Leaving the Factory* demonstrates the narrative spark inherent in the Lumières' filmmaking and in cinema more generally. It can be viewed as "the first work that aims at constructing a story, with a beginning and an end, solely by using the film image."[1] The Lumière brothers' films were subsequently made and shown in many countries, with the declared mission to "bring the world to the world." The tradition of featuring bicycles in films, inaugurated with *Workers Leaving the Factory*, continues throughout cinema's history.

The bicycle and its rider have repeatedly appeared on-screen as a composite vehicle at the intersection of reality and filmic storytelling. Human agency that mobilizes the bicycle image is key to its cinematic *frisson*.[2] The bicycle is a machine that, according to philosopher Gilles Deleuze, "only works when it is connected with another 'machine' such as the human body."[3] In this chapter, I argue that the bicycle (as well as the bicyclist) has become central to iterations of world cinema, from the post–World War II era onward, and is a recurring trope of realist narrative filmmaking. Examining films from Italy, Iran, and Saudi Arabia, I analyze the ways in which the synecdochic figure of the bicycle serves as a global cinematic emblem of human perseverance. Furthermore, I argue that the bicycle, as an image localized and hybridized within different cultural contexts, has been central to the assertion of national cinema.

Italian Neorealism and the Spinning of Film Theory

I contend that one particular film movement and film text have had a pervasive influence on the shaping of cinematic bicycle stories. This most celebrated landmark of bicycle-themed cinema, and a humanist world-cinema *ur-text*, is the Rome-set *Bicycle Thieves* (*Ladri di biciclette*, 1948), directed by Vittorio De Sica from an adapted screenplay by Italian neorealist proponent Cesare Zavattini. As an internationally and enduringly influential film movement, neorealism offers a representational and practical model of world cinema that formally strips away apparent artifice (using available light and nonstudio or soundstage "real" locations, in addition to nonprofessional actors) in aesthetic service to a realism informed by post–World War II economic exigencies. Conceptualizing neorealism as a "fruitfully open, polysemic term" recognizes the power of its influence on diverse filmmakers, manifestos, and global new cinema movements.[4]

Bicycle Thieves has been critically lauded for the ways it negotiates reality through the cinematic medium. Filmed on location in the streets of Rome, *Bicycle Thieves* features performances by nonprofessional actors including factory worker Lamberto Maggiorani, as protagonist Antonio Ricci, and eight-year-old street-discovery Enzo Staiola, as Ricci's son, Bruno. French realist film critic and theorist André Bazin underscores the impact of the quotidian and socially, morally, psychologically resonant incident of the theft of the impoverished workman's bicycle and his quest to recover it. Moving away from cinematic conventions of classical Hollywood cinema and minimizing narrative to focus on meaningful everyday moments that convey a sense of truth, De Sica's "supreme achievement," according to Bazin, "is to have succeeded in discovering the cinematographic dialectic capable of transcending the contradiction between the action of the 'spectacle' and of an event."[5] This is a point Bazin later reasserts in a discussion of the neorealist ideal articulated by both Zavattini and himself in his own expression of aesthetics and ontology, emphasizing a phenomenological image rather than exact reproduction of reality.[6] Bazin suggests that the depiction of chance is part of the achievement of *Bicycle Thieves* and neorealism, and he finds in them "the possibility of cinema encountering the world of contingency with open eyes, and thereby transcending the traditional notion of artistic realism as structured mimesis or imitation of the world."[7] Neorealism and *Bicycle Thieves*, as a key exemplar, convey a sense of lived human experience. Further, for Bazin, the metanarratives of auteurism and history provide a spectatorial appeal, an "emotional context for viewing."[8]

Bicycle Thieves, as a film that works within and beyond the frame of Italian neorealism, remains a treasured text in the world-cinema canon that Bazin helped to build. It received an honorary Academy Award for being an outstanding foreign-language film released in the United States during 1949. In 1952 the first poll of greatest films according to the British Film Institute's *Sight and Sound* magazine awarded its top spot to *Bicycle Thieves*, and the film's classic status endures.[9] A staple of film-history and film-appreciation courses, it is included in the auteur-centric catalog of the Criterion Collection, together with the later international bicycle-themed films *Muerte de un ciclista* (*Death of a Cyclist*, 1955) from Spain, *Close-Up* (1990) from Iran, and *Le gamin au vélo* (*The Kid with the Bike*, 2012) from Belgium. The creative affinities between these films and the iconic *Bicycle Thieves* help solidify their perceived connections with neorealism and their contributions to national and global cinema.[10]

However, a number of scholars, using bicycle examples, highlight and critique *Bicycle Thieves'* emotional manipulations in its combination of realism and narrative fiction. This fusion connotes the historical and cultural specificity of Italian neorealism, while also gesturing beyond the minimalist storytelling and universal appeal Bazin so deeply appreciated, to an exaggerated heightening of affect. Louis Bayman contends that Antonio's final desperate attempt to steal a bicycle in front of his son (and the final, tender handclasp between the two as they walk away together) mixes realism and "melodramatic strategies."[11] Frank Tomasulo, contesting the film's sociohistorical veracity, points out that when we first meet Antonio's son, Bruno, it is through the spokes of the bicycle as he polishes its frame.[12] Soon afterward, in a bonding moment flush with promise, father and son ride together on the bike before Antonio embarks on a new employment venture on the streets of postwar Rome. The bicycle, necessary for Antonio's new job, can be seen as a seemingly overdetermined symbol of "job, home, pride, faith, hope, Italy, physical and social mobility."[13] As such a "floating [or perhaps more appropriately, rolling] signifier" with flexible referents, the cinematic bicycle can be successfully dislocated and transplanted to other national and cultural contexts.[14]

Neorealism as an internationally influential movement offers a critical genealogical link to European and non-Western art cinemas. The French New Wave, for example, "embraced neo-realism as proof that filmmaking could be possible without a huge industrial structure behind it and that filmmakers could be as creative as novelists."[15] In turn, cinematic New Waves from the 1950s onward have proliferated around the world and are affiliated with expressions of global modernity beyond the West.[16] Iran in particular has emerged as a standout model of a national cinema with neorealist attributes. Exemplars of the New Iranian Cinema and its arthouse successors from the "globalizing era" of Iranian films following the postrevolutionary period include *The Cyclist* (*Bicycleran*, written and directed by Mohsen Makhmalbaf, 1987) and its reflexive, docu-fictive counterpart and counterpoint *Close-Up* (written and directed by Abbas Kiarostami, 1990), as well as the debut feature *The Day I Became a Woman* (directed and co-penned by Makhmalbaf's wife, Marzieh Meshkini, 2000).[17] In the following section, I address the ways such Iranian films narratively reconstruct and recontextualize the bicycle trope, assert authorship, and help set the stage for nascent national cinema elsewhere.

Reflexive Extensions and Narrative Machinery of New Iranian Cinema

In *The Cyclist*, an Afghan refugee, Nasim (played by Firouz Kiani), desperate to raise funds for his critically ill wife's medical care, agrees to ride a bicycle continuously for a week as a public street-circus attraction. According to director-screenwriter Mohsen Makhmalbaf, the film was inspired by an actual event that transpired in the Tehran coliseum.[18] Rumors of a Pakistani refugee cycling for ten days to help victims of a recent flood drew audiences, and a bazaar formed around the cyclist. Tragically, on the seventh day, the cyclist collapsed and died. Makhmalbaf had wanted the fictional cyclist in his film, upon completing his seven-day ride, to walk around in circles until he expired. Instead, Nasim continues to ride in circles, his spinning stilled only by a cinematographic freeze-frame that suspends his fate.

Poor and unemployed, cyclist Nasim endures a brutal ordeal. "Living" on his bicycle, he exhibits a kinetic relationship between machinery and subjectivity. However, he also demonstrates extraordinary depth of humanity in his relentless dedication as a husband and father. At different moments throughout the ride, his son, Jomeh, joins him on his bike (reminiscent of the tandem ride of Antonio and Bruno in *Bicycle Thieves*), bonding through the sharing of food while motivating and encouraging Nasim to stay the course. Nasim's societal disenfranchisement and displacement is emphasized by his former status as a champion cyclist in Afghanistan, now reduced to this exhausting challenge of nonstop riding in the blazing sunlight, freezing night, and drenching rain. The shady event organizer barks out grotesquely superheroic hyperbole: "He stopped a train in India in its tracks with the fierceness of his gaze; in Pakistan he lifted a couple of bulls with just one finger." Despite the ridicule and obstacles (protests, acts of sabotage), the cyclist retains a dignified (if masochistic) determination. In contrast, all motor vehicles in the film seem infected with abjection, from the motorcycle stunt drivers racing out of a spiral abyss, to the trucks that transport Afghan well diggers clamoring for day labor. As the week progresses, even after a nighttime fall (when Nasim has the chance for clandestine sleep as exhaustion and a substitute cyclist in disguise temporarily take over), body and bike seem melded together. He even manages to shift bicycles midpedaling when the tires of his first bike are intentionally damaged. As a break from the relentless realism, Nasim's ailing wife observes a surreal vision at one point, subtly reminiscent of the work of filmmakers such as Federico Fellini and Youssef Chahine, who blur the lines and codes of realism with fantasy. She witnesses a wheeled specter, just outside the hospital window: her husband in white on a bicycle, suspended on a cloud as a kind of *mise-en-abyme*, a film within a film. The woman's window-frame "movie," an apparent hallucination, functions as a fantasy projection, with the bicycle image a wish-fulfillment machinery of the imagination.

The Cyclist alludes to and amplifies the desperate need for a bicycle as a means for survival in *Bicycle Thieves*. Based on a true story with real-life characters playing themselves, about a man masquerading as Mohsen Makhmalbaf, Abbas Kiarostami's *Close-Up*, which has been called the "Iranian New Wave's seminal creation," repeatedly references Mohsen Makhmalbaf's *The Cyclist*.[19] Adding another layer of irony, *Close-Up* is made by Kiarostami, a director with a particular fascination with automobility. Jailed for fraud, Mr. Hossein Sabzian, the fake Makhmalbaf, sends a message with filmmaker Kiarostami to the real Makhmalbaf, informing him that *The Cyclist* is actually about Sabzian's own life struggles. Invested in a real-life "story about cinema," Kiarostami lobbies to get the case pushed forward and for permission to film in the courtroom. Ready for his close-up (not as a fame seeker but as a disenfranchised member of society to whom Makhmalbaf's films speak as art), Sabzian welcomes the opportunity to tell and (re)live his story on-screen.

As the trial proceeds, the film flashes back, in a reenactment, to the beginning of the story, suturing the director of *The Cyclist* with the protagonist-surrogate. Sabzian reads the published screenplay of Makhmalbaf's *The Cyclist* on the bus and gives the book to the woman next to him who expresses interest in it, while also claiming to be the filmmaker. In the courtroom, he explains the affinity with the director by relating how Makhmalbaf's films resonate for people like him. As fake Makhmalbaf, Sabzian had insisted that the Ahankhah family, who believe they will be in his next film, watch *The Cyclist* at a cinema "to acquire greater interest in cinema and have more respect for me as a director . . . who is aware of people's sufferings and difficulties" and who is "humble enough to mix with ordinary folk." "A true artist," Sabzian asserts in the courtroom, "is someone who is close to the people and is prepared to go to the cinema with them." His deception is apparently disclosed (as revealed in another flashback) during a conversation leading up to Sabzian's confrontation by a journalist and the police. Fake Makhmalbaf is congratulated for a prize he did not realize real Makhmalbaf had won, and his response does not match details in the newspaper report. Sabzian's actions are deemed by the court to be the result of "social malaise and unemployment," and he is finally pardoned and released from jail. In the film's final sequence, Kiarostami arranges and films a meeting of the real Makhmalbaf and Sabzian, who is overcome with emotions. (Kiarostami has said in an interview that Sabzian did not know he was being filmed in this scene, contributing to his vérité response compared with Makhmalbaf.)[20] The *Close-Up* director, in offscreen narration, notes some technical difficulties with Makhmalbaf's microphone and the uneven sound but nonetheless follows the two men as they ride off on a motorcycle together to make amends with the duped family, stopping along the way to buy a large pot of flowers as a gift.

Kiarostami's films frequently employ the automobile as a means to navigate the public sphere and provide a simulacrum of a private space. The precredit sequence of *Close-Up* takes place mainly in a taxi in which the journalist, together with the police officers in the back seat, reveals that he is motivated to catch and confront the Makhmalbaf imposter because it is a sensational media story. In the film's final sequence, Makhmalbaf and Sabzian are reflected in a rearview mirror in a tracking shot and glimpsed through the windshield of a parked car, enabling the viewer to apprehend the two Makhmalbafs together in a kind of mirror-reflected, unified ego ideal.[21] However, the challenges of mediated access to street-level reality and lived experiences are also realized in the film. Within the diegesis (i.e., narrative world) of *Close-Up*, *The Cyclist* (and in turn, *Bicycle Thieves*) is an intertext that invites the viewer to see the limits imposed on societal mobility. Kiarostami's final freeze-frame occurs after the real director, Makhmalbaf, informs Mr. Ahankhah that Mr. Sabzian has changed and should be seen in a new light and Mr. Akankhah replies that "he'll make us proud." Through Sabzian's face in profile nearly filling half the frame, with downcast eyes and mixed emotions, we are reminded that this tenuous *rapprochement* has occurred because of the movie we are watching.

Just as *Close-Up*'s Mr. Sabzian exalted his director-hero, Iranian auteurs and films came to occupy a prominent place in the international image market. By the turn of the millennium, Iranian cinema was one of the most globally acclaimed and prolific national cinemas.[22] To aspiring filmmakers in Middle Eastern countries with nascent national cinemas, Iranian art house cinema also potentially offered a viable alternative to spectacle and genre-driven production (dominated by Hollywood, Bollywood, and Egyptian commercial films) and Eurocentric art cinema.[23] As Saeed Zeydabadi-Nejad demonstrates, Iranian cinema offers an important case of "openings and opportunities" for filmmakers within, or despite, a system of state control.[24]

Realist reflexivity within Iranian cinema, and the productions of the Makhmalbaf Film House in particular, continued with *The Day I Became a Woman* (2000), another Iranian film that prominently features the image of the bicycle.[25] The film premiered in Venice at the world's oldest international film festival in the same year that Jafar Panahi's Tehran-set, gritty social drama *The Circle*, banned in Iran and also diffusely centered on the lives of multiple Iranian women, took the Golden Lion. *The Day I Became a Woman* won the UNESCO Award, the Isvema Award, and the CinemaAvvenire Award for the best first film. The structure of *The Day I Became a Woman* echoes Makhmalbaf's multicharacter triptych, *The Peddler* (1987), and his multiperspectival approach to representing subjectivity.[26] The film contains three fictional, loosely interlinked vignettes of girls and women at different life stages, filmed on the scenic island of Kish (a more relaxed, interstitial location compared to the rest of the country but still subject to cultural traditions and patriarchal rules).

In the middle section, young wife Ahoo rides in a bicycle race with women covered in a black chador (head and body covering). Focusing intensely on her pained and determined face, the camera subverts the gaze-deflection logic of the chador as culturally coded technology of gender.[27] Ahoo's marathon becomes a metaphor for the challenges she faces as a woman in her marriage, in her family, and in her society in general. As in *The Cyclist*, the bicycle and bicyclist are apprehended as a single, persistent vision, and we cannot see them separately. While Antonio in *Bicycle Thieves* spends little time on his bicycle, facing a crisis of masculinity and threatened livelihood should he fail to recover his lost machine, marginalized immigrant Nasim's situation in *The Cyclist* is even more abject. His need to stay on the bicycle is a matter of life and death, as he must ride to earn money to save his life but could die from exhaustion in the process. For Ahoo, the bicycle is a vehicle for freedom, however futile or illusory. Her participation in the race in the company of other women has broader social implications. Impediments to her mobility are intensifying acts of gendered psychic violence, physical obstruction, and brute fate.

The camera first shows the chador-clad women on the bicycles from a male point of view (that of Ahoo's husband), looking like a flock of undifferentiated dark birds in the distance. Ahoo, near the front of the pack, rides on her red bike with ever more determination, accompanied by the ambient sounds of the bike wheels, her breath, and her bell as she passes other cyclists. She is increasingly followed, flanked, and berated by galloping horses carrying male members of her family, tribe, and community who attempt to persuade her to stop riding her bicycle. Her husband expresses concern that she is riding with a leg injury, but he mainly objects to her defiance. And the mullah tells her cycling is devil's work. While she is still on her bicycle, her husband officially divorces her; and she concedes, continuing to ride on ahead alone in the hazy heat. She rolls past imposing cliffs at the edge of the sea and a sign indicating that "you are here"; past women who gossip about her; past her elderly grandfather, who begs her to dismount and return home to her husband; and past her father, who curses her for bringing shame on the family. Finally, she is forced to stop as her two brothers block the way; and the camera pulls away to an ambiguous but ominous tableau as the figures are dwarfed by the landscape.

Bookended by two other stories of female childhood and old age— the fable-like tale of nine-year-old Hava on her birthday and a surrealist episode about elderly Hoora, who is near the end of her life—Ahoo's neo-neorealist bicycle struggles in Meshkini's *The Day I Became a Woman* represent a critical stage of adult womanhood in Iranian culture. She must assert herself against patriarchy and societal strictures to realize her own ambitions. In the first segment, Hava enjoys her last hours of playful freedom with a neighborhood boy before being required to cover herself with a chador in her transition to womanhood (and the film's transition to Ahoo's story). In contemporary Iranian cinema, the societal exclusion, subjugation, and resistance of women are provocative topics that have been explored in the work of other women directors including Tahmineh Milani, Rakhshan Bani-E'temad, and Niki Karimi. However, Meshkini's film arguably breaks some new ground in addressing complicated and, at times, contradictory views on women across generations in Iran. Women's cycling is a particularly provocative topic for cinematic representation because of unevenly observed restrictions on the activity in public within the country. These constraints are based on perceptions of the female body on the bicycle, perceptions shaped by certain interpretations and applications of Islam. In addition to addressing such cultural realities, Ahoo's urgent cycling recalls previous landmarks of Iranian cinema: Nasim's desperate attempts to ride his bicycle nonstop in *The Cyclist* and the struggles of authorship and identity in its reflexive counterpart, *Close-Up*.

The narrative device of separated bicycle and bicyclist as cause for crisis recurs throughout contemporary world cinema, harkening back to film history's *Bicycle Thieves* as a primal scene of the loss of the bicycle as a traumatic event. In the Iranian film *The Day I Became a Woman*, cinematic humanism is further endowed with emotional potency through the connections between the narrative figure of the woman on the bicycle, the female filmmaker-author, and women more generally. In the next section, I examine the inauguration of national cinema in Saudi Arabia in a neorealist-inflected, bicycle-themed film by the country's first woman director, a film centering on the figure of the girl-child cyclist.

The Progeny of Neorealism and the Two-Wheeled Launch of Saudi Cinema

Italian neorealist films made between 1945 and 1949 "showed ordinary men and women *and children* struggling against inhumane social conditions."[28] As discussed earlier in this essay, Bruno, the child first seen through the spokes of the bicycle, is essential to the melding of reality and melodrama in the Italian neorealist classic *Bicycle Thieves*. Historically, significant postrevolutionary Iranian cinema—including formative films by Abbas Kiarostami, Majid Majidi, Bahram Beyzai, and Amir Naderi—was supported by funding from the film division of the Institute for the Development of Children and Young Adults (also known as Kanun). Kiarostami served as one of the division's founding supervisors and created films for and about children while also developing his own style.[29] Children became a central focus for Iranian filmmakers as a means to allegorize social and political issues while avoiding censorship and to view the world through a child's eyes, as in the case of Jafar Panahi's first two award-winning features, *The White Balloon* (1995) and *The Mirror* (1997). Iranian films featuring children became art house staples, and empathic cinematic images of children continue to hold broad potential for crossing national boundaries. In addition to citing Italian neorealist films expressing "the poetry of everyday life" and representing a rebirth of the nation in the aftermath of war and fascism, Haifaa Al-Mansour, the Saudi director of *Wadjda* (2012), has acknowledged Iranian cinema as her most immediate model for intelligent cinema in a cultural environment impacted by "censorship and conservative forces."[30] In order to create a movie focused on the lives of women in Saudi Arabia, Al-Mansour makes a film centered on a girl on the cusp of adolescence and her quest for a bicycle. *Wadjda* recasts the father-son dynamic of *Bicycle Thieves* as a "mother-daughter film centered around a bike."[31]

Wadjda hails from the most populous country on the Arabian Peninsula; however, Saudi film production and exhibition within a kingdom dominated by Wahhabi fundamentalism has, to date, been very limited and restricted.[32] German cofinanced, *Wadjda* premiered at the Venice Film Festival and has circulated throughout film festivals and the international art house. Widely described by critics as Saudi Arabia's first feature film, *Wadjda* is actually the first Saudi feature filmed entirely in Saudi Arabia and the first feature film made by a Saudi woman director. Distributed by high-profile Sony Pictures Classics, *Wadjda* also demonstrates mobility in its status as the first Saudi film to be submitted by Saudi Arabia to the foreign-language film category of the Academy Awards.

While *Bicycle Thieves* is narratively catalyzed by the loss of the bicycle and a crisis of masculinity as Antonio's livelihood is threatened, *Wadjda* foregrounds a young girl's quest to acquire and ride a bicycle as an assertion of public female agency—a quest ultimately inviting reflexive comparisons with the challenges faced by the film's writer-director. Originally from a small, conservative Saudi town, Haifaa Al-Mansour expresses that "it's very important to celebrate resistance, pursuing one's dreams."[33] Set in Saudi Arabia's capital and largest city, Riyadh, the film develops its title character, Wadjda Al Saffan (played by Waad Mohammed), through assertions of prepubescent individuality and entrepreneurial spirit in the cultural spaces she inhabits. Wadjda wears sneakers underneath her school uniform at the madrasa, makes pop song mixtapes, crafts friendship bracelets with football club colors, and does paid errands for the older schoolgirls, such as facilitating illicit meetings with boys. In contrast, her school-teacher mother is more compelled to obey societal restrictions, her inability to drive a car as a woman necessitating a long, shared commute to work in an un-air-conditioned van driven by a boorish South Asian migrant laborer (who is himself downtrodden and bullied). After Wadjda's best friend, Abdullah, playfully teases her, steals her breakfast and hijab, and compels her to chase him down the street, she calls out, "If I had a bike, you'd see," as the boy rides off with others to school. From this moment forward, Wadjda has a new focus: to acquire and ride a bicycle, a goal perceived by others as a rejection of conventional gender roles and behaviors. "Have you ever seen a girl on a bike?" her mother asks when Wadjda tells her she'd like to buy a bike to race her friend. Later her mother asks, "You think you can act like a boy?"

The film focuses mainly on its title character, but the contrasts between Wadjda and her mother underscore the film's vicarious sense of hope for the younger generation. Wadjda's mother is a sympathetic figure but one resigned to her limited mobility and limited independence. She expresses a combination of dissatisfaction and acceptance at her husband's choice to take on a new marriage and family, finding the situation unfair punishment for being unable to give birth to another child because of medical complications. Nevertheless, she tries to look and act like the ideal wife for her husband, refusing, for example, to cut her hair shorter as she'd prefer, since her husband prefers it long and smooth.

Wadjda's largely absent father, while expressing affection in the limited time he spends with her (playing a violent video game with her, giving her a magnetic rock for her collection, expressing pride at her school accomplishments), devotes his time and energies principally to his work and to his search for a second wife who will bear him a son. In a pivotal moment in the film, Wadjda pins a paper with her handwritten name to her paternal family tree (with only names of male relatives) and later discovers her addition removed, crumpled, and cast aside.

However, Wadjda is rebellious by nature and unwilling to accept defeat and to fully capitulate to imposed gender restrictions. Throughout the film, Wadjda is chastised by her school principal, Ms. Hussa, for not wearing full *abbayah*, for wearing sporty Converse sneakers to school instead of the requisite black shoes (Wadjda fills in her trainers with a black marker), for playing hopscotch in a courtyard where workmen on a rooftop might be able to see her, for having *haram* items in her backpack, and for her possible involvement with arranging a scandalous rendezvous for an older girl. At the madrasa, girls are reminded of the gendered rules of their religion and society, regulations that only tighten as the girls grow into womanhood. They are not permitted to touch the Koran if they are menstruating (to the girls' nervous amusement), and female friendship that is construed as romantic is publicly shamed in a "place of learning and morals."

The bicycle is narratively critical to the representation of Wadjda's defiance of stereotypes and expectations. A doodle of a bicycle in her notebook references her desire to occupy the public sphere on her own terms. She lobbies her mother with observations that she has seen some girls riding bikes on tv, and she is unconcerned or unconvinced by her mother's insistence that she'll never be able to have children if she rides a bike.[34] Wadjda befriends and repeatedly visits a shopkeeper to remind him that she intends to purchase a bicycle (and to reserve it for her), and she persuades her friend Abdullah to teach her how to ride a bicycle without training wheels. When the occasion to win bicycle money surfaces in the form of a Koran recitation competition, Wadjda opportunistically joins the school religious club and trains with fervor.

The direction, cinematography, and editing of *Wadjda* display a rather claustrophobic and circumscribed environment and existence, while also effectively gesturing toward openness. Freer and more mobile than the grown women in her life and community (and the film's director Haifaa Al-Mansour), Wadjda walks in the city streets, across construction-site rubble, to school, and to the shop. As revealed by the director in interviews, the film's style is informed by extradiegetic circumstances and attempts to work within—and circumvent—limits. As a woman, Al-Mansour was unable to freely film in public, especially when working together with men and giving them direction. Therefore, she directed her male crew via walkie-talkies from a van. Additionally, in Al-Mansour's script, partially developed in the Sundance and Rawi Screenwriter's Lab in Jordan, humor sweetens the pathos, as when Wadjda's mother reacts to her bicycle-skinned knee as if she's lost her virginity or when Wadjda brazenly announces to the school assembly that she plans to use her Koran-recitation prize to buy a bicycle with no training wheels "since I already know how to ride one."

By the end of the film, Wadjda becomes anything but a typically ideal Saudi girl, as defined by her teacher (who withholds and donates her prize money to a Palestinian charity), and is able to confront some of the hypocrisy around her that controls female desires and ambitions. She won't take Abdullah's bicycle when offered. ("How will we race?" she asks him.) After discovering that her father has married another woman, Wadjda becomes even more connected with the bicycle, which comes to symbolize movement away from dependency on men for survival. Her mother's enlightened gesture at the end of the film of surprising Wadjda with the bicycle she's rightfully earned and Wadjda's ebullient final race with Abdullah, which culminates in a shot of the girl looking out toward an offscreen horizon, suggest potential openness. As the first feature film made by a Saudi filmmaker within Saudi Arabia, *Wadjda* possesses a hopeful humanism conveyed through the girl on the bicycle and the woman with

the movie camera, creating a culturally specific and globally appealing filmic artifact that easily crosses borders and heralds the birth of
new cinematic possibilities.

Conclusion: Neo-neorealist World Cinema, Cycling On

In this essay, I have proposed that the bicycle, a component of early
cinema's investigations of the relationships between reality and storytelling and between human and machine, finds a seminal representation in the neorealist and world-cinema classic *Bicycle Thieves*. Tracing
the bicycle as a trope through subsequent films from Iran and Saudi
Arabia reveals the revitalization and recontexualization of neorealism
and the familiarity with the polysemic *Bicycle Thieves* intertext and
its humanist influence. The films I have discussed here foreground
narrative identification with the cyclist as an individualized figure
asserting a place within culture for both the outsider protagonist and
the outsider filmmaker. As Saudi filmmaker Haifaa Al-Mansour has
stated, "The bicycle has this heritage in cinema and I wanted to lean
on that because I felt it was important to continue something, to be
part of something."[35] (After the release of the film, the ban on women
riding bicycles in Saudi Arabia was reportedly lifted, although as of
this writing, the activity remains subject to restrictions.)

Throughout countries and decades, the bicycle has proven to have
extraordinary utility for critiques of social inequality and for exploration of the local and global mobility of cinema. With their innovative takes on neorealism, Iranian and Saudi films such as *The Cyclist*,
Close-Up, *The Day I Became a Woman*, and *Wadjda* assert national and
cultural specificity and agency, while establishing vital links with
one of the most globally beloved films and film movements in the
world-cinema canon.

Notes

1. Ion Martea, "*La sortie des usines Lumière* [*Leaving the Lumière Factory*]," *Culture
   Wars*, August 7, 2006. http://www.culturewars.org.uk/EF/ef7.htm.
2. As another striking example from early cinema, moving into a formally
   experimental realm of early documentary cinema (outside the scope of this
   essay), Soviet montage theorist and practitioner Dziga Vertov's anthropo-
   morphized camera in *Man with a Movie Camera* (1929) invites the viewer to

see man and machine as one, including a shopwindow tableau of a manne-
quin riding a bicycle.

3. See Claire Colebrook, *Gilles Deleuze* (London: Routledge, 2001), 56.

4. See Noa Steinmatsky, *Italian Locations: Reinhabiting the Past in Postwar Cinema* (Minneapolis: University of Minnesota Press, 2008), xxviii. This poly-
semy enables multiple interpretations, as in the neoformalist critique by
Kristen Thompson in *Breaking the Glass Armour* (Princeton NJ: Princeton
University Press, 1988).

5. André Bazin, "*Bicycle Thief*," in *What Is Cinema?* trans. Hugh Gray (Berkeley:
University of California Press, 1974), 2:60.

6. André Bazin, "De Sica: Metteur en Scène," in *What Is Cinema?* trans. Hugh
Gray (Berkeley: University of California Press, 1974), 2:76. Bazin suggests here
that De Sica's *Umberto D* (1952) comes even closer to the representational
ideal of neorealist cinema.

7. Geoffrey Nowell-Smith, "From Realism to Neo-Realism," in *Theorizing World
Cinema*, ed. Lucia Nagib, Chris Perriam, and Rajinder Dudrah (London: I. B.
Taurus, 2012), 157.

8. Greg M. Smith, "Reflecting on the Image: Sartrean Emotions in the Writings
of André Bazin," *Film and Philosophy* 10 (2006): 119.

9. I am grateful to film critic Eren Odabasi for this reminder about the first *Sight
and Sound* poll. It is also discussed on the Criterion Collection website in
an essay titled "*Sight and Sound* Poll 2012: *Bicycle Thieve*," November 13, 2012,
https://www.criterion.com/current/posts/2549-sight-sound-poll-2012-bicycle
-thieves. *Bicycle Thieves* is recognized there as being "hailed around the world
as one of the greatest movies ever made."

10. As this essay has evolved, I have removed my analyses of *Death of a Cyclist*
and *The Kid with the Bike* for purposes of concision, but I believe these films
also fit into my overarching thesis. My focus in this essay is primarily on
bicycle-themed Iranian and Saudi films after *Bicycle Thieves*.

11. Louis Bayman, "Melodrama as Realism in Italian Neorealism," in *Realism and
the Audiovisual Media*, ed. Lucia Nagib and Cecilia Mello (Basingstoke, UK:
Palgrave Macmillan, 2009), 56.

12. Frank Tomasulo, "*Bicycle Thieves*: A Re-Reading," *Cinema Journal* 21, no. 2
(Spring 1982): 7.

13. Tomasulo, "*Bicycle Thieves*," 8.

14. For a critical exegesis of the concept of the floating signifier, see Jeffrey Mehl-
man, "The 'Floating Signifier': From Lévi-Strauss to Lacan," *Yale French Studies*, no. 48 (1972): 10–37.

15. Peter Bondanella, "Italian Neorealism: The Postwar Renaissance of Italian
Cinema," in *Traditions in World Cinema*, ed. Linda Badley, R. Barton Palmer,
and Steven Jay Schneider (New Brunswick NJ: Rutgers University Press,

2006), 38. French New Wave auteurs François Truffaut and Bernardo Bertolucci in their respective films, *Jules and Jim* (1962) and *La Luna* (1979), represent complex facets of femininity in the rather fetishized or idealized figure
of what Germaine Greer calls the "cycling girl." See Germaine Greer, "Three's
a Crowd," *Guardian*, May 23, 2008, http://www.theguardian.com/books/2008
/may/24/francoistruffaut.worldcinema.

16. See James Tweedie, *The Age of New Waves: Art Cinema and the Staging of Globalization* (Oxford: Oxford University Press, 2013).

17. See Hamid Naficy's multivolume study of the social history of Iranian film,
A Social History of Iranian Cinema, especially vol. 4, *The Globalizing Era, 1984–
2010* (Durham NC: Duke University Press, 2010).

18. This story is related in a 1989 statement included in the extras of the 2005
Kimstim Collection DVD of *The Cyclist*.

19. See Michael Atkinson, "*Close-Up*: Iranian New Wave's Seminal Creation," *Village Voice*, March 24, 2010, http://www.villagevoice.com/2010-03-24/film/close
-up-iranian-new-wave-s-seminal-creation/full/.

20. See Abbas Kiarostami, interview by Geoff Andrew, *Guardian*, April 28, 2005,
http://www.theguardian.com/film/2005/apr/28/hayfilmfestival2005.guardian
hayfestival.

21. I refer here to Jacques Lacan's concepts of the mirror stage and the ego
ideal. See Jacques Lacan, "The Mirror Stage as Formative of the I Function as
Revealed in Psychoanalytic Experience," in *Écrits: The First Complete Edition in
English*, trans. Bruce Fink (New York: W. W. Norton, 2006), 75–81.

22. See Negar Mottahedeh, "New Iranian Cinema: 1982–present," in Badley,
Palmer, and Schneider, *Traditions in World Cinema*, 176.

23. This was one of my observations from examining the development of film
culture in Jordan, where Iranian cinema has helped diversify models of filmmaking. I examine Jordanian cinema in the essays "Digital Territories and
States of Independence: Jordan's Film Scenes," *Afterimage* 36, no. 5 (March–
April 2009): 3–6; and "Situating Jordanian Cinema: A Report on Contemporary Film Culture(s) in Amman," *Asian Cinema* 18, no. 2 (Fall–Winter 2007):
303–9.

24. Zeydabadi-Nejad, *The Politics of Iranian Cinema: Film and Society in the Islamic
Republic* (New York: Routledge, 2010), 6–7.

25. In the Afghanistan-set *At Five in the Afternoon*—a 2003 feature by Mohsen
Makhmalbaf's daughter (and auteur in her own right), Samira Makhmalbaf—a bicycle provides a striking visual image. *Joy of Madness*, Hana
Makhmalbaf's documentary about the making of her sister's aforemen-
tioned film, won the (three-wheeled) cycle-sourced festival award, the Vesoul
International Festival of Asian Cinema's Cyclo d'Or. As a further instance
of intertextuality, Samira Makhmalbaf had a small role as a gypsy woman's

young daughter (and a friend of the cyclist's son) in *The Cyclist*. There are also multiple international films about and directly inspired by *Close-Up*, including the documentary *Close-Up Long Shot* (Moslem Mansouri and Mahmoud Chokrollahi, 2005). Also of interest but outside the scope of this essay are international films that are in dialogue with *Bicycle Thieves* but that alter the vehicle, including the pedicab of *Cyclo* (Tran Anh Hung, 1995, released in Vietnam, France, and Hong Kong) and the motorbikes of *La promesse* (Luc Dardenne and Jean-Pierre Dardenne, 1996, released in Belgium, France, Luxembourg, and Tunisia) and of *Janji Joni* (Joko Anwar, 2005, released in Indonesia). Other key international landmarks or homages to *Bicycle Thieves* include the Sixth Generation—the urban generation—Chinese film *Beijing Bicycle* (Wang Xiaoshuai, 2001), discussed by Jinhua Li elsewhere in this collection, and the recent Belgian film by the Dardenne brothers, *Le gamin au vélo* (*The Kid with the Bike*, 2012).

26. See Rahul Hamid, "A Filmmaker at the Barricades: The Cinematic and Political Evolution of Mohsen Makhmalbaf," *Cineaste* 34, no. 4 (2009).

27. See Teresa de Lauretis's classic essay "The Technology of Gender," in *Technologies of Gender: Essays on Theory, Film, and Fiction* (Bloomington: Indiana University Press, 1987), 1–30.

28. Jan Wojcik-Andrews, *Children's Films: History, Ideology, Pedagogy, Theory* (New York: Garland, 2000), 85, my emphasis.

29. Khatereh Sheibani, *The Poetics of Iranian Cinema: Aesthetics, Modernity and Film after the Revolution* (London: I. B. Taurus, 2011), 21.

30. See the interview by Chris O'Falt, "Influences: The Movies That Inspired 'Wadjda' Director Haiffa Al-Mansour to Make History," *Hollywood Reporter*, December 18, 2013, http://www.hollywoodreporter.com/news/influences-movies-inspired-wadjda-director-665035. Al-Mansour mentions the representation of girls and their desire to occupy the public sphere as football fans in Iranian filmmaker Jafar Panahi's *Offside* (2006) as a particular influence.

31. O'Falt, "Influences."

32. I discuss Saudi film culture prior to *Wadjda* (2012), the first feature film made within the country, in "Saudi Arabia," in *Middle Eastern Cinema*, ed. Terri Ginsberg and Chris Lippard (Lanham MD: Scarecrow Press / Rowman and Littlefield, 2010), 355–57; and in "Cinema 'of' Yemen and Saudi Arabia: Narrative Strategies, Cultural Challenges, Contemporary Features," *Wide Screen* 3, no. 1 (June 2011): 1–16.

33. See the interview by Liz Hoggard, "Haifaa al-Mansour: 'It's very important to celebrate resistance,'" *Observer*, July 13, 2013, http://www.theguardian.com/theobserver/2013/jul/14/haifaa-mansour-wadjda-saudi-arabia.

34. This comment recalls nineteenth-century debates in Great Britain and America about bicycles, women's health, propriety, and morality—especially

negative impacts on the body and sexual development. While *Wadjda* is situated within the contemporary Saudi context, it exhibits global awareness and ultimately celebrates the girl on the bicycle as a figure of transgression and emancipation.

35. O' Falt, "Influences."

14 *Breaking Away* and Vital Materialism

Embodying Dreams of Social Mobility
via the Bicycle Assemblage

RYAN HEDIGER

The essential plotline of Peter Yates's film *Breaking Away* (1979) begins when Dave Stoller (Dennis Christopher), the protagonist, has the good fortune to win a high-quality Masi bicycle.[1] It is an exotic, Italian machine, its very presence interrupting a set of seemingly rigid identity and class dynamics in 1970s Bloomington, Indiana, Dave's midwestern home that is part working-class, part college town. So the story begins with the arrival of a strange new *thing*, an object, a bicycle. This alluring foreign object helps to spur Dave's interest in all things Italian, leading him to embrace the Italian language and a set of "Italian" personal habits, driving his father crazy. In our post–Lance Armstrong era, it can be difficult to recall that Dave's obsession with bicycle racing is itself somewhat unconventional, as the sport then enjoyed less popularity in the United States than it does now.[2]

Dave's performance as an exotic, Italian-inflected cyclist intensifies when, in a happy accident, the beautiful Indiana University student Katherine (Robyn Douglass), riding her motorized scooter, unknowingly drops her notebook. Dave retrieves it and chases her across the expansive midwestern campus, he on his Italian Masi and she on the scooter, an Italian Vespa (adorned with a USA sticker), to the soundtrack accompaniment of Felix Mendelssohn's *Italian* Symphony. When Dave catches her, he accidentally finds courting advantage in playing the role of a romantic foreigner; but in the plot's trajectory, Dave relinquishes his assumed Italian identity to find his ostensibly proper self, suggesting the falseness of his Italian claims. Indeed, as William C. Martell puts it, summarizing the narrative, Dave comes to realize not only that those he "admires most are liars and cheats" (both the Italian racing team and his own father) but that "*he's* a liar and a cheat."[3]

Martell's assessment rightly foregrounds the importance of identity in this film. But while Dave clearly is not the Italian he claims to be, to call his performed Italian self simply false obscures the complex dynamics of selfhood in this story. Instead, scenes like the campus chase present identity less as fixed or rigid and more as open, cosmopolitan, object entangled, even musicalized; identity is *performed*, amid a large cast, both human and nonhuman. In part, I contend that in the film's narrative arc, the characters first succumb to feeling trapped in themselves, only to find new opportunities in more expansive notions of self, a conception of identity made less visible by a true-or-false binary. The film's often lighthearted tone can soften or even disguise its central concern with matters of personal change, class, and social mobility. But then again, comedy is a genre that has long been used to engage the complex and fluid boundaries of identity, often in subtly serious ways.[4]

This chapter relies on "vital materialism" to make its case.[5] Vital materialism thoroughly unsettles conventional ideas of identity, complicating especially the distinction between animate and inanimate matter but also effectively reworking ideas about human class and national identities, species identity, and more. It offers the surprising recognition that ostensibly inert matter—traditionally the most fixed form of identity—has a kind of disruptive agency. Acknowledging the significant roles that seemingly inanimate objects like bicycles (and limestones, as shown below) play in the drama of human identity complicates our epistemological system of naming and identity much more broadly. This insight opens the way for a significantly more fluid sense of social class, which is part of what the dreaming Dave so desires in his Italian fascination. The comically sweet allure of the exotic in this film, therefore, is a kind of metaphor or synecdoche for open-identity systems in which desire and striving can lead us out of our former selves to something better. By the film's end, all the main characters have embraced change and thereby redefined themselves.

Thus, though in certain obvious ways Dave's Italian self is false, I argue that his adoption of it reveals a number of deeper truths. Most particularly, Dave's assumed identity shows—and enacts—his desire to become something better. In Dave's bicycle dreams, a larger self-transformation begins with an object, the bicycle, and a set of embodied practices. By the film's end, Dave has enrolled in college and successfully continued the journey of social mobility that his "fake" Italian identity reveals and initiates.

The title *Breaking Away* has multiple meanings: It signals both the move by a bicycle racer to break away from the pack and the need for each of the four cutters to break away from the cocoon of their adolescent social group (the nickname "cutters" refers to their fathers' jobs as limestone cutters). A third meaning emerges in this chapter's analysis that the cutters also break away from their stultifying class identities and the preestablished patterns of conventional life that would have them move from high school directly into labor. The resonances of these meanings are particularly well amplified from the perspective of vital materialism. It is clear that Dave begins to break away from his friends and his inherited family identity because of his unconventional interest in cycling, reinforced by his Italian obsession; the filmmakers' decision to accompany many of Dave's rides with classical music highlights the beautiful exoticism of his endeavors. Much of what is great and distinctive about cycling is evoked: the quiet and fluid movement through bucolic spaces; the harmonies among rider, bicycle, and place; the robust health a rider can feel.[6] Those scenes offer a kind of cycling dreamworld, a strange space apart, an alternative picture of selfhood.

Just how strange is cycling to conventional ideas of identity? A bicyclist is a combination of human and machine functioning as an identity category. The word itself places the machine ("bicycle") first and the human ("-ist") second. Bicycling vividly shows the materiality, often unacknowledged, of subjectivity; human identity is profoundly bound up with external materiality, with "objects," including bicycles. Conventional grammar often credits bicycle riders—the humans—with all the agency; they are said to "jump" or "sprint" or "break away."

We tend to elide the presence of the machine. But it is not difficult to recognize that this human action relies fundamentally on a partnership with a bicycle, with an object that translates human exertion into speed and more particularly, in regard to "breaking away," into a gap between riders and the pack they leave behind. This breaking away, then, illustrates the latent agency of the thing that is a bicycle, pointing not only to the significance of the labor practices and technical innovations that produced the bicycle but to the very characteristics of the materials themselves—the strength yet flexibility of the steel, the stick of the rubber tires, the harmony of the machine as a whole.

So when we discuss bicyclists as an identity group, we are actually discussing something like an assemblage, a set of identities cooperating, as Jane Bennett argues about bicycles in her compelling and demanding book *Vibrant Matter: A Political Ecology of Things*.[7] We are therefore implicitly crediting the value of the complex object that is the bicycle, its rider, and the communities across time that produced and refined bicycles. Much is at stake in such designations. As Bennett puts it, "The philosophical project of naming where subjectivity begins and ends is too often bound up with fantasies of a human uniqueness in the eyes of God, of escape from materiality or of mastery of nature" (ix). The desire to valorize human riders can lead us to ignore the importance of the cyclists' tools and even, strangely enough, of the cyclists' animal bodies.

Our bodies require nourishment in the form of ostensibly inanimate materials, food and water; yet these materials literally animate us. Food and water also comprise the very stuff of ourselves, our physical beings. As Bennett writes, for instance, discussing the "crisis of obesity" (39), "That food can make people larger is a fact so ordinary and obvious that it is difficult to perceive it as an example of a nonhuman agency at work" (41). What we eat, Bennett shows, can have surprisingly large impacts on the whole of a human life, affecting not just our physical being but our thoughts, moods, attitudes, our subjectivity itself. Sport magnifies this reality. Dave's cycling requires him to embrace particular material assemblages—diet, water, bicycles, training—to enable what the film designates as a breaking away. Failing to manage equipment well hinders a rider, and failing to manage food and fluid intake can result in a dramatic collapse of performance, so-called "bonking." Understanding better what happens in these scenarios as a human interacts with objects like bicycles and food helps to reshape other questions about relationships, including those between the cutters and the college students in the film.

Much more than in 1979, when the film was released, the human-bicycle relationship today is lauded for its potential to address key problems: not just obesity but pollution and global warming, urban traffic, and so on. Such ideas gain deeper resonance from a new or vital materialist perspective. As Bennett suggests, "The figure of an intrinsically inanimate matter may be one of the impediments to the emergence of more ecological and more materially sustainable modes of production and consumption" (ix). Her formulation, beginning with "the figure," underscores that our conventional understanding of "matter" relies on figuration, including figuration in language, particularly metaphorical language. Matter itself is distinct from our representations, models, and language about it. Thus, matter is constantly subject to being redescribed, from classical views of earth, wind, water, and fire, to Newtonian physics, to quantum theory. Bennett's book, and the work of other vital materialists, seeks to improve our errant descriptions and metaphors by showing that the notions of agency, animation, and life are more complex than they first appear.

While some may regard these vital materialist perspectives as denigrations of humans, they are also potentially liberating. As much as Dave's clearer understanding of who he has been helps him to pursue new hopes, a better sense of humanity's connection to the rest of matter opens many new possibilities for the way we live. Taking objects like bicycles and food a bit more seriously may be a crucial step toward change, as it was for Dave and his father. While I do not contend that Breaking Away was made with exactly a vital materialist consciousness about matter, the presence of this new theoretical field clarifies the film's insights into the material influence of our everyday practices of identity formation. That is important because it indicates how many of the claims in new materialism hinge on realities readily observable all around us.

One such reality is masonry. The cutters' name, we noted, indicates their status as descendants of the Bloomington working-class limestone laborers—workers who painstakingly cut the quarried blocks into usable shapes—and the tension that develops between the cutters and the university students directly relates to their class identities. The comic, sporting plot brackets these serious issues to some extent, since recreation can seem to operate, at least superficially, outside the realm of class. But some critics have recognized that this film pushes its class inquiries a bit further than is common in recent American cinema. Al Auster, for instance, finds "a great deal of early '60s British class consciousness" in the movie and credits this presence partly to the fact that "director Peter Yates worked in British cinema when films such as *The Loneliness of the Long Distance Runner* and *Saturday Night and Sunday Morning* were produced."[8] This class consciousness seemed lost on other critics, however. For instance, the brief 1979 review in *Variety* awards *Breaking Away* "no points for originality," finding it a "thoroughly delightful light comedy" that "is nothing more than a triumph for the underdog through sports, this time cycle racing."[9]

Underplaying the film's questions of class this way is characteristic of U.S. culture, argues M. Keith Booker. While Booker suggests "there is a somewhat richer tradition of working-class representations in American literature than has generally been recognized," he claims that "the American working class has historically had relatively few opportunities to generate a culture of its own—partly because ... historical denial of the existence of class in the United States leaves no space for the development of a specifically working-class culture."[10] He contrasts this paucity of class consciousness with "Great Britain, where class consciousness has long been more highly developed than in the United States and where there is a stronger tradition of working-class culture." Director Yates's British background seems particularly important, therefore, and Yates himself said of *Breaking Away*, as quoted in Auster's review, "I wanted to make a film about class distinctions in America. Coming from England, I was told they didn't exist here. But of course they do."[11] Still, Auster goes on to characterize the film as "too light, airy, and optimistic to get involved in intense social analysis, or to raise anything more than some of the milder ironies of social mobility." For Auster, the film's ending, with Dave enrolled at the university and now discussing the Tour de France with a female French exchange student, reiterates an essentially comic approach to class. Indeed, one could reinforce Auster's view by recalling the film's final frame, the comically outraged look on Dave's father's face when he hears his son resuming use of a language other than English.

But I contend that the conclusion, like the whole film, is comedy doing significant and artful cultural work. Dave's father, Ray Stoller (Paul Dooley), exemplifies the focus on social class and identity. Ray, a used-car salesman, verbalizes xenophobic phrases throughout the movie, in his resistance to Dave's exotic performances of new self-hood. For instance, in an early scene, Ray tells his wife, Evelyn (Barbara Barrie), that he sold "one of his worst cars" to a college boy, proof that "they ain't so smart."[12] Ray continues, "I think it's a good thing that Dave never . . ." He does not finish the sentence, which presumably would have ended, "that Dave never went to college." Instead of uttering those words, though, Ray is fittingly brought up short when he sees the sautéed zucchini Evelyn has served him for dinner. This food is a double signifier both of Ray's need to change his diet for health reasons and of Evelyn's sympathy with Dave's interest in the exotic—or the merely different. Ray rejects the food as "Iti," that is, Italian. "I don't want no Iti food," he declares. Comically, Ray continues, "I want some American food, dammit. I want french fries." The moment is performed compellingly by Dooley as Ray, attired in a short-sleeved collared shirt, tie still neatly clipped in place, and eyes narrowed with an ugly ethnic hatred.

Again, Ray's outbursts and his inconsistencies might play as comedy, but more is at stake than seemingly outdated offensive jokes. Ray wants Dave to confirm more conventional notions of identity, especially with regard to labor, partly to justify Ray's own life circumstances. This father is a familiar figure in American life, in his desire to have a "normal" son. Yet, of course, that begs the whole question of the film: what is it exactly to be a "normal" working-class son in the 1970s United States? Ray's resistance to "foreign" ethnic identity is not only nativism, then; it connects in rich ways to problems of class in American history. Ray's xenophobia reinforces his wariness about

Dave's desire to rise in social class by going to college. Ray rejects together both ethnic others and change, thereby affirming his narrowly conceived, static "American" identity.

But it is to the film's credit that the father is a complex character. Right down to the final frame, he urges his son to surrender his interest in all things foreign; yet Ray also finally recognizes that Dave should not feel tightly bound in his class and identity position. In the first scene depicting Ray's view, Ray talks to Evelyn at the dining room table. Ray agrees with Evelyn that cycling has improved Dave's health, his body, which Evelyn notes had been "sickly," but Ray says, "Well, now his body is fine, but his mind is gone." Ray continues, "He used to be a smart kid. I thought he was gonna go to college." Evelyn answers, "I thought you didn't want him to go to college," and Ray replies, in a more forceful tone, "Well, why should he go to college? I never went to college. When I was nineteen, I was working in a quarry ten hours a day." Evelyn notes, "Most of the quarries are closed," but Ray answers, "Yeah, well, then he can find another job." And there we have the dilemma not just of these four boys but of their social class and generation, coming of age in the late 1970s in the United States: what will they do with the future? We also glimpse Ray's internal conflicts about what future to imagine for Dave, a set of conflicts that Dave and his friends have internalized.

The problem of the closed quarries is present from the beginning of the film. *Breaking Away* opens by depicting the detritus of withered identity categories, represented, importantly, by objects.[13] The film's first image is a cast-off pile of limestone, with a rusty water tower in the background, near the water-filled former stone quarry. We hear the boyish, affected drawl of Dennis Quaid's character, Mike, singing about the A&P grocery store, where the four young men had recently worked. Mike was fired, so the other three quit, in a show of solidarity. Further, they have vowed not to get another job, preferring not to, like Melville's Bartleby. Thus in the film, the quarry, once a place of labor, has been transformed into a retreat of uneasy recreation, another place apart. Instead of joining labor unions, the sons of laborers join in a pact not to work at all. Further, the quarry, a place clearly designated "cutter" by its very status as quarry and by the many scenes set there, is repeatedly invaded by college students. In the second invasion, later in the film, Mike, the cutter star football player, is bested on his own turf by a college student in a swimming contest. Losing, Mike bloodies his head against the limestone, a moment emblematic of the quarry as a potentially damaging trap for the cutters. This scene sets the stage for the film's conclusion, the Little 500 bicycle race and the redemption of the cutters' hopes.

The beginning of the film, then, sets a tone that largely persists: though comic, there is a dark undertow in its treatment of class dynamics, particularly upon additional viewings. We learn in the opening that Mooch's father (never shown) is off in Chicago, unsuccessfully seeking work, and that Cyril's best imagined future is as a cartoon figure who can easily recover from the trauma of repeated injury. Cyril (Daniel Stern) may sum up these young men's plight best—in the specific terms of late-adolescent masculinity—when he recalls seeing a former crush and her then boyfriend, now husband, together at the quarry. As Cyril and his friends walk suggestively on the quarry's edge, Cyril yells for the crew to "stop!" and then exclaims, "It was somewhere right along here that I lost all interest in life." This moment is not just about romantic love. As in the film's opening image—the pile of limestones—this scene signals the worry that the potential of these young men has been cast aside.

The film's opening and its repeated staging of scenes at the quarry evoke the decline of the working class in Bloomington and in America more generally. In 1979 the United States was at the end of a pessimistic economic decade, of course, with growing unemployment and rising inflation—stagflation—injuring the hopes of many. It is not news to note that the plight of the working class in places like Bloomington has not improved since the 1970s, as David Leonhardt (among others) reports. Describing the recent work of economists on class mobility, Leonhardt indicates that "the odds of escaping poverty in some parts of the United States were much higher than in others" and that among the places with the least social mobility is "the industrial Midwest," precisely the region inhabited by this film's central characters.[14]

The sense of being trapped in a social structure that seems rigged against upward mobility is evoked by the film's first big bicycling competition, the Cinzano 100 race. Dave shows his ability to succeed by besting the whole field and catching the leaders, "the Italians," his idols, proving himself their equal. But Dave is cheated out of finishing when one of the Italian riders jams a frame pump into Dave's wheel, causing Dave to flip and crash. This trauma, compounded by Dave seeing his own father cheat his customers on the used-car lot, leads to Dave's pronouncement: "Everybody cheats. I just didn't know" (a piece of cynicism that the film proposes and then later effectively refutes, as the cutters win the Little 500 honestly). The trauma also leads Dave to surrender his "Italian" identity, drop his accent, and pull down all his bicycle posters in his bedroom. Dave is ready to quit all his striving. The moment is a crux in the film's treatment of identity, and it is in this context, late in the story, that his father helps to change Dave's mind in a subtle and effective scene on the Indiana University campus, worth analyzing in some detail.

Dave and Ray walk through the campus at night, Ray telling Dave that he cut the stone for one of the buildings they pass. Ray says to Dave that he enjoyed work as a cutter but resented feeling unwelcome on the campus, where the products of his labor could be seen. "It was like," Ray says, "the buildings was [sic] too good for us. Nobody told us that. Just . . . just felt uncomfortable, that's all." He is articulating the same class distinctions internalized by many of the film's working-class characters, who are alienated from the products of their labor. Ray then asks Dave whether he and his friends still swim in the quarry. When Dave answers yes, Ray says, "So the only thing you got to show for my twenty years of work is the holes we left behind." Ray's sense of those quarries as "holes" echoes the interpretation of the quarry offered by the film's opening scenes, discussed above. Dave then responds, "I don't mind." He has, we noted, surrendered his desires to be somebody else. But Ray answers, after a well-placed dramatic pause, "I do."

The conversation then turns to the college entrance exams. Dave is reluctant to admit that he did well, saying, "Hell, I . . . don't want to go to college, Dad. To hell with them. I'm proud of being a cutter."

Ray replies, "You're not a cutter. I'm a cutter." When Ray then asks Dave whether he is afraid of college, he sounds a theme that recurs throughout the film: the fear that those who receive better opportunities deserve them and that the likes of the cutters do not deserve them anyway. From that perspective, social class is basically static; those in better positions must belong in them, a form of circular thinking still very much present in the American political mind today. It is a version of class consciousness that holds back the cutters and sons of cutters, a point reiterated when Dave mentions "the other guys" in telling Ray of his wariness to go to college.

These class dynamics are reinforced by the cinematic treatment of the campus scene. The moment is appropriately liminal, the dark campus visually suggesting unclear and indefinite identities. Practically, the campus at night is also a marginal social space, with fewer students present and thus more physical and psychological room for these cutters to appear there; throughout the film the university has been designated as a realm they should not visit. When Dave confesses that he does not want to go to college, he and Ray embody their uneasiness on the screen; their *being* out of place and *talking* about their status as working class amount to a double dislocation. Reinforcing the internalized shame of defeat, father and son do not directly face each other. Ray leans slightly away from his son, awkwardly, and Dave's body language shows his unease. He faces away from the camera, swaying slightly, as he makes his confessions. These are "uncomfortable" bodies, to echo Ray's term for how he feels on the campus. Their discomfort is emphasized in this scene by the college students, their identities secure, comfortably using the brightly lit library directly behind them, inside the building that both Dave and Ray feel excludes them. Yet as the scene proceeds, Ray finds the resilience to encourage Dave, which seems crucial to Dave's ultimate decision to attend college after all. Dave's college hopes, then, are not purely individualist; they are also social and communal from the start. He resists going because he dreads the potential loss of ties to family and youthful friends, a problem presented in other texts about upward class mobility.[15] And he is able to go only when his social network encourages him.

But Dave's striving is more than just social. Father and son are on campus that night partly to be among the limestones that Ray had cut. Ray knows he has some right to occupy that space by virtue of its sheer materiality, entangled with his own labor; and that presence impacts their conversation and, ultimately, both Dave's and Ray's decisions and life paths. The performance of agency in this scene, then, is complex. Clearly much hinges on the agency of both father and son, but they rely on something like the agency of the constructed space and of the stones themselves. As Serenella Iovino argues, from the perspective of posthumanism and new materialist theory, we see not "the single agents but their inextricable connection in 'a new relational ontology,'" placing us at a "crossroads of multiple agencies and entanglements."[16] The space created in an assemblage of labor, limestone, and darkness offers tacit support for Dave's hopes and, finally, for the hopes of Ray and the rest of his now-growing family.[17]

Furthermore, the limestone is implicated in the larger semiotics of the film. The beautiful, pastoral space of the university campus, in its very existence, requires stone, workers, and a class and cultural system that bears within it agreements about who may and may not attend college, who may use these structures. In this way, the film shows how the undertakings of the elite Indiana college students rely explicitly and directly not only on the local labor practices but also on the presence of the physical campus and the characteristics of the limestone itself. The buildings at Indiana University borrow much of both their utility and their meaning—their aesthetic evocation of stability, grace, and so on—from that limestone.[18] Indeed, the semiotics of "college" more broadly in this film also signify using the stone. The images and ideas of universities, and by extension the notions of education and of other undertakings associated with universities, such as collegiate sports and events like the Little 500—all rely on the presence of these stones, the Indiana bedrock, and the labor required to cut and place them. The same is true of other colleges, each in its own way, so that our sense of higher education is always entangled with the physical presence of the campus, its materials, and the labor regime that built and maintains it.[19] That fact resonates in view of Bennett's and other new materialist arguments that we should be wary of the ostensibly absolute split between agency and materiality. Since colleges and college sports host many of the quintessential performances of human agency, this scenario is especially important.[20]

In effect, crediting the importance of the material campus changes what it means to be a cutter, which opens new futures for that whole social group. A reimagined past permits a reimagined future, and vice versa, since the future to some extent determines what the past *means*. In brief, it works like this: First, Dave appreciates more deeply the work his father has done, as does Ray himself. Second, this form of self-respect helps to facilitate the comparative freedom they both find; they are able to *break away* from their cutter status first by embracing it. Specifically, Dave cannot justify going to college without revising his ideas of being a cutter. The more general dynamics of community identity in this film work in similar fashion. Much of the plot's thrust suggests the necessity of individuation, of moving beyond high school friendships and youthful ties, and so renouncing cutter identity. Yet while the young men's adulthood does involve individuation— breaking away—it simultaneously requires a deeper and more rigorous sense of their community identity. Both movements happen together in the film, showing how the individual and community work in complex dialogue. This scenario is parallel to the arguments Bennett in particular makes about vital materialism, that *acknowledging* human status as ineluctably material offers the potential to live with and among the material in new, hopefully better ways.

Many of these ideas culminate in the film's staging of the Little 500. Dave must accept and finally triumph in his cutter identity by reclaiming his *cycling* identity in a new form. His opposed subjectivities— cutter versus cyclist—come together in a both-and, not an either-or, identity. And while the plot first casts Dave as a solitary champion who will do all the riding in the race, in fact all four cutters must participate to gain the victory. Partnerships are further emphasized when Dave is physically attached to the machine, his feet taped to the bicycle pedals to make them a better cooperating unit (with a nod to the unpretentious, working-class technology of tape). The Little 500 thus affirms bicycle riding as a personal practice, and it affirms a new version of the cutter identity, making the race a communal, object-entangled display of agency that impacts individuals and the culture both.

Indeed, in the film's semiotics, cycling is both example of and metaphor for what might be called *xenophilia*, an embrace of that which is foreign to the subject without and within, in contrast to Ray's xenophobia. The community—even the cutters' competitors—celebrates the success of these outsiders to the college. But the cutters are familiar strangers. Since the college students in the race are explicitly marked as being from out of town, the cutters are actually the home team, making them also insiders. Their strangeness derives from their class identity, so when the community praises them, it tacitly revises its class principles. Further, in celebrating cycling, the film embraces the familiar stranger that is the body. As much work in posthumanism asserts, the human body is also internally complex and heterogeneous, made of salt water and minerals, proteins and things that were once without, entities not homogenized entirely as parts of the body.[21] That robust physical reality is completely foreign to much of our conscious behavior. Yet success in sport requires practices that draw out particular performances from this strangeness within us: proper eating, hydration, a training regime that stresses the body enough, coaxing it to develop, without overtaxing it. Our knowledge of how to do all of this has itself had a long, complex, object-entangled social development.

In *Breaking Away*, change spreads through the physical to the social body, and across generations, as Ray's conversations with his son have also been two-way. Although he is not quite prepared (yet) to go as far as Dave in pursuit of a new self, Ray's cycling at the film's end and his healthy, "un-American," unconventional meals suggest his slow acceptance of his own need to change—or perhaps better, his gradual recognition that his identity is not, so to speak, set in stone. Not only has Dave come to a new appreciation of his father's work, but Ray has learned real admiration for Dave's talent as a cyclist and new pride in his own cutter identity. Further signs of these changes are his renaming his car dealership to Cutter Used Cars and the dynamics of his support for Dave in the Little 500. In that episode, Ray is reluctant to show or admit the intensity of his partisanship for Dave and his friends, even believing his presence at the track might bring bad luck. So Ray first listens to the race on his car radio. As the pressure mounts and the cutters' success grows more likely, Ray roars to the track in his car, driving for a moment as Mike drives throughout the film. Mike and Ray both, in these additional examples of object-entangled agency, express unrest in their subordinated identities by acting with their machines (Mike's machine, fittingly, is borrowed).[22] While this episode with Ray can be read as a touching and realistic rendering of a father's (conventionally conceived) laconic form of support, it is also very clearly about Ray's own identity. He vacillates between an unease with this strange bicycle racing and a growing pride in Dave's reworking of cutter or descendant-of-cutter identity. In the end, significant barriers have been broken for Ray personally and for the whole group of cutters.

For all these reasons, I do not accept Auster's view, quoted above, that *Breaking Away* does not take class seriously. Instead, even though it is ultimately optimistic, I find the film to show the real challenges involved with escaping the confinements of social class, displayed clearly by Ray and Dave both. While the final frame's joke about a wary father, resistant to change, can be read as reactionary, it can also remind us of the radical and even dangerous potential of comedy. The father responds with unsettled outrage because he recognizes he cannot finally control his own son's pursuits; further, Ray is himself drawn into these identity changes. He has already changed his own business name, his personal behaviors, his diet—who knows what future changes he may yet undergo. The look on his face signifies all these hazards, the hazards of being the mortal, changeable material beings we are.

This chapter's argument adds depth of meaning to the view that the bicycle is well suited to help solve contemporary environmental, social, and biological problems. Indeed, rethinking the role of the bicycle in human culture can help us recognize the *vital* realities of *objects* more generally. Undertakings such as stone masonry or bicycling appear more as partnerships—with matter, with other people, and with other forms of life, typically—and that recognition complicates default ideas of solitary individualism. Instead of isolationist, neo-Hobbesian notions of identity and of nature, we find relationships, intersubjectivity, indeed interobjectivity.[23] In place of regarding relationships as external to who "we" are, a robust vital materialism helps to reveal that we are always, and have always been, a congress of matter.

Notes

1. *Breaking Away*, directed by Peter Yates (1979; Beverly Hills CA: Twentieth Century Fox, 2001), DVD.
2. See David V. Herlihy, *Bicycle: The History* (New Haven CT: Yale University Press, 2004). He reports a "recreational boom of the late 1960s and early 1970s [which] rekindled American interest and participation in the competitive sport." *Breaking Away* follows not far off the heels of that boom. But Herlihy notes that the success of Greg LeMond in the 1980s and Lance Armstrong in the 1990s and 2000s led to Americans taking "a much greater interest in the professional sport" (394).
3. William C. Martell, "Dramatic and Cinematic," *Scr(i)pt* 12, no. 1 (2006): 22.
4. For instance, tracing her argument back to Northrup Frye's definition of comedy and engaging Mikhail Bahktin's work, Kathleen Rowe discusses the way that comedies often critique insistent social norms pertaining to gender, power, and freedom. See Kathleen Rowe, *The Unruly Woman: Gender and the Genres of Laughter* (Austin: University of Texas Press, 1995), 14.
5. Various terms have been attached to this critical focus on objects: new materialism, thing theory, object-oriented ontology (or ooo), guerilla realism, and the term most often used in this essay, vital materialism. For more background on this movement, see Jane Bennett, *Vibrant Matter: A Political Ecology of Things* (Durham NC: Duke University Press, 2010); Serenella Iovino, "Stories from the Thick of Things: Introducing Material Ecocriticism," *ISLE* 19, no. 3 (2012); Timothy Morton, *Hyperobjects: Philosophy and Ecology after the End of the World* (Minneapolis: University of Minnesota Press, 2013).
6. The filmmakers also keep these paeans to cycling grounded in several ways: For example, they interrupt Dave's pretty backroads ride with a sudden flat tire, and they add piquancy, or even irony, to the spontaneous cooperation between Dave on his bicycle and the Cinzano truck driver when the police stop the driver for speeding (we should note that Dave and the driver's cooperation is a moment of community driven by their shared material orientation—both are involved with cycling).
7. Bennett, *Vibrant Matter*, 38. Subsequent references to Bennett's book appear parenthetically in the text.
8. Al Auster, review of *Breaking Away*, *Cineaste* 10, no. 1 (Winter 1979/1980): 48.

9. Unsigned review of *Breaking Away*, *Variety Movie Reviews*, January 1, 1979.

10. M. Keith Booker, "Set Introduction," in *Blue-Collar Pop Culture: From NASCAR to Jersey Shore*, ed. M. Keith Booker, vol. 1, *Film, Music, and Sports* (Santa Barbara CA: Praeger, 2012), xii–xiii.

11. Auster, review of *Breaking Away*, 48.

12. All transcriptions of the film's dialogue in this essay are my own. The dialogue is sharply written, as reflected in the many awards the film won, including an Oscar in 1979 for Best Writing, Screenplay (the writer was Steve Tesich).

13. The ordinary fact that this film and other forms of representation rely heavily on objects to produce meanings itself demonstrates a vital materialist idea: our vaunted, meaningful art is entangled with "things."

14. David Leonhardt, "Upward Mobility Has Not Declined, Study Says," *New York Times*, January 23, 2014, Business Day.

15. See, for instance, Richard Rodriguez, *Hunger of Memory: The Education of Richard Rodriguez* (New York: Bantam, 1982).

16. Iovino, "Stories from the Thick of Things," 456.

17. Evelyn is pregnant by the film's end, raising questions of gender norms worth exploring, though I lack the space to do so here.

18. The film makes a point of telling viewers that it was produced on location in Indiana. It matters to this paper's argument that we see the real limestone and the actual campus produced by laborers.

19. This point has many implications that stretch beyond the scope of this essay. For instance, acknowledging the materiality of college life offers an orienting principle in questions about what is gained and lost in online education, where the edifices of the buildings, the shared social spaces formed by the campus, and the face-to-face encounters among faculty, students, and staff are all made virtual.

20. To be clear, I do not mean to suggest that the "agency" of the limestone, say, or of the buildings, or even of the planetary movement that produces night and enables exactly this kind of conversation, is the *same* as the agency of Ray or Dave. Indeed, even in the much narrower confines of human agency, we must recognize significant differences between father and son. And the need to differentiate forms of agency is all the more pressing when we widen notions of agency to include nonhuman materiality. While much of the work in new materialism insists—usefully—on flattening the differences between humans and other forms of materiality, we should be cautious of, well, overflattening those differences. Limestone does not have a cerebral cortex and does not make decisions in the same way human animals do, or other animals do, or even plants do. But there is a kind of agency in limestone's very materiality, much as there is a kind of agency that rises from human materiality.

21. For instance, consider Donna J. Haraway's reminder "that human genomes can be found in only about 10 percent of all the cells that occupy the mundane space I call my body; the other 90 percent of the cells are filled with the genomes of bacteria, fungi, protists, and such, some of which play in a symphony necessary to my being alive at all, and some of which are hitching a ride and doing the rest of me, of us, no harm." See Donna J. Haraway, *When Species Meet* (Minneapolis: University of Minnesota Press, 2008), 3–4. Her terminology of "symphony" and ride "hitching" are particularly well suited to this chapter. Also relevant is Timothy Morton's point that what we call oxygen is "bacterial pollution from some Archean cataclysm" and that our cells' energy producers, mitochondria, are "anaerobic bacteria hiding in my cells from the Oxygen Catastrophe." See Timothy Morton, *Hyperobjects: Philosophy and Ecology after the End of the World* (Minneapolis: University of Minnesota Press, 2013), 58. Cary Wolfe's important work in posthumanism is also crucial, especially as series editor of the Posthumanities Series from the University of Minnesota Press, which published both Morton's and Haraway's books cited above; Wolfe's own scholarship is also widely influential. His *What Is Posthumanism?* (Minneapolis: University of Minnesota Press, 2010) offers theoretically compelling ideas.
22. We watch these symbolic displays of machine-entangled agency via another machine assemblage—this one cinematic, stretching from the cameras and recording equipment to the replay devices in cinemas and at home, all of which is analyzed here through another machine assemblage that is the publishing industry.
23. See Timothy Morton's chapter "Interobjectivity," in *Hyperobjects*, 81–96.

15 *Beijing Bicycle*

Desire, Identity, and the Wheels

JINHUA LI

China's Sixth Generation director Wang Xiaoshuai's (王小帅) *Beijing Bicycle* (*Shiqi sui de danche* 十七岁的单车, 2001) is the previously independent filmmaker's first attempt to reconcile art cinema with popular entertainment.[1] Although temporarily banned by the Chinese Film Bureau, *Beijing Bicycle* received both international critical acclaim and box office success with its winning of the Jury Grand Prix at the 2001 Berlin International Film Festival.[2] As the third installment of the Tales of Three Cities series—a transregional collaboration among filmmakers in mainland China, Hong Kong, and Taiwan—*Beijing Bicycle* signals the coming of age of the new urban cinema that represents Beijing as a paradigmatic urban space that exists in the intersections of old and new, tradition and postmodernity, and memory and desire.[3]

Beijing Bicycle's international commercial success attracted critical attention from scholars both at home and abroad. While many scholars writing both in English and in Chinese on *Beijing Bicycle* focus either on the film's representation of the socioeconomic conflicts between the city and rural areas or on the realistic portrayal of the disillusion of youthful aspirations and identity anxiety (often comparing it to Vittorio De Sica's 1948 film *The Bicycle Thieves*), they overlook the symbolic and political use of the bicycle as a visual trope and cinematic signifier that is subtly subversive and intricately layered.[4] The bicycle, while necessarily invoking nostalgia and being reminiscent of a bygone era, becomes a contested site where the relationship between the individual and the society, globalization and tradition, upward mobility and social stratification, desire and dystopia, and belief and disillusion destabilizes and fluctuates.

This chapter investigates *Beijing Bicycle*'s employment of the bicycle as a politicized trope that visualizes a society in transition when discursive social forces and individual uncertainty interact in the increasingly consumerized urban space of Beijing. It argues that although the mechanical functionality of the bicycle connotes mobility, speed, and freedom, the cinematic representation of the bicycle highlights the young protagonists' social immobility, emotional incapacity, and futile attempts to find reconciliation between reality and youthful dreams, between socialist localized values and postsocialist globalized consumerism. *Beijing Bicycle* captures the confusion and anger of the youth in a society in transition, as they try to gain control over their lives through a misplaced fixation on the false promise of speed and on the adolescent desires of love and mobility. The bicycle, while simply a means of transportation to the adults, symbolizes something that is dangerously alluring yet mundanely comforting to the teenage protagonists. Therefore, *Beijing Bicycle*'s ambiguous ending, when the bicycle finally loses its motion, alludes to the uncertain future of the two protagonists.

Bicycle: Historicized Signifier and Politicized Trope

Beijing Bicycle dramatizes the lives of two teenage boys in Beijing as both project their dreams onto the bicycle. Young migrant worker (*mingong*) Gui (Lin Cui) finds a job with a delivery company in Beijing and works diligently so that he can own the company-issued bicycle through a profit-splitting arrangement. To his despair, Gui's bicycle is stolen the night before he can take ownership of it, and it is subsequently sold to Jian (Bin Li), a Beijing high school student who shares a passion for bike stunts with his close friends. By mere chance Gui discovers that Jian's bicycle is the same one that he lost, and he tries to take it back from Jian. Since neither Jian nor Gui is willing to relinquish his right over this bicycle, they reach an agreement that they will take turns using it, each using it on alternate days. When the film ends, no one owns the bicycle, because Gui is involuntarily involved in Jian's fight with local hooligans, during which the bicycle is smashed.

Beijing Bicycle reconfigures the bicycle's historical social significance and its political association by focusing on a different kind of bicycle—the mountain bike (*shandi che*)—than the typical bicycle that was popular in the 1970s and 1980s in China, which is of a plainer appearance and has limited functions (no speed changes, thin wheels, etc.).[5] While the regular bike is a much more modest machine, the fashionable and expensive mountain bike (which does not become popular until the early 1990s) is built for off-road cycling as a popular sport and is therefore designed to negotiate complex terrains such as sudden drops, unpaved roads, and zigzagging tracks. Compared with the regular bicycle, the mountain bike has a suspension system, knobby tires, bigger and wider wheels, and more powerful brakes. While the mountain bike is apparently not meant for commuting in the city, it gained national popularity almost overnight in urban China starting in the early 1990s, typically among the young, urban generation. Sold at almost triple the price of a regular bicycle, the mountain bike now replaces the regular bike's original status as a sign of social affluence and has become the embodiment of a modernizing China.

Just as the regular bike used to indicate wealth and social status in the 1970s, the mountain bike represents an urban youth subculture characterized by desires for material goods, financial excess, Western consumerism, and fashionable coolness. The mountain bike thus displaces the regular bike's historical association with government-controlled economy and an era of communist social politics, and it serves as a symbol of encroaching Western values defined by material wealth and consuming power. The ruggedly cool appearance of the mountain bike invokes a powerful image of a Western lifestyle that promises fashion, freedom, and leisure. For the first time in the Chinese imagination, riding a bicycle has purposes other than mere transportation; and this reconfiguration of what used to be mundane and ordinary perfectly captures the nation's excitement and expectation when the country is embarking on national economic reformation and ideological transformation. Young, urban, Chinese Gen Xers quickly identify with the technical dexterity, mechanical precision, and defiant attitude represented by professional mountain bikers and deem themselves the embodiment of a youthful cultural fever that idolizes everything Western. Mountain bikes allow these teenagers to perform stunts that are gratifying, exciting, and empowering, all feelings that set them apart from their parents' generation. In other words, the mountain bike becomes symbolic of the "disappearance of the thing we always count on in life," and it is therefore the projected site for youthful social nonconformity and inevitable changes.[6]

It is within such historical and political contextualization that *Beijing Bicycle* opens with a scene where the mountain bike represents two opposing tendencies: upward mobility and fossilized class differentiation. Accompanied by home video–style cinematography and loud ambient noise, the camera cuts through a series of subjective, close-up one-shots, each focusing on individual workers with messy hair and dowdy, country-style clothes, who stare blankly into the camera. Their physical appearance and awkward interaction with the camera indicate their alienated social status as migrant workers from either rural areas or small towns. Confronted with these migrant workers, the audience unwittingly assumes the position of the cold and domineering female interviewer who asks questions in a disembodied voice. Such spectatorial point of view subtly reveals a social unevenness by placing these migrant workers under the debilitating, urbanized gaze of the camera.[7] As the interviewer goes through the list and talks to her interviewees in a tone that is obviously condescending and impatient, the unequal social exchange is powerfully reminiscent of a police interrogation. What is even more unsettling is that these interviewees have internalized such deep-rooted social inferiority that their compliance and passivity at being treated as pariahs seems to be a natural and necessary step before they are offered a job. Among all the questions, only one really matters in this interview: "Can you ride a bicycle?" Without depicting the bicycle, the film effectively reminds the audience of the essential functionality of the bicycle, its ubiquitous usage in a not-so-remote past, and its reconfigured socioeconomic relevance in a globalizing urban space characterized by unmistakable geopolitical class stratification.

However, the politically symbolic and historically reimagined bicycle is strategically visualized, albeit out of focus, in the title sequence, where the camera remains stationary while fragmented and blurry images of the regular bicycles in motion dominate the frame. The bicycles' movements are shot in slow motion and are superimposed on one another, creating a decontextualized, abstract flow of images. Notably, unlike the regular color scheme in the opening scene, here the bicycles are visualized in black and white, which subtly yet powerfully reminds the audience of old pictures showing large crowds of people on bicycles, a common scene from the past that earned China the befitting nickname of Country on Bicycles. This cinematic representation of the mundane bicycles in black and white against a muted cityscape is reminiscent of a historical period when bicycles represented limited social mobility and slow economic development; but more significantly, the nostalgic visual style underlines the regular bicycle's declining social value and symbolic meaning in a rapidly consumerized society. The blurred images of bicycles, therefore, serve as a powerful visual trope for their ambiguous social significance in the present era and challenge the bicycle's historical importance. Just like the indistinct bicycles that are reduced to the background of the city, young migrant workers and poor urban youth are marginalized in a quickly stratified Beijing. By employing these fragmented and shadowy images during the title sequence, *Beijing Bicycle* strategically foreshadows its social critique of market consumerism and urban dystopia.

Beijing: Urban Dystopia and Wheels for Consumption

Following the blurry representation of the regular bicycles in the opening scene, the camera cuts to neatly lined mountain bikes in a crisp and sharply focused close-up tilt shot, highlighting the mountain bikes' advanced mechanical design and high consumer values. Paralleling this cinematic upgrade from the regular bicycles to the fancy mountain bikes is Gui's own makeover. Following the order of the company manager, Gui and his fellow peasant workers take a shower and have a haircut, so that they don't look like country bumpkins and can therefore "represent the company and fit in the society." In a few shots, the camera focuses on Feida Fast Delivery Company's logo and emphasizes Gui's transformation from an outsider of Beijing's rapid marketization to a "homo economicus," as he dons the uniform and stands beside his company-issued mountain bike, excited about his new job and his soon-to-be-assumed socioeconomic identity.[8] Contextualized within Beijing's economic development and consumerist globalization, Gui's brand-new mountain bike now becomes both a consumer product for which Gui has to pay and a tool that generates income. Therefore, the mountain bike serves as an inseparable connection between Beijing's urban space and Gui, providing him with a concrete and manageable goal in the alienated society.

Gui's urban transformation reveals a third layer of significance when his relationship to Beijing's sociocultural landscape is defined through a well-known literary allusion. The manager calls Gui and his coworkers "rickshaw camel Xiangzi in the new era" at the end of their job orientation, right after they are told how the profit is split between the individual couriers and the company.[9] This comparison captures some of the essential similarities between Gui and Xiangzi, the Beijing protagonist in Lao She's 1936 novel *Rickshaw* (*Lo-t'o Hsiang Tzu* 骆驼祥子).[10] Both Gui and Xiangzi use wheels as their work tool, both come from low social class, and both depend on their navigation of Beijing's cityscape as a means of living. But such a comparison has a rather gloomy undertone, because Xiangzi tragically ends up a homeless, hopeless, and rickshawless beggar. In this novel, Beijing is portrayed as a city of false promises and a ruthless society, a place where social circumstances and character flaws cause Xiangzi's downfall. Therefore, by calling Gui a modern rickshaw Xiangzi, the Beijing manager not only implies Gui's disfranchised socioeconomic status and his alienation from the city but more significantly reminds Gui that Beijing is not a land of plenty, nor will it welcome migrant workers, who are always outsiders. Instead, it is essentially an urban dystopia and a society that feeds on consumerism and on labor as capital.

It is uncertain if such implications in the manager's comment are lost on Gui and his coworkers or if they think long and deep enough to question the exploitative arrangement of the company taking 80 percent of the earnings until the couriers make enough to own the mountain bike and taking 50 percent thereafter. Yet Gui seems quite happy with such a deal, as he smiles for the first time in the film at this prospect, filled with hope and ambition, just like Xiangzi. As if the oral allusion does not quite suffice, Gui's similarity with Xiangzi is painstakingly represented in the following sequence, when Gui enjoys the fast mountain bike and its speed, taking every delivery seriously, working industriously, and above all, keeping close track of his earnings and of the days left before he owns the mountain bike. Unlike the Beijing native Xiangzi, Gui has yet to familiarize himself with both the geographic and cultural landscape of the city. But Gui's first encounter with Beijing's urban space is characterized by an empowering speed, freedom, and hope similar to Xiangzi's.

Gui's work experience in the first half of the film crystallizes Beijing's dystopian metropolitanism and the economic values of the mountain bike. Gui's first day at work sends him to a commercial building downtown, and his anxiety over losing the mountain bike is apparent when he locks it carefully and keeps looking back to check on it. His worry is not unwarranted, given the high percentage of bicycle theft in Beijing; and it foreshadows the mountain bike's fateful disappearance.[11] Gui's social marginality is underscored when he is confronted with a revolving door, something that is unfamiliar and intimidating to a country boy. As soon as he clumsily jumps into the lobby, Gui enters into a space where no verbal communication occurs. The entire interaction between Gui and the faceless secretary is shown in silence, as Gui waits for her to fill out the delivery confirmation. In a subjective shot from Gui's point of view, the camera only frames the woman's torso from below the neck as she silently writes on the receipt book. The woman's anonymity suggests not only Gui's social insignificance and hence his negligibility but more revealingly the commonality of such coldly dismissive attitudes toward migrant workers like Gui. In other words, by employing the no-face woman in this shot-and-countershot scene, the camera creates an unequal power dynamic between Gui and the urban citizens, highlighting Gui's inability to look her in the eyes because of his low self-esteem as a social outsider. Under the camera's gaze, the woman's well-manicured and bejeweled hands become a fragmented visual symbol that stands for unalterable social stratification, futile communication, and ultimately xenophobic rejection in Beijing's urban dystopia. More significantly, the woman's alienating and discriminating treatment of Gui reveals the illusive allure of the mountain bike and highlights the futility of the mountain bike's promises of social recognition and self-realization. Additionally, her treatment of Gui points out the cold truth that riding a mountain bike does not change the fact that Gui is still a worthless outsider who will never become part of Beijing's modern glamorization. Thus, Gui's first delivery job reveals Beijing as an alienating urban space defined by an absence of human connection and by a fascination with materialistic consumerism.

The mountain bike's illusory allure is reemphasized in Jian's story in the next sequence. Having reemerged when the narrative bifurcates to focus on Jian's life, the mountain bike is consumed symbolically as an insider's badge of urban youth culture and as evidence of Jian's alternative coolness. But just as the bike cannot realize Gui's urban dream, it will never bring Jian the masculine confidence and independence he craves. According to Haomin Gong, the mountain bike embodies a material "superfluity" for Jian, because "the basic use of the bike has almost shrunk to nothing."[12] In other words, Jian cares nothing about the bike's basic function as his transportation. Instead, he attaches great significance to what it symbolizes: coolness, fashion, and freedom. However, a closer reading of the cinematic narrative reveals otherwise. Although it is not explicit in the film if Jian simply *wants* a mountain bike to be socially acceptable among his friends or if he actually *needs* a bicycle to commute between school and home, logic and common sense dictate that Jian needs transportation to get to school, which in turn suggests that the mountain bike to Jian is first and foremost a necessity of daily usage and is only afterward a fancy toy with symbolic value.

Similarly, the mountain bike is not essential to Gui either. Yingjin Zhang argues that for Gui the mountain bike is a "crucial" necessity for his work because "it can hold up under its condition of use," and Zhang uses Gui's frustrating and futile attempt to ride Qiu Sheng's (Mengnan Li) old bicycle for his delivery jobs to illustrate the mountain bike's central significance for Gui's work.[13] However, Zhang overlooks the fact that Qiu Sheng's old bicycle is already in a state of dilapidation because of disuse and negligence and that it would not have lasted very long even for minor or regular daily use, let alone for frequent delivery rides. If Gui would use a brand-new regular bicycle, it would be an adequate, if not excellent, alternative to his mountain bike, because it would be cheaper and involve lower maintenance. Thus, whether in Gui's spatial imagination of Beijing—with its busy streets, imposing high-rises, and congested traffic—or in Jian's familiar territory of Beijing's old-style *hutongs* (small alleyways) with traditional, single-story houses, the mountain bike assumes comparably practical significance.

Seventeen's Bicycle: Displaced Desire and Identity Anxiety

The mountain bike is also intimately connected to the protagonists' youthful sexual awakening and erotic imagination, for the bike becomes the site of displaced desire. Not only is the bike often visualized as an object under the camera's male gaze; it is also closely associated with masculine identity formation and sexual competition between older and younger men. Both Gui and Jian's relationship with the bike is mediated through their respective encounters with desirable women, and both have to navigate their desire while simultaneously feeling threatened by competition from either a familiar elder (Qiu Sheng) or a social superior (Da Huan). Therefore, possession of the bike signifies success in ritualized heterosexuality and triumph in the rite of passage to manhood through masculine competition.

Through the camera's point of view, the mountain bike is represented as the objectified projection of Gui's sexual awakening. Gui's encounters with Qin (Xun Zhou), a young maid from the countryside who likes to dress up in her employer's fancy clothes when left alone, needs to be contextualized within his sense of pride and fulfillment at his soon-to-be-realized ownership of the mountain bike. Gui's interaction with the city is punctuated with his regular visits to his friend Qiu Sheng's corner grocery store in an old neighborhood of Beijing's inner city. On Gui's first day of work, he brings the mountain bike to Qiu Sheng's grocery store to show it off like a trophy of his successful first step in the assimilation into the city. When both Qiu Sheng and Gui admire the glossy finish and mechanical crafts-manship of the mountain bike, the camera uses an eye-level close-up shot that glamorizes the bike as if in a commercial in which the product is visually consumed for its surface appearance.

The same commodifying gaze is reenacted immediately after when Qiu Sheng and Gui fetishize Qin through their masculine, voyeuris-tic gaze. Significantly, the camera positions Qin under a similar cine-matic gaze as it does the mountain bike and thereby alludes to Qin's symbolic connection with the bike. Through a crack in the wall, both men look at Qin, who is seen framed within a large window, all dressed up and looking bored. Each time when the camera cuts from Qiu Sheng and Gui's mesmerized look to Qin, she is seen in a differ-ent outfit and in a different posture. This scene is crucial as it pres-ents Qin in a clearly recognizable style: she is a commodity behind a display window, performing her female physicality as a commer-cial product. What she symbolically sells to Qiu Sheng and Gui is a dreamlike urban lifestyle of surplus and leisure, one that is desirable but unobtainable, just like the elevated glass window that lures them in yet keeps them at a distance.

Gui's male gaze at Qin is never fulfilling because it is always policed by Qiu Sheng's caution against Gui's youthful sexual desires. When Gui first looks at Qin, his gaze is interrupted and cut short by Qiu Sheng's admonition that "if you look more, it will hurt your psycho-logical and physical health." Arguably, Gui's fascination over Qin is indicative of what Elizabeth Wright refers to as his "avid desire to attain material possessions in the fast-paced metropolis"; thus, the carefully visualized symbolic similarity between Qin and the mountain bike shows that Qin becomes a projected site where Gui's obsession over material possessions and sexual longings intersect.[14]

If Gui's sexual awakening results from his displaced desire for the mountain bike, then Jian's relationship with the mountain bike is pre-determined by his romantic infatuation for his beautiful classmate Xiao, by his identity anxiety resulting from peer pressure, and by his frustration at his patriarchal family. Yingjin Zhang points out that the mountain bike's "intimate tie to eroticism works itself out as Xiao leaves the infuriated Jian for Da Huan (Li Shuang)," but Xiao does not leave Jian only because Jian lost his mountain bike or because Da Huan has a better bike and enjoys a celebrity reputation for his biking stunts.[15] Rather, Jian becomes a completely different person when he coldly distances himself from Xiao, despite her efforts to console him after he lost the bike, and refuses to communicate with Xiao because of his hurt dignity and pride. Confronted with Da Huan's popularity, gentlemanly help, maturity (Da Huan ridicules Jian's adolescence by asking him for a lighter, which Jian fails to provide), and rightful possession of a mountain bike, Jian realizes he is undoubtedly a social inferior in this courting competition.

While the mountain bike gives Gui a glimpse of what he could be, for Jian the mountain bike defines who he is. In other words, while Gui's life would be better with the mountain bike, Jian's life would certainly become worse without it. Despite his instant advantage as a Beijing native, as opposed to being a migrant worker like Gui, Jian has to resist social marginality due to his family's difficult financial circumstances and limited economic means. To Jian's father, it is simple to choose between sending his step-daughter to a good high school and purchasing a luxury item like a bicycle for his son that is not absolutely necessary and is obviously beyond his means. But to Jian, the bike symbolizes a coveted identity, an identity constructed around a globalized Western lifestyle, autonomy, and erotic love.

It is precisely because of the mountain bike's significance that it is also the reason for Jian's youthful anxiety and identity crisis. Since so much of his self-image and identity formation is determined by his ability to claim sole ownership of the mountain bike, Jian establishes his social relationships around this bicycle. Therefore, when the mountain bike is taken from him, Jian inevitably experiences fear and disorientation, and his world becomes decentered. *Beijing Bicycle* spares no efforts to highlight the central position of the mountain bike in all of Jian's social relationships: it stands for recognition from his father, camaraderie and respect from his friends, and romance between him and Xiao. When confronted with his father's furious accusation that he stole the money that his father stashed away for his step-sister's tuition, Jian refuses to be called a disgraceful son by claiming that he earned the money with good grades at school and that the bicycle was already promised to him by his father as a reward for those grades. Jian needs the mountain bike to fit in with his friends at school and to form a close bond with them when they spend time after school practicing bike stunts. But more significantly, the mountain bike is a luxurious and cool piece of equipment that allows Jian to feel socially adequate despite his family's precarious financial situation.

However, this sense of empowerment is only illusory, and Jian can mature only when he sees who he really is after realizing the futility of his commodity fetishism. Jian's maturation begins when he crosses paths with Gui, as they share ownership of the mountain bike. Because neither is able to persuade the other to give up the bike, Gui and Jian agree that each will use the bike on alternative days, and every day at dusk they will trade the bike. While Jian is sharing the bike with Gui, the audience does not see Jian perform bike stunts with his friends any more, nor does Jian succeed in regaining Xiao's favor, and Jian's relationship with his family becomes even more strained. Thus, Gui's involvement in Jian's life becomes an antidote to Jian's obsession over the mountain bike. Jian comes to see the mountain bike as an inadequate symbol of his identity and thus begins to confront reality with bravery and independence. When Jian finally decides to give up on the mountain bike after he attacks Da Huan with a brick, the mountain bike eventually loses its glamour and becomes what it is on a fundamental level: a mundane mode of transportation.

Youth on Wheels: Transient Spatial Temporality and Mobile Immobility

Gui, Jian, and the mountain bike become sociopolitical coordinates that triangulate Beijing's rapidly changing cityscape. Metaphorically, it is through the stories of Jian and Gui, who are connected through the mountain bike, that Beijing is represented three dimensionally as a city in transition. In *Beijing Bicycle*'s cinematic remapping of the city, if Gui symbolizes the axis of Beijing's spatiality through his delivery job as well as his migrant background, then Jian represents the axis of Beijing's palimpsestic temporality as he lives in a traditional courtyard house in an inner city hutong, the most characteristic architectural style of historical Beijing.[16] The mountain bike, therefore, reflects the ephemeral reality of the ever-changing city when the bike's urban signification becomes layered and fluid.

The axes of Beijing's spatiality and temporality converge when Gui's experience of Beijing is juxtaposed with Jian's, through a shared ownership of the mountain bike, so the bike serves as the crucial third axis through which the city's transient reality is captured. The mountain bike therefore witnesses the superimposition of a Beijing that aspires to be a glamorous and vibrant world metropolis onto a Beijing that mourns the disappearance of cultural traditions and historical heritage. When Gui rides through Beijing's high-rises and imposing infrastructures, he is often framed in high-angle shots of Beijing with its intimidating skylines and giant buildings towering over him. Such cinematic style captures Gui's admiration and infatuation with the modernity of the city, while simultaneously obliterating the city's traditional characteristics and singularity. However, from Jian's point of view, Beijing is flatter, narrower, and much older. From the rooftop of Jian's family's apartment building, Beijing is seen in two altitudes: single-level courtyard houses and old city corner towers form the lower foreground, and skyscrapers dominate the background. Although a Beijing native, Jian seems removed and alienated from Beijing's future, as he is framed within the restrictive space of the past, whereas Gui, an outsider in many aspects, enjoys an accommodating Beijing, whose changing cityscape is made possible by many migrant workers like him.

In this rapidly changing and multidimensional Beijing, moral uncertainty and gray areas of social ethics are portrayed through the mountain bike's contested ownership. Jian's reliance on a material object as a centripetal force that holds his life together is more symptomatic of social problems in contemporary China's postsocialist consumer society than of Jian's personal journey into adulthood. Although Wang Xiaoshuai cautiously explains that *Beijing Bicycle* is "a story about fate and the experience of growing up," emphasizing that "all are equal before fate,"[17] his critical dramatization of "increasingly divided social realities" and "an obvious indictment of . . . material possessions" is not lost among critics.[18] If allowing Gui and Jian to share the mountain bike is Wang's allusion to nominal social fairness, then this awkwardly shared ownership creates more problems than it solves. It is not difficult to predict that in a foreseeable future, both Gui and Jian will revisit this argument unless one party relinquishes his right to the bicycle or unless they settle it in the manner of businessmen, with one of them paying the other for half of the bike.

The ending of *Beijing Bicycle* reveals the mountain bike's ambivalent significations. Although it metaphorizes youthful sexual awakening and erotic desire in the first half of the film, the bike facilitates the disappearance and dissolution of the protagonists' projected sexual attraction in the second half of the film. Earlier in the film, when the young maid Qin is about to sell her employer's clothes, Gui accidentally knocks her over with his bicycle, thereby revealing Qin's true identity as a petty thief. Since Qin's attractiveness is primarily predicated on her assumption of an urban identity, this bike accident deglamorizes her pretentious appearance and wakes Gui up from his admiration and yearning. For Jian, it is the mountain bike that enables him to follow Da Huan and Xiao on their way home. In the scene when Jian attacks Da Huan with a brick, the camera adopts a low angle where the bike is seen in close-ups, while Jian's body is fragmented, suggesting the breaking down of his identity that is so closely linked to the mountain bike.

The final scene juxtaposes the mountain bike's promise of mobility with its symbolically debilitating power, for the mountain bike's unsurpassable efficiency in Beijing's narrow hutongs leads to Jian and Gui's total defeat and immobility. In this scene, everybody is riding mountain bikes in hutongs at a breathtaking speed. The mountain bike is portrayed as an effective transportation choice because it effortlessly maneuvers the labyrinthine hutongs, whose mazelike design is dizzyingly visualized in the climactic chase scene when Da Huan and his gang beat up Jian and Gui. While the bicycle should have been empowering to Gui, who has just obtained its sole ownership and is therefore closer to his Beijing dream, it is precisely his possession of the mountain bike that makes him a victim of Da Huan's vengeful beating. Thus, while the bike is supposed to give Gui speed, freedom, and happiness, it instead brings pain, loss, and helplessness. The incapacitating effect of the bicycle is also subtly implied when Jian warns Gui not to get involved in the imminent fight between Jian and Da Huan and his gang. Gui cannot get away, because he does not know his way around these hutongs. The audience cannot help but wonder, then, if Gui were not riding the bicycle, would he still have been victimized? It may be true that Gui just happens to be in the wrong place at a wrong time, but Gui eventually realizes that the bicycle can also bring disillusion.

The bicycle's destruction represents a climactic moment when Jian and Gui's identities are in flux. The wrecked bicycle signals the breaking of a material link between Jian and Gui, but it also allows Gui and Jian to become each other's mirrored half. Gui turns into Jian when Gui uses a brick to knock down the teenager who destroyed his bicycle, which is exactly how Jian attacks Da Huan in the previous scene; Jian is lying on the ground shrouded in white, vulnerable and defenseless, powerfully reminiscent of how Gui looked when Jian and his friends beat up Gui. The broken mountain bike therefore subverts the power dynamics between Jian and Gui, allowing Gui to gain agency and win the fight, both literally and symbolically. Gui visually represents the last person standing and assumes the dominant position in the mise-en-scène, when he looks down at Jian for the first time on-screen and carries the bike over his shoulder, like a champion carrying his trophy.

Beijing Bicycle ends on an ambivalent tone when Gui carries the useless bicycle on his shoulder and walks through Beijing's busy street. It is easy to interpret this ending as an allusion to frustrated desires and crushed dreams, as Yingjin Zhang argues, or as an indication that Gui will persist in realizing his Beijing dream and hold on to what is most valuable to him, as Ling Chen observes.[19] Yet if, as the director Wang Xiaoshuai claims, "owning the bicycle symbolizes maturity and their [the teenage protagonists'] ability to possess something in society," then does the wrecked bicycle sustain such symbolic significance after all?[20] Furthermore, since Gui possesses the bicycle at the end, does it indicate that Jian fails his rite of passage to maturity and adulthood? And if so, could it also suggest that Beijing's urban space defies a simple understanding as an unsympathetic place for migrant workers? The answers to these questions rely on a careful reading of the mise-en-scène of the last shot, in which the camera employs a panoramic high-angle shot that allows the audience to see a nondescript Beijing street filled with cars and bicycles. What dominates the frame are not people on bicycles, who are positioned at either side of the frame, but cars in different sizes, colors, and shapes, at the foreground and center of the frame. While the flow of bicycles is disrupted as the bicycle lane becomes invisible midframe, cars are driving toward Beijing's vastly expanded cityscape on the main road that leads straight to the horizon. In the end, the contested bicycle has lost its motion and functionality, and the bicycles in the urban space are subtly appropriated as a signifier of the teenage boys' lives: marginalized in Beijing's cityscape but inseparable from its cultural imagination.

Beijing Bicycle presents the bicycle as a signifier of identity anxiety among the young generation and as an externalization of material and psychological desires in the postmodern society. Wang's bittersweet dramatization of a lost-then-found bicycle poignantly reveals the contested urban social space, especially between urban residents and migrant workers, and employs the bicycle to serve as a visual metaphor that problematizes the identity politics of the urban youth subculture. The bicycle, therefore, paradoxically connects and alienates people in this urban melodrama. As a representative film of the Sixth Generation directors, *Beijing Bicycle* serves as a searching cinematic gaze that is directed at the subtly stratified yet transparent and impenetrable class differences in contemporary Chinese society.

Notes

1. A loosely grouped generation of filmmakers, the Sixth Generation directors are typically identified as a group of young directors who graduated from Beijing Film Academy in the late 1980s and early 1990s and began their filmmaking career in the 1990s. They include some of the most recognized directors in Chinese cinema, such as Wang Xiaoshuai, Lu Xuechang, Jia Zhangke, and Lu Chuan.
2. *Beijing Bicycle*, directed by Wang Xiaoshuai (2001; Culver City CA: Columbia TriStar Home Entertainment, 2002), DVD.
3. The term "new urban cinema" was first used in promotional materials in early 2000 and later used in the journal *Popular Cinema* (*Dazhong dianying*

大众电影). For an excellent and informative examination of the new urban cinema and its sociopolitical engagement with Chinese urban culture, see Yomi Braester, "'This Is the Story of Our Street': Urban Preservation and the Post-Maoist Politics of Memory," chapter 6 in *Painting the City Red: Chinese Cinema and the Urban Contract* (Durham NC: Duke University Press, 2010), 224–80.

4. Among English critiques, Haomin Gong, Elizabeth Wright, Harry H. Kuoshu, Gary Xu, and Yingjin Zhang, all discuss the contrast between city people and migrant workers and its thematic connection to De Sica's 1948 film. In Chinese criticism, both Ling Chen and Lei Chen point out the contrasts and the similarities between the city and the rural; Xiaoyan Feng focuses on the identity crisis of young people; Peng He compares Wang's and De Sica's similarities in filmic language and cinematic narrative; and Wei Nie examines the power dynamic between the city and the rural in *Beijing Bicycle*. For articles mentioned here, see Lei Chen 陈磊, "On Sixth Generation Directors from *Beijing Bicycle* 从《十七岁的单车》看新生代导演," *Journal of Shanghai University (Social Science 10)* 上海大学学报（社会科学版）2 (2003): 50–53; Ling Chen 陈凌, "Uncertain 'Search': Thematic Interpretation of *Beijing Bicycle* 寻找的彷徨—评电影《十七岁的单车》主题阐释的意义," *Movie Literature* 电影文学 18 (2008): 50–51; Xiaoyan Feng, 冯晓燕, "Walking at the City's Edge: A Cultural Strategy of Sixth Generation Directors 在城市边缘行走—第六代导演的一种文化策略," *Journal of Liaoning Educational Administration Institute* 辽宁教育行政学院学报 7 (2008): 116–19; Peng He 何鹏, "When Wang Xiaoshuai Meets De Sica: *Beijing Bicycle* and *The Bicycle Thief* 当王小帅遭遇德•西卡—以《十七岁的单车》和《偷自行车的人》为例," *Movie Review* 电影评介 8 (2011): 52–54, DOI:10.3969/j.issn.1002-6916.2011.08.022; Harry H. Kuoshu, *Metro Movies: Cinematic Urbanism in Post-Mao China* (Carbondale: Southern Illinois University Press, 2011); Wei Nie 聂伟, "Part Three of the Study of New Generation Films: On Wang Xiaoshuai 新生代电影研究之三：王小帅论," *Journal of Hangzhou Teachers' College (Social Science Edition)* 杭州师范学院学报 (社会科学版) 2 (2005): 85–91.

5. The bicycle played a significant socioeconomic role in China's modernization era during the decade from the late 1970s to the mid-1980s, when the country's large bicycle production and consumption earned it the nickname of Kingdom of Bicycles, or Country on Bicycles. The bicycle has since then become a politicized visual trope for an underdeveloped Chinese society, a government-controlled economy, and a socialist ideology because of its intimate association with a historical period that is defined by these conditions. As China undergoes tremendous economic developments in the twenty-first century, the once coveted bicycle is now a cheap substitute for cars for low-income city residents, while also serving as a nos-

talgic reminder of the bygone days. Once a symbol of modernization and affluence in the 1970s in China, the bicycle often connotes economic under-development, low-income urban living, and limited financial means in contemporary society. This change in the bicycle's socioeconomic connotations is especially significant in contemporary urban spaces, where the bicycle is an undesirable mode of daily transportation for people living and working in Beijing, China's largest metropolis. For a more detailed report on the history of bicycles in China, see Yuhan Luo 骆昱含, "The Bicycle's China Spectacle 自行车的中国奇观," *Chinese Heritage* 中华遗产, no. 89 (2013): 70–86. For a portion of this article, see *Chinese Heritage*'s web page at *China National Geography Online* 中国国家地理网, http://www.dili360.com/ch /article/p5350c3d83bd9428.htm.

6. Interview with Wang Xiaoshuai in Michael Berry's *Speaking in Images: Interview with Contemporary Chinese Filmmakers* (New York: Columbia University Press, 2005), 175.

7. Haomin Gong engages the concept of uneven modernity in his discussion of *Beijing Bicycle*'s social critique. For further reading, see Haomin Gong, *Uneven Modernity: Literature, Film, and Intellectual Discourse in Postsocialist China* (Honolulu: University of Hawai'i Press, 2012), 120–29.

8. Yingjin Zhang, *Cinema, Space, and Polylocality in a Globalizing China* (Honolulu: University of Hawai'i Press, 2010), 79.

9. This phrase in Chinese is 新时代的骆驼祥子. Xiangzi is the central character in Lao She's *Rickshaw*, a novel set in Beijing in the 1930s. Xiangzi is a hard-working rickshaw boy who makes a living by pulling passengers in his rickshaw in Beijing, a job that is comparable to modern taxi drivers. He rents the rickshaw from the company and fixates on saving enough money to buy his own rickshaw and thereby achieve financial comfort.

10. Lao She, *Rickshaw: The Novel Lo-t'o Hsiang Tzu*, trans. Jean M. James (Honolulu: University of Hawai'i Press, 1979).

11. In his interview with Michael Berry, director Wang Xiaoshuai also mentions that bicycles were often stolen while he was in college in Beijing. Berry, *Speaking in Images*, 174–75.

12. Gong, *Uneven Modernity*, 126.

13. Zhang, *Cinema, Space, and Polylocality*, 80.

14. Elizabeth Wright, "Riding Towards the Future: Wang Xiaoshuai's *Beijing Bicycle*," *Sense of Cinema*, no. 18 (December 2001), http://sensesofcinema.com /2001/feature-articles/beijing_bicycle/.

15. Zhang, *Cinema, Space, and Polylocality*, 80.

16. Typically a familial adobe for extended Chinese families in the Yuan, Ming, and Qing Dynasties, the courtyard house, or *Sihe yuan* (四合院), refers to a rectangular courtyard with houses built along its three sides. Because of its

popularity in history, the courtyard houses are almost exclusively associated with Beijing's historical cityscape.

17. Berry, *Speaking in Images*, 176.
18. Zhang, *Cinema, Space, and Polylocality*, 79; Wright, "Riding Towards the Future."
19. Zhang, *Cinema, Space, and Polylocality*, 80–81; Ling Chen, "Uncertain 'Search,'" 50–51.
20. Berry, *Speaking in Images*, 175.

16 "Swerve! I'm on My Bike"

Mediated Images of Bicycling in Youth-Produced Hip-Hop

MELODY LYNN HOFFMANN

Although African Americans are reported by the League of American Bicyclists to be among the fastest growing group of bicyclists in the United States, this growth is not reflected in the media.[1] Bicyclists in television and film are typically representations of white men, but these portrayals are not necessarily positive or progressive. Pop-culture representations of bicycling emasculate white men by depicting them "as childish, eccentrics, sexually odd characters, geeks, and/or financial failures."[2] Some of the most well-known characters associated with adult cycling, including Pee Wee Herman and Steve Carell's character in *The 40 Year Old Virgin*, point to the danger in riding a bike as an adult male: you will be seen as a queer, virginal, childish loser.[3] There are exceptions to media representations of the "loser on a bike" image, but these positive representations in the media are still overwhelmingly white men.[4]

There have been some recent exceptions to the absence of black-bicyclist images, primarily with young black artists producing their own media. In 2012 two underground rap artists released bicycle-themed music videos. BlocBoi Fame's "Disrespectful" and YnG RobB's "Speedin' on My Fixie" both feature black men riding on and rapping about fixed-gear bicycles. This style of bike is popular in urban spaces because of the minimalist construction (e.g. no gears, no brakes) and the trend in color-coordinated parts and accessories. In both videos, the artists focus on the aesthetics of the bikes and on the riders' connected cultural capital, or social status, gained through symbolic means such as their dress, style, and music.

Both artists use the coolness of fixed-gear bikes to help construct their bad boy performances. In "Disrespectful," BlocBoi Fame develops a bad boy image as he rides his fixed-gear bike while drinking alcohol, gesturing wildly, and rarely holding onto his handlebars. His image is also articulated through the song's hook, bragging about his "disrespectful" behavior when he is "doin' wheelies all in traffic" and "blowin' through them red lights." YnG RobB, in "Speedin' on My Fixie," focuses on the coolness of riding fast. The video highlights the bike's aesthetics, showcasing a clean, sleek, and brightly color-coordinated fixed-gear bicycle that sits behind YnG RobB as he raps, "Speeding on my fixie / You can't slow me down / Like Critical Mass / Yeah I'm leading / If you can't keep up then I'm leavin."[5] YnG RobB also brags about the high cost of his bicycle: "Pay five hundred for each rim on my bike / You ain't gotta believe it." The video showcases his crew riding on the streets erratically, showing off their ability to ride backward in circles. These videos are significant in that they deviate from the "loser on a bike" image. The artists also do the difficult job of making biking seem cool within an urban culture that has long championed the car as the coolest form of transportation. Through these music videos, BlocBoi Fame and YnG RobB suggest which aspects of the bicycle are important to young black men, including aesthetics, speed, and expensive components.

Because riding a bicycle as an adult is still seen as atypical, mainstream media chooses to represent adult bicyclists as atypical, leaving underground media to fill in those gaps. In contrast, it is common for children to ride bicycles. Yet even media representations of children bicycling follows the same loser framework. Films such as *The Way, Way Back* (2013) reiterate the problematic representations of adult bicyclists, featuring young white boys who seem inept at impressing girls due to their reliance on bicycles. The audience is encouraged to laugh at and feel sorry for the young boy who rides away from a pretty girl on his pink cruiser bike with streamers. Perhaps unsurprisingly given people of color's underrepresentation in the media, images of black youth on bicycles are also difficult to find. However, like their

adult counterparts, black youth have produced their own representations of bicycling through music videos.

In this chapter, I analyze two youth-oriented rap groups, both of
which have produced videos with probicycle messages that directly
conflict with the hegemonic coolness of car culture that permeates
their social circles. Although these artists operate within underground
music scenes, their mediated images are still important to understand
considering the dearth of "biking while black" images in the media. I
also understand these videos as promotion to encourage young people of color to bicycle. Mainstream bicycle culture and advocacy in
the United States is dominated by middle- to upper-class white bicyclists, and this domination can skew perceptions of who can ride a
bicycle. It is important for people of color to have mediated images
of bicycling that they can identify with so as to make the bicycle a
plausible form of transportation for them.

This chapter's focus is on the Oakland-based Original Scraper Bike
Team's "Scraper Bike" video and Minneapolis's Y.N.RichKids' "My
Bike" video. Through these videos, I explore how the artists represent bicycling in underserved urban spaces. I analyze the songs' lyrics,
music-video imagery, and relevant historical and geographical context
to argue that these performances produce a unique vision of bicycling for black youth. Although the bicycle is typically associated with
environmentalism and health, these young artists show how a bike is
also an intervention in urban street culture, a marker of pride in forgotten neighborhoods, and a mode of survival within the capitalist
system that typically disenfranchises young black people. My focus
on youth-produced hip-hop is an important and otherwise-missing
contribution to cultural and media studies. Beyond academia, the
interventions made through the music videos are important because
these youth are on the margins of urban bicycle culture as they work
to push the boundaries of what bicycle activism can look like.

Hip-hop and bicycles are a unique mix, but one thing they have
in common is a struggle for respect. Although there is plenty of critique of the misogyny, violence, and love of wealth embedded in the
hip-hop genre, some scholars have argued for its potentiality. For
example, Bakari Kitwana argues that hip-hop and rap "just may be

the vehicle for Black America's next major political movement," in part because rap gives young African Americans unprecedented visibility in a larger society often trying to make them invisible.[6] Kitwana gives specific praise to off-the-radar, neighborhood kids who use hip-hop as "a place of sustenance for an oppressed people's spirit" and as a site of resistance.[7] Similarly, people have long used bicycles for activist purposes, most notably the women's liberation movement in the nineteenth century.[8] More recently, scholars have studied the ways in which bicycles are used to communicate radical political messages about war and capitalism.[9] The Original Scraper Bike Team and Y.N.RichKids bring together the positive activist potential of both hip-hop and bicycles to craft songs and videos with unique messages about mobility in urban spaces.

What makes the Original Scraper Bike Team and the Y.N.RichKids unique compared to other representations of urban bike culture is the specific space the performers occupy in the videos and the construction of the highlighted bicycle scenes. The significance of black youth writing songs about bicycling reaches beyond representational disparities. It is important for young African Americans to represent themselves through the media. But also these young artists are constructing new frameworks for encouraging their peers to take up a marginalized form of transportation in the face of the ubiquitous car culture and the stereotypes of riding a bicycle in the inner city.

Rollin' Deep on MCs: Background on the Artists

The Original Scraper Bike Team and Y.N.RichKids both come from underserved areas of major cities and were formed in part as a response to their troubled environments. The scraper bike movement comes out of one of the poorest neighborhoods in Oakland, California, where a then-teenaged African American man, Tyrone Stevenson Jr., invented the scraper bike. Stevenson Jr. originally constructed his scraper bike to stay out of trouble and showed off his bike in hopes of getting other kids more interested in bikes than in gang culture. Scraper bikes get both their name and their visually engaging aesthetic from the Oakland original scraper cars. The name comes from the cars' huge, shiny rims, which often scrape the inside of the wheel wells. Scraper cars are clean and eccentric with flashy colors and booming sound systems. Inspired by these cars, scraper bikes stand out because of the bright colors and clever use of materials, including what some people would consider garbage. For example, the Original Scraper Bike Team suggest using candy bar wrappers, aluminum foil, and duct tape to embellish the wheels' spokes.[10] The team's music video helped them gain nationwide attention, including 4.6 million views to date on YouTube and numerous media spots.

The Y.N.RichKids, based in North Minneapolis, also focus on creating a positive and safe space for youth. Whereas the Original Scraper Bike Team produced a music video to promote its bicycle group, the Y.N.RichKids are primarily a hip-hop group that produced a music video about biking. Similar to Oakland, North Minneapolis has a concentrated population of African Americans and struggles with high rates of unemployment, foreclosed homes, and health disparities. The group started in the Beats and Rhymes program at the North Minneapolis YMCA in which kids are able to write and record songs with help from established music producers. The Y.N.RichKids gained national attention with their "Hot Cheetos and Takis" video, garnering 7.8 million views on YouTube; at the time of this writing, the "My Bike" video has over 800,000 views.

To maintain ridership, the Original Scraper Bike Team had to find something besides bicycle rides to keep the at-risk youth from going astray, and making a hip-hop video seemed like an obvious choice. The video's images are comprised of fellow team members dancing, lip-synching lyrics, and biking around the neighborhood streets. The lyrics convey pride in the scraper bike crew and its home in Oakland. There is continual bragging regarding Stevenson Jr. being the originator of scraper bikes: "Scraper bikes was invented in the towns / By a champ [Stevenson Jr.] who loves to get around."[11] The majority of the lyrics are descriptions of the bikes, with the catchy hook, "Yellow, green, orange with bling / Scraper bikes is on the scene." The production value of the song and video are rather low due to the team's limited resources.

In contrast, the Y.N.RichKids are known for having high production values in both their songs and videos because of their connections to veteran music producers, and "My Bike" is no exception. The video takes viewers on a whirlwind tour of Minneapolis as members of the group ride on BMX bikes in spaces typically forbidden for bicyclists. The Y.N.RichKids are filmed riding through the Mall of America, showing off their coordinated bike moves on the Minnesota Vikings' practice field, and riding around the Minnesota Twins' field with the team's official mascot. Both "Scraper Bike" and "My Bike" illustrate why and how riding a bike is a desirable activity for young people of color, despite the barriers to and perceptions of bicycling in their inner-city communities.

Fresh Bicycle Advocacy

Some bicycle advocates are invested in promoting bicycling with people of color and in lower-income communities, but the benefits of riding discussed by advocates do not always resonate with these communities. This is because of unique barriers to and perceptions of bicycling, including racial profiling by the police and a lack of storage for bicycles at their homes.[12] This divergence from mainstream bicycle advocacy is represented in both the "Scraper Bike" and "My Bike" music videos as the artists reshape common reasons for riding a bicycle. Mainstream bicycle advocates focus on increasing ridership by educating people on how to ride safely and explaining the benefits of bicycling, including lessening one's impact on the environment and saving money.[13] The artists do not directly consider these benefits in their videos but instead suggest that to engage and empower young people of color to ride bicycles, a different framework of reasoning needs to be used in their communities. For example, bicycle advocates typically do not use "looking cool" as an incentive to ride a bicycle, but this incentive is brought up continuously in both videos. These artists understand that biking needs to look and seem cool before some young adults will even consider taking up this marginalized form of transportation.

For many advocates, bicycling is an inherently political act based on radical anticar and antioil sentiments. In both music videos the artists do in fact boast about not needing a car. Additionally, the young artists push the boundaries of what the intersection of politics and biking can look like. For example, the politicization of the Original Scraper Bike Team's work happened after making their video. Stevenson Jr. said that people had to tell him that there was something bigger to his project than just making cool bikes.[14] In the "Scraper Bike" music video, there is no mention of utilizing the bicycle as a more sustainable transit option. Only *after* the making of the video did he start defining his crew as dedicated to "creating a sustainable, positive, educational, and 'Green' way of life in the inner city."[15] The Original Scraper Bike Team now use their bicycles in local social-justice protests. Although bicycles have historically been used in many political spaces, the Original Scraper Bike Team use their bikes to push for an end to gun violence in their community, which is an issue largely untouched by bicycle advocates.[16]

Similarly, the Y.N.RichKids do not promote overtly political reasons for bicycling in their video, but they do complicate why lower-income people ride a bicycle. When asked in an interview whether bicycling is understood as cool in their social circle, Lady J responded that "it's normal" to ride a bike. G-6 of Y.N.RichKids explained that biking is "better than walking," to which Ben-on-Ten added "and it's exercising!"[17] G-6's position on biking being better than walking illustrates some agency in choosing his form of mobility. If there are two choices to get to a friend's house, biking just seems better. None of the artists argued that bicycling was their *only* option; it was in fact their preferred transportation option. This complicates the stereotype that some lower-income people are forced to ride a bicycle because they are too poor to afford other modes of transit; or as bike activist and writer Elly Blue articulates the stereotype, "Everyone who rides a bike is a broke ne'er-do-well."[18] Ben-on-Ten's statement about exercise is telling of the messages he receives in his community, because it reflects a benefit of riding that advocates promote primarily in lower-income communities, including North Minneapolis.[19]

These videos are also productive in recruiting inner-city youth to bicycling in a fresh way, because neither group celebrates or utilizes a proven tool to increase the number of people riding: bicycle infrastructure (e.g., bicycle lanes).[20] In fact, the artists seem to purposefully eschew the infrastructure. Instead of showcasing the miles of bicycle lanes in Minneapolis, the Y.N.RichKids chose to ride in typically forbidden ways, including taking over an entire street and riding inside sports stadiums and a mall. The Original Scraper Bike Team are filmed riding erratically through the streets of Oakland. In one scene, Stevenson Jr. is riding against traffic and in the middle of the street while a designated bicycle lane quickly goes out of frame. In many U.S. cities, bicycle advocates have struggled with encouraging lower-income residents to ride in bicycle lanes. There is not conclusive research as of yet that explains *why* lower-income people are less likely to use bicycle infrastructure. But these two music videos clearly speak to the different ways in which people can bicycle through a city—and they are not necessarily through normative bicycle-sanctioned spaces. So if the artists either do not address or reframe common persuasive points for riding a bicycle, then what is their approach to advocating for young people to ride? In short, it is through making this form of transportation look cool.

Cool Bikes, No Cars

In the music videos, the bicycles' aesthetics are the most significant way the artists demonstrate the coolness that comes with riding a bicycle. "My Bike" features the Y.N.RichKids riding BMX bikes, a style of bicycle that is designed for doing tricks rather than long rides through the city. Dame Jones specifically references BMX trick riding when he raps, "Ridin' down the street showing off my tricks / Tellin' these haters to get off my pegs."[21] When I asked three group members whether they typically rode BMX bikes, they responded with a synchronized "No," and Lady J told me they usually ride "just Huffys." Throughout the music video, they are filmed standing up while riding because sitting down on the small frame of a BMX bike is difficult to do. Using BMX bikes is a purely aesthetic choice because they are typically not used as a form of transportation, despite the video being based on taking a long journey through the city.

The lyrics in "My Bike" send a strong message about how bicycling can make you cool. By boasting positively about bicycling, the artists break down negative associations with biking in the inner city. Lady J specifically speaks to how cool she looks when she raps, "I whip my hair back and forth / When I'm riding on my bicycle / Cute outfit / Fresh shoes on." Kid Nas argues that he is "fresh to death" on his bicycle and "that I can do it with no hands / I'm the man." G-6 says that when he is on his bike, he is "Flyer than a kite." What stands out with these successive lyrics is a total focus on bragging about how great they look on a bicycle. Being able to do tricks on pegs and with no hands is also seen as a marker of coolness. In short, the question of "why ride a bike?" is answered in the song with the resounding answer "because they make you look cool."

In the "Scraper Bike" video, the Original Scraper Bike Team promote the bicycle *design*, rather than the act of biking, to encourage youth to get involved. The whole point of the scraper bike is its distinctive look; and like the BMX bikes, functionality is severely downplayed. A blur of blue, orange, and red wheels fill the screen as the camera pans riders on a variety of bike builds, including a three-wheeled bike with a stereo system, a low-rider bike with long handlebars and a banana seat, and an ordinary department store bike. Just as the Y.N.RichKids boast continuously about their coolness when riding bicycles, the entirety of "Scraper Bike" is used to argue that scraper bikes are desirable. Lyrics focus on unique elements of the bike—"What do we have here? / Handlebars I don't even have to steer"—and the attention people receive when riding "hype" scraper bikes: "When we come around / They know who we be." Both groups make a strong claim that *how* the bicycle looks is just as, if not more, important to youth than the mobility allowed by that bicycle. This is significant because bicycle advocates focus on the functionality of bicycles, such as being able to get to places quicker than cars in cramped urban streets, rather than how a person looks when they ride.

Not only are these artists articulating the social status one can gain from riding a cool-looking bicycle; they are also boldly and creatively rejecting car culture, a culture that is heavily embedded as a marker of success in their communities. Dame Jones of Y.N.RichKids rhymes, "I don't need a car / These two wheels gon' take me far." And Stevenson Jr. similarly states, "My scraper bike go hard / I don't need no car." These lyrics are bold because bicycling is not typically seen as a cool form of transportation for young black people in urban spaces. Rather, these young adults aspire to drive stylish cars. It is typical for people in this community to spend a lot of time and money on their cars, with booming sound systems, tricked-out interiors, and flashy rims. Cars are symbols of high status and wealth and are a way to move beyond one's immediate surroundings. Although the Original Scraper Bike Team rejects car culture by promoting bicycling as a cooler form of mobility, the team also creatively coopts the aesthetics of their localized car culture to recruit new members.

Stevenson Jr. was savvy enough to craft a bicycle design based on a popular car in hopes of recruiting young adults attracted to the scraper car culture. Those too young or without the resources to own a scraper car can build a scraper bike for very little money and still participate in the scraper culture. Moreover, Stevenson Jr. used a familiar style of car to encourage people to try bicycling. To lower-income people of color, bicycling can be both undesirable (i.e., a marker of poverty) and, with low rates of cycling in urban spaces, unfamiliar. By combining a desirable and familiar form of mobile cultural capital, Stevenson Jr. lessens the apprehension to ride a bicycle in Oakland. In other words, youth can identify with and recognize the scraper-style bike more than a road bike with a lot of gears and shifters.

From Cool Bikes to Cool Cities

Although the artists focus on bicycles as aesthetic objects rather than functional modes of transportation, another way in which the artists show how cool biking can be is by demonstrating how bicycles allow them unique access to various parts of their cities, both culturally and geographically. In "Scraper Bike" this access is evident in the cultural references to a Bay Area–specific rap genre; in "My Bike" the artists gain access to parts of the city typically prohibited or cut off to young black bicyclists. And in both videos, impoverished neighborhoods gain positive attention. The "Scraper Bike" video has made a small group of black youth highly visible in a city where they are often forgotten. One way they mark their existence is by capitalizing on the hyphy movement, a popular rap subgenre and lifestyle that artists created in Oakland.[22] Scraper cars, Stevenson Jr.'s original inspiration, were born out of the hyphy movement. Stevenson Jr. also gives a nod to the hyphy scene through his lyrics. Those within the movement refer to their hyphy behavior as "getting stupid" or "going dumb."[23] Stevenson Jr. directly references the hyphy movement when he raps, "I go stupid, dumb, retarded / Scraping my bikes looking hella retarded." Here Stevenson Jr. uses specific slang (i.e., stupid, dumb, retarded) popularized in the hyphy movement. Although not the most politically correct language, these lyrics signify the scraper bike movement's association and identification with the hyphy movement. As with the cooptation of scraper car design, the Original Scraper Bike Team's association with the hyphy movement is important for recruitment of young adults. Young adults can identify with the hyphy movement and thus feel more at home with bicycles connected to the local hip-hop scene.

Beyond the hip-hop scene, the Original Scraper Bike Team often attend events advocating for social issues that impact their community. For example, scraper bicyclists were credited with instigating a massive freeway shutdown in Oakland during a week-long protest against the George Zimmerman verdict in July 2013.[24] The scraper bicyclists encouraged other protestors to clog the street; and "once the scrapers had made the first move on to the freeway, the freeway shutdown was no longer their action. . . . [F]amilies, young people and activists . . . soon made it their own."[25] In sum, members of the Original Scraper Bike Team not only encourage people of color to use bicycles; they also use bicycles to address racialized social issues. This is another example of how these artists politicize bicycling in a new way, one that promotes social justice for young black people.

As for the Y.N.RichKids, their lyrics and their use of major Minneapolis landmarks signifies a complicated relationship with the city. Many of the places showcased in the video are usually geographically, culturally, and economically off-limits to many black youth. But the Y.N.RichKids chose to reconnect to the city, outside the isolated North Minneapolis, and bring their unique message about bicycling to places that do not prioritize the voice of young black bicyclists and artists. Although the music video does not identify any North Minneapolis landmarks, one member does give a shout out to their community, when Lauren rhymes, "Northside, Northside stay strong." North Minneapolis, or the Northside, is often a site of struggle for residents. This isolated area of the city has massive health and income disparities compared to the rest of Minneapolis.[26] Mayor of Minneapolis R. T. Rybak outlined in his 2012 State of the City speech the disparities of the Northside, including an 11 percent drop in population and new initiatives he would be launching to address violent crime, unemployment, and "reconnection" to the rest of the city.[27]

Members of the Y.N.RichKids told me that they found great joy in getting inside access to typically forbidden spaces. But there is something peculiar about their celebration of the sports facilities, especially the Minnesota Twins field. The construction of the field led to turmoil in the African American community and North Minneapolis in regards to equal-employment opportunities.[28] Beyond employment concerns, many residents felt that the stadium's location would isolate North Minneapolis even further. The stadium is built on the edge of downtown and the Northside. Although the upper-class North Loop realtors advertise the area as "blissfully isolated," residents farther north found the additional isolation problematic. And because new public transportation planning has nearly abandoned parts of North Minneapolis, it is not surprising that Northside kids use bicycles as a form of transportation.[29]

In lower-income areas of the city, bicycles may initially signify people's isolation and disenfranchisement from public transit, but the Y.N.RichKids and Original Scraper Bike Team have reappropriated biking in the inner city to be not a necessity but a choice. By choosing to ride bicycles, these youth combat the stereotype that poverty is linked with riding a bicycle. This stereotype is localized in lower-income neighborhoods, as higher-class people on bicycles are typically read as having the *privilege* to ride a bicycle. These artists are trying to harness the higher-class understanding of bicycling by opting into riding, not being forced into it. And even if it is a necessity for some people, they want people to feel pride, not shame, in their mode of transportation. The positive message of choosing to ride a bike over other potentially "cooler" modes of transit and being able to access new parts of the city via a bicycle is articulated by Lauren as she raps in "My Bike," "You can catch me and my crew on our bikes / Rollin' past haters as we cruise our town."

From Cool Bikes to Cold Hard Cash

Although both groups show pride in their underserved neighborhoods, the pride does not necessarily work to romanticize their inner-city roots. Michael Eric Dyson argues that when hip-hop artists refer to ghettos, "it's not the ghetto that is being romanticized [it's the] intellectual attachment and intimacy that it breeds, a bond established among those who suffer and struggle together."[30] Despite the obvious struggles happening, none of the artists call for an exodus from their communities. Rather, they use bikes in the music videos to move within, not away from, their communities. These young adults are bragging through the songs about their cool crews and hot bikes, all the while avoiding violent gang culture and other pitfalls on a daily basis.

Both groups work as socially conscious spaces for youth to expend energy in otherwise-dangerous neighborhoods. They have also had to confront the realities of survival in the inner city. Stevenson Jr. is excited to be taking his scraper bike movement into economically supportive and celebrity territory. On his Facebook page, Stevenson Jr. often posts messages about his goals of being famous and powerful. Posts include "Back On The Grind . . . CEO Status Is Plastered On My Mind."[31] A more direct sign that Stevenson Jr. is seeing the scrapers beyond a community group is his post "Not Just an Artist . . . But a Brand." He is also teaching youth the important skills of bicycle mechanics, custom design, and stereo-system building, all of which can be used in more traditional forms of employment. The Y.N.RichKids have faced a more dramatic shift in their economic goals. After the success of their "Hot Cheetos and Takis" song and video, they began doing numerous public appearances in Minneapolis. However, despite a viral video and a four-star review in *Rolling Stone*, the artists have seen very little money from their celebrity status.[32] In 2013 they broke ties with the YMCA and started working with Alonzo Jackson, a former executive at Dr. Dre's Aftermath Records. The hope is for the kids to finally make money off their talents. To start, Da Rich Kidzz, as they are now known, signed on to a national advertising campaign with Kmart.

There is nothing inherently dubious in Stevenson Jr.'s and the Y.N.RichKids's intentions to create fame and an income based on hip-hop or biking, especially considering the ways in which young black adults are forced to interact with capitalism in underground and creative ways. This approach to capitalism is a strategy to survive within its system. It allows black youth to avoid dead-end and low-paying jobs and to devote their creative energies to something pleasurable. The creativity and passion seen in both groups reflects Robin D. G. Kelley's theory on African Americans' relation to leisure and labor in which "the pursuit of leisure, pleasure, and creative expression is *labor*, and some African-American urban youth have tried to turn that labor into cold hard cash."[33] Kelley does not argue that this approach to leisure is emancipatory or resistive; rather, he argues that it is a way to survive in a system that actively works to disempower young African Americans. Da Rich Kidzz are now on a money-making venture, while maintaining their "positive achievements."[34] Due to the lack of job opportunities in Oakland, Stevenson Jr. said that he had no choice but to sell scraper bikes.[35] In other words, the hobbies that the Y.N.RichKids and the Original Scraper Bike Team took up to stay busy and out of trouble are now working to make them that cold hard cash.

Conclusion

The interventions made by the Y.N.RichKids and the Original Scraper Bike Team in the hip-hop and bicycle movements should not be ignored by scholars and bicycle advocates. The Beats and Rhymes program in North Minneapolis gave the Y.N.RichKids an impressive outlet to craft both high-quality songs and videos about their lives. The kids capitalize on their exposure by being role models for their peers. This includes positive boasting about bicycling, rather than the typical bragging about money and violence found in many rap songs. As for the scraper bikes, Stevenson Jr. admitted that without them he would either be "dead or in jail."[36] The survival mechanism he attributes to the bicycle is unprecedented in the current context of bicycle activism. People in the inner city use bicycles to quickly and safely get to friends' houses or to a work shift that starts before the first bus runs. Whereas many middle-class urban bicyclists use their bikes to commute to work and lessen their carbon footprints, Y.N.RichKids and the Original Scraper Bike Team show people that there is much more to riding a bicycle in the inner city.

In these videos, the bicycle signifies an intervention in urban street culture, a marker of pride in forgotten neighborhoods, and a mode of survival within the capitalist system. This signification diverts from more typical understandings of the bike as being a tool for healthy living and improving the environment. Although African Americans are part of the "New Majority" of bicyclists, bicycle advocates and organizations are still concerned with diversifying who rides.[37] By looking at how black youth define and understand the bicycle, advocates can use this imagery as a point of connection with youth and people of color. It is imperative for bicycle advocates to look to young people of color to understand how they relate to bicycling instead of mapping already-established frameworks for riding.

The Y.N.RichKids and Original Scraper Bike Team showcase unique and creative means of bicycle advocacy. This analysis illustrates the importance of paying attention to how people reshape what biking can be. There is a strong focus on the aesthetics of the bike in both music videos. Although having a nice-looking bike is not a new phenomenon (e.g., fixed-gear bikes), what counts as nice looking to these youth is different than what people can find in a typical bike shop. In other words, black youth may be more interested in riding a bicycle if they can look "fresh to death" while doing so. If bicycle advocates are truly committed to increasing ridership across classes and ethnicities, it is worth taking their mediated suggestions seriously.

Notes

1. *The New Majority: Pedaling towards Equity* (Washington DC: League of American Bicyclists / Sierra Club, 2013), http://www.bikeleague.org/sites/lab.huang .radicaldesigns.org/files/equity_report.pdf.

2. Zack Furness, *One Less Car: Bicycling and the Politics of Automobility* (Philadelphia: Temple University Press, 2010), 109.

3. Furness, *One Less Car*, 110–14.

4. For example, the 2012 film *Premium Rush* features a young, white, male bicycle messenger protagonist and no major roles for people of color.

5. All transcriptions of the lyrics for "Speedin' on My Fixie" are my own, from Choppa Wesst, "YnG RobB 'Speedin' on My Fixie' World Premiere"," YouTube video, 3:44, August 29, 2012, https://www.youtube.com/watch?v=enVqsljZtEw. YnG RobB invokes leading a Critical Mass ride, which is an international monthly bike ride dubbed an "organized coincidence." Riders gather at a designated spot and embark on a bike ride, purposefully taking over entire street lanes. Critical Mass seeks to perform a reality in which bicycles are the dominant mode of transportation. Critical Mass rides in many cities have hundreds of participants and dominate streets during rush hour.

6. Bakari Kitwana, "The State of the Hip-Hop Generation: How Hip-Hop's Cultural Movement Is Evolving into Political Power," *Diogenes* 51, no. 3 (2004): 115.

7. Kitwana, "State of the Hip-Hop Generation," 203.

8. Late nineteenth-century feminists such as Elizabeth Cady Stanton fought against the moral panic over women riding the bicycle by arguing that the bicycle was the quickest way to release women from the confines of patriarchy (perhaps a reason for such a moral panic). Lisa Brown and Robert Brown, "The Bicycle, Women's Rights, and Elizabeth Cady Stanton," *Women's Studies* 31, no. 5 (2002): 609–26.

9. Dave Horton, "Social Movements and the Bicycle," *Thinking about Cycling* (blog), November 25, 2009, http://thinkingaboutcycling.wordpress.com/social-movements-and-the-bicycle/.

10. "Customizer-in-Residence @ the Oakland Museum of California," *Original Scraper Bikes* (blog), March 22, 2013, http://originalscraperbikes.blogspot.com/2013/03/customizer-in-residence-oakland-museum.html.

11. Song lyrics for "Scraper Bike" transcribed by Trunk Boiz Lyrics, "Scraper Bike," Urban Lyrics, n.d., http://www.urbanlyrics.com/lyrics/trunkboiz/scraperbike.html (accessed September 28, 2015).

12. *Understanding Barriers to Bicycling: Interim Report* (Portland: Community Cycling Center, 2010), http://www.communitycyclingcenter.org/wp-content/uploads/2010/07/understanding-barriers-report.pdf; Elizabeth Rusch, "Biking while Black," *Mother Jones*, September/October 2002, http://www.motherjones.com/politics/2002/09/biking-while-black.

13. A Google search for "why ride a bicycle" produces endless web pages listing reasons to ride a bicycle. Health, the environment, and saving money are listed on the vast majority of pages.

14. Jacob Fenston, "Scraper Bike Fever Spreads, Thanks to YouTube," *National Public Radio: Weekend Edition*, September 13, 2008, http://www.npr.org/templates/story/story.php?storyId=94318161.

15. "Original Scraper Bikes," *Original Scraper Bikes* (blog), October 20, 2009, http://originalscraperbikes.blogspot.com/2009_10_01_archive.html.

16. In July 2009 the Original Scraper Bike Team organized "Healin' from the Killin'." Over one hundred cyclists took to the streets to ride against gun violence. At the time of the ride, sixty people had already been murdered in Oakland that year. Dara Kerr, "I'm Moving on My Scraper Bike," *Oakland North*, July 27, 2009, http://oaklandnorth.net/2009/07/27/im-movin-on-my -scraper-bike/.

17. Da Rich Kidzz, in discussion with the author, August 10, 2013.

18. Lindsey Abrams, "The Unstoppable Rise of Bikes," *Salon*, January 12, 2014, http://www.salon.com/2014/01/12/the_unstoppable_rise_of_bikes/.

19. For example, the Minneapolis-based bicycle-share program Nice Ride intentionally installed bike stations in neighborhoods with "historic issues of poverty and high incidence of heart disease, diabetes, high blood pressure and obesity," to "enhance active living opportunities in low-income populations." North Minneapolis was listed in Nice Ride's 2011 annual report as a target neighborhood. *Nice Ride Minnesota: 2011 Annual Report and 2012 Mid-Season Update* (Minneapolis: Nice Ride Minnesota, 2012), https://www.niceridemn .org/_asset/9n2z8n/NICE_RIDE_2012_ANNUAL_REPORT_OPT.pdf.

20. This is significant because many transportation planners and bicycle advocates argue that bicycle infrastructure is the best way to increase ridership.

21. Song lyrics for "My Bike" transcribed by Jeremy Dean, "My Bike, Y.N.RichKids," Rap Genius, n.d., http://genius.com/Ynrichkids-my-bike-lyrics (accessed September 28, 2015).

22. Steve Jones, "Hyphy Pulls a Bay Area Breakout," *USA Today*, April 13, 2006, http://usatoday30.usatoday.com/life/music/news/2006-04-13-hyphy-main_x .htm.

23. *Ghostride the Whip: The Hyphy Movement*, directed by DJ Vald (Los Angeles: Rugged Entertainment, 2008), DVD.

24. George Zimmerman was found not guilty of second degree murder in the killing of black teenager Trayvon Martin. For more on the Oakland protests, see "Zimmerman Protestors Shut Down Oakland Freeway," KTVU, July 15, 2013, http://lee.house.gov/news/in-the-news/zimmerman-protesters-shut-down -oakland-freeway.

25. Jaime Omar Yassin, "Scraper Bike Heroes and Other Gloriously Chaotic Casualties of the 'Outside Agitator' Narrative," *Hyphenated-Republic* (blog), July 24, 2013, http://hyphenatedrepublic.wordpress.com/2013/07/24/scraper -bike-heroes-and-other-gloriously-chaotic-casualties-of-the-outside-agitator -narrative.

26. The Northside has almost triple the rate of unemployment as the rest of the city, and half of the residents in the Near North neighborhood are living

below the poverty line. These statistics were gathered from the Minnesota Compass website (http://www.mncompass.org). Minnesota Compass is "a social indicators project" that is often cited by the Minnesota government.

27. R. T. Rybak, "One Minneapolis, Growing North," *The Mayor Blog* (blog), April 13, 2012, http://themayorblog.wordpress.com/2012/04/13/one-minneapolis -growing-north/.

28. Ron Edwards, "City Failed to Monitor Hiring during Twins Stadium Construction," *Minnesota Spokesman-Recorder*, May 12, 2010.

29. Eric Roper, "Minneapolis North Siders Demand Transit Improvements," *Star Tribune*, May 12, 2014, http://www.startribune.com/local/minneapolis/258843021 .html.

30. Michael Eric Dyson, *Know What I Mean: Reflections on Hip Hop* (New York: Basic Civitas Books, 2007), 11.

31. Scraper Bike King, "Back on the Grind," Facebook, April 30, 2010, http:// www.facebook.com/ScraperBikeKing (accessed April 30, 2010; site discontinued). See also Tyrone Stevenson Jr.'s updated Facebook page, https://www .facebook.com/pages/Baybe-Champ-Da-Scraper-Bike-King/53305105853.

32. Joe Gross, song review of "Hot Cheetos and Takis," by Y.N.RichKids, *Rolling Stone*, August 15, 2012, http://www.rollingstone.com/music/songreviews/hot -cheetos-takis-20120815.

33. Robin D. G. Kelley, *Yo' Mama's Disfunktional! Fighting the Culture Wars in Urban America* (Boston: Beacon Press, 1997), 45.

34. Chris Riemenschneider, "'Hot Cheetos' Kids Get a Lesson in Cold, Hard Facts," *Star Tribune*, February 17, 2013, http://www.startribune.com/entertainment/music /191430461.html.

35. *The Scraper Bike King*, directed by Rafael Flores (San Francisco: Green Eyed Media, 2009), DVD.

36. *Scraper Bike King*.

37. *New Majority*.

Afterword

Form and History in the Bicycle Sculptures of Ai Weiwei

DANIEL P. SHEA

Read collectively, the essays in this volume argue for the relevance of the bicycle as a rich subject for analysis in literature and film. As Jeremy Withers and I argue in our introduction, ever since the invention of the bicycle, in the nineteenth century, authors have employed bicycles as "rolling signifiers," as devices whose multifarious and continuously shifting cultural connotations render them ideal for use as literary or cinematic devices. That is, bicycles are material vehicles that have always worked extremely well as figurative vehicles, carrying a host of complex ideas and meanings on the page and the screen. At the same time, however, it is abundantly clear that many or most of the scholars working to unpack the significance of the fictional or representational bicycles depicted in fiction and film are motivated by their devotion to actual bicycles, which they see as transportation; entertainment; sport; and, most importantly, the potential solution to a number of all-too-real, real-world environmental and social crises.

In order to continue the momentum of the essays in this collection and to steer the conversation in a direction that will suggest avenues for the continued expansion of scholarship on bicycles in culture, this brief afterword considers a series of artworks that present a unique fusion of bicycles as signifiers and as material objects, of bicycles as both content and form—the bicycle installations of Ai Weiwei (b. 1957), China's best-known contemporary artist and one of its most powerful and persistent cultural critics. Ai Weiwei's sculptures, beginning with *Forever* (2003) and appearing in larger formats as *Forever Bicycles* in 2011 and again in 2013, are in fact unique fusions of real, physical bicycles; each site-specific installation consists of multiple bicycles—42 bicycles in 2003; 1,000 in 2011; and 3,144 in 2013—that are dissected and reassembled, joined together to form shapes and patterns that are at once familiar in their repetition of the instantly recognizable geometry of the standard bicycle frame and surprisingly alien in their fusing together of interlocking bicycles in strange and unintended configurations. With the front forks of one inverted bicycle sharing the rear wheel of the frame above it, frames attached to one another at the seat posts and the handlebar tubes, and the seats of upside-down frames sometimes supporting the entire structure, Ai Weiwei's bicycle installations present both a chaotic perversion of function and, alternately, a beautiful, complex symmetry of form in expansive, unanticipated patterns. The *Forever* installations demand that we reconsider the bicycle; they place this ubiquitous and easily overlooked vehicle in a prominent position, forcing us to *see* bicycles again and to consider anew their promise and possibility. Like the figurative fictional or cinematic bicycles that are the subject of analyses in the essays of this volume, the multiple bicycles that are conjoined to make the sculptures are more than just bicycles; they play a role in an artwork both as themselves and as representations of—and carriers of meanings beyond—themselves.

The hermeneutic possibilities of Ai Weiwei's bicycle sculptures begin with their titles. "Forever" ("Yongjiu") is the name of one of the iconic bicycle brands in China, and it was "the nation's most popular bicycle" from the 1940s through the early 1990s, during which time utilitarian bicycles were so plentiful as a mainstay of daily transportation that China came to be known as the Kingdom of Bicycles.[1] The Forever bicycle was, as Huang Hung writes, a status symbol in the seventies and eighties, when it was so popular that it was sold by lottery and "was the must-have item on any respectable wedding list."[2] In the years preceding the 2003 appearance of the *Forever* installation, however, the popularity of bicycling in China had plummeted. Bicycles, which once connoted success and progress in China, "came to represent Chinese backwardness," its underdevelopment compared with the automobile-centered West.[3] As China's economy blossomed, its economically empowered citizens were quick to abandon their bicycles. The Earth Policy Institute reported that between 1995 and 2005 the number of bicycles in everyday use in China had dropped by 35 percent, while, not unrelatedly, the number of cars on the roads grew from 4.2 to 8.9 million.[4] In the same time period, Sherley Wetherhold reports, Chinese cities began closing bicycle lanes and designating some streets as off-limits to bicycles.[5] Effectively conveying the changing attitude in China and perhaps unwittingly alluding to the name of the bicycle brand and the sculpture, in 2005 the ambassador to Finland, Yu Qingtai, retorted, "We should not be expected to stay forever as a kingdom of bicycles!" after Western journalists spoke critically of China's growing reliance on cars.[6]

Thus, Ai Weiwei produced *Forever* at a moment when it began to seem unlikely that the Forever cycle brand, or the centrality of bicycling in China in general, would in fact last forever. The fundamental irony of the title carries over into the form of the piece itself. The forty-two interlocking bicycles that make up *Forever* are fused together, one inverted frame on another about three bicycles high, to form a wide circle. This circle, along with the interlocking and interchangeable uniformity of the bicycle frames patterned within it, does suggest an endless, looping infinity. The sculpture's cycles form an endless cycle, reassuringly implying that bicycling and the Forever brand will be permanent, will go on forever. In the context of the decline of bicycling in China and the decline of the Forever bicycle, however, Ai's sculpture appears to make a more acerbic critique. While, as My T. Le writes, *Forever*'s infinite loop of bicycles may offer "a sense of protection, unity, and harmony," it seems rather more "like a heroic and frivolous act of resistance, echoing the slow disappearance of bicycles ... from all major Chinese cities as the country is modernizing."[7] Anthony Pins likewise interprets *Forever* as a commentary on the bicycle's "diminished utility [and] social status" and on the "waning significance" of bicycling in China.[8]

Like Marcel Duchamp's *Bicycle Wheel* (1913), in which a bicycle wheel on a front fork is bolted upright to the top of a stool, Ai Weiwei's *Forever* makes its point in part by rendering the bicycle functionally useless, a reflection of the declining Chinese interest in and reliance on the bicycle, which the artist no doubt perceived in the years leading up to the production of the sculpture.[9] Indeed, the sculpture's most evocative quality is its frustrating containment of potential energy that will never be realized: its bicycles contain implied energy and force, they are built to move but can move no longer. In Chin-Chin Yap's words, the bicycles in *Forever* are "devoid of practical purpose, robbed even of conventional function and motion."[10] If the Forever bicycle was, for the previous generation of Chinese citizens, a vehicle of both individual and economic mobility, it has become static, arrested, in Ai Weiwei's *Forever*. Each bicycle is frozen, locked in place and upright alongside many others in an enforced, confined stasis that runs contrary to the nature of a machine that is designed to move forward independently and that, as anyone who has learned to ride a bike will attest, falls over if it stands still. Though the circular *Forever* takes on the shape of a bicycle wheel, it is a wheel that lies flat on its side, incapable of motion and therefore entirely superfluous. For Pins, the looping structure of *Forever* ultimately "evokes only an ill-conceived carousel in which half the riders find themselves oriented upside down."[11] If the sculpture, which seems as though it is "about to lurch into motion," were to enact the movement its form implies, it could merely turn in circles, carrying out a banal repetition.[12]

In *Forever*, the bicycle already *is* what it appeared to be becoming in China as a whole—a museum piece, a relic. The bicycles in the sculpture are removed from their practical, utilitarian purpose and have become aesthetic objects, even representations of themselves. As Chin-Chin Yap remarks, however, Ai Weiwei's works unfailingly "remain acutely germane to the world . . . declining to close themselves off in self-contained aesthetic systems."[13] In particular, Ai Weiwei's art maintains a close contact with, and stands in complex relation to, Chinese history. Even as he moves the bicycles from the material-historical to the aesthetic sphere, Ai comments on and calls our attention to this transmutation of the object. *Forever* is in this regard closely aligned with Ai's other artworks of the period, many of which feature objects with particular symbolic significance to Chinese culture, which are transformed—sometimes even destroyed—by the artist. In

Fragments (2005), *Template* (2007), *Through* (2007, 2008), and *Map of China* (2008), Ai assembles installations and sculptures out of architectural elements, including timbers, doors, and windows, salvaged from Ming and Qing Dynasty structures destroyed by modern urban development. In *Coca-Cola Vase* (2007), Ai prints a Coca-Cola logo on an antique vase, while in *Colored Vases* (2007–10), he dips a series of Han Dynasty vases in bright industrial paints. And in *Dropping a Han Dynast Urn*, a photographic triptych depicts the artist holding and then intentionally dropping and shattering a two thousand–year–old urn. Considered alongside these related pieces, *Forever* calls attention to the Forever bicycle as an important element of Chinese culture from a period (the Kingdom of the Bicycle era?) that is giving way to the forces of modernity. Like the broken urn and the vases dipped in paint or branded with an American corporate logo, the bicycles are transformed by Ai Weiwei in an act that simultaneously destroys them, decries their destruction, and calls for their preservation. Or as Chin-Chin Yap argues, Ai's use of historical objects "runs the gamut from preservation ... to irreversible destruction ... to reconstruction."[14]

We might argue that the real medium of these works by Ai Weiwei is not door frames, vases, or bicycles but instead the longing and sense of loss that accompanies the passage of the tangible, useful, and culturally significant object into the dustbin of history—and its simultaneous reemergence within the ephemeral field of our own, or China's, collective memory. While *Forever* does not evoke the same degree of shock or sense of historical loss as *Colored Vases* or *Dropping a Han Dynasty Urn*, a sculpture made of modern bicycles bereft of their functional mobility does elicit a strong, almost physical reaction from the viewer. The bicycle is, after all, built to the scale of the human body. A machine designed to be powered by human bodies, the bicycle's form is determined by the nuance of the human corporeal design. As a result, the viewers confronting a sculpture made of bicycles are implicated in the work and inevitably respond to it in a unique way: we *feel* the bicycle seat, the push of the pedals, the grip of the handlebars, and all the motions and forces of the bicycle that we associate with a learned physical skill—the ability to ride a bicycle—so central to our experience that, as the saying goes, we can never forget it once we've learned it (all the more so if we were raised riding Forever-brand bicycles in China). Although the installation may be grand, weighty, and foreboding, its basic, elemental building block is patterned to the human body and the very intimate relation our bodies develop with the machine. Accordingly, *Forever* speaks to its audience with an unusual corporeal immediacy.

Because the bicycle is scaled and designed to the specifications of the human body and because we as individuals develop, often painstakingly in early childhood, a very intimate and unshakeable physical relationship with it, the bicycle, when employed as a basic sculptural building block, serves as a very powerful conduit for Ai Weiwei's statements about the tension between the individual and society. Just as the individual bicycle is very intimate and personal despite being manufactured to uniform specifications on an industrial scale, the sculpture made of multiple bicycles speaks to our sense of individuality while subsuming the individual identity within the multitude. Proceeding from the assumption that all of Ai Weiwei's work is informed by a Foucauldian awareness of the fraught discursive codependence between individual freedom and social power, Chin-Chin Yap asserts that the bicycles in *Forever*, each having begun as an "atom," "have transmuted into an organism."[15] This sense of the individual relation to the social whole, to the multitudes, may be unnerving, but it offers the potential for a kind of fulfillment or even liberation. Karen Smith concurs, noting optimistically that in *Forever* "individual components come together to achieve a cogent physical structure and enjoy a symbiotic relationship with space."[16] Given Ai Weiwei's fierce devotion to his own individual artistic freedom and, consequently, his consistently antagonistic relationship with the Chinese government (Ai has been beaten and imprisoned by the Chinese government; his passport was confiscated; and he remains under constant surveillance—all events that receive due treatment in his art), Anthony Pins's more circumspect interpretation of the sculpture's commentary on the relation of the individual to society probably comes closer to Ai Weiwei's intent. *Forever*, Pins argues, "subjugates the value of any particular bicycle to the composition as a whole."[17] Each bicycle,

Pins continues, is effectively "indiscernible from the next" and is consequently "marginalized" and reduced to little more than "a cog in a giant geometric sculpture."[18] To be sure, each of the bicycles in *Forever* is compromised because of its relation to the multitude of bicycles in the sculpture as a whole; none of the bicycles can move independently as they were designed to do. Even if some could escape, the frames are locked to shared wheels, and there aren't enough wheels to go around.

To this point, I've focused on the first version of Ai Weiwei's bicycle sculptures, *Forever*, and will turn now, in conclusion, to the later, larger-scale sculptures of 2011 and 2013, both titled *Forever Bicycles*. Constructed of 1,000 bicycles and 3,144 bicycles, respectively, the *Forever Bicycles* installations might seem to offer an exponentially more pessimistic account of the plight of the individual than the 2003 *Forever*, with its comparatively cozy 42 bicycles. Instead, however, the larger-scale bicycle sculptures seem more inviting and more promising. Commenting on the 2011 version, which was installed in the Taipei Fine Arts Museum, Pins captures the more optimistic tone of the work, remarking that with its lofty aerial thrust and the delicate outward expansion of the bicycle frames, which interlock in a precarious yet flowery balance, *Forever Bicycles* "literally appears to extend into infinity" as it "explodes into space and recedes to an unseen horizon."[19] While the 2003 iteration of the sculpture seemed immobile and heavy, the much larger *Forever Bicycles* versions appear lighter. The mass of bicycles seem poised for motion, reaching up and out from their foundation. Employing language that suggests flight and lightness, one spectator reviewing the 2013 sculpture installed in Toronto for the city's Nuit Blanche arts festival writes that "Ai Weiwei's stunning sculpture *floats* 3,144 bicycles above Toronto square" and goes on to say that this "*ballooned*" version of the original sculpture "evok[ed] a blurred sense of motion from every angle."[20] Both the 2011 and 2013 sculptures, with their very intricate, fractal repetition of patterning of the bicycles, do suggest motion and continuation, a liberatory sense of possibility heightened by the apparently greater ratio of wheels per bicycle frame—the individual bicycles seem capable of realizing their inherent inclination toward freedom of movement. Perhaps not coincidentally, the timing of the installation of *Forever Bicycles* coincides with what Sherley Wetherhold identifies as the 2011 "U-turn in transportation policy," during which the Chinese government began again to encourage bicycling by instituting a series of bicycle-advocacy programs in multiple cities.[21] (It's important to note that even at their lowest levels, rates of daily bicycle usage in China outstripped those of nearly every Western country.)

While the spectators of the 2003 *Forever* were kept outside the circle of bicycles, viewers were invited to walk between and through the numerous corridors and arches created by the fused bicycle frames of the later versions of the sculpture. (The 2013 *Forever Bicycles* was one hundred feet long and thirty feet high, and both *Forever Bicycles* installations contained channels through which spectators were invited to walk.) Viewers immersed in the bicycle frames saw everchanging patterns appear as they explored the installation, gaining new perspectives at every turn as they viewed the multitude of bicycle frames from different angles. The bicycles created meaningful patterns because of their connections with each other. The bicycle, this latter manifestation of Ai Weiwei's bicycle sculptures suggests, connects us as individuals with a global network. It connects us with history—as Zack Furness notes, the bicycle is a "nineteenth-century solution to a [quantity of] twenty-first-century problem[s]."[22] And increasingly the bicycle connects us with each other, with a network of other bicyclists around the globe. The bicycle indeed has global implications in the age of global warming and critical resource scarcity: our transportation decisions have global consequences, and the simple, utilitarian bicycle remains a global force. Moreover, as the essays in *Culture on Two Wheels* demonstrate, the bicycle carries a lasting cultural significance. Its appeal crosses cultural and demographic barriers, as it serves as both a vehicle and an expressive medium in multiple cultural forms and genres, offering opportunity for renewal and understanding even after we thought its necessity had faded. *Forever* surely seems like a rich, apt name for Ai Weiwei's bicycle sculptures, though he might also consider using the brand name of one of the other most popular Chinese bicycles: Phoenix.

Notes

1. Anthony Pins, "Forever," in *Ai Weiwei: Spatial Matters—Art Architecture and Activism*, ed. Ai Weiwei and Anthony Pins (Cambridge MA: MIT Press, 2014), 38.
2. Huang Hung, "ChinaFile: New Lease on Life for Some Old Brands," *WWD* (blog), July 11, 2012, http://wwd.com/fashion-news/fashion-features/chinafile -new-lease-on-life-for-some-old-brands-6067554/. Bicycles were such important icons of respectable modernity that they constituted one of the four necessities of the young newlyweds' household in China, the so-called "three rounds and sound": a watch, a spindle sewing machine, a bicycle (each with round features), and a transistor radio.
3. Sherley Wetherhold, "The Bicycle as Symbol of China's Transformation," *Atlantic*, June 30, 2012, http://www.theatlantic.com/international/archive /2012/06/the-bicycle-as-symbol-of-chinas-transformation/259177/.
4. Earth Policy Institute, quoted in Wetherhold, "Bicycle as Symbol of China's Transformation."
5. Wetherhold, "Bicycle as Symbol of China's Transformation."
6. Yu Qingtai, quoted in Robert Dreyfuss, "China: A Kingdom of Bicycles No Longer," *Nation* (blog), November 24, 2009, http://www.thenation.com/blog /kingdom-bicycles-no-longer#.
7. My T. Le, "Culture Matters: Contemporary Art as a Philosophy of Society," Human Rights in China, December 12, 2009, http://www.hrichina.org/en /content/3189.
8. Pins, "Forever," 38.
9. The influence of Duchamp, as well as Andy Warhol, on Ai Weiwei has been widely acknowledged among critics, and many critical discussions of Ai's bicycle sculptures cite Duchamp's *Bicycle Wheel*. See, for example, Anthony Pins, "Forever"; Chin-Chin Yap, "A Handful of Dust," in *Ai Weiwei. Works: Beijing 1993–2003*, ed. Charles Merewether (Beijing: Timezone 8, 2003).
10. Chin-Chin Yap, "Handful of Dust," 15.
11. Pins, "Forever," 40.
12. Pins, "Forever," 40.
13. Chin-Chin Yap, "A Handful of Dust," 17.
14. Chin-Chin Yap, "A Handful of Dust," 14.
15. Chin-Chin Yap, "A Handful of Dust," 8, 15.
16. Karen Smith, "Giant Provacateur," in *Ai Weiwei*, ed. Karen Smith, Hans Ulrich Obrist, and Bernard Fibicher (New York: Phaidon, 2009), 94.
17. Pins, "Forever," 38.
18. Pins, "Forever," 38.
19. Pins, "Forever," 41.

20. Aaron Souppouris, "Ai Weiwei's Stunning Sculpture Floats 3,144 Bicycles above Toronto Square," *The Verge*, October 9, 2013, http://www.theverge.com/2013/10/9/4819360/ai-weiwei-forever-bicycles-toronto-nuit-blanche-photos, my emphasis.
21. Wetherhold, "Bicycle as Symbol of China's Transformation."
22. Zack Furness, *One Less Car: Bicycling and the Politics of Automobility* (Philadelphia: Temple University Press, 2010), 203.

CONTRIBUTORS

NANCI J. ADLER is an adjunct professor of humanities at Valencia College in Orlando, Florida. In 2012 she earned a master's degree in liberal studies from Rollins College, Winter Park, Florida, for which she wrote the thesis "The Bicycle in Western Literature: Transformation on Two Wheels." Ms. Adler's undergraduate degree is also from Rollins College, with a major in economics. Prior to teaching, Ms. Adler worked in donor relations and development for Rollins College; and in a previous career path, she worked in the telecommunications industry in both operations and regulatory-compliance positions. An avid bicyclist who uses bicycles for commuting, exercising, and touring, Ms. Adler has cycle toured in over ten countries and finds self-supported bicycle touring the perfect way to experience new places.

UNA BROGAN is a PhD student at Université Paris–Diderot, where she is researching the role of the bicycle in British and French literature in the period of 1880 to 1914. She has completed degrees in French, history, literary translation, and comparative literature at Oxford, Warwick, and Paris-Sorbonne universities before embarking on her doctorate. Originally from Northern Ireland, she has worked as a translator, bicycle courier, and migrants' rights researcher. She both commutes and tours by bicycle and is involved as a mechanic and activist in DIY bicycle-workshop, Critical Mass, and advocacy projects in Paris.

DAVE BUCHANAN works in the Department of English at MacEwan University in Edmonton, Alberta, where he teaches eighteenth-century literature as well as courses on creative nonfiction and travel literature. He is the editor of a new edition of the Pennells' first two cycle-travel books, *A Canterbury Pilgrimage* and *An Italian Pilgrimage* (Edmonton: University of Alberta Press, 2015). He blogs about the semiserious cycling life for the *Dusty Musette*.

ANNE CIECKO is an international-cinema educator, academic researcher, writer, and curator. She is currently an associate professor in the Department of Communication and a core faculty member in the interdepartmental program in film studies at the University of Massachusetts–Amherst, where she coordinates the graduate certificate in film studies. Her writing has appeared in *Afterimage, Asian Cinema, Asian Journal of Communication, Cinema Journal, Cinemaya, Continuum: Journal of Media and Cultural Studies, Diogenes, Film Quarterly, History, Journal of Film and Video, Journal of Popular Film and Television, Jump Cut: A Review of Contemporary Media, Literature/Film Quarterly, Quarterly Review of Film and Video, Spectator: Journal of Film and Television Criticism, Tamkang Review, Velvet Light Trap, Wide Screen*, and numerous edited volumes.

CORRY CROPPER, professor of French, researches the political and cultural significance of sports in French literature. His recent publications include *Playing at Monarchy: Sport as Metaphor in Nineteenth-Century France* (Lincoln: University of Nebraska Press, 2008), a book on nineteenth-century French leisure activities; an article on poachers in French literature, published in *French Forum*; and an article on games in the short stories of Prosper Mérimée, published in *Cahiers Mérimée*. Professor Cropper currently serves as the cochair of the Nineteenth-Century French Studies Association and is the chair of the Department of French and Italian at Brigham Young University.

AMANDA DUNCAN earned her PhD in English from the State University of New York at Buffalo. Her dissertation, "Irish Modernism and the Problem of Metaphor," examines the interactions between the imagination and the materiality of language in the literature of Beckett, Joyce, and Yeats. She currently teaches at Pacific University.

ZACK FURNESS is assistant professor of communications at Penn State University, Greater Allegheny, and author of *One Less Car: Bicycling and the Politics of Automobility* (Philadelphia PA: Temple University Press, 2010). He is also editor of *Punkademics* (New York: Minor Compositions, 2012), coeditor of *The* NFL: *Critical and Cultural Perspectives* (Philadelphia PA: Temple University Press, 2014), and has published various articles and book chapters on bicycling, media, punk culture, and teaching.

RYAN HEDIGER is associate professor of English at Kent State University at Tuscarawas. He has published essays on a range of subjects, including military dogs in the U.S. conflict in Vietnam in *Animal Studies Journal*, hunting and violence in the *Hemingway Review*, and Werner Herzog's film *Grizzly Man* about Timothy Treadwell in *Interdisciplinary Studies in Literature and Environment*. He coedited the volume of essays *Animals and Agency* (Leiden, NL: Brill, 2009) and edited another volume of essays, *Animals and War* (Leiden, NL: Brill, 2013). He is currently at work on a monograph, "Homesickness: Posthumanism, Eco-cosmopolitanism, and the Desire for Place in U.S. Literature and Culture."

MELODY LYNN HOFFMANN is a journalism instructor at Anoka-Ramsey Community College. Her research focuses on community responses to bicycle advocacy and processes that seek to make bicycling a more equitable form of transportation in urban spaces. She is engaged in bicycle-equity advocacy work, including serving on the Minneapolis Bicycle Coalition's diversity task force and working with the Nice Ride Neighborhood program. More of her work can be found at phmelody.com.

PETER KRATZKE is a senior instructor for the University of Colorado, Boulder's Program for Writing and Rhetoric. He has published in a variety of journals and serves as an editor for the CEA *Critic*. When not involved with academic activities, he enjoys repairing and riding bicycles, whether those wheels are fleet steeds for racing or sturdy plodders for touring. Kratzke, in this respect, happily agrees with the optimism of Charles Pratt.

JINHUA LI is assistant professor of Chinese studies and language at the University of North Carolina–Asheville. She received her PhD in comparative literature from Purdue University, where she specialized in comparative cinema studies, transnational cultural studies, and gender politics. Dr. Li has published several journal articles and book chapters on gender politics in contemporary Chinese cinema, has contributed book reviews regularly to journals on China studies, and is currently working on a monograph on gender politics in contemporary Chinese cinema.

MATTHEW PANGBORN is assistant professor of English and writing and chair of the Department of Modern Languages at Briar Cliff University in Sioux City, Iowa. In addition to publishing on eighteenth- and nineteenth-century American literature and the Gothic, he has contributed to edited collections on popular-culture topics such as Alfred Hitchcock and the ABC television series *Lost*. His primary book project, titled "Founding Others: Oriental Tales of the Early American Republic," examines early American challenges to the oriental other constructed by period authors to ease the nation's entry into an imperialist Franco-British world system.

DANIEL P. SHEA is associate professor of English at Austin Peay State University, where he serves as coordinator of the English graduate program and teaches courses in nineteenth-century British literature and culture, critical theory, and film studies. He has published on William Morris, Richard Jefferies, and Olive Schreiner and is currently pursuing research projects on Victorian bicycling and the literature of the late-Victorian agricultural depression.

CHARLES L. P. SILET is professor emeritus at Iowa State University, where he taught courses in film and twentieth-century literature and culture for more than thirty years, including classes on Truffaut. During that time, he published numerous articles, reviews, encyclopedia entries, and books on a wide variety of cultural, literary, and film topics in such publications as the *Quarterly Review of Film Studies*, the *Hitchcock Annual*, *American National Biography*, *Journal of Popular Film and Television*, and others. His latest book is *The Films of Woody Allen: Critical Essays* (Oxford, UK: Scarecrow Press, 2006).

ALYSSA STRAIGHT is a doctoral candidate at Miami University in Ohio, where she studies late nineteenth- and early twentieth-century

British and Irish literature as well as women's, gender, and sexuality studies. She is currently working on a dissertation that investigates the importance of the material body in relation to women's technological and spiritual mediation. She teaches courses in literature, women's studies, and first-year composition and rhetoric.

DON TRESCA has a master's degree in English from California State University, Sacramento, where he specialized in twentieth-century American literature and film studies. Previous publications of his include essays focusing on the horror genre both in literary and cinematic form, and on the works of Joss Whedon, Stephen King, and Clint Eastwood. He is currently working on a book-length study of found-footage horror films.

BENJAMIN VAN LOON is a writer, researcher, and former bike mechanic from Chicago, Illinois. He is the cofounder and editor-in-chief of Anobium, an experimental literary publisher, and holds a master of arts in communication, media, and theater from Northeastern Illinois University. He holds multiple awards for his research and writing and more of his work can be found online at www.benvanloon.com.

JEREMY WITHERS is assistant professor of English at Iowa State University, where he teaches classes on science fiction, literary theory, and British literature. His previous articles have appeared in *ISLE: Interdisciplinary Studies in Literature and the Environment*, the *Wellsian: The Journal of the H. G. Wells Society*, the *Journal of Popular Culture*, and the *Journal of Ecocriticism*. Currently, he is working on a book-length study of bicycles and cycling in the works of H. G. Wells.

INDEX

Page numbers in italics refer to illustrations.

abject, concept of, 195–96, 248, 252
Accommodating the Chaos (Dearlove),
 168n5
The Adoration of the Magi (da Vinci),
 227, 234, 236–37
aesthetics of perception, 122
Agostinelli, Alfred, 129
airplanes, 87–88, 93n36
Ai Weiwei, 318–25; *Coca-Cola Vase*, 322;
 Colored Vases, 322; *Dropping a Han
 Dynasty Vase*, 322; *Forever*, 319–25;
 Forever Bicycles, 12n8, 319, 324–25;
 Fragments, 322; *Map of China*, 322;
 Template, 322; *Through*, 322
Albergotti, Reed, 110
Allen, Grant: *Charles Darwin*, 76n60;
 The Type-Writer Girl, 59–60, 66–72,
 73n19
Al-Mansour, Haifaa, 254–55, 257, 258,
 261n30
American Bicycle Company, 53
The American Bicycler (Pratt), 42, 43–
 46, 48
An Bèal Bocht (Beckett), 153
Andrei Tarkovsky (Bird), 229
And Soon the Darkness (film), 206n26
Angel in the House, 61, 66–67
Anti-Oedipus (Deleuze and Guattari),
 163, 167n4

Armstrong, Lance, 13n28, 108, 110–11,
 278n2; *Comeback 2.0*, 115n73
Armstrong, Tim, 60
"The Arrivals Gate" (DiFranco), 8
The Art of Winning at Cycling, 99
Asp, Anna, 240n4
Astérix series, 112n6
At Five in the Afternoon (film), 260n25
athleticism, disease of, 75n46
Attridge, Derek, 169n22
Auster, Al, 268–69, 277
automobiles: bicycles' obsolescence
 and, 53–54; debt of, to bicycle, 87–
 88; and foreshadowing in *Jules and
 Jim*, 214, 218–20; Iranian films and,
 250; primitiveness of bicycles relative to, 194–96, 205n12; rejection
 of culture of, 308–9; replacement
 of bicycles by, in Paris, 139, 148; in
 Stephen King's fiction, 172, 182–83,
 184n3; *The Wizard of Oz* and, 193,
 199, 200–204, 207n39

Bachman, Richard. *See* King, Stephen
Bahktin, Mikhail, 278n2
Bair, Deidre, 139
balance bicycles, 205n12
Balzac, Honoré de: *Les paysans*, 112n7
Bani-E'temad, Rakhshan, 253

Barathieu, Marie-Agnès, 119, 122
Bardem, Andrei, 226
Barthes, Roland, 155; *Mythologies*, 107
Baudelaire, Charles: "Le Gâteau," 112n7
Baudry de Saunier, Louis, 105
Baum, L. Frank: *The Wonderful Wizard of Oz*, 192
Bauman, Zygmunt, 200–201
Bayman, Louis, 246–47
Bazin, André, 245–46
Beard, Dan, 49
Beats and Rhymes program, 304, 313
Beauvoir, Simone de: *The Blood of Others*, 136–48; *The Ethics of Ambiguity*, 141; *The Second Sex*, 137
Beckett, Samuel, 9, 226; *An Béal Bocht*, 153; cyclical structure of novels of, 152–54; "Dante . . . Bruno.Vico . . . Joyce," 154; experimentation of, with language, 166–67; late works of, 170n30; *Malone Dies*, 161; *Molloy*, 152–54, 167n4, 170n30; *More Pricks Than Kicks*, 226; nonrelational aesthetics and, 154–56, 168n5; nonrepresentational vehicles and transgressive process and, 153–62, 168n11; rejection of formal English by, 153–54; "Three Dialogues," 154–55, 156; *The Unnamable*, 161, 162, 166
"Beckett's Bicycles" (Menzies), 167n4
"Beckett's Three Critiques" (Rabeté), 161
Before the Suffragettes (Rubenstein), 74n28
Begam, Richard: *Samuel Beckett and the End of Modernity*, 168n5
Beijing Bicycle (film), 226, 260n25, 281–96, 297n4
Bellamy, Edward: *Looking Backward*, 195
Bennett, Jane, 196, 202, 274; *Vibrant Matter*, 266–67

Ben-on-Ten, 306
Béraud, Jean: *Le chalet du cycle*, 123
Bergman, Daniel, 240n4
Bergman, Ingmar, 227, 240n4
Bernard, Claude: *Study of Experimental Medicine*, 97
Bernard, Ernestine, 211
Bernhardt, Sarah, 124
Bertolucci, Bernardo, 259n15
Better Off Dead (film), 201
Beyzai, Bahram, 254
Bicycle (Herlihy), 15n46, 211, 224n7, 224n10
"bicycle face," 64, 71–72, 197
"A Bicycle Gymkhana" (Norris), 51
bicycles: balance, 205n12; BMX, 2, 7, 305, 307–8; "boneshaker," 3, 43, 44; fixed-gear, 300–301, 314; gender and French words for, 124, 133n49; high-wheeler, 3, 13n25, 37n19; as metaphor for French national character, 98–99; "ordinary," 41–43, 45, 47–48, 49; quintuplet, 103; safety, 3, 28, 42–43, 50, 138, 149n10, 244. *See also* cycling; tricycles
bicycle-share programs, 1, 11n2, 316n19
"bicycle stoop," 197
Bicycle Thieves (film), 260n25; *Beijing Bicycle* and, 281, 297n4; film theory and, 245–47; Iranian films and, 248, 250, 251–52, 253; Saudi films and, 254, 255
A Bicycle Tour in England and Wales (Chandler and Sharp), 22
Bicycle Wheel (Duchamp), 320–21, 326n9
Bird, Robert, 233, 236–37; *Andrei Tarkovsky*, 229
BlocBoi Fame: "Disrespectful," 300–301
Bloch, Marc, 103
The Blood of Others (Beauvoir), 136–48

bloomers, 119, 124, 129, 198, 211. *See also* rational dress for women cyclists

BMX bikes, 2, 7, 305, 307–8

Bockett, F. W.: *Some Literary Landmarks for Pilgrims on Wheels*, 19–20, 29–35, 39n70

"The Body" (King), 184n3

"boneshakers," 3, 43, 44

Booker, M. Keith, 268

Bordeaux–Paris bike race, 100

Borysewicz, Eddie, 110

Botz-Bornstein, 229, 234–35

Boulder Report, 110

Breaking Away (film): agency and materiality in, 274–75, 279n20; class identity and, 267–73, 275–78, 278n6; comedy's role in, 268–69, 271, 277, 278n4; limestone, agency, and identity in, 264, 268, 270–71, 274–75, 279n18, 279n20; performance of identity and self-transformation in, 263–65; vital materialism and human-machine combinations in, 265–67, 278n6, 280n22

Brooks, Charles S.: *Thread of English Road*, 34

Brotchie, Alastair, 95

The Brothers Karamazov (Dostoyevsky), 138

Buckman, Kitty Jane, 74n28

Burrell, Margaret, 149n9

Butler, Judith, 129

Campbell Davidson, Lillias, 71; *Handbook for Lady Cyclists*, 59–63

A Canterbury Pilgrimage (Pennell and Pennell), 19, 22, 23–26, 23, 26, 28, 37n17, 37n21, 39n45

The Canterbury Tales (Chaucer), 23–26

Carlyle, Thomas, 19–20

Carrie (King), 173, 182

"The Cartesian Centaur" (Kenner), 167n4

Cartesian idea of body, 167n4

Cell (King), 173

Centennial Exposition, 44, 48

Chahine, Youssef, 248–49

Chandler, A. D.: *A Bicycle Tour in England and Wales*, 22

Chant, L. Ormistan, 65

Chapman, Raymond, 35n6

Charles Darwin (Allen), 76n60

Chaucer, Geoffrey: *The Canterbury Tales*, 23–26

Chin Chin Yap, 321, 322, 323

Christine (King), 173, 182–83

"Christ's Passion Considered as an Uphill Bicycle Race" (Jarry), 108

The Circle (film), 251

Close-Up (film), 246, 247, 249–51, 253, 258, 260n25

Coca-Cola Vase (Ai Weiwei), 322

Collier's Weekly, 51

Collings, Michael, 177

Colored Vases (Ai Weiwei), 322

Columbia ordinary bicycle, 41–43, 45, 47–48, 49

Comeback 2.0 (Armstrong), 115n73

The Compleat Angler (Walton), 30, 32

Comte, Auguste: *Course in Positive Philosophy*, 97

Conan Doyle, Arthur, 138

A Connecticut Yankee in King Arthur's Court (Twain), 42, 43, 46–50

Cook, Thomas, 38n32

Cook's tickets, 23, 38n32

Course in Positive Philosophy (Comte), 97

Cowley, Abraham, 32

Critchley, Simon, 106

Critical Mass rides, 301, 315n5

Critique of Judgment (Kant), 160–61

cross-dressing, 126–28, 215–16

Crowe, Eyre, 78–79, 80

Cujo (King), 183

cycling: Chinese interest in, 319–21; as liberation, 2–5; popularity of, 278n2; scholarship on transportation and, 7–10; symbolic dichotomies and, 6–7, 12n23, 13nn25–30; twenty-first-century interest in, 1–2, 11n2, 12n8. *See also* bicycles; tricycles; women's cycling

Cycling and Society, 9–10

Cycling and Society Research Group, 10

"Cycling for Ladies" (Everett Green), 62

The Cyclist (film), 247–49, 250, 251–52, 253, 258, 260n25

"cyclist's figure," 64

Cyclo (film), 260n25

Dalton, Joseph G., 47

Dame Jones, 307, 308–9

"Dante . . . Bruno.Vico . . . Joyce" (Beckett), 154

Da Rich Kidzz, 313

The Dark Half (King), 182

The Dark Tower III (King), 184n3

Darwin, Charles, 67, 76n60; *The Descent of Man*, 72n5

da Vinci, Leonardo: *The Adoration of the Magi*, 227, 234, 236–37

Day, Thomas: *The History of Sandford and Merton*, 32

The Day I Became a Woman (film), 247, 251–53, 258

Dearlove, J. D.: *Accommodating the Chaos*, 168n5

Death of a Cyclist (film), 226, 246, 259n10

de Gaulle, Charles, 107

Deleuze, Gilles, 196, 203, 206n32, 244; *Anti-Oedipus*, 163, 167n4

DeLillo, Don: *Falling Man*, 8

de Maupassant, Guy, 105

Denham, John, 32

Derrida, Jacques: "Structure, Sign, and Play in the Discourse of the Human Sciences," 160, 169n22

The Descent of Man (Darwin), 72n5

de Sica, Vittorio, 245–46, 281, 297n4

"desophistication" of language, 159–60

Dickens, Charles, 8, 25–26, 33, 39n70

Diesbach, Ghislain de, 127

DiFranco, Ani: "The Arrivals Gate," 8

Directed by Andrei Tarkovsky (film), 242n42

"Disrespectful" (BlocBoi Fame), 300–301

Doctor Sleep (King), 173, 184n3

Dodge, Pryor, 143

doping and human performance, 94–111; cycling culture and, 13n28, 107, 108–11; in French literature and culture, 94–95, 96, 99–100, 112nn6–7; French positivism and, 97–99, 110; and *The Supermale*, 95–96, 100–108

Dostoyevsky, Fyodor: *The Brothers Karamazov*, 138

Dropping a Han Dynasty Vase (Ai Weiwei), 322

Duchamp, Marcel: *Bicycle Wheel*, 320–21, 326n9

Duffour Kola, advertisement for, 99–100

Duncan, H. O., 100

Duthuit, Georges, 154–55

Dyson, Michael Eric, 312

Ellis, Reuben J., 52

Elly Blue, 306

Epperson, Bruce, 42, 44

Erskine, F. J., 71; *Lady Cycling*, 62

The Ethics of Ambiguity (Beauvoir), 141

eugenics, 119

Everett Green, Evelyn: "Cycling for Ladies," 62

The Experimental Novel (Zola), 97

Falling Man (DeLillo), 8
Fellini, Federico, 248–49
"female masculinity," 125
Findley, Mary, 183
Fiske, Fred C., 87, 93n36
Fitzgerald, F. Scott: "Three Hours between Planes," 8
Fitzpatrick, Jim, 93n46
fixed-gear bicycles, 300–301, 314
Following the Equator (Twain), 48
F-One initiative, 110–11
Forever (Ai Weiwei), 319–25
"Forever" bicycle brand, 319–23, 326n2
Forever Bicycles (Ai Weiwei), 12n8, 319, 324–25
Foucault, Michel, 124
Fournel, Paul, 94, 198
Fragments (Ai Weiwei), 322
France (Jackson), 139
freedom and women's cycling, 59–60, 66–72, 73n19, 76n60
French New Wave cinema, 247, 259n15
Freud, Sigmund, 199, 206n32
Frye, Northrup, 278n2
Furness, Zack, 13n25, 325

G-6, 306, 308
Gagnon, Carolle, 142
Gaillard, Françoise, 121
Gallon, Tom: *The Girl behind the Keys*, 75n57
Garin, Maurice, 109, *109*, 115n67
The Gay Science (Nietzsche), 239, 242n37
gender fluidity. *See* cross-dressing
The Girl behind the Keys (Gallon), 75n57
Gladiator Cycles, 209–10, *210*
Goddard, Stephen, 42, 44
Gong, Haomin, 288

Goscinny, René, 112n6
Graetz, Friedrich, 47
Gray, Henri, 211, 224n7
Greer, Germaine, 259n15
Greville, Violet, 76n62
Grossman, Jonathan H., 8
Gruault, Jean, 213, 225n11
Guattari, Felix, 196, 203, 206n32; *Anti-Oedipus*, 163, 167n4
Guerra, Tonino, 229

Halberstam, Judith, 125
Handbook for Lady Cyclists (Campbell Davidson), 59–63
Haraway, Donna J., 280n21
Harmsworth, Alfred, 79, 91n3
Hart Cycle and Automobile Company, 53
"Healin' from the Killin'" bicycle ride, 316n16
Hemingway, Ernest: *The Sun Also Rises*, 8
heredity, 57–58, 64–66, 67, 72n5, 75n46
Herlihy, David, 4, 9, 42, 43, 73n19, 139, 278n2; *Bicycle*, 15n46, 211, 224n7, 224n10
hermeneutical philosophy, 231–34, 238
Herzog, Maurice, 107
high-wheeler bicycles, 3, 13n25, 37n19
Hill, Joe: *NOS4A2*, 187n54
hip-hop music videos, 300–314, 315n4, 316n16
The History of Sandford and Merton (Day), 32
Holveck, Eleanore, 141
Hopper, Keith, 153
horse-versus-bicycle issues, 41–54, 129–30, 219, 220
Horton, Dave, 13nn29–30, 83, 92n18
"Hot Cheetos and Takis" (Y.N.RichKids), 304, 312
Howells, William Dean, 48

human-machine partnership: in
  Breaking Away, 265–67, 278n6,
  280n22; and desire in *The Wizard
  of Oz*, 196–99, 206n23, 206nn26–
  27, 206n30; and doping, 13n28, 107,
  108–11; and *The Supermale* and perpetual motion, 95–96, 100–108; in
  The Type-Writer Girl, 70–72
The Human Motor (Rabinbach), 97
Hung Huang, 319
Hurd, Jim, 48
hyphy movement, 309–10

Illich, Ivan, 83, 91, 117
*Increasing Output of the Human
  Machine* (Querton), 97–98
In Search of Lost Time (Proust), 116–
  30; appearance, physical exercise,
  and independence in, 119–21; and
  The Captive, 121–23, 125, 126–30; and
  cross-dressing and queer desire,
  126–28; and cycling, travel, and
  desire, 121–23; death of cyclist in,
  128–30; and *The Fugitive*, 126, 129;
  gender fluidity and, 123–26; histori-
  cal era of, 116–19; and *Sodom and
  Gomorrah*, 127; and *Within a Bud-
  ding Grove*, 116–17, 119–21, 122
Institute for the Development of Children and Young Adults, 254
In the Trail of the Three Musketeers
  (Newman), 34
Iovino, Serenella, 274
It (King), 173, 179–82, 186n29, 186n35,
  187n54
An Italian Pilgrimage (Pennell and
  Pennell), 36n15

Jackson, Alonzo, 312
Jackson, Julian: *France*, 139
Jameson, Frederic, 233
Janji Joni (film), 260n25

Jarry, Alfred, *101*; "Christ's Passion
  Considered as an Uphill Bicycle
  Race," 108; *The Supermale*, 95–96,
  100–109, 111, 112n8, 114n53, 121
Jennings, Oscar, 65
Jeppson, Janet, 171–72
Johnson, Vita, 229, 235
Josephson, Erland, 240n4
Joyce, James: *Work in Progress*, 154, 160
Joyland (King), 184n3
Joy of Madness (film), 260n25
Jules and Jim (film), 208–23, 259n15;
  Catherine's contradictions in, 214,
  217–18, *219*; compression of Catherine's personality in, 221; fin de
  siècle posters in, 208–11, *210*, *212*,
  215, 219–21, *220*, 224n7, 225n13; foreshadowing in, 214, 218–20; freedom,
  sex, and desire in, 214–17, *216*; hats
  in, 225n12; New Woman and, 208–
  9, 212, 224n8; posters in, 208–11, *210*,
  212, 215, 219–21, *220*, 224n7, 225n13;
  as reflection of early 1960s, 221–23;
  screenplay for, 213–14, 225n11

Kanun. *See* Institute for the Devel-
  opment of Children and Young
  Adults
Kant, Immanuel: *Critique of Judgment*,
  160–61
Karimi, Niki, 253
Kaufmann, Walter, 238
Kaun, Axel, 153
Keefe, Terry, 137
Kelley, Robin D. G., 313
Kenealy, Arabella: "Woman as Ath-
  lete," 63–65
Kenner, Hugh: "The Cartesian Cen-
  taur," 167n4
Kern, Stephen, 78
Kiarostami, Abbas, 247, 249–50, 254
Kid Nas, 308

The Kid with the Bike (film), 246, 259n10

King, Gilbert, 50

King, Stephen, 171–83; automobiles in work of, 172, 182–83, 184n3; "The Body," 184n3; *Carrie*, 173, 182; *Cell*, 173; *Christine*, 173, 182–83; *Cujo*, 183; *The Dark Half*, 182; *The Dark Tower III*, 184n3; *Doctor Sleep*, 173, 184n3; hand washing in work of, 186n29; *It*, 173, 179–82, 186n29, 186n35, 187n54; *Joyland*, 184n3; *Mr. Mercedes*, 183; *Needful Things*, 173, 176–79, 182n27, 186n29; *The Regulators*, 175–76, 185n18; *'Salem's Lot*, 172, 176; *The Shining*, 172–75, 185n6, 185n14; stuttering in work of, 180, 181, 187n43; *The Talisman*, 184n3; *Thinner*, 182; trains in work of, 171–72, 184n3; werewolves in work of, 180, 187n39; "Willa," 184n3

Kitwana, Bakari, 302–3

Kraus, Karl, 107

Kreutz, Elizabeth, 115n73

Kristeva, Julia, 195–96, 197

Kron, Karl, 36n12, 37n19

Kubrick, Stanley, 185n14

Kunstler, James Howard, 193

Lady Cycling (Erskine), 62

Lady J, 306, 307–8

Lagrange, Fernand, 98

La Luna (film), 259n15

Lamb, Charles, 31

Lao She: *Rickshaw*, 286–87, 298n9

La promesse (film), 260n25

Latour, Bruno, 203; *We Have Never Been Modern*, 198

L'Auto, 108

L'Auto-Vélo, 124

Lays (Marie de France), 94–95

Le, My T., 320

League of American Wheelman, 44

Leblanc, Maurice: *Voici des ailes*, 123–24, 130

Le chalet du cycle (Béraud), 123

Le Fanu, Mark, 229, 233

"Le Gâteau" (Baudelaire), 112n7

LeMond, Greg, 278n2

Leon, Philip L., 49

Leonhardt, David, 271

Le Portrait de Garin, 109, 115n67

Les paysans (Balzac), 112n7

Lettres d'Espagne (Mérimée), 112n7

Linton, Eliza Lynn, 61

literary language, 152–67, 168n5, 168n11, 170n30

literary tourism, 19–35; bicycle racing contrasted with, 20, 22, 36n12; cycling as, 20; F. W. Bockett and, 19–20, 29–35, 39n70; and nostalgia, 20–21, 34, 35n3, 35n6; Pennells and, 19–20, 21–29, 23, 26, 36n15, 37n17, 37n21, 38n24, 39n45; revival of, 34; sentiment and, 23, 25, 30–31, 37n21

Lloyd, Rosemary, 124

Looking Backward (Bellamy), 195

Lovell Cycles, 50–51

Lucas-Championnière, Juste, 121

Lumière, Auguste, 244

Lumière, Louis, 244

Maggiorani, Lamberto, 245

Magistrale, Tony, 174

Majidi, Majid, 254

Makhmalbaf, Hana, 260n25

Makhmalbaf, Mohsen, 247–51

Makhmalbaf, Samira, 260n25

Mallarmé, Stéphane, 124

Malone Dies (Beckett), 161

man versus machine. *See* horse-versus-bicycle issues; human-machine partnership

Man with a Movie Camera (film), 258n2

Map of China (Ai Weiwei), 322

Marasco, Robert, 171

Marie de France: *Lays*, 94–95

Marinetti, Filippo Tommaso Emilio, 79

Martell, William C., 264

Martin, Clancy, 229

The Matrix (film), 193, 204n10

memorial tablets, 32–33, 39n70

Menzies, Janet, 9, 168n11; "Beckett's Bicycles," 167n4

Mérimée, Prosper: *Lettres d'Espagne*, 112n7

Meshkini, Marzieh, 247, 252–53

Messenger, Christian, 97

Meynell, Alice: "The Woman in Grey," 57–58, 65–66, 67, 72n5

Milani, Tahmineh, 253

Miller, Henry, 5

Minneapolis, 302, 304–7, 310–11, 312, 313, 316n19, 316n26

The Mirror (film), 254

"mobility turn," 7

The Modern Bicycle (Spencer), 44

A Modern Utopia (Wells), 86–87

Molloy (Beckett), 152–54, 167n4, 170n30

More Pricks Than Kicks (Beckett), 226

Morley, Christopher, 5

Morton, Timothy, 280n21

Mr. Mercedes (King), 183

Mucha, Alphonse, 211

Murphy, Neil, 153

music videos. *See* hip-hop music videos

"My Bike" (Y.N.RichKids), 302, 303, 304–5, 307–12

Mythologies (Barthes), 107

Nabokov, Vladimir: *Speak, Memory*, 226

Naderi, Amir, 254

Nagornaya, Alexandra, 186n27

Nathanson, Paul, 192–93, 207n39

Native Kids Ride Bike exhibit, 12n8

Needful Things (King), 173, 176–79, 182n27, 186n29

Nenilin, Alexander, 173

neorealism: in Iranian films, 246, 247–54, 261n30; in Italian films, 245–47; in Saudi films, 253–58

Newman, Bernard, 40n72; *In the Trail of the Three Musketeers*, 34

new urban cinema, 281, 296n3

New Women: cycling and, 58–59, 198, 202–4; *Jules and Jim* and, 208–9, 212, 224n8; Marcel Proust and, 120; versus Angel in the House, 61, 66–67

Nietzsche, Friedrich: *The Gay Science*, 239, 242n37; *On the Genealogy of Morals and Ecce Homo*, 241n8; *Thus Spoke Zarathustra*, 228, 232, 238–39

nonrelational aesthetics, 154–56, 168n5

Norcliffe, Glen, 3

Norris, Frank: "A Bicycle Gymkhana," 51; *The Octopus*, 42, 43, 50–53

NOS4A2 (Hill), 187n54

Nykvist, Sven, 240n4

O'Brien, Flann: *The Third Policeman*, 152–54, 156, 158–59, 162–67, 170n30, 226

O'Casey, Sean, 153

O'Connell, Vanessa, 110

The Octopus (Norris), 42, 43, 50–53

Offside (film), 261n30

On the Genealogy of Morals and Ecce Homo (Nietzsche), 241n8

Original Scraper Bike Team, 303–4, 306–7, 308–9, 310, 311, 313–14, 316n16; "Scraper Bike," 302, 303, 305–6, 308–12

O'Rourke, P. J., 194–95

Ostlund, Lars, 236
Our Journey to the Hebrides (Pennell and Pennell), 36n15
Our Sentimental Journey (Pennell and Pennell), 19, 22, 26–29, 37n17, 38n24, 39n45
Ousby, Ian, 20–21
Outing, 43, 47

Paige, James, 48
Paléologue, Jean de (Pal), 211, 224n7
Panahi, Jafar, 254, 261n30
Paris–Brest–Paris bike race, 100
Pearl Izumi catalog, 110
The Peddler (film), 251
Pennell, Joseph and Elizabeth Robins: *A Canterbury Pilgrimage*, 19, 22, 23–26, 23, 26, 28, 37n17, 37n21, 39n45; *An Italian Pilgrimage*, 36n15; *Our Journey to the Hebrides*, 36n15; *Our Sentimental Journey*, 19, 22, 26–29, 37n17, 38n24, 39n45; *To Gipsyland*, 36n15; *Two Pilgrims' Progress*, 36n15; on women and cycling, 61, 76n62
performance-enhancing drugs. *See* doping and human performance
Perry, David B., 54
Petrie, Graham, 229, 235
Pickwick Bicycle Club, 35n3
Pins, Anthony, 320, 321, 323–24
Police Gazette, 211
Poovey, Mary, 74n37
Pope, Albert A., 41–43, 44, 45, 47–48, 49, 53–54
Pope Manufacturing Company, 41–42, 47–48
positivism, 95–96, 97–99, 100–108, 110
posthumanism, 274, 276, 280n21
Pratt, Charles: *The American Bicycler*, 42, 43–46, 48
Premium Rush (film), 315n4

Pridmore, Jay, 48
Proust, Marcel. *See In Search of Lost Time* (Proust)
Puck, 47

Querton, Louis: *Increasing Output of the Human Machine*, 97–98

Raab, Alon, 9, 15n46
Rabeté, Jean-Michel: "Beckett's Three Critiques," 161
Rabinbach, Anson: *The Human Motor*, 97
racing, literary tourism contrasted with, 20, 22, 36n12
railroads, 3, 22, 25–26, 37n18, 52–53, 102–4
rap. *See* hip-hop music videos
rational dress for women cyclists, 61–62, 73n26, 74n28. *See also* bloomers
Ratkoff, Fiona, 119
Rautio, Anna-Maria, 236
readerly tourism. *See* literary tourism
Redwood, Thomas, 226, 229, 230–31, 233, 235, 237
The Regulators (King), 175–76, 185n18
Remington, Frederic, 51
Reynolds, Siân, 120
Rickshaw (Lao She), 286–87, 298n9
Ritchie, Andrew, 4, 9, 100
Rockefeller, John D., 50
Rolling Stone, 312
Rosa, Harmut, 117
Rowe, Kathleen, 278n2
Rubenstein, David, 73n26; *Before the Suffragettes*, 74n28
Ruczai, Maciej, 164–65
Ruskin, John, 37n18
Rybak, R. T., 311
Ryley, J. Beresford, 75n46

Sabzian, Hossein, 249–51

The Sacrifice (film): Andrei Tarkovsky's hermeneutical philosophy and, 231–34, 238; Apocalypse in, 231–33, 238; bicycle as poetical metaphor in, 226–40, 241n5, 242n42; bicycle's appearance, dreams, and narrative texture in, 228, 230–35, 239–40, 242n32; characters in, 227; eternal recurrence and, 228, 232, 238–39; music in, 238–39, 243n49

safety bicycle, 3, 28, 42–43, 50, 138, 149n10, 244

'Salem's Lot (King), 172, 176

Samuel Beckett and the End of Modernity (Begam), 168n5

Saunier Duval company, 111

Savage, Jon, 200

Schaberg, Christopher, 8

"scorching," 120

"Scraper Bike" (Original Scraper Bike Team), 302, 303, 305–6, 308–12

scraper bike movement, 303–4, 308–10, 312–14

Sculpting in Time (Tarkovsky), 227, 229, 235, 240, 242

The Second Sex (Beauvoir), 137

A Sentimental Journey through France and Italy (Sterne), 19, 20, 22, 26–27

Shadwell, A., 64, 71

Sharp, J. C.: *A Bicycle Tour in England and Wales*, 22

The Shining (film), 185n14

The Shining (King), 172–75, 185n6, 185n14

Simpson, Tommy, 13n28

Sixth Generation Chinese directors, 281, 296, 296n1

Smith, Karen, 323

Smith, Robert A.: *A Social History of the Bicycle*, 9

social Darwinism, 119

A Social History of the Bicycle (Smith), 9

Some Literary Landmarks for Pilgrims on Wheels (Bockett), 19–20, 29–35, 39n70

Sorokine, Nathalie, 148, 150n37

Speak, Memory (Nabokov), 226

"Speedin' on My Fixie" (YnG RobB), 300, 301

Spencer, Charles: *The Modern Bicycle*, 44

Staiola, Enzo, 245

Stalker (film), 240, 240n3

Stanton, Elizabeth Cady, 315n8

Starrs, James E., 9

"Starvation Strings," 236, 242n38

Sterne, Laurence: *A Sentimental Journey through France and Italy*, 19, 20, 22, 26–27

Stevenson, R. A. M. (Bob): *Travels with a Donkey in the Cévennes*, 22, 37n17

Stevenson, Robert Louis, 22, 37n17

Stevenson, Tyrone, Jr., 303, 304, 306, 307, 308–10, 312, 313

"Structure, Sign, and Play in the Discourse of the Human Sciences" (Derrida), 160, 169n22

Study of Experimental Medicine (Bernard), 97

The Sun Also Rises (Hemingway), 8

The Supermale (Jarry), 95–96, 100–109, 111, 112n8, 114n53, 121

Suranyi, Clarissa, 66–67

The Talisman (King), 184n3

"Taming the Bicycle" (Twain), 48

Tarkovsky, Andrei, 226–27, 240n3; *Sculpting in Time*, 227, 229, 235, 240, 242

Taylor, Charles E., 93n36

"technological maturity," 83

Template (Ai Weiwei), 322
Terront, Charles, 100
"The Thing from Inner Space"
    (Žižek), 233
Thinner (King), 182
The Third Policeman (O'Brien), 152–54,
    156, 158–59, 162–67, 170n30, 226
Thompson, Christopher, 119
Thread of English Road (Brooks), 34
"Three Dialogues" (Beckett), 154–55,
    156
"Three Hours between Planes"
    (Fitzgerald), 8
Through (Ai Weiwei), 322
Thus Spoke Zarathustra (Nietzsche),
    228, 232, 238–39
Tissié, Philippe, 98–99, 113n30
Todd, Marlin C., 87, 93n36
To Gipsyland (Pennell and Pennell),
    36n15
Tomasulo, Frank, 247
Tour de France, 13n28, 95, 107, 108–11,
    150n15
The Tour of France by Two Children
    (textbook), 96
Travels with a Donkey in the Cévennes
    (Stevenson), 22, 37n17
tricycles, 22, 37n19, 61
Truffaut, François, 259n15
Twain, Mark, 41; *A Connecticut Yankee
    in King Arthur's Court*, 42, 43, 46–50;
    Following the Equator, 48; "Taming
    the Bicycle," 48
Two Pilgrims' Progress (Pennell and
    Pennell), 36n15
The Type-Writer Girl (Allen), 59–60, 66–
    72, 73n19

Uderzo, Albert, 112n6
The Unnamable (Beckett), 161, 162, 166
urban bicycle culture. *See* hip-hop
    music videos

Urry, John, 7
utopian world state, 86–87, 92n25

van Velde, Bram, 155
vélocipédards, 120
Vertov, Dziga, 258n2
Vibrant Matter (Bennett), 266–67
Virilio, Paul, 103, 105, 107
Voet, Willy, 111
Voici des ailes (Leblanc), 123–24, 130

Wadjda (film), 254–58, 261n34
Walton, Izaak: *The Compleat Angler*,
    30, 32
The War in the Air (Wells), 78–91
Watson, Nicola J., 20–21, 31
Wave, 51
The Way, Way Back (film), 301
Weber, Eugen, 117
We Have Never Been Modern (Latour),
    198
Wells, H. G., 138; *A Modern Utopia*, 86–
    87; *The War in the Air*, 78–91; *The
    Wheels of Chance*, 4–5, 83
Wetherhold, Sherley, 320, 325
Wheel, 47, 49
Wheelman, 48
The Wheels of Chance (Wells), 4–5, 83
A Wheel within a Wheel (Willard), 6–7
The White Balloon (film), 254
Whorton, James, 64, 75n46
"Willa" (King), 184n3
Willard, Frances E., 72; *A Wheel within
    a Wheel*, 6–7
The Wizard of Oz (film), 191–204,
    204n8, 205n12, 206n23, 206nn26–27,
    206n30, 207n39
Wolfe, Cary, 280n21
"Wolf Man" dream, 199, 206n32
"Woman as Athlete" (Kenealy), 63–65
"The Woman in Grey" (Meynell), 57–
    58, 65–66, 67, 72n5

women's cycling: and hereditary theory, 57–58, 65–66, 67, 72n5; physical aspects and propriety of, 59–63;
and reproduction and heredity, 63–
66, 74n34, 75n46; technology and
freedom of, 59–60, 66–72, 73n19,
76n60
women's liberation movement, 303,
315n8
The Wonderful Wizard of Oz (Baum),
192. See also The Wizard of Oz
(film)
Workers Leaving the Factory (film), 244
working-class status, bicycles and, 6,
13n26
Work in Progress (Joyce), 154, 160
World War II, 137, 139, 149n5
Wright, Elizabeth, 290
Wright brothers, 88, 93n36

Xiaoshuai, Wang, 226, 281, 293, 295–96

Yates, Peter, 263, 268
YnG RobB: "Speedin' on My Fixie,"
300, 301
Y.N.RichKids, 302–14; "Hot Cheetos
and Takis," 304, 312; "My Bike," 302,
303, 304–5, 307–12
Young, Silvie, 114n53
Yu Qingtai, 320

Zavattini, Cesare, 245, 246
Zeydabadi-Nejad, Saeed, 251
Zhang, Yingjin, 288–89, 295
Zimmerman, George, 310, 316n24
Žižek, Slavoj: "The Thing from Inner
Space," 233
Zola, Émile, 138; The Experimental
Novel, 97

www.ingramcontent.com/pod-product-compliance
Lightning Source LLC
Chambersburg PA
CBHW030422100426
42812CB00028B/3059/J